# SHAKE & BAKE

# SHAKE & BAKE

## The Life and Times of
## NBA Great Archie Clark

**BOB KUSKA** with **ARCHIE CLARK**

University of Nebraska Press

LINCOLN

Library of Congress Cataloging-in-Publication Data
Names: Kuska, Bob, author. | Clark, Archie, 1941– author. |
University of Nebraska Press.
Title: Shake and bake: the life and times of NBA great Archie
Clark / Bob Kuska, with Archie Clark.
Other titles: Life & times of National Basketball Association
great Archie Clark
Description: Lincoln: University of Nebraska Press, 2021.
Identifiers: LCCN 2020011783
ISBN 9780803226548 (Hardback: acid-free paper)
ISBN 9781496224811 (ePub)
ISBN 9781496224828 (mobi)
ISBN 9781496224835 (PDF)
Subjects: LCSH: Clark, Archie, 1941– | Guards (Basketball)—
United States—Biography. | African American basketball
players—United States—Biography. | Basketball players—
United States—Biography. | Detroit Pistons (Basketball
team)—History. | Los Angeles Lakers (Basketball team)—
History. | National Basketball Association—History. |
Veterans—United States—Biography.
Classification: LCC GV884.C55 K87 2021 |
DDC 796.323092 [B]—dc23
LC record available at https://lccn.loc.gov/2020011783

Set in Minion Pro by Mikala R. Kolander.

When people talk about my NBA career, they always mention the phrase "shake and bake." It was my signature crossover move. Rarely mentioned is the move went nameless for years. It was just a dribble crossover move that I did to get my shot. No name required. In the early 1970s, an NBA radio broadcaster named Sonny Hill started saying on the air that I was "shaking and baking" whenever I used the move, and the name just stuck like glue.

—ARCHIE CLARK

SHAKE & BAKE

# 1

A spring shower pattered like a drumroll through the streets of downtown Minneapolis on a busy day in mid-May 1966. Archie Clark hustled along the sidewalk and into the fashionable Leamington Hotel. Archie, a star basketball player at the University of Minnesota, brushed the raindrops from his jacket and followed his nose to the coffee shop. He was looking for Lou Mohs, general manager of the NBA Los Angeles Lakers. The two had never met, though they'd spoken by phone to arrange that day's meeting. Archie scanned the old-fashioned lunch counter. There, hovering over a plate of fried food, was Mohs, his briefcase at the ready.

Mohs, a silver-haired man with black horn-rimmed glasses and clad in a dark business suit, introduced himself in a bone-dry monotone. Archie took a seat at the lunch counter, and a waitress placed a glass of ice water in front of him. But Mohs wasn't buying. He was eager to catch the next flight to Salt Lake City. In the days when college draft choices negotiated their rookie contracts directly with management, Mohs needed to be in Utah to sign his top draft choice in the 1966 NBA draft. Archie was the Lakers' third-round selection. As Mohs calculated, this wouldn't take long.

"I happened to be in Minneapolis, and I wanted to sign my fourth draft choice to a contract," said Mohs, stretching out the word "fourth" like a lawyer introducing a winning legal strategy. Mohs falsely insinuated that because the Lakers had drafted two high-priced first-round choices, Archie deserved the lower pay of a fourth-round selection.

Archie sipped the ice water and tried to size up the seventy-year-old Mohs, whom he found as stiff as a starched shirt. At age twenty-four Archie was older than most NBA draft choices. He had spent three years in the army saluting officers, and as a young black man from working-class Detroit, Archie was streetwise and confident enough to deal with most situations. Yet he had no idea how to talk money with Mohs. Archie had never negotiated a pro contract, and, like most NBA draftees that year, he had to learn on the spot against a seasoned adversary and potential employer who, as Archie had just heard, was willing to stretch the truth to save a few dollars.

"What are you offering?" Archie answered.

"A one-year, $11,000 contract," said Mohs with feigned enthusiasm intended to obscure his lowball offer. The average NBA player salary was reportedly $15,500 per season in 1966.

"I don't know," hemmed Archie, instinctively trying to up the ante. "I want to look into playing major league baseball. That's always been my dream."

"I've seen you play baseball," Mohs answered dismissively. "Basketball is your best sport."

"Do you offer signing bonuses?" Archie finally asked.

"No, we don't give signing bonuses," Mohs fibbed. "But I'll tell you what we can do. I can write a check for $2,000 right now and front you some of the money from your contract. That will leave you $9,000."

The thought of instant cash was too appealing. Mohs unclasped his briefcase and produced a dog-eared standard NBA player contract written in a circuitous jumble of clauses that arrived at the same potentially deal-breaking point. For the contract to be valid Archie had to pay his way to Los Angeles and earn a spot on the Lakers' opening-season roster. Archie digested the text as best as he could amid the lunchtime clatter. He finally signed on the dotted line. Mohs handed him a $2,000 check, paid his bill at the cash register, and hurried off to the airport. The negotiation had taken no more than ten minutes.

When he got back to his apartment, Archie called home to Detroit to share the good news. He had signed a one-year contract to play professional basketball. In the NBA. With a team called the Los Angeles Lakers. Yes, he would be moving to California at the end of the summer.

Archie couldn't offer many more details to his parents. He had no idea what to expect in Los Angeles, nor did he understand how the business of professional basketball worked. Like most college players, he had nobody to call or write for more information—no agent, no lawyer, no helpful pro players. Like his ten-minute contract negotiation, he would have to figure out the dealings—and double dealings—of the NBA on his own.

# 2

*I got the $2,000 check from Lou Mohs and cashed it. I had never owned a car in my life. So a few days later I went car shopping in Minneapolis. I wanted a Cadillac, but it was out of my price range. So I bought a 1966 Ninety Eight Oldsmobile, which was the next best luxury sedan at the time. The Ninety Eight came with a "super rocket" v8 engine, or so the ads said. Mine was black with a white convertible top. Let me tell you, it was a great car.*

---

Archie Clark packed his Ninety Eight Olds, taking care not to scratch the new paint. Helping him was his pretty young bride, Valerie. Their wedding had been spur of the moment, a college romance that both agreed with heavy heart shouldn't end. If they hit the road today, Archie figured they would reach Los Angeles in time for the Lakers staff to show them to their hotel room so that Archie could grab some needed rest before training camp opened on September 9, 1966.

Archie maneuvered his new car one last time through downtown Minneapolis. In his rear-view mirror the skyline descend slowly, eventually giving way to flat, open Minnesota prairie. U. S. Highway 14 blew across western Minnesota into the flatlands of South Dakota and, four uneventful hours later, slanted south near the state's capital, Pierre. Every forty minutes or so the two-lane highway slowed through another dot on the map, a small town with its predictable scramble of brick buildings, grain elevators, pickup trucks, and fifty-foot water towers standing guard on the edge of town. The towns and water towers eventually gave way to magnificent stands of ponderosa pine and spruce, and he saw a large yellow road sign with a silhouette of a cowboy riding a bucking bronco: "Wyoming Welcomes You."

Wyoming was cowboy country, and Archie wondered whether he had relatives riding horses on the open range. His parents, Sadaler and Houston, grew up dirt poor in rural Arkansas, and long-lost relocated relatives seemed to pop up everywhere. Most had left the Ozarks to go north to look for better jobs and a chance at a middle-class life. In 1942, with World War II reaching a full geopolitical boil, Archie's parents migrated too, with their four children in tow—two-year-old Archie, three-year-old Evans, and the older girls, Christine and Willistine.

The Clarks settled temporarily with Houston's older brother, Willie, and his family in the township of River Rouge on the outskirts of southwest Detroit. Uncle Willie, the patriarch of the family who was the first to move to the Detroit area, helped Houston find an entry-level job in the iron foundry at the Ford Motor River Rouge plant, which then touted an around-the-clock workforce of about eighty-five thousand to supply the American war effort. More Clark babies arrived—twelve would come in all—and the family settled in Ecorse, one township over from River Rouge, into a squat, three-bedroom home in a new public-housing project that had been specially constructed to house black factory workers and their families. Times grew harder when Houston quit his union job at Ford. He had asthma, and the dust and swelter inside the factory had left him wheezing too many times. Soon thereafter Houston started driving a cab.

Sadaler, a strong-willed optimist, took great pains to fill their modest home with love. But her responsibilities for cleaning, cooking, and tending to newborns never ceased. She let her pre-adolescent boys be boys during the day, as most parents did back then. Archie rarely strayed far from the projects. He spent his free time playing baseball with the older boys, his younger brother Charles always by his side. The two had grown especially close, and although their father had neither the time nor the inclination to throw the ball with them, Archie and Charles had baseball in their blood soon after they learned to walk.

When Archie was nine, tragedy struck on a hot summer's day. Archie, his now ten-year-old brother Evans, and their friend Billy Brock decided to cool off in nearby Ecorse Creek. The three boys headed down the street en route to the creek when Archie turned back and noticed Charles scurrying after them.

"Go home, Charles," Archie finally called out, always eager to protect his little brother. At age seven Charles wasn't old enough to swim in the creek.

"Quit picking on him," Evans snapped. "You're always picking on Charles."

The boys continued on their way, and Charles tagged tentatively along several yards behind. "All right; you sit right here," Evans commanded Charles in a big brotherly tone, pointing at the wet, heavily silted bank of the creek. The older boys untied their shoes and inched into the green soupy water. None knew how to swim. But they disappeared into the shallow water along the bank, where they could hold their breath and wiggle underwater like fish for about thirty seconds.

"Where's Charles?" Archie called out to Billy when he came up for air.

They heard a splash off in the deep end of the creek. It was Charles. Fear and adrenaline seized them at the moment, and the boys paddled desperately through the murky creek water in the general direction of the splash. Archie held his breath as long as he could, groping to feel a hand or a foot. Nothing. A few minutes later they were back on the shore, dripping wet and scared. Fighting to catch his breath, Evans raced home to tell his mother. Archie stayed behind, searching in tears for an older boy who could dive in and save Charles.

Archie struggled to make sense of Charles's death. Why hadn't he forced his little brother to go home? Why had God taken away his best friend? Archie suddenly felt alone in his big family. He and Evans never really saw eye to eye, and his next closest sibling was four years younger. Archie remained a good kid, obedient and loyal to his parents. But he withdrew into himself. When confronted by strangers, Archie could be slow to warm up, parsing their words, weighing their intentions, and, unlike that awful day, sticking to what he knew was right. His wariness wasn't personal. He had to be cautious. Life was safer that way.

Months passed without incident. But Archie remained guarded. Every day was an education, only more so in Ecorse. The town of twelve thousand, squeezed into 2.7 square miles along the Detroit River, bordered the Motor City's far southwest side, making it the first in a chain of eighteen then suburban "downriver" communities. This urban-suburban divide imbued Ecorse with a hybrid culture. During work hours Ecorse bustled like a blue-collar extension of Detroit with its smokestacks and blast furnaces, freight trains, and busy urban storefronts. But after quitting time Ecorse settled back into its own quaint downriver identity. The streets around the large Municipal Park, better known as "the Muni," were lined with cars on summer evenings to watch the softball games; cigarette boats zipped along the Detroit River; and kids roller-skated in the streets until the inevitable call of "time for supper." Under the cover of night the urban edge returned. The corner taverns bustled, and the Stroh's beer flowed. If you weren't union, you weren't right.

Unlike the blatant racism that haunted Archie's parents as Arkansas sharecroppers, blacks and whites were generally civil in Ecorse. They worked shoulder to shoulder in the factories, paid the same union dues, sent their kids to the same public schools, and shopped at some of the same stores.

But barriers remained firmly in place. Whites went home at night to their own all-white neighborhoods; blacks went home to the public-housing units that covered about one hundred acres on the other side of the railroad tracks. That was the way the whites liked it. In River Rouge it was the same segregated tale of two townships. Further downriver Lincoln Park and Wyandotte townships were whites only. In Dearborn, Mayor Orville Hubbard campaigned successfully for decades on a platform to keep his city "lily white." Even Detroit, the nation's fourth largest metropolis with nearly two million residents, was almost completely segregated. White children on the Northwest Side could go days without seeing a black person, even at the ballpark. The Detroit Tigers didn't have a single black player on their roster back then, and owner Walter Briggs vowed to keep it that way, as though it were a matter of civic pride. Nobody in power called his bluff.

In the instances that Archie crossed the railroad tracks into white Ecorse, he noticed the names printed on the mailboxes: Nagy, Zukonik, King, Vukovich, Poremba, Kozma, Gambino. Each block was a melting pot of European ethnicity and its shared New World culture. On Friday nights the Catholics gathered at the Pulaski Club on Southfield Road for fried perch-and-frog-leg dinners. At High and Labadie Streets white kids in matching mittens and scarves mobbed the

Muni's 220-foot ice rink, where the policy and source of bottomless town pride was "Free skating until nine o'clock." Afterward everybody piled off to the A&W Root Beer stand or, better yet, to Frankie's, where the pizza was so good (according to legend) that astronaut John Glenn took a slice with him into space.

It was the white folks' party, and tradition dictated that Archie stay on his side of town. White people didn't care what he thought about them, their ice skating, or their fish fries. The funny thing was that the white teenagers had started shaking their hips to the hottest black music of the day. Many would have braved a blizzard to hear Nat King Cole or meet black baseball star Willie Mays. If they could have it both ways, why couldn't he?

Archie heard people in his neighborhood decry the double standard. The black auto and steel workers who gathered after hours to blow off steam alternately laughed and grumbled with a wry, better-wake-up-boy wisdom that the game of life was rigged. Black people weren't going to get ahead standing on assembly lines. Postwar America was headed away from manufacturing, and all of the big factories were cutting capacity and jobs. In Detroit black unemployment had bumped over 25 percent and would climb to 37 percent by 1960. Most of the people doing the talking in the neighborhood had been born and raised in the South, like Archie's parents, and had shallow roots in the Motor City. They dreamed of seeing California palm trees and riding cable cars halfway to the stars. Mostly it was just talk, but their blunt assessments of Detroit only further ingrained Archie's worldview. Life was uncertain, change was constant, and he had to stay strong to survive.

But survival only grew harder. With four and five children crammed into each tiny bedroom at night, home was a crawling, hair-pulling, I'm-telling-Mom headache. Archie had embarrassingly few clothes hanging in the closet and little or no money jingling in his pocket. At school while the other kids ate lunch in the cafeteria, he had to race home to meet his father, who, if he was there, handed him a dollar or two that he had collected plying the streets in his cab. Archie dashed to the store and grabbed a loaf of bread, bologna, a pint of milk, or whatever other sustenance he could afford. He blew back home, choked down a sandwich, and then hurried to class to beat the tardy bell. At night the meal was equally modest: beans, beans, and more beans, often with a square of cornbread and a vegetable on the side.

Archie's parents did the best they could under the circumstances. But Archie, still missing his brother Charles, came to realize that he was on his own to make his way in this often unjust world. He found structure in school, where his careful, attentive nature made him a quick learner. He also found meaning scrapping on the sandlot with the other kids. In the fall Archie was a regular in after-school tackle football games. In the winter he moved over to the asphalt basketball court next to the water fountains, where he had learned to flip a hook shot at the basket to compensate for his still scrawny boyish frame. But his childhood dreams still resided a stone's throw across the playground on the baseball diamond.

In the summer of 1954, a few months shy of his thirteenth birthday, Archie registered as one of two blacks to play in the local American Legion League. His manager was an African American recreation worker in his late twenties named James Bibbs. Mr. Bibbs, as the kids called him, quickly became a mentor and second father to Archie. The loquacious Mr. Bibbs had been a state champion sprinter at Ecorse High School in the 1940s. He attended what is now Eastern Michigan University and returned home with a polite, winning way with people and a commitment to progressive ideas. In the coming years he would become one of the first blacks to live on the white side of Ecorse.

When he wasn't coaching, Mr. Bibbs played on a local semi-pro baseball team. Archie was the team's batboy and often sat on the bench absorbing the dugout chatter. One evening a batter lined a pitch out of play, and a spectator corralled the foul ball, cocked his arm, and fired the baseball straight into the wire fence a few feet in front of Archie.

"Archie slipped up and yelled, 'Good, kill your damn self,'" said Mr. Bibbs. "I talked to him about it afterward, and he apologized for his language. But I went home that night, and there was a twelve-year-old black girl from Baltimore named Gloria Lockerman on television. She had won $16,000 on a game show spelling words. So I copied down all of her words, and I gave them to Archie the next day.

I said, 'Archie, I want you to learn all of these words because if you're swearing, it just means your vocabulary isn't big enough.' I handed over about twenty-five words and told him to spell and define them. I thought it would take him two or three weeks. Archie brought them back in two days. That's when I said, 'This boy is bright.'"

The boy also was fast and extremely coachable. "If I hit him fly balls, Archie ran from one side of the field to the other to catch them," said Mr. Bibbs of their daily practice sessions. "He never begged off. Sometimes, if it was raining, I'd tell him, 'The sun is shining, and it's a beautiful day. Let's go.' And off we'd go. Archie didn't take any shortcuts."

As often was the case, the two sat around talking about baseball. How do you get in front of a ground ball? Was Willie Mays better than Mickey Mantle? As the conversation wound back to life in Ecorse, Mr. Bibbs grew serious and said, "Archie, you're going to make it."

"Why's that, Mr. Bibbs?"

"Because when times get tough, you don't lose your head like most kids. You know how to adjust and keep going."

Mr. Bibbs might have been referring to conditions on the baseball field. Or maybe he was referring to life in general? Archie wasn't quite sure. But this moment of affirmation stuck with him. Archie Louis Clark was going to make it. It had to be true. Mr. Bibbs had said so.

UTAH WAS MORMON COUNTRY. The desert and sagebrush of northeastern Utah hardly looked like a place of latter-day miracles. Then the Wasatch Mountain Range heaved into view, and Archie approached the first of the nine-thousand-foot peaks that his Oldsmobile would need to conquer before descending into the Salt Lake valley. Valerie had curled up in the passenger seat, and Archie stared ahead at an empty Interstate 30 South, the news fading in and out on the AM radio.

The mountains brought back a flood of bittersweet memories. Archie had spent fourteen months in the army after high school, staring up at the craggy mountaintops of Korea. He had never given military service much thought as a kid. Major league baseball had been his dream of course. But circumstances intervened during his teens, and the cautious boy who didn't take shortcuts had to go all the way to the windswept mountains of the 38th parallel to keep his life on track. Where the army would push him in life, he had no idea. It just seemed like the right choice at the time.

Archie got the idea to join the army from Richard Garrett. Everybody called him Fish Man because he was as popeyed as a flounder. Archie and Richard grew up in the projects, attended public school together, and—unbeknown to Mr. Bibbs—belonged to the same neighborhood gang in high school. They called themselves the Siege'uns, as in those ready to lay siege. As to whom they planned to attack, none had a clue. But the name sounded sinister, and that's all that really mattered.

Archie could snicker now about his double life as a high school jock and juvenile-delinquent-in-training. His membership in the gang as a 5-foot-7, 119-pound high school sophomore came with the territory. Ecorse, the neighborhoods along Detroit's far southwest side, and Ecorse's downriver neighbor River Rouge had long-standing rivalries that could turn ugly for anyone in the wrong place at the right time. Out of necessity many teens banded into fraternal, got-your-back gangs that romped off to parties at night flaunting their strength in numbers and, in the case of the Siege'uns, gathered in the projects by day to pass the hours shooting pool and mouthing the *West Side Story* bluster of the era.

Archie rarely landed in the inevitable dustups. Richard and the others made sure to shield him from trouble. He was more important to the gang as an athlete who did his scrapping for the Ecorse High Red Raiders. By his junior year Archie had grown to about 6 feet and, with his wiry physique and quickness, had become a pretty good basketball player. He liked the competition and camaraderie, but the sport remained an afterthought. Baseball remained his game of choice and ticket to a better life.

In Ecorse, like in most industrial towns in the 1950s, once students completed their high school graduation requirements, they marched off to jobs in the nearby factories, where many would punch the clock for the next forty years. In the winter of 1959 Archie graduated in the middle of his senior year and thus ended his prep basketball career in mid-dribble. His coach had mentioned that he could work out a deal for Archie to play college basketball for all-black North Carolina

A & T. Archie thanked him, but he wasn't interested in four years of watching his back in the segregated South. He'd get a $65-per-week factory job like everybody else and maybe save enough money to attend college in a few years.

The trouble was that the local steel workers were striking for higher wages, and the other downriver factories were slumping. Archie found himself living at home, jobless and unsure of his immediate future. He started hanging out more with the Siege'uns, and his buddies promptly voted him their president and leader. Being perceived as a tough guy had its perks, but his pensive, careful nature told him there was no future in it. He needed to get back on track. Archie tried out at a free-agent baseball camp sponsored by the Detroit Tigers. A scout wrote down his name and thanked him for coming. If the Tigers wanted to talk further, they'd send him a letter.

That's when Richard floated the idea. What about joining the army on the buddy plan? They'd serve their country with honor, and the buddy plan would allow them to attend basic training together. Archie mulled over the idea in his usual cautious manner. He kept thinking about his brother Evans. Several months earlier Evans had enlisted in the army, and his life was literally going places. The army sent him to Germany, and Evans wrote home about buying fine European suits and gadding about with his army buddies on weekend trips to Copenhagen and Amsterdam. That sure beat racking 'em up at the Salliotte Pool Room, one of Archie's daily haunts, and scuffling with rival gangs for no good reason.

Archie and Richard rode the bus one balmy summer day to the army recruitment office in Wyandotte township. They shook hands with the uniformed recruiter, informed him of their intentions, and hunkered down to take the entrance examination. A few days later an envelope bearing the army logo arrived in the mail. Archie unsealed the flap, pulled out the folded sheet of paper, and felt the adrenaline rush through his body. He was in. The letter instructed him to report to a local reception center and then Fort Linderwood in Missouri for basic training. Archie found Richard a few hours later and asked him if he'd opened his letter. Richard changed the subject. He'd flunked the test.

*I left for basic training in September of 1959. Ten days later a letter arrived from the Detroit Tigers. They invited me to spring training in Lakeland, Florida, and a chance to try out for a big league contract. I was heartbroken, to tell you the truth, about missing out on seizing my big league dream. I thought, "Why did you go and join the army?" But it was too late. I belonged to the military for the next three years. As the end of my basic training approached, I really wanted to be stationed in Germany. My brother was there, and it sounded like a good place to be. The talk in the barracks was, "Don't ask to be sent to Germany. If you asked for Germany, they'll send you to Korea." So you know what I did? I tried to outsmart them. I asked for Korea. And, sure enough, they sent me straight to Korea.*

*The Korean War had ended, but the tension between the two sides remained palpable. If the enemy attacked along the DMZ, my reconnaissance unit was the first line of defense. Our job was to hold off the enemy until the big guns arrived. Ours was basically a suicide mission, and we knew it. Luckily no gunfire was ever exchanged. Our commanders just had us playing war games to stay sharp. I did that for a few months until they broke up my company and reassigned me to the Fourth Cavalry across the river. I started out as what they called a "runner." I carried equipment between the main headquarters of the Fourth Calvary and its Third Platoon, positioned high up on a mountain.*

*I can remember one afternoon dragging myself back to headquarters after hours of performing field training exercises. I was completely gassed. It took about thirty minutes to scale the mountain and reach the Third Platoon and then another thirty minutes to climb back down. I wasn't in that kind of shape yet. I had only been there maybe five days. Anyway I was sitting in a communal tent when the first officer walked in and called out, "Who is the runner for the Third Platoon?"*

*"I am, sir," I answered.*

*"The Third Platoon just called down to headquarters. They need more batteries up on the hill."*

*I wasn't trying to cause any trouble, but I could still feel the burning in my lungs from the earlier trip. I had nothing left in my tank to run up that mountain again in full army gear, clutching my rifle and lugging a pack filled with ten-pound batteries.*

*"Sir, I can't make it," I finally answered.*

*"What did you say?"*

*"Sir, I can't make it up that mountain again."*

*The first officer glared at me for a second and exited the tent without a word. A few minutes later the captain arrived and called out, "Who is the runner for the Third Platoon?," knowing full well it was me.*

*"I am, sir."*

*"Well, Clark, they need batteries up on the hill."*

*"Sir, I can't make it up that mountain again."*

*"But you will, won't you?"*

*For one long second I was ready to tell the captain that he could have all of this. Just send me to the brig right now. But I got myself together and, like Mr. Bibbs said, just kept going. I grabbed my gear, and an hour later I crawled up the last of that miserable mountain. When I staggered into the Third Platoon command to deliver the batteries, the officers were all laughing at me. I had been hazed.*

*After that I got with the program and became a heck of a soldier. I realized that if the North Koreans attacked, we would be facing a life-or-death situation. It was kill or be killed, and I preferred to stay in the land of the living. The army taught me discipline and provided me with a daily structure. Don't get me wrong. I had discipline as a kid. But my resolve was a little loose. In the army, my resolve to win became air tight, and I carried that with me into sports.*

IN LATE 1960 ARCHIE, then a private and soon to be a specialist fourth class, was transferred to the headquarters of the First Missile Battalion, Seventy-First Artillery, in Suitland, Maryland, just outside of Washington DC. The headquarters oversaw the network of heavy artillery units that protected the capital from a possible Soviet attack. But his new posting offered no Cold War intrigue. Archie served in the recreation and welfare office, where he drove visiting soldiers and VIPs on sightseeing tours of Washington. After sliding down mountain trails and wading chest high through Korean rice paddies, Archie had no complaints. He was happy to be back in the United States.

He also was happy that the First Missile Battalion would be the final stop on his three-year tour of duty. Although proud to be a soldier, he had no interest in becoming career military and shipping off to Vietnam, the latest flash point in the war against communism. Archie looked forward to returning to civilian life in September 1962, landing a decent job, starting a family, and making good in this uncertain world. Or so he thought. Little did he know that making good would involve basketball and a white guy named Buzz.

It all started rather innocently. To stay in shape Archie joined an intramural basketball team at nearby Andrews Air Force Base. The competition was stiff, but Archie more than held his own. In Korea he had spent most of his off-hours scrapping in pickup games in the unit's makeshift gymnasium. As Archie would say, he always had been a pretty good basketball player. He had worked on his fundamentals as a kid, developed a soft jump shot in high school, and could dribble well with either hand. The difference now was that he had added muscle to his once rail-thin frame, polish to his game, and a hard-nosed army resolve to win. Onlookers started asking, "Who is this sergeant from Detroit?"

One day after a game in the Andrews Air Force Base gymnasium, a trim, light-haired man in his early thirties introduced himself in the flat monotone of his native Duluth. His name was Buzz Bennett. Bennett, a basketball star at the University of Minnesota in the mid-1950s, said he coached the base team at Andrews and wanted to invite Archie to try out for the squad. The conversation confused Archie. How could he play basketball for the air force? He was in the army.

His fellow gym rats advised him not to worry. Try out for the team; work out the logistics later. When Archie made the air force squad, common sense dictated that the army would never allow him to represent a rival branch of the military. So one day in between leading sightseeing tours, he tested the waters with Captain Johnson, his immediate superior. To his astonishment Captain Johnson returned a few minutes later holding signed orders that permitted Sergeant Clark to suit up for the air force as long as it didn't interfere with his official army duties. Captain Johnson never explained why he had bucked tradition and went out on a limb for him.

Captain Johnson's good deed transformed Archie's final months in the military into the basketball equivalent of a Horatio Alger story.

Archie came out of nowhere to lead Bennett's team in scoring and earned all–air force honors. Bennett began telling his friends in Minnesota that this Clark kid had it all—speed, quickness, smarts, and desire.

"Archie, would you be interested in college?" Bennett asked one day. "I might be able to arrange something for you."

College was very much in Archie's plans. Since enlisting, he had socked away a few hundred dollars for college when he got out of the army. But there had been a recent development. While on leave to visit his family, Archie had gotten a girl pregnant. Her name was Barbara, and Archie planned to marry her and help raise their child. If Coach Bennett came through with a full basketball scholarship to cover room and board, he might be able to swing both.

A few weeks later Bennett accompanied Archie to a restaurant on one of the numbered streets in downtown Washington. Waiting to greet them was a young, blond assistant basketball coach from the University of Minnesota named Glenn Reed. Bennett and Reed had been teammates at Minnesota in the early 1950s. The three sat down and talked about military life, Big Ten basketball, and the educational opportunities that waited in the Twin Cities.

"How were your grades in high school?" Reed asked.

"Good," Archie answered. "I took college preparatory classes in high school."

With that all-important first hurdle cleared, Reed explained that Minnesota, or the "U," as everybody called it, had never had a black basketball player on its roster. But that was due largely to tradition, not overt racism. The Twin Cities, mostly white but politically progressive, weren't as hung up on race as the rest of the industrial North or the Jim Crow South. Minneapolis–St. Paul had cheered black pro athletes on the baseball Twins, the NFL's Vikings, and the departed NBA Lakers. What's more, Reed said, the University of Minnesota football team already suited up black football players, as did other Big Ten football and basketball teams.

Reed said Minnesota head coach John Kundla, a former successful NBA head man in his third season at the U, planned to get with the times. After two subpar seasons and waning fan support, Kundla realized that Minnesota's traditional recruiting base of white all-state players from Minnesota, Wisconsin, and the Dakotas was no longer sufficient to compete for Big Ten championships. He wanted to bolster his roster with a few black players, and that meant recruiting in cities along the eastern seaboard, where the Minnesota football team already had made contacts with high school coaches. The strategy worked like a charm, and Reed said two outstanding black players already had agreed to attend Minnesota in the fall as freshmen. They were Lou Hudson, a 6-foot-5 athlete extraordinaire from Greensboro, North Carolina, and Don Yates, a 6-foot-3 Adonis who was the Pennsylvania high school player of the year.

Archie was impressed with the sales pitch and remembered telling Reed, "If you take me, you won't have to worry about me flunking out. I've been in the military for a few years, and at this point in my life, I just want to get my degree."

About a week later Sergeant Clark got the good news. His grades had checked out, and Minnesota would award him a full basketball scholarship. To the best of his knowledge neither Reed nor Kundla had watched him play. Was this a good or bad sign? Archie didn't really care. At age twenty-one his life was headed in the right direction. Archie would be a first-time father in a few months, the first member of the Clark family to attend college, the first Big Ten basketball player from Ecorse, and a civil rights pioneer to boot.

# 3

**W**elcome to Fabulous Las Vegas, Nevada. After six hours of Archie's staring down the ashen moonscape of the West, the Las Vegas Strip now blinked in a garish assault on sense and scruple. On the facades of the big casinos, neon signs flashed, popped, and glittered in synchronized, thousand-watt shouts to passersby to step right up and take a chance. At the Golden Nugget Casino chance wore the spurs and ten-gallon swagger of the Old West. At the Stardust the moon, the stars, and the heavens were rumored to be in perfect alignment. At the brand-new Circus Circus Hotel and Casino life was a Barnum and Bailey world. It was just as phony as it could get.

Archie had never seen anything like it. Las Vegas ran on light, illusion, and (at the green felt gaming tables inside the casinos) sleight of hand. At the sportsbook in town gamblers bet the ranch on the outcomes of college and pro games. Maybe Archie had made somebody rich during his college career.

Oh, that college career. The transition from soldier to first-time father to student athlete was tougher than Archie had thought. Barbara and their baby, Tonetria, had remained in Ecorse. That had Archie feeling homesick. He spent most of his free time alone in his dorm room. By January of his freshman year Archie had secured an apartment, allowing Barbara and the baby to move to Minneapolis. But all was not well. Barbara couldn't find a job, and between classes and basketball Archie had no time to work. The bills piled up, and Archie wondered whether attending college was such a bright idea.

Hoping to pay down a few bills, Archie applied at the Ford plant in River Rouge. It was supposed to be a summer job, but if he got his foot in the door, Archie knew he'd never leave. He couldn't endure the thought of three more years of the hand-to-mouth student life. He was tired of being poor. But life can be fickle. Archie flunked the physical for the Ford job. Having played freshman basketball and baseball at Minnesota, Archie was in such fantastic physical shape that his resting heart rate was abnormally slow. The examining physician erroneously concluded Archie had a congenital heart condition and was unfit for factory work. After figuring out the snafu, Archie confided in Mr. Bibbs about the difficulties at home. Mr. Bibbs advised Archie to secure a student loan, return to college for his sophomore year, and lock in on earning his degree.

Deep down, Archie couldn't shake his childhood dream. If the Detroit Tigers had wanted to give him a tryout once, he could catch the eye of a Major League scout again. Archie vowed to have a break-out sophomore season on Minnesota's varsity baseball team and thereafter ink a Major League contract. Just as important, the big-league money would enable him to buy a car and a house and otherwise get on with his life. Coach Kundla wouldn't be happy. But college basketball was strictly a means to a higher education. Who played professional basketball anyway? Maybe Wilt Chamberlain or do-it-all superstars like Oscar Robertson or Jerry West. But Archie wasn't in their class. Or so he thought.

In 1964 Minnesota won the College World Series in Omaha, with sophomore center fielder Archie Clark chasing down fly balls like a big leaguer. He was that good. Archie's woes resided in the batter's box. Determined to show Major League scouts that he could hit for power, he too often swung for the fences. "Archie, just make contact," his manager, Dick Siebert, pleaded. But Archie couldn't help himself. Savvy opposing pitchers, seeing him step to the plate with his big swing, hurled a steady diet of slow curves, pitches that Archie struggled to hit, and the big-league scouts sniffed at the strikeouts.

Archie returned home in the summer of 1964. His marriage was on the rocks, and his Major League dream had fizzled. The scouts wouldn't take a chance on a twenty-three-year old prospect who would need to spend his peak physical years in the Minor Leagues learning to smack a curve ball. A factory job was a possibility, assuming he could pass the physical. But why settle for the status quo? He had reached the halfway point at college and could see the metaphorical light at the end of the tunnel. Archie vowed to leave Minnesota in two years with his degree in physical education, maybe find a teaching job, and—most important—settle into a stable, middle-class life.

BY HIS JUNIOR year Archie had settled like a rock into his role as the basketball team's leader. His job on offense was to sprint ahead with the ball on the fast break, force defenders to cut off his path to the basket, and then flip a pass to the trailing Lou Hudson or Don Yates on the wing for easy scores. Assuming the opposition cheated back on defense, Archie set up Minnesota's half-court offense and ran one of Kundla's set plays for Hudson. Or he simply rotated the ball to the sharp-shooting Terry Kunze in the corner for an open twenty-foot jump shot. The opposition couldn't keep up with Minnesota's speed and ball movement. Around campus the early-season domination had some whispering that the U might just have its greatest hardwood combination ever.

The buzz, though probably true, was short lived. Minnesota entered Big Ten play with two strikes against its championship hopes, the first obvious and the second known only to insiders. Strike one came when Kunze was caught cheating on a chemistry test and was ruled academically ineligible. There was nobody on the bench capable of replacing Kunze's scoring and snappy passing. Strike two was Coach Kundla. On paper Kundla was just the man to lead Minnesota to the Big Ten title. In the 1950s he had won five professional basketball championships while coaching the hometown Minneapolis Lakers, the NBA's first dynasty. With his personable, easygoing disposition, Kundla was an enormously popular figure around the Twin Cities. He was the embodiment of Minnesota's growing big-league image and a prime example of a hometown boy who had made good on the national stage.

Kundla's legend was at best a half truth. In the 1940s Kundla had been a successful high school and small-college coach in Minneapolis. That's where he planned to stay until the Lakers came knocking for a hometown face to lead their team. Kundla inherited pro basketball's equivalent of the New York Yankees. Four of the five starters on his 1950 NBA champion Lakers would land in the Naismith Basketball Hall of Fame. The players on his bench were nearly as good.

Kundla drew up his pet plays on the chalkboard and called for the dominating George Mikan to take most of the shots. But that's where his influence ended. Kundla kept a low profile on the bench during games and let the superstars, particularly playmaker and coach-on-the-floor Slater Martin, run the show. Some NBA writers dubbed Kundla "the coach nobody knows." Several players considered him lazy.

At Minnesota Kundla was lazy. Or maybe distracted is the better description. "Which way are they going to tip the basketball?" Kundla often whispered to his assistants at the start of games. Kundla's perpetual state of strategic confusion left Archie and crew locked into the same nuts-and-bolts strategy game after game—play tight defense, rebound, fast break, and punch the ball inside to Hudson. It also left Minnesota vulnerable to the more creative coaching minds at Michigan, UCLA, Kentucky, and the other powerhouse college basketball programs.

Strike three came when Michigan defeated Minnesota for the Big Ten title. In these days when only the Big Ten champion advanced to the NCAA men's basketball tournament, the second-place Gophers, who were 19–5, the school's best record in nearly two decades, never appeared in a postseason tournament.

---

*I'll tell you what finally made me think about playing pro basketball. I was a junior at Minnesota, and we traveled to Madison to play the University of Wisconsin. Our team had an assistant coach named Dan Spika. He knew his stuff and was real passionate about the game. Dan stopped by my hotel room the night before the Michigan game and started talking basketball with me and Don Yates. Dan turned real serious and said, "I don't know what's wrong with you guys. Don't you know how good you are?"*

*What Dan meant was the team was built around Lou Hudson. Lou was our All-American, and our job was to get him the ball. But Dan was challenging us to stop deferring to Lou and showcase our talent. He said, "You guys are good enough to play pro basketball."*

*Well, Don Yates might have already known how good he was. He had been the high school player of the year in Pennsylvania. But I didn't come from that kind of a basketball pedigree. Dan was the first per-*

*son to broach the possibility of me playing pro basketball. I remember*
*thinking to myself, "Maybe there is a future in this game"*

IN THE SUMMER of 1965 Archie returned to Ecorse and focused on
the possibility of playing in the NBA. In addition to the usual daily
playground battles, Archie worked hard to improve his jump shot.
Rotating from spot to spot around the perimeter of the basket, he
fired away five hundred shots per day—just the echo of a bouncing
ball and soft ripple of the net. As Archie imagined, he would carry
more of the scoring load in his senior year, and if Coach Spika was
right, he'd need a more accurate jump shot to make the NBA.

Coach Kundla had never spoken to Archie about the NBA. As
Kundla would later recall he had never received calls from NBA teams
or picked up the phone on Archie's behalf. Although Kundla remained
on paper the most successful coach in NBA history and clearly had
connections, college coaches in the mid-1960s rarely peddled their
players to pro teams. Or they did so at their own peril. The ethical
line between professional and amateur sport was still rigid and not to
be crossed cavalierly. Rumors that a college coach was openly entertaining NBA offers on behalf of a player could only lead to bad publicity and scandal.

Archie was literally on his own to ponder his place in the NBA. He
knew little about the NBA. Sure, Archie could rattle off the names of
the big NBA stars, among them Wilt Chamberlain, Bill Russell, Jerry
West, Elgin Baylor, and Oscar Robertson. But he couldn't name a
single starting lineup. If he happened to switch the channel and an
NBA game was on television, Archie usually watched for only a few
minutes. The games bored him. He preferred playing basketball, not
watching it.

Better yet, he preferred to make some money playing basketball.
Although Archie had done well in school, he had grown uninter-
ested in his major of physical education. He was certain that he didn't
want to spend his life teaching. In fact, now that he was single again,
Archie wasn't sure what he wanted to do with his life. A pro basketball career would give him some money and breathing room to
decide. So Archie practiced five hundred jump shots the next day . . .

and the next day. He planned to have a great senior year at Minnesota and then, with a little luck, earn an NBA contract.

"HEY, ROOMMATE, YOU went and broke my personal record," laughed Lou Hudson, angling himself next to Archie in the cramped visitors' locker room at the University of Detroit on the night before Christmas 1965.

"I apologize," Archie mumbled, preoccupied with cutting away the sticky layers of white tape from his foot.

Hudson, wearing a dark, loose-fitting suit, gestured with a bulky white plaster cast covering most of his slender right hand. The cast came after a nasty, bone-breaking tumble five nights earlier. As the sidelined Hudson acknowledged, his career high as the team's go-to guy over the last two seasons was thirty-six points. In his first game as the featured offensive weapon, Archie netted thirty-eight points to push the U to a hard-fought victory.

Waiting outside the locker room was a smiling Mr. Bibbs. He and a small entourage from Ecorse had arrived early to watch Archie's first showdown against Detroit's outstanding guard and River Rouge native Lou Hyatt. "Hyatt was averaging twenty-something points a game," said Mr. Bibbs. "Archie shut him down. That's when he convinced the boys back home that he was the truth. He was the real deal."

While Mr. Bibbs beamed with pride, Coach Kundla glowered with obvious concern. He continued to view his team—and prospects—through Hudson, and the doctors had ordered his star out for the duration of the Big Ten schedule. Adding to his woes, Don Yates had flunked out of school.

Kundla wondered how Clark, his tried-and-true team captain, could survive as a one-man band who ran the offense, defended the opposition's top scorer, and now shot his team to victory. As Mr. Bibbs could have told him, Archie had survived the projects, scaled mountains in Korea, and endured a tough divorce. Playing basketball was easy. He'd adjust and just keep going. By early February Kundla was genuinely astonished. Maybe Buzz Bennett and Dan Spika were right. Maybe Clark was one of the best players in the country. Nobody in the Big Ten could stop him.

When Hudson made an unexpected one-armed return to the lineup at midseason, his heroism raised an awkward question. Who was Minnesota's All-American candidate? Hudson or Clark? In the 1960s tradition dictated that colleges promote one All-American candidate at a time, even if they had two on their roster.

For Archie the question was critical for his NBA future. He had spent much of his collegiate career obscured by Hudson, and Archie's All-American honors and a twenty-four-points-per-game average, fourth best in the Big Ten, would boost his chances of an early—and more lucrative—selection in the upcoming NBA draft.

"Based on what has developed so far this season, I have to say that Archie Clark is the most deserving on our team," said Kundla in early February, before turning his loyalty and attention back to Hudson. "It's too bad that most of the votes are taken at this time of the year. You can never tell what Louie Hudson will do once he has the cast removed from his arm." Kundla, though certainly respectful of Archie's ability, never got around to pushing him as an All-American candidate. The other coaches voted him first-team All–Big Ten honors, but Archie received not a single All-American nod.

The lack of support left a sour taste in Archie's mouth. He had given his all during his senior year, piloting a thin Minnesota squad to a winning record and an unlikely fifth-place finish in the Big Ten. Wasn't that worth picking up the telephone, calling a reporter or scout, and otherwise helping him get ahead in life? To Archie it didn't seem fair.

By May the All-American Hudson was the fourth pick in the 1966 NBA draft. Archie wished his roommate the best. He was a great player. But without the All-American tag before his name Archie was a great player who fell to the Los Angeles Lakers in the third round. As a third rounder, he'd have to fight off the challenges of the other draft choices and free agents to make the team.

AFTER A TAME night in Las Vegas Archie and Valerie awoke the next morning, ordered breakfast, and made a point of hitting the road early. Los Angeles wasn't far now. They'd spend the next several hours along U.S. 466, crossing more of the barren Mojave Desert.

Once they hit Barstow, they'd bend south down to San Bernardino and then head west straight into LA. Archie wanted to reach the city by early afternoon while Lou Mohs and the Lakers staff were still in their offices at the Los Angeles Sports Arena. That way somebody could escort them to their hotel room. It had been a long trip, and Los Angeles was such a hopeless sprawl of buildings and boulevards.

Archie still hadn't heard where the Lakers planned to put up the players and their families during training camp. Two months earlier the team had flown Archie to town to attend rookie camp at Loyola College in West Los Angeles. He and the others had stayed for a week at the Airport Marina Hotel, which overlooked the undulating blue waters of the Pacific Ocean. Palm trees were everywhere. With the Spanish Colonial–style architecture and the sunny pastel colors, it was like waking up in a postcard each morning.

Archie and Valerie now planned to call Los Angeles home. As Archie reminded himself every day, he would work hard in training camp, impress the coaches, and make the Lakers' opening-season roster. He had no choice. An NBA career was his only chance to make good money. He'd already been through one tough marriage, and Archie wanted this one to work.

But first things first. He and Valerie would need to get to the hotel room that the Lakers had reserved for them and spend the next day recovering from their long trip out West.

## 4

*I'd had a solid rookie camp in June. When the Lakers invited me back in September to participate in their preseason training camp [with the veterans], I thought I had it made. I didn't understand that now I had to beat out the other veterans, rookies, and free agents to actually make the team.*

---

A rchie saw the brake lights flash red in front of him and tapped his brake pedal. Traffic on the Pasadena Freeway slowed for an instant and then sailed onward. Along the roadside thirty-foot palm trees rustled exotically overhead. In the distance Archie glimpsed row upon concrete row of single-level stucco homes and backyards landscaped with citrus trees and swimming pools—mass-produced, middle-class haciendas to celebrate sun, surf, and the good life. Archie had heard that without a car to ply the city's vast freeway system, the California dream and its perpetual state of motion ground to an unpleasant halt. Thank goodness for his trusty Olds Ninety Eight. The thing ran like a top.

As the traffic neared downtown Los Angeles and the usual rush-hour snarl, Archie spotted the green overhead sign for exit 26, Figueroa Street. Bingo. He signaled to exit, merged left into heavy midday traffic, and noticed in the distance the LA Coliseum and beside it the modern, glass-and-steel façade of the 15,300-seat Los Angeles Sports Arena, home of the NBA Lakers. Ten minutes later Archie stood in the air-conditioned lobby of the Lakers' office suite, exchanging another predictably awkward hello with general manager Lou Mohs.

"Mr. Mohs, my wife and I just got into town. I was wondering if you have a place ready for us to stay?"

Mohs frowned. "No, we don't offer accommodations," he answered tartly. "You have to find your own place to stay. Didn't you get our letter?"

Archie felt his heart begin to pound. What letter? Maybe he could afford another night in a hotel. Then again, maybe he couldn't. Finding an apartment was a lot to dump on a rookie from the Midwest with the start of training camp just around the corner. Archie didn't know his way around Los Angeles, nor did he have any idea of where black people were welcome. Los Angeles was just as self-segregating as Detroit, although a little more informal about it.

Mohs, anxious to get back to his desk, wasn't offering any advice. In fact Mohs seemed to want to be rid of his third-round draft choice altogether. "You know, Archie, there are other teams out there that need guards," Mohs shrugged. "Baltimore and Chicago will need help in the backcourt this season. You might have a better chance of making one of those teams."

The words cut through him like daggers. If the poker-faced Mohs was being truthful—and he seemed to be—the Lakers planned to cut him. At age twenty-five Archie's NBA career was over before it had started. He would be back in Ecorse by October, dead broke and scrambling to find a factory job to make his car payment. The thought chilled him. But Archie regained his composure, looked Mohs in the eyes, and chuckled politely, "I didn't come all this way to play for Baltimore or Chicago."

Archie headed back outside into the California dream, took a deep breath, and tried to remain calm as he told Valerie about the change in plans. He found a telephone booth nearby and dialed his mother. She had an idea. Archie's father Houston had a cousin whom everybody called Aunt Ruby. She and her husband lived in Los Angeles. Maybe Ruby could take them in until they got settled.

Archie dropped another dime into the pay phone and carefully dialed the number his mother had dictated. He heard the line crackle, followed by the first dull ring. What if nobody's home? What would he tell Valerie?

"Hello," a woman's voice answered.

Archie identified himself as Houston's son and, trying to sound upbeat, recounted his saga and predicament.

"Come on over here, baby," the warm, melodic voice answered.

Archie felt his tension ease. He jotted down the directions to the house, repeated them to her, and hurried back to his car.

Thank God for his big family.

"HELLO, BABY. YOU'VE come a long way," Aunt Ruby called out to Archie when he arrived. "How're your mother and father doing in Detroit?"

Aunt Ruby and her husband owned a single-story bungalow in the then racially mixed Crenshaw neighborhood in the city's southwest section. As Archie would discover, nobody had a bigger heart than Aunt Ruby. He and Valerie were in good hands.

That night Archie tossed and turned and replayed his brief encounter with Lou Mohs. Why had Mohs even drafted him? The only positive comment that Mohs had ever made publicly about Archie was that he already had completed his military service, a plus in these Cold War days.

Did Mohs have the final say on the Lakers' opening-season roster? Or did Lakers coach Fred Schaus? If it was Schaus, that gave Archie a fighting chance to make the Lakers. He did the math. The Lakers invited five guards to camp, and four would make the team. Jerry West, the team's superstar, was a seven-time all-NBA player. He wasn't going anywhere. Neither were second-year guards Gail Goodrich and Walt Hazzard. Both had starred for UCLA and were extremely popular around Los Angeles. That left rookie John Wetzel as Archie's sole competitor for the fourth and final guard spot. Archie paused. John Wetzel? He was the team's eighth-round draft choice. Why would Mohs prefer to keep a seemingly obscure eighth-round pick from the Virginia Polytechnic Institute over a third-round choice with All–Big Ten credentials who had been a standout in rookie camp? It didn't make sense. And if it didn't make sense, it couldn't be true. Could it?

SEVERAL MILES AWAY at his home in Inglewood, Lou Mohs lay in bed that night hoping not to feel the pain. His doctors said he was down to months, maybe a year, before he would lose his battle with cancer. Although Mohs maintained the tanned, buttoned-down appearance of a Los Angeles business executive by day, he had dropped a great deal of weight over the last several months. For many at work, it was hard to believe this tall, frail, sixty-something-year-old had played three seasons in the National Football League back in the 1920s and answered to the nickname "Big Lou."

Mohs continued to push himself through the daily aches and fatigue. The Los Angeles Lakers were his baby, and it was hard for him to let go. Six years ago, in the summer of 1960, Big Lou had signed on as general manager of the Lakers to relocate the failing franchise from his native Minnesota to Los Angeles. The Lakers' nearest NBA neighbor would be more than eighteen hundred miles away in St. Louis.

Bob Short, the team's forty-two-year-old majority owner, advised Mohs that he would stay behind in Minneapolis and tend to his trucking company. As Short told Mohs, he and his investors had lost a hefty $300,000 on the Lakers. They couldn't afford to fritter away much more. If Mohs could turn a quick profit for them in Los Angeles, they could cover their losses and sell the team to the next sucker. Before Mohs departed, Short reportedly handed over $5,000 in seed money, wished him Godspeed on behalf of the stockholders, and repeated the half-serious instructions: "Go out there and don't let me hear from you; if you have any money left, send it back to me; if you need any money, forget where you came from."

Through much trial and error Mohs sold Southern California on the Lakers. In this city of stars his main attraction was the high-scoring Elgin Baylor. Although the team's leading man was black, Mohs wasn't worried about selling tickets. Not in Los Angeles, where entertainment came in all colors, though presumably in the right proportions, and Baylor had the magnetic presence of a hip jazz musician. Most considered the price of admission a bargain to experience Baylor's virtuosity, the float and the flourish that no other American in a pair of sneakers could equal.

The other leading man was Jerry West, a skinny, 6-foot-3 white kid with a crooked nose and crew cut. As his more worldly teammates joked, Jerry was just "Zeke from Cabin Creek." He was a Walt Disney throwback character—a shy, self-critical, socially awkward backwoodsman who felt more at home in Boomer, West Virginia, than on Wilshire Boulevard. And there was absolutely no hiding it. "When he first came to L.A., he had an accent only a few squirrels could understand," wisecracked *Los Angeles Times* columnist Jim Murray.

Mohs realized that if he could get fans to the games, Zeke from Cabin Creek would take care of the rest. Nobody played harder than

West, and nobody was more clutch with the ball in his hands and the shot clock winding down.

Although some questioned the wisdom of promoting a two-man show in a sport that historically offered fans intricate, five-man offensive patterns, Mohs would hear none of it. In 1954 the NBA owners had voted in a twenty-four-second clock to speed up games—and to make a statement. The NBA was in the entertainment business. If fans wanted to watch deliberate offensive sets and cheer final scores of 46–42, they could take a seat in a college gymnasium. But if they wanted to watch basketball's greatest stars go head to head every twenty-four seconds and light up the arena with their extraordinary talent and 120 guaranteed shots per game, the NBA was their ticket.

"Willie Mays comes up to bat just four times in a game for the [baseball] Giants," Mohs shrewdly explained the comparative advantage of paying four bucks to watch the Lakers. "But there's nothing in the basketball rules that says we can't have our best shooters try fifty baskets a game if we want them to."

Describing those fifty baskets a game was Chick Hearn, one of the best play-by-play announcers in the business. Hearn, a chatty Art Linkletter clone, had turned a struggling, seemingly self-conscious basketball team into a trusted, entertaining, fifty-thousand-watt friend: "Rudy LaRusso—and isn't he a handsome young man, folks?—passes the ball from the corner to Jerry West. Zeke from Cabin Creek . . . dribbles in the backcourt, showing no signs of favoring his injured knee while his lovely wife Jane watches from courtside. . . . West passes ten feet into the right forecourt to Elgin Baylor. Elg yo-yos the dribble in front of the key, fakes Bob Pettit into the popcorn machine, jumps, hangs suspended ten feet in the air, is hit, shoots twenty feet straightaway. It looks good, it'll count if it goes, it goes, it is good!"

All that was left for Mohs, before the cancer took him, was to beat the Boston Celtics. The Celtics had bested the Lakers two out of three seasons in the NBA finals. As hard as it was to admit, the Celtics were just better. They were like an old battle-tested army platoon that fought as hard as necessary—but they always pulled together and won in the end.

The Lakers also had absolutely no answer for the dominating,

6-foot-10 Bill Russell. He was an explosive leaper, quick as a cat, and always in position to rebound, block shots, and otherwise intimidate opponents. Mohs had tried his damnedest to find Russell's 6-foot-11 match. In fact he'd rotated more big men into Laker uniforms than he could count—Jim Krebs, Ray Felix, Wayne Yates, Gene Wiley, LeRoy Ellis, Tom Dose, Darrell Imhoff. None could handle Russell.

The hole in the middle bothered new owner Jack Kent Cooke. The fifty-two-year-old self-made media mogul paid a record $5.175 million to purchase the Lakers from Bob Short in June 1965. It was a startling—no, a jaw-dropping—figure. Short and his stockholders had purchased the team eight years earlier in Minneapolis for $150,000. As recently as 1960 Laker stockholders had sold their shares in the team for ten cents on the dollar; others had simply handed back their shares to Short and called it even. Was any basketball team really worth $5 million? Or was this new, emerging breed of sports entrepreneurs just crazy? In Cooke's case he knew zero about the sport other than that the garages of many Southern California homes were decorated with wooden backboards and that owning a pro basketball team might make a promising investment.

Cooke grinned like a fox at those who questioned his sanity, having privately appraised the team's worth at $4.5 million. "I know it is a high price to pay, but eventually it will be worth it," said Cooke, a short, balding Canadian ex-patriot with slits for eyes and the affected voice and air of a Shakespearean actor. "Bob Short is a hard man to do business with, but I like him. Not enough, however, to sell it back to him for a million-dollar profit when it dawns on him next week or next year what he has done. The Lakers are here to stay."

The NBA and its mostly undercapitalized, hand-to-mouth arena owners who still operated many of the franchises had never seen anything like Cooke's pushy, conquer-the-world ambition. Most insiders simply bristled at his megalomaniacal behavior. "He [Cooke] was the number one asshole that ever lived," said former player Rod Hundley, who now teamed with Chick Hearn in the broadcast booth. "He was totally, absolutely, unbelievably wrapped up in himself and had no respect for anyone but himself."

Mohs, though stoic, seasoned, and sixty years savvy, clearly walked on eggshells around Cooke. The new boss, with his whirlwind mind, left little in his path unscathed. He grilled Mohs about the team's finances, rewrote the team's fight song to his liking, sent memos to Chick Hearn on proper word pronunciation, and consolidated press row in the Sports Arena to create a special section where he could lounge at courtside with the Hollywood stars. Mohs didn't push back. He was too tired for that now. His health continued to decline, and his days with the Lakers were numbered. Mohs checked his ego at the front door and got with the program of hailing the emperor and his new pajamas. "I have worked with many brilliant and aggressive men, but Mr. Jack Kent Cooke has to be the most versatile, experienced, and eloquent of all," Mohs pandered. "I don't think you can say enough about this man's drive and enthusiasm. It's catching—or better be—and affects his entire organization, escalating even greater successes."

In truth Mohs benefited from Cooke's arrival. He no longer had to worry about the administrative bean counting nor about planning promotional giveaways. He could focus his energy, as Cooke called it, on the "day-to-day operations" of the team under his new title as vice president and general manager. In other words Big Lou would work more closely with Fred Schaus to produce a winning product for Cooke and his minions to sell. In addition to deciding which players to keep, Mohs spent more time on the road scouting college players. Mohs, after all, considered himself to be one of the best talent scouts in the business. His secret: look for players with long arms. They played taller than their height.

While on the road, Mohs noticed a lanky, long-armed, 6-foot-5 white kid from the Virginia Polytechnic Institute named John Wetzel, probably in the first round of New York's National Invitation Tournament (NIT). Wetzel wasn't mentioned prominently in any of the standard college basketball magazines that scouts then used as cheat sheets. And yet number 24 had a real presence about him on the court and a soft shot. Mohs made a mental note. He may have just stumbled onto the next Jerry West.

That May, Mohs selected Wetzel in the eighth round of the 1966 NBA draft. Mohs might have chosen him earlier, but Wetzel had broken the navicular bone in his right wrist. He was back in Blacksburg, Virginia, wearing a cast and hoping to begin rehabbing his wrist in a couple of months.

"When the Lakers drafted me," Wetzel recalled, "I went into Howard Shannon, my college coach, and asked him, 'What would you do if you had a cast on your hand and you had a chance to try out for a pro team?' He said, 'I'd cut the damn cast off and go try out.' So I walked up to the college infirmary, and I had one of the guys take a saw and cut it off."

"I flew to Los Angeles and played well in rookie camp," Wetzel continued. "At the end of camp Fred Schaus and Lou Mohs called the players individually into a room to meet with them. That's when they'd either let you go or invite you back to attend the veterans' camp. I got in there, and they said, 'Wow, we like what you did. We want you to come back in the fall.' Of course, nobody had agents back then. They just pulled out an NBA contract and offered me $11,000 on the spot to sign with the Lakers."

Wetzel signed on the dotted line and flew home to Blacksburg. An orthopedist replaced a plaster cast on his broken wrist, and Wetzel lugged the thing around for another six weeks. Just long enough to pack his bags and say his goodbyes. John Wetzel was headed to California to play for the Los Angeles Lakers.

---

*The Lakers held training camp at Loyola University in the hills of West Los Angeles. It was a beautiful setting, with lots of palm trees and the blue waters of the Pacific Ocean in the distance. The Loyola gymnasium was small and really pretty basic. Nothing fancy at all. When camp started, I was polite and introduced myself to everyone. But my focus was completely on making the team. I was all business, especially after Lou Mohs had told me a few days earlier to consider trying out for another NBA team. Elgin Baylor started calling me Toughie. Elgin would see me sitting there by myself at practice, staring straight ahead and trying to gather my thoughts. He'd walk up and say, "Calm down, Toughie; you look like you want to go out and kill somebody." Elgin was just that way, always joking around and saying things to get a rise out of you. I just smiled and got back to business. I had to make the team.*

COACH SCHAUS TOOTED his whistle, and about a dozen tall men in practice gear immediately rotated around the perimeter of the basket, shooting jump shots, one after the other. The mass shooting drill turned the Loyola gymnasium into a rhythmic, thudding, squeaking echo chamber. Seated in the wooden bleachers of the gymnasium was Lou Mohs. He had made up his mind. The Lakers had to keep rookie John Wetzel as their fourth and final guard.

Mohs had no problem with Archie Clark. In fact Clark had looked real sharp at the start of training camp, but the businessman in Mohs said that he had no choice. Clark was a small guard, and the Lakers already had two good ones in Walt Hazzard and Gail Goodrich. Wetzel was a big guard at six feet five inches, and he could reliably spot West for a few minutes per game and even fill in at forward if needed.

Mohs also had to worry about the Lakers' "balance," a code word for too many blacks on the roster. Although every team defined "balance" differently, Mohs drew the line at five black players on his twelve-man roster, up from four African Americans in the early 1960s. His gut told him that average white fans would start calling the team "too black" past that point. They'd quit identifying with the team and attendance would suffer.

That's why Mohs had traded forward Tommy Hawkins, one of his favorite black players, to the Cincinnati Royals at the start of the 1962–63 season. Mohs had always regretted that trade. As the sentimental last wish of a dying man, Mohs planned to trade for Hawkins and forward Jim "Bad News" Barnes, another of his favorite black players, and bring them home for what might be his final season. If Mohs kept Clark, he would have six whites and six blacks or, in the strange math of the NBA, an imbalance.

Mohs met with the team publicist Warren Turnbull to begin preparing the annual Laker yearbook and the other standard promotional materials. His orders: keep the photo of Wetzel; don't worry about Clark.

Before Mohs could meet with Clark to deliver the pink slip, the Ax struck again. The Ax was Laker center Darrall Imhoff, who had earned the nickname for constantly hacking opponents on shots. During a team scrimmage Wetzel saw an opening, drove hard to the basket, and Imhoff reached in for the steal. The 6-foot-11, 225-pound Ax got all wrist and no ball. "Darrall broke my wrist for a second time," said Wetzel. "So that was the end of training camp for me."

Mohs now faced a dilemma. He could keep Clark, the only viable fourth guard in training camp, and imbalance his roster. Or he could work the phones to see if he could orchestrate a trade for a decent white guard. Big Lou started dialing.

# 5

B altimore, October 15, 1966. A steady rain fell over Baltimore, sending a line of raincoats and black umbrellas scampering for cover into the Maryland Avenue entrance of the Civic Center, tickets in hand. The lobby reeked of cigarette smoke, but that came with the territory. The NBA placed no restrictions on smoking in its arenas, and every adult in this solidly working-class city seemed to puff away, sending a collective choke of white smoke to the ceiling, where it formed cotton candy clouds.

"Ladies and gentlemen, welcome to the Baltimore Civic Center for the opening contest of the 1966–67 National Basketball Association season between the visiting Los Angeles Lakers and your Baltimore Bullets," began the public address system. The usual whoops and whistles from the three-dollar seats greeted the announcement. About eight thousand Baltimoreans had passed up their regular Saturday night television date with the TV show *Gunsmoke* to watch the shootout between Elgin Baylor's Lakers and their Bullets, picked to finish dead last in the NBA Eastern Division. "At this time, please extinguish all smoking materials, remove all hats, and rise for the playing of the national anthem."

At courtside Fred Schaus and his Los Angeles Lakers, clad in their road blue jerseys, jostled into place and squared their shoulders toward the flag. Among them was number 21, Archie Clark. Lou Mohs couldn't trade Archie and, shrugging a let's-see-how-it-goes, kept him on his opening-night roster. The Lakers were a little too black by NBA standards, but Schaus could care less. He had clapped Archie on the shoulder in the locker room and told him to be ready. With Jerry West injured, Archie would log several minutes tonight off the bench.

As Baltimore's Pier 5 Dixieland band tooted out the familiar first stanzas of the national anthem, Archie's mind drifted: "Make sure to push the ball up court on offense, get the ball to Elgin in the corner early in the twenty-four-second clock, and hustle back on defense." Archie felt a tad nervous, but the butterflies weren't so bad. He belonged in the NBA.

Training camp had taught Archie that management was coy and not to be trusted. Think about it. He had averaged twenty points and ten assists per game in preseason, and Lou Mohs had still intended to cut him. Why? Was he too small, too black, too tough, too dime-a-dozen? Archie hadn't a clue. He remained naïve to the backroom wheeling and dealing of the pro basketball moguls, as they were called, and their fixation on roster balance. All he could fathom was that the pro game operated according to its own slippery, arcane logic. Teams sold their individual stars and touted their rock-solid starting fives like brand names to keep the turnstiles clicking. But management could replace the supporting cast arrayed on the bench as quickly as it poured its next cup of coffee in the morning. For every Archie Clark there was a John Wetzel itching to take his place for the going rate of $11,000 per year or less.

Unbeknown to Archie, Mohs probably would have traded him if he could have found a taker. But none of the teams wanted to take a chance on a third-round draft choice sight unseen, especially if he was black. And therein hung a historical tale.

In the early 1950s the first black players in the NBA were strictly blue-collar workers. Their job: set solid screens, rebound, and do the dirty work to help their white teammates. In 1955 Rochester's black rookie forward Maurice Stokes changed everything. Stokes was then an utterly unique talent, combining the brawn of a center with the agility and ball handling of a guard. Rochester had no choice but to run plays for Stokes and turn him loose. Other NBA general managers took note. A black star didn't hurt attendance. The Stokes epiphany dovetailed with the NBA debuts of Bill Russell, Wilt Chamberlain, Elgin Baylor, and other game-altering African American players. Management now rolled out the red carpet for the best black players, although it remained keenly aware of the roster balance. To keep up appearances most teams reserved their final roster spots for white players. That made a capable white reserve a far more valuable commodity to an NBA general manager than a capable black reserve.

Archie didn't know Lou Mohs had cancer. He wasn't too fond of his general manager and his dry, overbearing demeanor; but Archie was willing to play for the wrinkled hand that fed him, especially if it meant staying in Los Angeles. He loved everything about LA, from the ninety-degree temperatures to the laid-back lifestyle to the easy camaraderie in the Lakers' locker room. Valerie was expecting their first child, and Archie hoped they could settle down in a nice neighborhood somewhere in one of the sun-splashed valleys and chase that California dream.

Chasing that dream, of course, meant taking on the uphill battle of boosting his NBA earning power to $20,000 or more per season. Although it was taboo for NBA players to discuss their contracts, he'd heard mumblings that only the superstars inked meaty multi-year deals. Everybody else got the scraps—standard, one-year agreements that were renewed at the start of each season. Because very few players dared to hire legal representation and challenge the team's authority in financial matters, the negotiation process sometimes was as perfunctory as a "Just say 'Ah'" physical examination. General managers pulled out a standard league contract and filled in a conservative dollar figure that balanced the team's financial needs and their own personal druthers about a player. They then asked each veteran to sign on the dotted line and remember to count his lucky stars that the NBA existed to give him a chance to travel and play pro ball.

As the Lakers huddled in the Baltimore Civic Center before the start of their season opener, Archie listened intently as Fred Schaus barked out his pregame instructions one last time: "Keep Gus Johnson off the boards, and don't let Kevin Loughery dribble to the basket." Elgin Baylor had nicknamed Schaus "Stomp" for pounding his foot on the floor like a clap of thunder whenever he got excited. Whatever Stomp wanted, Archie planned to give—and more. Archie just wanted to win, earn a reputation as a quality NBA guard, and sign a $20,000 contract.

THE DOWNTOWN STREETS were still. Big cities always seemed so groggy on Sunday mornings. The storefronts near Baltimore's Holiday Inn, where the Lakers spent the night, remained dark as pitch, except for the neighborhood bakeries and the corner newsstands with their bundled newspaper stacks piled high out front. Over breakfast Archie bought a newspaper and glanced at a long synopsis of last night's Lakers victory: "Baby-faced Gail Goodrich gave an excellent impersonation of ailing all-pro Jerry West and Elgin Baylor was just his old destructive self as the Los Angeles Lakers ran the Bullets dizzy in a front-running 126–115 victory at the Civic Center last night."

True enough. Goodrich got hot early, and Baylor took charge in the fourth quarter. Archie finished with an easy nine points in his pro debut. He tried not to get too high or low about the game. The NBA wasn't like college, where bragging rights came with beating a Big Ten rival. As the veterans advised him, it was one game down, another eighty to go. Next stop: Madison Square Garden for a Tuesday evening clash with the New York Knickerbockers.

NEW YORK, OCTOBER 18, 1966. The New York Knickerbockers had missed the playoffs for ten of the last eleven seasons, and they had bombed in their season opener on the road in Philadelphia. The *New York Daily News* opined, "Knix Up to Old Trix, But. . . ."

The "but" was Knicks coach Dick McGuire. "Mumbles," as everyone called him for his indecipherable rapid-fire Brooklyn brogue, was no John Wooden (the innovative college coach at UCLA) or even a Fred Schaus. "Dis is a team game. I wan' ya to run," he had offered as his only words of pregame inspiration last season to launch the McGuire era. But Mumbles was, if nothing else, Brooklyn tough, and maybe he could toughen up the Knicks. The *New York Daily News* and its thousands of readers hoped to get the answer tonight in their home opener against the Lakers.

Mumbles's minions cruised to a double-digit lead, and, as often happens in the NBA, the intensity picked up in the second half as the Lakers' Rudy LaRusso and the Knicks' Willis Reed began to tangle inside. With the third quarter winding down, a now nameless Laker shanked a free throw. As the ball caromed off the rim, LaRusso and Reed tussled once again for the rebound. Reed, built like Hercules, swung an elbow, and LaRusso answered with a punch that glanced off Reed's chin.

"The two fired-up youngsters tore into each other as they spilled along the 50th Street side of the arena and then waltzed their way along the Eighth Avenue end,." wrote the *New York Daily News*. Or directly in front of the Lakers' bench. Reed looked ready to tear the leaner LaRusso limb from limb. Seeing their teammate had met his match, Lakers guard Walt Hazzard and rookie forward John Block leapt off the bench and grabbed Reed from behind to restrain him. Big mistake. As a child, Reed had been grabbed from behind by two boys and badly beaten. Reed felt the tug from behind and panicked. He clocked Block, breaking his nose.

Archie stood across the court next to Baylor. Neither made a move to dive into the fray. LaRusso was the team's tough guy, after all, and the fight would be over in a minute. Basketball fights always were. "Whoa, look at that," Baylor chuckled. "He got a good one in."

When order was restored, Reed, who walked away with only a gash on the inside of his lip, and the largely unscathed LaRusso had been ejected. Though the Lakers came out ahead on ejections, the Knicks would win the contest on points.

Before sunrise the next morning Archie and crew already had checked out of the Statler Hilton Hotel on Eighth Avenue and boarded a bus to JFK Airport. The league's early years had been punctuated with embarrassing, weather-related no-shows and late arrivals by road teams. No more. Per NBA rules the Lakers had to catch the first available flight to Chicago to ensure that come hell or high water, they arrived as soon as possible for the next game against the Bulls, the league's first expansion team. Archie had never felt more tired in his life.

INGLEWOOD, CALIFORNIA, OCTOBER 20, 1966. The Lakers returned to Los Angeles humbled by their brief stop in Chicago. The expansion Bulls, tossed together like a salad from the league's leftover talent, outdueled the Lakers. The star of the game was Chicago's crafty veteran Guy Rodgers, whom Archie admittedly struggled to defend in his third pro game. "I never played against Bob Cousy, but I'd seen him on TV," said Archie. "Guy did everything that Cousy did with the ball—only twice as fast."

Despite the embarrassing loss, things were looking up for the Lakers on the newsstands. *Sports Illustrated*, the full-color magazine and weekly oracle of the nation's sports junkies, had sent out its NBA season-preview issue. On the cover was none other than Elgin Baylor. With a little help from Lou Mohs and the Lakers publicists, Baylor had been all over the newsstand this autumn under the heading of miracle recovery. Contrary to those who had written him off after two knee surgeries in as many years, Baylor had regained much of his former offensive magic, although at a lower altitude, and Mohs and the NBA wanted to get the word out. "Elgin Baylor is back, his knees restyled and his magnetic quality reconstituted, so that he is again the player of basketball legend, of his own elegant moves, all smoothness, all power," wrote *Sports Illustrated*.

Archie wasn't sure what to make of Baylor. Archie of course had heard of Baylor in college, but, as a baseball fan, he had never had reason to embrace his legend. At first Archie thought Baylor was just lucky on the court. He would bull to the basket and throw up shots that seemed to glance randomly off the backboard, thudded two or three times on the rim, and, as though succumbing to some magnetic force, dropped through the net. It had to be all luck.

"Hey, Toughie," Baylor yelled to Archie one day after practice. "Come here a minute." Baylor ran Archie through his complete repertoire of spin shots. Each whirled through the net over and over and over again. Archie got the point. Baylor was a master of his craft, and he seemingly had 365 different ways to put the ball through the basket. There was nobody in the NBA like him.

Now into his eighth pro season Baylor was like an aging heavyweight champion in boxing. He sucked all attention to himself whenever he entered a room. But everyone wondered how much longer the champ could keep weathering the punishment. "Baylor no longer can and probably never will again be able to sustain peak efforts game after game," wrote an NBA insider. "It's not a case of not wanting to but rather one of too much surgery and pain."

And it was also a case of too much susceptibility to further injury. About a week after his *Sports Illustrated* cover (does it qualify as the *Sports Illustrated* curse?) Baylor made a quick move near the basket against the Knicks. He felt a sharp pain, like he'd been shot in his right knee, and collapsed to the hardwood. According to the team physician, it was only a strained ligament. But Baylor and his then league-leading thirty-nine points per game would be out of action "indefinitely," which in the 1960s must-play NBA roughly translated to "at least a week." With West still wearing a soft cast on a foot that was slow to mend, Schaus and the Lakers were stuck "indefinitely" in a holding pattern.

INGLEWOOD, CALIFORNIA, NOVEMBER 19, 1966. Lou Mohs had quietly finagled a deal eighteen months ago to take All-American Rick Barry in the 1965 NBA college draft. The Lakers owner at the time, Bob Short, had put his foot down. Short wanted the other All-American white kid, Gail Goodrich. Mohs still grumbled; if not for that blankety-blank Short, the Lakers would feature West, Baylor, and the handsome, boy-next-door Barry, who instead joined the rival San Francisco Warriors. Barry now ranked "second in popularity in San Francisco only to the five o'clock martini."

Barry certainly didn't hold any hard feelings toward the Lakers. But Super Rick always seemed to save his best for his in-state rivals, and tonight Barry dropped a cool forty-five points on Elgin Baylor's return from the injured list. Following the thirty-three-point drubbing, which included a second-half chorus of boos from the Laker faithful (likely with owner Jack Kent Cooke at courtside), Fred Schaus was stomping mad and lit into his team behind closed doors for a full twenty minutes.

Jerry West, also just back, continued to struggle mightily. His jump shot was sometimes as crooked as his nose. Without the Dynamic Duo, Baylor and West, clicking in Los Angeles, the Western Division belonged to Barry and the Warriors. As if to emphasize that point, the Warriors crushed the visiting Lakers 130–107 in their next meeting a month later without Barry. Nate Thurmond, the Warriors center extraordinaire, snatched thirty-seven rebounds in that one.

"Everyone talks about Wilt Chamberlain and Bill Russell," said Archie. "They were great players, don't get me wrong, but they had little holes in their game that you could always use to your advantage. That wasn't the case with Nate Thurmond. He had no holes in his game. Nate was strong, athletic, fundamentally sound, and did everything well for a big man."

NEW YORK, DECEMBER 27, 1966. Fred Schaus shuddered about the other night. The Boston Celtics, the NBA team that Schaus hated above all others, had run roughshod over his Lakers. They'd lost five of their last six games, nine of their last fourteen. What was he going to do about his ailing, underachieving team? The league was starting to gossip. "We've just been talking about it," admitted Celtics reserve forward Don Nelson. "But we can't understand it. Baylor's playing up to par. Imhoff's having a great year. West has been good. I'm stumped."

Jack Kent Cooke, meanwhile, kept breathing down Schaus's neck to bring back the title-contending Lakers of old. But how? Stuffed in his briefcase, Schaus had a detailed statistical breakdown of the season to date. In the first thirty games or so, opposing NBA teams had scored two-thirds of their points against the Lakers from the backcourt, meaning that Goodrich and Hazzard weren't, in coach-speak, getting the job done on defense. What about Clark? He was the team's lone bright spot against the Celtics. He played defense, according to a courtside observer, with "the furtive look of a hold-up man on his first job, stalking his prey on the balls of his feet, eyes scanning right and left like a radarscope seeking potential threats, blocking shots, intercepting passes." What if he moved Clark into the starting lineup against the New York Knicks? It was worth a try, Schaus thought.

Archie gazed down from his hotel window at the yellow cabs and delivery trucks bunched like bumper cars. How did anyone drive in Manhattan anyway? Archie and his teammates had a day to themselves before their Wednesday afternoon game at Madison Square Garden. In the NBA a day off usually meant killing time.

Life on the road was a case study in human disorientation. NBA players marched to a sensory-numbing beat of 1 a.m. hotel arrivals, breakfast at 2 p.m., wet jerseys draped and drying over the backs of hotel chairs, smoke-filled arenas, roaring crowds, word-twisting reporters, postgame bull sessions with teammates in twenty-four-hour burger joints, and early morning wake-up calls to catch the first flight out of town. Over and over again.

Archie went out with his teammates occasionally. But he mostly stayed put at the hotel or ventured out on his own to go shopping or grab a bite to eat. It was just easier that way. Archie was still very much the kid from the projects. Survival came first, and survival now meant staying focused on his pro career. As the past several months had taught him, the NBA was full of surprises. You had to stay on your toes.

As a matter of fact, Fred Schaus had asked Archie real cheerfully to meet him in the hotel lobby. It might be nothing. Then again, everyone knew that Lou Mohs had been trying to finalize a trade before the Lakers embarked on their eastern trip. Archie was a little on edge because Schaus also wanted to meet downstairs with Tommy Hawkins. His name always came up in trades.

Archie, bracing for the words "You've been traded to Chicago," spotted Stomp downstairs and made the slow march over. The losing season clearly was wearing on Schaus. A sturdy man with the alternately stoic and friendly demeanor of his native working-class Ohio, Schaus was the consummate coach. "I always kept notebooks, diagrams of plays and things," he once said. "I did that when I was in college, when I was in the service, and when I was in pro ball." Schaus had forsaken most of his notebooks in Los Angeles. His job was to get the ball to Baylor and West.

After the usual hellos Schaus turned to the veteran Hawkins and said, "It's going to disrupt the team somewhat, but I'm putting you and Archie in the starting lineup tomorrow against the Knicks." Hawkins nearly fell out of his chair. "Archie and I had no idea this was coming," he recalled. "We were speechless."

As Schaus explained his decision, the two nodded as if their coach were diagramming a play on a chalkboard. Inside they were ready to burst. Schaus told them to keep the news under their hats until tomorrow. He just wanted to give them a heads-up.

The thirty-year-old Hawkins had played his heart out just about every night of his eight-year career as an athletic but undersized

6-foot-5 forward. All of the hard work finally had paid off. He was back in the starting lineup.

Archie and Tommy the Hawk, as everyone called him, decided to have dinner and replay what had just happened. "As soon as we hit the front door of the hotel, we started dancing," said Hawkins. "We danced all the way to the restaurant. Over dinner I remember us vowing that we would never relinquish these positions."

# 6

*I was the thirty-seventh player selected in the 1966 NBA draft. By mid-season I ranked third among NBA rookies in minutes played and started for the Lakers opposite Jerry West. So my professional basketball career was coming together. Valerie and I moved out of Aunt Ruby's house and into a two-bedroom duplex in Inglewood, then an overwhelmingly white, middle-class suburb. A lot different than it is today. The duplex was owned by my teammate Walt Hazzard. He and his wife Jaleesa lived on one side; we stayed on the other. The duplex was near the airport, and that turned out to be a real advantage. After a long road trip back east it was nice to land at LAX and be home in a few minutes. And I wanted to be home as much as possible. Valerie was expecting our first child in March.*

---

Inglewood, California, January 3, 1967. Since the starting lineup had been shuffled eleven days ago, the Lakers had showed they could play hard-nosed, cohesive defense, and Jerry West's jump shot finally found the bottom of the net as in seasons past. Fred Schaus attributed West's turnaround to his professionalism. While certainly true, Schaus had forgotten another major catalyst: Archie had made the game easier for West.

"I'd noticed sitting on the bench that Jerry and Elgin wanted the ball early in the shot clock," said Archie. "Walt [Hazzard] wouldn't do it. He'd try to break down the defense off the dribble to create shots for everybody. Not out of spite but because that's what he did in college. He controlled the basketball and made the plays. . . . But Jerry and Elgin could create their own shots," he continued. "They didn't need Walt to set them up. When Fred put me in the starting lineup, I made sure to get them the basketball when and where they wanted it."

Archie also greatly reduced the defensive wear and tear on West. Archie could guard the other team's best backcourt player, and that meant West was free to roam the passing lanes to block shots, swipe passes, and run the floor. "When people think of Jerry, they think of his offense," said Archie. "But he and Philadelphia's Hal "Bulldog" Greer were two of the best off-the-ball defenders in the history of the game."

The team's core problem remained as obvious as the San Gabriel Mountains, however: the Lakers didn't match up well against teams with dominant frontlines. Laker center Darrall Imhoff had played well, even earning an appearance in the NBA All-Star Game, but he remained the Ax on defense and a butter knife on offense.

Lou Mohs had traded for Bad News Barnes during training camp, convinced that he would be the final piece to the Laker championship puzzle. According to Mohs, Barnes would neutralize the Reeds and Russells with his girth and gritty play, and West and Baylor would take care of the rest.

If only it had been that easy. Barnes had been a flop, Baylor and West had been hobbled, and the team's still lackluster 18–26 record had everyone in Lakerland on edge. Making matters worse, Jack Kent Cooke had begun to meddle in personnel decisions. Against Schaus's objections and an appeasing shrug of the shoulders from Mohs, Cooke traded the popular Rudy LaRusso to Detroit. LaRusso refused to go, claiming Cooke hurt the team's confidence, and Schaus had become a nervous, foot-stomping wreck. "I've never been anything but kindness personified to Rudy," Cooke countered. "My rooting hasn't affected Elgin Baylor, Jerry West, Archie Clark, Jerry Chambers, or that wonderful Fred Schaus." Nevertheless, Cooke quickly canceled the trade to stop its run of bad publicity. When the NBA owners intervened to enforce the trade, LaRusso retired in protest.

INGLEWOOD CALIFORNIA, FEBRUARY 1, 1967. The games kept coming and coming in a blur of towns and testosterone. Archie and Walt Hazzard commuted by car to home games from their duplex at 102nd Street and First Avenue, just around the corner from where Jack Kent Cooke was building his new arena. Although they played the same backcourt position, Archie respected Hazzard's game—and vice versa—and that gave them space to reach out to each other off the court. They were, as Hazzard's wife Jaleesa recalled, "two guys in the same business." A decade ago two young black players wouldn't have thought to compare notes; they would have been grateful just to be in the league. Now, like their white teammates, they had ten-year careers and fatter contracts to ponder.

Both Archie and Walt found their chosen profession perplexingly random. Take the LaRusso mess. Rudy had given his heart and soul to the Lakers for going on eight seasons, punishing his body night after night against bigger men and getting injections of God knows what to numb the pain. Then in early January the Lakers looked terrible at home against the Knicks, and a fuming Jack Kent Cooke pinned the blame on LaRusso and his roughhouse tactics. He ordered Lou Mohs to get rid of him. Mohs, who was like a father to LaRusso, acquiesced, but who did he try to get for LaRusso? LeRoy Ellis—the same player that the Lakers had shipped to Baltimore six months earlier. When Baltimore wouldn't budge on Ellis, Mohs took Mel Counts off its hands. Poor Mel. Red Auerbach, Boston's crazy-like-a-fox coach, had traded him to Baltimore two years ago for the beloved Bailey Howell. Auerbach laughed all the way to the 1966 NBA championship, while the Bullets languished in last place. The Baltimore fans never let Mel forget it, though he had had absolutely no say in the trade or the subpar talent that surrounded him. Now his once promising career was on the rocks.

Hazzard certainly could relate. His NBA career had stalled badly in its third season, ironically because of his outstanding basketball pedigree. Hazzard had been a first-team All-American and star of UCLA's 1964 men's national champion team. His coach, John Wooden, the "Wizard of Westwood," taught crisp, five-man, textbook basketball, and as the team's playmaker, Hazzard had become Wooden's eyes and ears on the court. Hazzard now grumbled that Schaus, though a nice guy, couldn't hold a chalkboard to Wooden, and he resented playing the Lakers' watered-down, two-man game.

Hazzard figured his days with the Lakers were numbered. The NBA had plans to add two expansion teams next season in San Diego and Seattle, and the Lakers likely would throw his name into the hopper for the expansion draft. Another possibility was the American Basketball Association (ABA). Yes, a second pro basketball league was in the works. These guys were going to play with a red, white, and blue ball. The thing looked like a beachball. Between the ABA and two NBA expansion teams the American pro game would more than double in size next year, pushing the number of roster spots from roughly 120 to about 250. That would give Hazzard more than enough room to find a better fit for his playmaking skills.

The sun had now set over the San Fernando Valley, leaving behind a soft purple twilight and the glitter of lights along the boulevards below. A half-moon hovered above. Archie exited the Harbor Freeway and wound his Olds Ninety Eight down the off-ramp onto Figueroa Street. A block later the Sports Arena rose through the twilight like a giant glass mushroom. He and Walt found an open door into the arena for tonight's game against the Philadelphia 76ers and meandered through the concrete hallways to the Laker locker room and nostril-numbing wintergreen odor of muscle-soothing lineaments. Ankles already were being mummified in white tape, and Baylor's usual silly chatter filled the room. Last week Baylor had become so violently ill at Boston's Logan Airport that he had torn the lining of his stomach and thrown up gouts of blood. He was rushed to the hospital, and the doctors advised him to sit out a week. But here he was. Too proud to quit.

Coach Schaus strode into the locker room looking like emcee Ed Sullivan in his suit and gathered his players, in various states of dress, around the chalkboard to outline tonight's keys to victory. Schaus jotted down the usual points—play tight defense, win the battle of the boards, run the fast break, and get the ball to Jerry and Elgin on offense. This was the same crude, warmed-over game plan that irritated Hazzard. But Schaus had a trick up his sleeve tonight: a full-court zone press. The 76ers were in the midst of a two-week road trip, and Wilt Chamberlain had a cranky Achilles tendon. He would be slow to trot up and down the floor. If Schaus could sucker Philadelphia into an up-tempo game, the dominant Chamberlain and his fellow bruiser Luke Jackson would be lost huffing and puffing in transit.

Philadelphia wasn't the best team in basketball for nothing. The 76er starters shredded the soft zone press and jumped to the early lead. But the Lakers kept pushing the pace, and the great Hal Greer, Wally

Jones, Billy Cunningham, and Chet Walker couldn't help themselves. They started running with the Lakers, and a winded Chamberlain retreated to the bench for air. Jack Kent Cooke, per usual, cackled at both teams from his courtside seat, sounding like Burgess Meredith, the Penguin in the popular new TV show *Batman*. Archie heard the shrill cackle from time to time, but he mostly blocked it out. Not so for Hazzard. The big boss openly heckled him. Walt's days in Laker-land were numbered.

The Lakers trailed the 76ers, 64–61, at halftime. Schaus had another brainstorm: scrap the zone press. It was too soft. Greer and Jones were in foul trouble and would need to play passively in the second half to remain in the game. Press them man on man. Keep the tempo up, up, up.

With Archie, Tommy Hawkins, and Jerry West at their ballhawking best, the Lakers swarmed the 76ers in the third quarter, and for one night arguably the greatest team in NBA history crumbled under the pressure. "I looked up at the scoreboard one time, and we were ahead by twenty or something," Schaus said. "Unaccustomed as I am to leading that team by that much, I almost went into a state of shock."

Archie's defender kept sagging off him to double team West. So Archie cut into the clear, arms extended, and the unselfish West hit him again and again with passes to knock down mid-range jump shots. Archie finished with twenty-four points, tying his NBA career high. But most of West's twenty-three assists went to Baylor. Looking five years and three knee operations younger, Baylor was a one-man highlight reel in the third quarter, scoring twenty points on a mix of jump shots and hanging, dipsy-doodle moves up and around the towering Chamberlain. Just as Magic Johnson and Kobe Bryant would in the years ahead, Baylor had the usually mellow LA crowd "screaming themselves hoarse" over his then amazing sleight of hand, the shrill Jack Kent Cooke included. Baylor ended with a game-high forty-four points. Like Mark Twain, the rumors of Baylor's athletic demise had been greatly exaggerated.

The Lakers (22–32) were two games back of second-place St. Louis and twelve games behind San Francisco, the Western Division front-runner. The late-season jockeying for playoff position had taken its annual turn for the bellicose. The other night the St. Louis defenders had roughed up Baylor and West to send the message that second place belonged to the Hawks. While Schaus lambasted the Hawks for their antics, Lou Mohs went after the San Francisco Warriors. He accused the delightful Bill King, the San Francisco radio announcer, of bating NBA referees during his broadcasts and forcing them to favor the Warriors. Everything was insidious; nothing was too small to contest.

The Lakers had tomorrow off, followed by back-to-back home games against the Warriors and Philadelphia. Then came a whirlwind three-games-in-four-nights East Coast trip that would send them to New York, Charleston (West Virginia), and Philadelphia. Winning the division was still the longest of long shots. But a second-place finish was in reach. They just had to take it from St. Louis.

NEW YORK, FEBRUARY 7, 1967. "Too late. Fall back, baby." Dick Barnett leapt into the air, leaning his body backward at about a forty-degree angle and holding the basketball like a loaded revolver in his left hand. Barnett curled his legs under him, kicked backward and released his soft, arching shot just past the peak of his jump. "Basket by Barnett," a nasally voice mumbled over the public address system.

Archie had heard Barnett repeat his signature "fall back" line (meaning his shot would be good, and his teammates on the New York Knicks should trot back on defense) ever since the veteran guard had entered the game early in the second quarter. How Barnett could be so ready to play basketball on a wretched night like this was a complete mystery. The worst blizzard to hit Gotham in twenty years had dumped 12.6 inches of snow on the sidewalks and streets. Although the snow had stopped falling about three hours ago, the heavy winds continued their relentless howl between the midtown skyscrapers. Few pedestrians stirred outside, and everything was closed or canceled for the evening—except, of course, tonight's NBA game. God forbid. About 3,600 mostly stranded travelers trickled into Madison Square Garden to kill a few hours as the city workers began to salt and dig out the main avenues. How the Lakers would get to Charleston, West Virginia, for tomorrow night's game against the Baltimore Bullets was anybody's guess.

By the third quarter Knicks coach Mumbles McGuire made a point of rotating Barnett, Willis Reed, Walt Bellamy, and his other regulars in and out of the game to keep their minutes down. He had no choice. New York had a game tomorrow night against the Chicago Bulls in tough-to-reach Evansville. Why the owners kept scheduling games in these mid-sized cities was beyond most of the coaches and players. There were no direct flights into Evansville or Charleston. What should be two-hour trips for both teams to the next NBA city on the map morphed into five-hour, puddle-jumping odysseys.

With 7:30 left in the game and the Knicks ahead by eleven points, McGuire rotated Barnett back onto the court to ice the victory and lead the team into the locker room to begin preparations for tomorrow. Number 12 dribbled down the floor and rose into the air. "Too late. Fall back, baby."

*Clank.*

The streak-shooting Barnett suddenly couldn't buy a bucket, and West, Baylor, and Goodrich soon couldn't miss. When Goodrich knocked down a pair of free throws with under a minute to play, the Lakers had escaped with a 122–117 gift.

The next morning at JFK airport a small fleet of yellow snowplows finished clearing Runway 31 at around 11:30. A few minutes later, TWA Flight 97 rumbled down the runway and lifted off, marking the first flight out of the city in a day. Schaus made a phone call to Charleston. Tonight's game would be a go.

By early afternoon the Lakers were en route to Pittsburgh, where they would catch their connecting flight to Charleston. Archie didn't mind flying. The friendly skies sure beat bumping along for hours in a train or bus. Archie mostly talked or slept, while the veterans invariably huddled to play cards. Travel and cards went together like peanut butter and jelly in the NBA, and every team had its preferred card game. For the Laker veterans it was hearts.

Archie felt the first butterflies flutter in his stomach as the plane began its descent into Pittsburgh. "Please return your seats and food trays to their upright positions," the stewardess clicked over the intercom. Archie saw the runway down below and soon felt the torrid thump, thump, thump of the jet's wheels striking the asphalt.

After waving good-bye to the stewardesses, the veterans moved the card game into the cramped airport terminal. They had no choice. There was another delay. Vice President Hubert Humphrey was due to land at Charleston's Kanawha Airport. Until Air Force Two landed, the airport was under Secret Service lockdown. Although the flight from Pittsburgh to Charleston was under an hour, game time was 8 p.m. They were starting to cut it close. By 4:45 p.m. Air Force Two had arrived to whisk Humphrey off to a conference, and the Lakers reached snowy Charleston about an hour later.

Archie had never been to West Virginia, but he'd heard West mention its lush mountains and diehard basketball fans. Like in Detroit, big industry clearly ran the show. Charleston, the state capital, called itself the "Chemical Capital of the Universe," a nod to the miles of billowing chemical factories along the pea-green Kanawha River. West had grown up several miles downriver in a land of coal camps and county seats. Tonight would mark the latest triumphant homecoming of West Virginia's Mr. Basketball and the eponym of youth basketball leagues across the state. Also on the VIP list was Schaus, an adopted West Virginian and another of the state's college basketball greats.

Left unmentioned was some bad chemistry from the Lakers' trip here back in January 1959. The then Minneapolis Lakers, still minus West and Schaus, had come to Charleston to play a regular-season game against Cincinnati. A few hours before the game the team checked into the Daniel Boone Hotel, the city's most posh downtown address, and a clerk reminded Lakers coach John Kundla that the hotel was "whites only." Arrangements had been made for Baylor and two black teammates to stay at a "Negro" motel. Kundla and his players refused to be split up, and the team rode off to check into a "Negro" motel on the other side of town. Baylor, who had grown up resenting the Jim Crow policies of his native Washington DC, refused to play in Charleston.

Baylor's refusal cast him correctly as a man of tremendous principle. Lost in the retelling was Kundla, later Archie's distracted college coach, had tacitly agreed in writing a month earlier for the team to be Jim Crowed.

Now eight years later Jim Crow had been mostly run out of the state.

The Lakers, black and white, were checked into the Daniel Boone, and Baylor had been greeted like a long lost friend at Charleston's modest, six-thousand-seat Municipal Arena. But most of the praise was reserved for West and Schaus, or "Furnace Fred," as the reporters sometimes jokingly called him.

"How are things going with the team?" the reporters asked Schaus. "I think we're beginning to move now," Schaus answered. "We've added Mel Counts, and the club is really playing well. We've won seven of our last nine games, and I think we can finish second."

The Baltimore Bullets were tonight's opponent. Most on hand came to see "their Jerry" play once more. Archie obliged them. He passed the ball to his backcourt mate early and often in their set offense, and West answered with forty points to lead the Lakers to an easy win.

By sunrise the Lakers were off to catch a flight to Philadelphia. The Daniel Boone Hotel and the Municipal Arena would soon be distant memories. But had Archie and his teammates stuck around, they would have noticed an interesting tidbit a few days later from local sports columnist Shorty Hardman: "Sideliners visiting here with the Lakers last week hinted strongly that this might be the last year for Furnace Fred Schaus as L.A. coach," wrote Hardman. "They say he's fed up with traveling, wants to spend more time with his family, and is in so solid with the new Laker owner Jack Kent Cooke, that he may move into the job as general manager of the club." As time would tell, Hardman and his sideliners were correct on all three counts.

LOS ANGELES, FEBRUARY 24, 1967. In the summer of 1960 Lou Mohs had brought professional basketball to Los Angeles with a pat on the back and a $5,000 check stuffed in his pocket. Nearly seven years later Mohs's Lakers were being pulled from their provincial NBA orbit into a larger corporate galaxy of Jack Kent Cooke's opportunistic creation. It was called California Sports, Inc., a revolutionary concept in American sports. Cooke had positioned himself as the first mogul of professional sports properties. These included the Lakers, the expansion Los Angeles Kings hockey team, the nearly completed arena called the Forum, a prominent stake in the Washington Redskins football team, and likely a soccer team in the not-too-distant future. As Cooke pontificated at cocktail parties, sports entertainment and its myriad marketing opportunities were the wave of the future. He planned to corner the market.

But first Cooke cornered Mohs with a friendly business proposition. What about a promotion to executive vice president of California Sports, Inc.? The timing was odd since Mohs was losing his battle with cancer. Big Lou now winced through more low-energy, sick-as-a-dog days than he cared to count, and he didn't need the pressure of kowtowing full time to Cooke. And yet Cooke had a point. The two had a moderately respectful working relationship, and Mohs, as the consummate front-office manager and experienced hand at the business of sports, could help Cooke greatly in an expanded role.

Whatever Mr. Cooke wanted, Mr. Cooke got. Now America's sports mogul needed "that fabulous Fred Schaus" to become the new vice president and general manager of the Lakers. As Schaus had tipped his hand in Charleston, Cooke's offer was too good to refuse.

In the meantime the Lakers had lost two of their last three games since returning from the east and remained two games behind St. Louis. And the schedule was about to take a sharp turn for the worse. The Lakers would play ten games over thirteen days, starting with must-win scraps on the road against rivals Detroit and St. Louis. "Operation Survival," the Laker beat reporters described the next two weeks. Others preferred "Mission Impossible."

# 7

*I looked forward to playing in Detroit and seeing family and friends. I didn't have a lot of time, though. We usually got into Detroit, played the game a few hours later at Cobo Arena, and caught the next flight out of town. That was the rhythm of the NBA. In and out. But this was cool about Pistons games: there would be what they called the Downriver Contingent. It was a bunch of guys from mostly Ecorse and River Rouge. Some were Dave Bing fans; others were Archie Clark fans. They wanted to see how we matched up on the court.*

---

Detroit, February 24, 1967. The Downriver Contingent was out of luck tonight. Dave Bing had tonsillitis and, under doctor's orders, would play sparingly, if at all, against Archie. Sliding over to take Bing's ball-handling duties was his backcourt mate Tom Van Arsdale, whom Archie had faced in college. Running the offense wouldn't be a problem for him. The Pistons ran only six offensive plays.

Doing most of the scoring on this cold Friday night was Eddie Miles, the team's sixth man, or first substitute off the bench. He answered to the nickname "The Man with the Golden Arm," a nod to his sweet jump shot. It was the same name as that of a controversial movie (starring Frank Sinatra) that delved into the seedy underworld of heroin addiction. So unrelated in popular culture were drugs and athletes, at least for a few more years, that the nickname remarkably seemed cool.

In the third quarter, almost like clockwork, Elgin Baylor went off. He faked his defender out of position, whirled to the hoop, and spun shots up and around the lumbering Detroit big men. Everybody talked about his legs, but his hands were equally amazing. Archie remembered earlier in the season when Baylor had called him over after practice, his large right hand palming a basketball: "Come on, Toughie; try to knock the ball out of my hand." Archie slapped and punched to no avail. Baylor's hand strength was like something out of a medieval tale.

But it was Miles who went medieval in the fourth quarter. He drilled a twenty footer and then another to give the Pistons a one-point advantage with thirty-nine seconds left. Time out, Lakers. Schaus called a play for West. Everybody knew the drill: crash the board in case of a miss, get the win. The inbounds pass lobbed into Darrall Imhoff near the free-throw line. He was the initiator. West cut hard to the basket, and the Ax heaved the ball in his direction—and straight into the first row. Game over.

Archie was back in his hotel room around midnight. The temperature along the Detroit River was two degrees and sinking. Frank O'Neill, the Lakers' stout, 5-foot-something trainer whom the players had nicknamed "Little Hawg," would deliver wake-up calls at sunrise, or in roughly six hours. The Lakers had to catch the first flight in the morning to St. Louis, per NBA rules, and Archie already could hear O'Neill's baritone: "Clark, you up yet?" But falling asleep wouldn't be so easy after such a tough loss. Archie had logged fewer minutes than usual when Schaus, for whatever reason, benched him in the second quarter.

Tomorrow night he needed to bounce back. Schaus already had reminded everyone that the St. Louis game was a must win. The fourth-place Lakers (28–38) now trailed the Hawks for second place by only two and a half games with fifteen regular-season games left.

Archie had heard that the difference between finishing in second and fourth place was $10,000 in team playoff money. That came to about $900 per player or, in Archie's case, enough to cover a few car payments and, more important, to help out with the hospital costs when Valerie delivered their baby in March. And what if the Lakers won it all? The players would split $35,000, plus another $20,000 for winning the Western Division title.

The extra cash would be a Godsend, but the thought of the playoffs looming was too much to process. Archie was exhausted from an NBA season that seemed as long and episodic as Tolstoy's novel *War and Peace*. Nothing could have prepared him for the mental and physical strain of packing eighty-one "wars" into five months. Nor could he have prepared himself for the travel. The Lakers flew east every two weeks, usually for two or three games at a time. When

Archie had left his condo in Inglewood en route to the airport, the temperatures were mild, the grass was green, and many cars cruised the freeways with their tops down. A five-hour flight later he was scuffling along sidewalks covered in snow with people who looked like Eskimos bundled in winter jackets and fur hats. After six months in Los Angeles Archie wondered why anyone would want to spend four months of the year shoveling snow? It was too much. . . . *Zzzzzz. Ringggg.* "Clark, you up yet?"

Kiel Auditorium was still empty. In a few hours, the nine-thousand-seat venue, the most cramped in the NBA, would be teeming like a gladiator pit, and the hecklers would be out en masse: "Go back to Los Angeles. Clark, you're terrible." But for now basketball existed on its most peaceful, elemental level. A dozen guys shooting baskets, swapping advice, and loosening up before another game on the NBA tour.

Archie briefly said hello to his college roommate Lou Hudson, now with the Hawks. Richie Guerin, the Hawks' thirty-four-year-old player-coach, frowned on his players mingling with the opposition. Guerin, a former Marine leatherneck and street-smart native of the Bronx, didn't like fraternizing with the enemy. Loose lips sank ships.

The Hawks (31–36) had yet to conquer the world or the Western Division. Center Zelmo Beaty had blown out his Achilles tendon early in the season, and the Hawks had no one to fill in to battle a Chamberlain, Russell, Thurmond, or even an Imhoff. But Beaty was back, and the fiery Guerin and his Hawks were preparing to make a run deep into the NBA playoffs.

Guerin preached a relentless, Marine Corps defense that was the grumbling talk of the league. "The Hawks put their bodies on you and tried to get under your skin," said Archie. "We heard that Guerin didn't want opposing teams driving to the basket. If an opposing player got to the rim and didn't get hit, the guilty Hawk received an automatic fifty dollar fine. Whether this was true or not, that's what we went into games believing."

So did the referees. To control tonight's game, they whistled every nudge and bump in the early going, and that spelled frustration for Archie as an aggressive, unheralded rookie and an easy mark for foul calls. Midway through the first quarter he retreated to the bench with three quick misdemeanors, plopping down near Schaus and the nearest Dixie cup of water.

"Clark, you're terrible."

Others followed him to the penalty box. By the fourth quarter Guerin had banished himself to the bench, and the younger, fast-breaking Hawks took over to send the game into overtime on a backboard-rattling dunk by Joe Caldwell. Then West, per usual, willed himself to greatness. He hit big shot after big shot, found Baylor for the go-ahead lay-up, and then stole the ensuing inbounds pass to ice the 134–133 nail-biter.

Archie toweled off and dressed after the game. He'd finished with one basket tonight. His minutes remained down, and Schaus had been giving the offensive-minded Gail Goodrich more playing time in the fourth quarter. Archie reminded himself again to stay focused, be aggressive, and look for his shot a little more.

His mind over matter worked. Archie was spectacular in the next game in a blow-out win over Cincinnati at the Sports Arena. He pitched in most of his twenty points in the second half showing that if called upon, he could help West and Baylor in the scoring column with his quick, stutter-step moves.

Now "Operation Survival," the Lakers' late-season, ten-games-in-thirteen-nights endurance test, continued with an East Coast swing that would eventually drop them in hated Boston.

BOSTON, MARCH 5, 1967. Fred Schaus loved to tell the story about the time he flew to New York—and nearly crashed in Boston. According to Schaus, the flight approached New York and circled . . . and circled. The pilot finally announced that the plane had mechanical problems, and he had been ordered to prepare for an emergency landing in Boston. "I thought, 'Just my luck, the plane has to go out of its way to crash with me in Boston,'" said Schaus, though the plane landed safely. The irony was that Schaus and the Lakers had crashed nearly every year since 1961 in the Boston Garden during the NBA finals.

Now Schaus had landed on the unlucky Boston Garden parquet floor one last time as an NBA head coach. His Lakers would meet the Celtics at 2 p.m. in the NBA's *Game of the Week* on ABC TV, an imperfect melding of traditional 1960s sports and newfangled video technology. The ABC boys routinely wheeled their 250-pound, metal RCA TK-41 box cameras onto the court during games, bumping referees and players aside at times for a better view of the action. More irritatingly, the ABC producers frequently signaled referees that they needed to cut to a commercial, forcing coaches to sacrifice valuable timeouts in the fourth quarter to sell America more beer, razors, and potato chips. "The NBA televised productions are so controlled by the network that when a player misses a shot, you almost wait for a guy to run out and yell, 'Cut, we gotta do that one over,'" joked a St. Louis reporter.

Operation Survival was off to a groggy start. Last night, just past 10 p.m., the Lakers' plane had waffled down safely onto the runway at Logan Airport, and with everyone's bodies and minds still dialed into Pacific time, Frank O'Neill's wake-up calls several hours later seemed like a cruel prank. The players shook off the cobwebs, gathered in the Garden's antiquated visitors' locker room, and trotted out in their road blue uniforms to a sold-out, playoff-like atmosphere. The Celtics didn't draw well during the regular season. Why the full house now?

It was just Schaus's rotten Boston luck. It was KC Jones Day, a full-course tribute to the popular Boston guard who would retire at the end of the season. Bill Russell, the team's cackling, crazy-as-a-fox player-coach and Jones's long-time teammate, was prepared to do whatever it took to win this one for his old pal.

Winning didn't take much for Russell and the Celtics. The Lakers couldn't find their sea legs or their jump shots, much to the dismay of the ABC producers and living rooms around the country. "We just played lousy basketball," Schaus grumped to reporters after the 130–105 shellacking, which included the Celtics converting twenty-two points off of twenty Laker turnovers.

Mr. Cooke wouldn't be happy, nor would he understand. Dropping a game behind St. Louis in the standings was bad enough. But flopping on national television was embarrassing for his California Sports, Inc. Schaus could expect a condescending phone call. Mr. Cooke always had to offer an uncomfortable, sometimes one-glass-too-many synopsis of the game. Schaus took it like a man. Whatever Mr. Cooke wanted, Mr. Cooke got.

The forlorn Schaus exited Boston Garden with his players. The temperature was thirty-five degrees, and a hailstorm thumped the pavement. Not a cab in sight to drive them back to their hotel. It was par for the course. At least Schaus would be out of here in the morning, never to crash and burn again. Good riddance, Beantown.

BOSTON, MARCH 6, 1967. Archie glanced out the airplane window. The first snowflakes had begun to waft onto the runway. Eight inches were predicted today in Boston, and the way things were going, the Lakers and their commercial flight to Pittsburgh would never beat the coming squall. The plane ahead of them had broken down on the runway, and they'd been waiting for twenty-five minutes to be bumped ahead of the ailing jet to hurry into the air before the snow started accumulating.

Five minutes later Archie felt the airplane lurch forward. They finally had been cleared for takeoff. After the plane ascended through the clouds, Archie settled into his cramped seat and thought of Wilt Chamberlain and the Philadelphia 76ers tonight. Wilt, known as Goliath around the league, had turned himself into a seven-foot assist machine, palming the ball like a grapefruit and feeding his teammates for easy shots.

Archie remembered facing the Sixers earlier in the season and beating his defender off the dribble for a series of quick drives to the basket. "You'd better stop coming in here," Chamberlain bellowed, a word of warning that guards weren't allowed in the land of the giants near the basket. "Wilt, just get the ball," Archie answered. "Don't get me."

As Archie had learned early in his rookie year, the NBA operated on a self-policing code of respect for its superstars and top teams. The veteran players knew it, the referees validated it, and the fans expected it. Challenge the pecking order, and the testosterone spiked. Many of the running disputes amounted to pure gamesmanship, often involving Boston's "villainous" general manager, Red Auerbach, the NBA's prime practitioner of psychological warfare. Whenever Auerbach spoke, Schaus and the other NBA coaches and general managers usually bristled.

With all of the bad blood flowing through the NBA's ten cities, the league should have been one big nightly, bench-clearing, Hatfield-and-McCoy brawl. And yet an underlying gravitational force kept the jostling and jawing within proscribed bounds. Archie and his fellow NBA players referred to this governing force generically as "the commissioner's office." Cross the line, and the commissioner's office would mete out fines and suspensions. For a player or coach who earned $25,000 or less per annum the threat of lost income was sufficient to make most think twice before racing into the crowd to throttle a heckler or pop off in the press about the referees.

The pilot's voice suddenly scratched over the intercom. He was awaiting final clearance to land at the Greater Pittsburgh Airport. Five minutes stretched to twenty. When the plane finally landed and off-loaded its passengers, the luggage hatch wouldn't budge. Twenty minutes of elbow grease later Archie and the other Lakers jumped onto a waiting bus and soon were en route to the hotel. The bus threaded through a long and disorienting maze of tunnels and bridges to reach downtown Pittsburgh and its glass-and-steel skyline.

After checking into the hotel, Archie frittered away a few remaining hours of daylight. At nightfall Archie shivered to the Civic Arena, a large, stainless steel orb located just a few blocks from the hotel. The temperature hovered in the low thirties, and snow was predicted for later tonight. By game time the seventeen-thousand-seat arena was maybe half full. But those on hand could witness a small piece of history. With a win the Sixers would tie the NBA record for most victories in one season at sixty-two.

Before exiting the locker room, Schaus offered his standard pre-game speech: play tight defense, rebound, get the ball to West and Baylor, and run at every opportunity. The last was more a hope than an expectation. His team was tired and had must-win games upcoming against New York and St. Louis on Tuesday and Wednesday nights. Schaus certainly wanted to win every game. But he could live with a loss to the best team in NBA history and a quick exit to regroup tomorrow night in New York.

Midway through the first quarter Schaus was ready to throw in the towel. West and Baylor couldn't find their jump shots. But Archie and the supporting cast somehow kept the Lakers alive through three quarters. Then Baylor got hot, and the Lakers grabbed the lead to start the fourth quarter. The trip to New York could wait. With 1:05 to play and his team now trailing 117–115, Schaus yelled to foul Chamberlain, a notoriously poor free-throw shooter. The odds dictated that Chamberlain would shank his old-fashioned underhanded shots, his latest attempt to master the free throw, and the Lakers could rebound his second miss and send the game to overtime.

Sure enough, Chamberlain shanked both, but the odds bit Schaus in the rump when Philly's 6-foot-9 Luke Jackson snatched the second miss, stumbled, and scooped the ball to Chamberlain. Goliath rammed the basketball through the basket and watched the unflappable Baylor hurry downcourt to answer with a fourteen footer. The Sixers' lead was back to two.

When the Sixers misfired on the next possession, the Lakers set up Baylor for the final shot. As he lifted into the air to send the game into overtime, Jackson's muscular right arm dropped like a tree branch toward his head. Baylor hurried and flicked his wrist, sending the shot too high and glancing off the rim into Chamberlain's outstretched hands. He fired the ball to teammate Hal Greer, who took a few dribbles and passed the ball onward to kill the clock.

Archie trudged back to the hotel as a heavy snow fell. Schaus had told everyone to sleep in tomorrow morning. To hell with NBA rules; they would catch a mid-morning flight to New York. He wanted everyone rested and ready to go tomorrow night in Madison Square Garden. But Archie had a hard time putting tonight's game to bed. It was always that way with the close ones. The images were more intense, and they cycled spontaneously through his head. There was the Jackson rebound, the Chamberlain dunk. All of the what ifs, churning like a load of wash. What if Elgin had just. . . . *Ringggg, ringggg, ringggg.*

Archie peeled his eyes open. What time was it? Seven forty-five a.m. He fumbled for the telephone on the nightstand. "Hello."

"Archie, you've got to get up," the voice boomed. It was Laker trainer Frank O'Neill. "It's been snowing all night," he continued. "We've got to go by train. Get dressed, get your breakfast, and be in the lobby in forty-five minutes."

Archie opened the blinds and beheld a foot of snow that was already covering the ground. The snow looked extra heavy and wet. No wonder the airport was closed. An hour later Archie trudged three blocks, knee-deep in snow, to reach the train station. As a rookie, he had to pitch in and help carry the equipment bags while Baylor, Imhoff, and the other veterans shuffled ahead. Grunt duty. It was as though he were back in Korea slogging up mountains. Next season and veteran status couldn't come fast enough.

By nine o'clock the Lakers had dried off and were safely aboard a passenger train to New York. It had no café car, just a snack bar with day-old, prepackaged sandwiches and the usual brands of soda. At least the train was moving—well, sort of. A tree had fallen onto the tracks near Harrisburg. That killed an hour. And snowdrifts had to be cleared frequently along the way. That killed another two hours. "We felt we had to have one out of three on this trip," Schaus confided, trying to pass the time and remain focused on tonight's game. "We've already lost two. Regardless of what St. Louis does, we have to win tonight and have to win tomorrow [against St. Louis]."

Day turned to night. Everyone had grown restless on the rails about twenty miles back. They had been cooped up in the quaint Pullman cars for ten hours, and New York was still sixty minutes away. Telephone calls were made to the Knicks. At 8:05 p.m. the train finally creaked into New York's Penn Station. The game was scheduled to start in twenty-five minutes. A bus was waiting on Eighth Avenue and shuttled the team fifteen blocks to the old Madison Square Garden. By 8:45 and without any pregame warm-ups the Lakers set out to secure their claim on second place in the Western Division. Mr. Cooke wouldn't be happy.

Then again, maybe Mr. Cooke would have been amazed. With no time to prepare, the Lakers played purely on instinct. Basketball was a simple schoolyard game again, and the footloose Lakers broke open a tight first quarter against the banged-up Knicks to take a commanding 70–51 lead at halftime. West, after his two-game shooting funk, suddenly couldn't miss.

If only he'd missed Knicks forward Willis Reed in the third quarter. While stepping around a screen on defense, West plowed face first into the stationary, 6-foot-10 Reed. Something had to give, and it was West's fragile nose. For the sixth time in West's playing career—and third time as a pro—it broke into a bloody, game-halting mess.

West took his place on the Lakers bench, wads of white gauze shoved up each nostril and an ice pack to his face. Although Archie and Gail Goodrich assumed the scoring load, the Knicks roared back early in the fourth quarter to cut the Laker lead to nine.

"Can you play?" Schaus called out to West.

"It's up to you."

"No, it's not up to me. It's up to you."

"Okay, I'll play," West snapped.

West gutted out five more minutes, sinking two shots and dishing two assists, to secure the win. In the locker room Archie caught a glimpse of West's swollen, misshapen face. He looked like boxer Jerry Quarry after a fifteen-round brawl. But West refused to have his broken nose reset for a few days. Once the nose was reset, West explained, the extra bleeding would make him nauseous, and he didn't want to feel sick during the St. Louis game.

Archie glanced around the locker room. Baylor had bulky bags of ice draped over knees broken by too many seasons on the NBA circuit. Walt Hazzard stood nearby in street clothes. He had an inflamed heart, of all maladies. In the New York locker room many of the wounded and missing weren't walking. Dick Barnett was out for the rest of the season with a bum leg, forward Dave Stallworth remained hospitalized from a heart attack, Em Bryant had his knee slip out of joint in the first half, and Howie Komives had torn ligaments in his ankle in the third quarter.

And so it went across the league. The NBA remained rooted in the traditional 1920s barnstorming model of pro basketball that held two truths to be self-evident: (1) pro basketball promoters started at a financial disadvantage because they sold tickets to small indoor venues, not seventy-thousand-seat football stadiums; (2) teams had to squeeze as many games into a season as humanly possible to keep the turnstiles clicking, the bills paid, and the show on the road. Although barnstorming was a tough row to hoe in the first half of the 1900s, basketball was a simpler game then. The players were smaller, the tempo was slower, the competition was uneven, and the distances between games were mostly a few train whistles away. In the NBA, with teams bouncing from coast to coast and city to city and facing the best players in the world nightly, it took a terrible toll on the body. The NBA locker rooms told the tale.

Management didn't want to hear players grump about the grim life on the road. Pro basketball was a tough, nickel-and-dime business, and the barnstorming model worked. But more ailing players had begun to wonder: would management be there in twenty years to pay for their hip replacement surgeries?

Archie pulled on his street clothes. His body ached from the rigors of the day, and he felt like he probably could have slept for the next forty-eight hours. But the NBA show must go on. The Lakers were scheduled to depart New York tomorrow at noon and land in Los Angeles about five hours before the game. That would make four games in four nights on both American coasts. The good news was tomorrow night's showdown would mark the end of Operation Survival.

SOMEWHERE OVERHEAD, UNITED States, March 8, 1967. Elgin Baylor couldn't stop marveling at the verbal speed and dexterity of heavyweight boxer Muhammad Ali: "That man talks even more that I do." The Lakers and Ali had stayed last night at the same hotel in New York, and Ali had invited Baylor, Walt Hazzard, and former UCLA star Fred Slaughter to his room for a few hours to unwind after the Knicks game. "I said to him, 'I got a man here who can whip you,'" Baylor continued in a serious, confiding tone. That man was the 6-foot-5, 280-pound Slaughter, now a law student at Columbia University.

Baylor leapt to his feet and stepped into the aisle of the airplane, waving his arms like a professional boxer. "Cassius looked him over and started jabbing and giving him the Ali shuffle, and Slaughter's eyes got *t-h-i-s* big." Baylor cupped his fingers into saucer-sized circles, and everybody burst into laughter.

Archie already had heard the Ali stories. He preferred to try to get some rest, but his tiny, hopelessly uncomfortable seat wasn't cooperating. Why were airplane seats built for people six feet and under? After a few hours of Archie's drifting in and out of the Land of Nod, the airplane started its gradual descent into LAX. Archie glanced out the window. He saw the San Gabriel Mountains in the distance, the pleasure boats of Marina del Rey, and sunshine. Lots of sunshine. The voice of a stewardess came over the intercom soon thereafter and welcomed everyone to Los Angeles, where the temperature was seventy-three glorious degrees and the local time was approximately 3:30 p.m. Forty minutes of bumper-to-bumper traffic later Archie and Walt Hazzard pulled their bags from the trunk and trudged into their respective condominiums.

Archie kissed Valerie and asked how she was doing. Valerie was nine months pregnant, and the doctor said the labor pains could start at any time. No sooner had Archie begun to unwind than it was time to go again. As dusk now settled over Los Angeles, Archie and Walt dragged themselves back to work. Both were dog tired, but this evening there could be no excuses. A win would give the Lakers a one-game advantage over St. Louis. That translated to a two-game lead over the Hawks with just five games remaining in the regular season. If the Lakers lost, they were sunk.

In the locker room West arrived sporting two black eyes and a badly swollen nose that was as crooked as the state of New Jersey. But he was his usual edgy, withdrawn, win-at-all-costs self. Whatever it took, West was ready. He was, as Laker announcer Chick Hearn liked to say, "Mr. Clutch."

But clutch against the Hawks meant running the gauntlet each time the Lakers set up their half-court offense. The Hawks' strategy was for Richie Guerin or Joe Caldwell to funnel Jerry into the middle, where their big men would be waiting in the paint to hit him "with their elbows, knees, hips, chainsaws, and bazookas," said Archie.

Sure enough, just over six minutes into the game, West broke into the paint for a driving lay-up and met all 6 feet 8 inches and 230 pounds of Paul Silas. West landed splat on his left side, grabbing for his face and sending a hush through the Sports Arena. Silas missed the nose but left a nasty, two-stitch gash in the corner of West's left eyelid. West wobbled to the bench, wrapped for a second straight night in bloodied white towels.

With the referees now calling the game tightly to maintain order, Hawks guard Lennie Wilkens went to work. He cleverly bounced Archie off of screens set by Beaty and Silas, forcing slower-footed Lakers to switch onto him. Wilkens then beat them off the dribble for an assortment of running lay-ups, hook shots, and passes to teammates. But the Lakers, through sheer will and Elgin Baylor, kept the game close until the closing minutes of the second quarter, when West returned with his two black eyes, a stitched eyelid, and a crooked nose and looking, as sports columnist Jim Murray quipped, "like an embroidered raccoon."

Somehow West, who would finish with thirty-four points, and Archie, who would net seventeen, clicked in the third quarter, and the Lakers built an improbable ten-point lead. But the road-weary Laker defense tired, and the swifter Wilkens rallied the Hawks to an early fourth-quarter lead. The Lakers roared back and cut the lead to two with twenty seconds left.

The crafty Wilkens began dribbling out the final seconds. Somehow Wilkens blundered into a corner, where Archie and West immediately trapped him. West grabbed at Wilkens, and the referees signaled for a jump ball. The scoreboard showed fourteen seconds.

Up went the ball, and West tapped it ahead to Archie, a good thirty feet from the other basket. He pivoted and dribbled in an all-out blur down the left sideline, Baylor and Tommy Hawkins a good two steps in his wake. Seeing the 6-foot-9 Zelmo Beaty back on defense, Archie hesitated with nine seconds left and launched a nineteen-footer for the tie. The shot fell halfway down—and whooshed out.

"I got the rebound," said Hawkins. "I went around Beaty—I don't know if I got fouled—and tipped it to Elg. Elg put it back up [missing a point-blank shot]. Then three or four guys tapped it."

The basketball finally trickled into the hands of the Hawks' Lou Hudson, followed by the blare of the final horn and quiet resignation on the Lakers bench. "You can't fault the players," Schaus said afterward. "They fought and scratched out there, but it wasn't quite enough."

Archie was numb afterward in the Laker locker room. He kept seeing that game-tying shot whoosh out. A few lockers away West looked like he had been to hell and back. But the nose and the stitched eyelid were the least of his worries now. In the third quarter the Hawks had funneled him into the middle again, and West had swooped to the basket for an apparent lay-up. A defender walloped West in midair, forcing him to land awkwardly and sending pain stabbing through his right hamstring. By morning West could barely walk.

INGLEWOOD, CALIFORNIA, MARCH 21, 1967. Merv Harris was the Lakers' beat reporter for the *Los Angeles Herald-Examiner*. Portly, in his late twenties, and blessed with a gift for gab, Harris had developed a friendly rapport with the players in these days when journalists traveled with NBA teams, sharing the same bad airplane food and early morning wake-up calls.

In the waning days of the regular season Harris entered the Lakers' locker room after another tough home loss and spotted Archie looking the worse for wear. "How're you holding up, Archie?"

"I've never been this fatigued," he told Harris. With Jerry West sidelined, Archie had logged forty minutes three nights in a row. He also had a brand-new baby at home. Valerie had given birth to their 6-pound, 3-ounce daughter Kelley a few days earlier. Between the rigors of pro basketball and a newborn's irregular hours, Archie never seemed to rest and recover.

Now the fatigue would intensify. The Lakers opened the playoffs in a best-of-five series against the Western Division champion San Francisco Warriors. The "best-of" format was yet another relic of pro basketball's barnstorming days, when the top teams strung together a series of championship showdowns to popularize their rivalry and cash in at the box office. Although anything could happen in the playoffs, the Lakers' prospects appeared bleak. The Warriors had owned them during the regular season.

SAN FRANCISCO, MARCH 26, 1967. Archie stepped outside the Cow Palace after the final blowout loss. It was mid-afternoon on Easter Sunday. A breeze blew. The Pacific Ocean glimmered to the west, and San Francisco's terraced skyline clustered on the hills to the east.

Archie took a deep breath. The Warriors had just swept the Lakers in three games. His interminable rookie season had come to an abrupt and bittersweet end. The bitter, of course, was the Lakers' resounding playoff defeat. The sweet was Archie's stellar performance in the losing effort. He had stepped up in the series to lead the banged-up Lakers in scoring with 25.7 points per game, up from his season average of 10.5 points.

Archie kept thinking about a conversation he'd had with Lakers broadcaster Chick Hearn near the end of the regular season. The team was traveling by bus, and Hearn sidled up to Archie, waving a stat sheet in his right hand. "Hey, Archie, take a look at this. Since joining the starting lineup, you've been averaging eighteen points per game."

Archie smiled at Hearn. He knew to be polite but to keep up his guard. Anything he said to Hearn could be used against him. Hearn was close with Lou Mohs and Fred Schaus and beholden to Jack Kent Cooke.

"I know what you've been making," Hearn continued, referring to Archie's one-year, $11,000 rookie contract. "You deserve a nice raise. You should be able to get $18,000 next season. If you were to ask me for $25,000, I'd kick you out of my office."

Archie thought about the two figures and then about Hearn. Why hadn't Hearn asked him how much he might want next season? Why was he telling him what to expect? Had Mohs put him up to this to plant an $18,000 idea?

Hearn patted Archie on the shoulder and moved on. The conversation gave him the creeps. It reminded Archie that he badly needed a mentor who would teach him how to negotiate an NBA contract without getting rolled by management. As luck would have it, Archie was about to get one.

# 8

rchie had been relaxing at his condominium in Inglewood. His only pressing need was finding an offseason job to supplement his monthly NBA income. His one-year, $11,000 rookie contract, which ran through September, brought in around $800 per month after taxes. That was more than double the salary of most folks back in Detroit who worked the assembly lines. But $800 per month was harder to stretch in go-go-go Los Angeles.

The telephone rang in the kitchen. Archie walked over, reached for the receiver, and immediately heard the dull, muffled crackle of a long-distance call in these days of cable telephone lines. "Hi, my name is Eddie Holman," cooed a soft, unassuming Midwestern voice. "I'm the general manager of the Minnesota Muskies of the American Basketball Association."

Archie's first emotion was surprise, followed by skepticism. Minnesota Muskies? American Basketball Association? But he couldn't hang up. As Chick Hearn had hinted, the Lakers planned to resign him for what amounted to a mid-level salary, jumping from $11,000 to $18,000 per year. That was fine and good, but Archie still wondered why the Lakers had the right to dictate his earning power. He had proved his worth as an NBA player. Shouldn't the free market determine his value? Maybe Holman could sweeten the pot.

The crackle continued, and Holman confided that the Muskies were now in secret negotiations with his college roommate Lou Hudson. Was Archie open to returning to the Twin Cities too? Archie hemmed for a moment, trying to digest the news. Lou was jumping to the ABA? Archie told Holman that he might be interested if the price was right. Holman said he'd be in touch.

Archie dug up Hudson's telephone number and left a message. Days passed. No return call. When Bad News Barnes signed with the ABA in mid-April, a reporter asked Archie about the new league with the crazy red, white, and blue ball, and he admitted his conversation with Holman. At Lakers headquarters the prospect of another ABA defection drew a clipped response. Archie Clark was the exclusive property of the Los Angeles Lakers.

April turned to May, and there was still no word from Hudson or Holman. Archie turned his attention back to finding that summer job. He'd heard that former Laker Rudy LaRusso had arranged for Gail Goodrich and other Lakers to spend the summer in Beverly Hills as entry-level stockbrokers. Archie got the okay to join them.

On a Wednesday night in mid-May Archie came home after a long day in Beverly Hills. The phone rang. It was Hudson.

"Archie, I signed," Hudson said in a slow Southern drawl.

"You did what?"

"I signed."

Hudson explained that he now was seated with Holman and colleagues at a popular Minneapolis steakhouse called Murray's. They were celebrating Hudson's three-year, $50,000-per-season contract with the Muskies. It made "Sweet Lou" the first legitimate NBA star to jump leagues.

Hudson passed the phone across the table to Holman. He asked if Archie wanted to join Hudson and college teammates Don Yates and Terry Kunze in the ABA. Archie repeated, "If the price is right." Holman repeated that he'd be back in touch. *Click.*

Archie's mind raced. What if the Muskies offered him $50,000 per season? That kind of money didn't grow on trees. He'd need a lawyer. Archie recalled hearing his teammates talk about a recent UCLA Law School graduate named Fred Rosenfeld. He had played softball with several Lakers and, as a small favor, had agreed to represent LaRusso last summer during his pro forma contract renewal with the Lakers. Jack Kent Cooke didn't like it one bit, but the twenty-seven-year-old Rosenfeld held his ground.

Other Lakers soon ran their contracts past him, and Rosenfeld launched Professional Management Associates. He was the first West Coast–based lawyer—or, in modern parlance, "agent"—to represent NBA players.

Rosenfeld agreed to squeeze in a meeting with the Muskies. He reminded Archie that the Muskies and the ABA needed him a lot more than he needed them. Rosenfeld advised that they negotiate from a position of strength. Archie soaked up the advice like a sponge, and the two talked ahead to a stout dollar figure. They agreed on a three-year contract at a then substantial $80,000 per season. If Holman countered with a figure closer to Hudson's $50,000 salary, Archie could either sign with the ABA or use the offer, again from a position of strength, as leverage to force Lou Mohs to match the dollar figure.

Rosenfeld flew to Minneapolis, not sure what to expect. This would be his first negotiation with an ABA club, and he worried about the league's long-term stability. If the ABA folded in a matter of months, like most new pro leagues, would the Muskies honor a three-year contract?

Then there was the forty-nine-year-old Holman. He had spent most of his adult life as the owner of various Minneapolis watering holes, earning a reputation as a gambler and card shark. In 1959 Holman, an eighth-grade dropout, sold his last bucket of suds to gamble his future on the Holman Oil and Gas Drilling Corporation. Eight years and a big gusher later Holman, a short, trim man with jet black hair, bought a 10 percent stake in the Muskies and, in between oil prospecting, agreed to run the team's day-to-day operations. Holman's basketball credentials? He was a neighbor of ABA commissioner George Mikan.

Mikan had recently done Holman a huge favor. He had coaxed former Minneapolis Lakers star Jim Pollard into coaching the Muskies. Pollard, with six NBA championship rings on his fingers, brought the team immediate credibility. He also thankfully freed Holman from assembling the team's roster, a tough task for a man who drilled holes in the ground for a living.

The transition to Team Pollard a few days ago had made Archie more of a wish than a need. Pollard had solid basketball contacts around the country to help him find low-budget talent, and cost had become an immediate priority. The Muskies were about to get slammed with three lawsuits, totaling over $3 million, courtesy of Hudson's St. Louis Hawks. If Holman raided Jack Kent Cooke's cupboard too, he almost certainly would get hit with another million-dollar grievance, which would drown the franchise in legal fees before its first game.

Rosenfeld, unaware of these developments, steamrolled ahead with his offer of three years at $80,000 per season. Final offer. Pollard frowned. Not in a million years. "We told our attorneys to drop negotiations with Clark's attorney when he started to talk about those figures," Holman described the encounter.

When Rosenfeld flew home, Archie took the news in stride. In pro basketball, as in love, timing is everything, and Archie had missed a big ABA offer by maybe a week. Another lesson learned.

Two weeks later, just like the other early NBA defectors, Hudson jumped back to the St. Louis Hawks for a handsome raise. Yes, timing and a new word in Archie's vocabulary—leverage—were everything in pro basketball.

Despite its tall talk of competing head to head with the NBA, the ABA clearly was treading water. As of mid-June 1967 the ABA had managed to sign just six NBA players, all of whom were prepared to jump back to their former teams for more money. The ABA's only tangible inroad came from snapping up a handful of players who had been banned by the NBA for allegedly associating with gamblers in college. Among them were two of the game's more exciting performers, forwards Connie Hawkins and Roger Brown. But their checkered pasts preceded them, and having never occupied the national spotlight, Hawkins and Brown lacked the celebrity to bring credibility to the league. The ABA remained a minor league with big league ambitions.

Then, in the NBA's equivalent of Pearl Harbor, the ABA finally struck. On June 20, a day that would live in infamy in NBA front offices and change the course of pro basketball history, Rick Barry signed a three-year contract with the ABA Oakland Oaks.

Archie heard the numbers afterward, and his jaw dropped. Oakland reportedly paid Barry a then astounding half-million bucks, plus incentives and a 15 percent ownership stake in the Oakland franchise. That came to roughly $160,000 per year. To put this figure into perspective, we must know that Boston's Bill Russell, the NBA's highest-paid star, made $125,000 per season as a player and coach.

The money sounded way too good to be true—and indeed it was. Barry actually signed a three-year, $250,000 contract (or $75,000 per season), plus the previously announced extras, a package that still sounded impressive. But the ABA allowed the inflated figure and the word "million" to waft through the sports world like a smoke ring from a victory cigar.

Wafting less ceremoniously was the 1967 college draft. The NBA, hoping to starve the ABA of young talent, signed the best of the college seniors to larger, more cost-prohibitive first contracts. NBA veterans cried foul. "When they start paying huge amounts to untried rookies like Bill Bradley, it isn't fair," said Elgin Baylor, referring to Bradley's reported four-year, $500,000 rookie contract with the New York Knicks.

In the summer of 1967 this first whiff of high finance changed the game forever. For twenty-five-odd years NBA owners had survived on the backs of their players. They had kept their labor costs low to increase their chances of earning a profit and (as they grumbled) to keep the NBA going. This organized exploitation, while still operative and vital to the survival of both leagues, now became a sideshow.

The main event had become the battle within pro basketball's ownership class. Despite the all-encompassing moniker of the "NBA-ABA war," the players in both leagues had no beef with each other. They were tall, long-armed brothers caught in the middle of a millionaires' feud. This feud, war, spat, misunderstanding, or whatever the millionaires preferred to call it would reshape most aspects of the business and marketing of pro basketball. Out of this conflict emerged the more fertile financial terrain that would nurture the minds of millions to celebrate future cultural icons named Larry Bird, Magic Johnson, Michael Jordan, Kobe Bryant, Lebron James, and a really long-armed Greek freak called Giannis Antetokounmpo.

ARCHIE WASN'T SURPRISED when he heard the news in mid-August 1967. Lou Mohs was dead. The seventy-year-old father of the Los Angeles Lakers had passed away in his sleep from an apparent heart attack. "I haven't had a day off in seven years, and I work at least one-half of all Saturdays and one-third of all Sundays," Mohs had grumped last year about his life with the Lakers. In the end, if it hadn't been his heart, the cancer would have killed him. Or his failing kidneys.

Archie had seen "Big Lou" several weeks ago. Although he looked more fragile than ever, Mohs was his old crusty self in his new position as executive vice president of Jack Kent Cooke's California Sports, Inc. "Archie, are you ready to sign your new contract?" he had asked. "We're ready to offer you a nice raise up to $18,500 for next season."

The figure confirmed that Chick Hearn worked for management. It also kind of hit Archie in the solar plexus. All he could think to say was, "Call my lawyer, Fred Rosenfeld."

"I don't talk to lawyers."

"But Fred is representing me now."

"Why don't we do this, Archie," Mohs snapped. "The Lakers have lawyers too. Have your lawyer call our lawyers, and they can talk. In the meantime, come into my office and sign your contract for next season."

Archie thought at first that he might have a more sympathetic ear in Fred Schaus, the Lakers' new general manager. But Archie already had two strikes against him. For one thing, Mohs had trained Schaus to follow in his penny-pinching footsteps. For another, Schaus now spent his days shaking hands, attending meetings, tweaking operating budgets, and otherwise appeasing Mr. Cooke. "Fred Schaus was the ultimate loyal employee," said Mike Waldner, then the Lakers beat reporter for the *South Bay Daily Breeze*. "He took a lot of heat from the players [as general manager] because Cooke had made up his mind, and there was no arguing with him. Cooke had to make every decision."

So Schaus kept dragging his feet on Archie's new contract. Archie figured the delay wasn't personal. Elgin Baylor wanted a pay raise. So did Jerry West. Of course, as the stars of the Lakers show, their financial interests came first. But Archie certainly rated too, and he desperately needed a new one-year deal to rescue his bank account. The go-go-go California lifestyle wasn't cheap, neither was the baby, and Archie felt obligated to help his family in Ecorse. The bills had started stacking up on his kitchen table, and Archie's summer job as a stockbroker, though interesting, provided little breathing room. If Schaus kept stalling, Archie would have to skip a car payment. Then what?

Archie vented his frustration to Woody Sauldsberry, his summer workout partner. Big Woody, as his friends called him, was a 6-foot-7 free-agent forward who, at age thirty-two, wanted one last shot at a pro contract. By his own description Sauldsberry had seen it all. A former Harlem Globetrotter and the 1958 NBA Rookie of the Year, he had gotten caught in back-door NBA politics and, seven seasons and five teams later, was out of the league.

Nobody understood the NBA and the challenges that mid-level black players faced to stick in the league any better than Sauldsberry. Unlike other NBA veterans he openly discussed money and contracts. For Archie, Sauldsberry's straight talk made him as profound as an Indian guru.

Sauldsberry advised Archie to be careful. He repeated that rule number one in an NBA contract negotiation was leverage. With the ABA's Minnesota Muskies out of the equation, he said, the Lakers had all of the leverage. Sauldsberry explained that Schaus would assure Archie that a generous contract was in the works. He'd tell Archie to be patient about the contract and to bust a gut in training camp. Then, Sauldsberry predicted, a few weeks before the start of the season Schaus would magically call Archie into his office, produce a standard NBA contract, and ask him to sign on the dotted line. Just like Lou Mohs had done in Minneapolis. No lawyers, no questions asked. If Archie didn't sign the usually lowball contract on the spot, Schaus would call him disloyal to Mr. Cooke, the Lakers organization, his teammates, and even his family. That's how NBA general managers saved their teams a few thousand bucks. According to Sauldsberry, the trick was not to take the bait. With Walt Hazzard out of the picture the Lakers needed Archie in the lineup more than ever to secure the backcourt.

The second rule of an NBA negotiation was to focus on one's overall productivity to the team, from scoring to assists. As Sauldsberry liked to say, business executives couldn't argue with numbers. The longer that Archie stuck to his guns and worth to the team, the more impatient Schaus and Jack Kent Cooke would become. Cooke was so rich—unlike the old arena owners who had started the league—that he'd probably counter with a higher offer to close the deal and get on with the season.

Archie mulled Sauldsberry's words. So that's how the system worked? As Archie told himself, Lou Mohs was gone, and so was the naïve rookie that Mohs had steamrolled a year ago in Minneapolis at the Leamington Hotel. This time around Archie planned to stand up and, with the help of Fred Rosenfeld, fight for a fair wage.

# 9

*I worked hard on my game over the summer. I played a lot of one-on-one with Woody Sauldsberry. He was 6 feet 7 inches, with real long arms, and I mean he could defense you. All of the bumping and tussling helped me hone my offensive moves and prepare for my second NBA season. You see, one of the things that stuck with me from my rookie year was that after I crossed half court with the basketball, Elgin and Jerry always broke in my direction. As the playmaker, my job was to give them the ball and clear out. That meant I always moved without the basketball and hoped they'd find me to get my shots.*

*In my second season I wanted to create my own shot. But I knew that wasn't going to be easy. If I held the ball too long, Jerry and Elgin would look to the bench, as if to say, "What's Archie doing?" They weren't necessarily being selfish. They were just used to getting the ball. That was Lakers basketball. I needed some quick moves, especially in running the ball upcourt on the fast break, when there was more freedom to look for my shot.*

*I already had a quick crossover. But that summer I developed what players today call a step-back move. I used it in college a little bit, but I really refined the move playing against Woody. In order to get my shot off I had to fake, step into Woody, step back, and then shoot over him. I worked on it all of the time and pretty much perfected it. Woody couldn't block the shot, and neither could anyone else. Some say that I was the first NBA player to use a step-back move. I don't know. I certainly didn't copy anyone, so maybe it's true. Nobody else in the NBA was using it in 1967. It was my own unique move.*

---

**W**hittier, California, August 22, 1967. Lou Mohs might have passed, but his community-outreach bandwagon rolled on. Call it "Meet the Lakers." Mohs's plan was to hit a different suburban gym every week of the summer to shake hands, play an intra-squad game, and hopefully sell a few season tickets.

Most players hopped aboard the promotional tour. There were no organized pro summer leagues in the late 1960s, and most viewed these intra-squad showcases as their best chance to stay in shape and score brownie points with the Lakers' new head coach. His name: Willem Hendrik Van Breda Kolff. His friends just called him Butch.

Butch was another of Jack Kent Cooke's late-night Eureka moments. Last February Cooke had been flipping through *Sports Illustrated* when he happened upon an article about the forty-five-year-old Van Breda Kolff, then the head basketball coach at Princeton University. Cooke liked his spunk, but mostly he liked his Ivy League pedigree. He told Schaus to encourage Van Whatever-His-Name-Was to apply for the Lakers coaching vacancy. Van Whatever-His-Name-Was got the job, and the Lakers got a New York–sized ego wrapped in the schlumpy, happy-go-lucky demeanor of Oscar Madison from the Broadway play *The Odd Couple.*

Princeton had been Van Breda Kolff's Felix Unger (Oscar Madison's roommate in *The Odd Couple*). He had coexisted with the college's white-gloved image and ridden the coattails of its elite reputation. But high teas and tailor-made suits were too namby-pamby for him. Butch bopped around campus in Bermuda shorts and floppy hats, smoked cheap cigars, told dirty jokes, frequented ale houses, and wobbled home at night like a commoner.

Van Breda Kolff's life had been a case study in eat, drink, and be lucky. The quick-witted son of a successful stockbroker, Butch had grown up in the 1930s in New Jersey playing basketball and eschewing academics. He had barely gotten into Princeton, flunked out, enlisted in the military, and served as a Marine drill sergeant during World War II. While drunk and wobbling back to his barracks one night, Butch had whacked an MP with a shoe and landed in the brig to sleep it off. That's where he met his fellow prisoner and future wife, Florence. He called her "Sarge."

After the war Butch flunked out of Princeton again and spent three years warming the bench for the New York Knicks. When the Knicks cut him in 1950, Butch had a job lined up with a company that sold industrial-strength adhesive tape when sheer luck rode to the rescue. On his way out of Madison Square Garden, Van Breda

Kolff noticed a job posting for a basketball coach at tiny Lafayette College. "I never thought about college coaching," he guffawed, "but I decided to see if it was for me."

Fifteen years and three coaching positions later Van Breda Kolff stood at the top of his profession and, improbably, back at Princeton. He had earned national coach of the year honors for transforming an Ivy League nobody into a Top Ten college program. Butch could have leveraged it all into a higher-paying position at a larger university. But he had grown tired of coaching, and when the Lakers came calling, Van Breda Kolff saw the NBA as another lucky coincidence. "The way things are in the NBA today, with [yearly] expansion, a guy can come in, coach one or two years, make a name for himself, and then become general manager of a new team," he explained his unorthodox decision to jump from college to the pros.

Doubly unorthodox was Butch's disdain for pro basketball. "Pros in general are great in their specialties when they have the ball. But they want to keep it," he explained. "They could be better at moving without the ball, working together and circulating. There are five guys on the court and only one ball. It's silly to let a couple of guys have it all the time."

Van Breda Kolff warned reporters that the days when everyone had stood around to watch Baylor or West dribble on most offensive possessions were over in Los Angeles. He expected his two All-Pros to transition into their new roles as cogs in *his* tightly synchronized, five-man motion offense, the same one that he had run at Princeton.

So what was this magic offense? "Just go fast, stay out of one another's way, pass, move, come off guys, look for one-on-ones, two-on-twos, three-on-threes," Butch explained its basic give-and-go, screen-and-roll geometry. "That's about it."

Van Breda Kolff was a product of the 1930s and 1940s. He liked his music to swing and his basketball to snap. But for an eastern-style offense, as they called it, to work with the NBA's twenty-four-second shot clock, Van Breda Kolff needed a strong playmaker to run the show. He needed somebody to be his eyes and ears on the court, manage the shot clock, get everyone involved in the offense, and set the tone defensively. Tonight, at California High School in Whittier, rookie playmaker Ben Monroe had shown promise. But Monroe wasn't quite what Van Breda Kolff needed.

The good news was that the Lakers already had a quality playmaker in Archie Clark. The bad news was that Clark had missed most of the intra-squad games. He was waiting to sign his contract for next season.

SALT LAKE CITY, October 6, 1967. Still no contract. Tonight, on their preseason tour, the Lakers made short work of the Baltimore Bullets. Tomorrow night both teams would be back in action at Minidoka County High School in Rupert, Idaho. Where was Rupert, Idaho? Archie hadn't a clue. The better question was what would he be doing eleven days hence, when the NBA regular season started? Archie hoped he'd still be a Laker. But until he and Schaus settled their contract dispute, all options remained on the table—a roster spot, a trade, holding out.

Archie's contract woes traced to the NBA-ABA war. The NBA had preemptively inflated rookie salaries to keep the best college grads out of ABA hands. This cost of war had turned NBA payrolls upside down, with unproven first-round draft choices suddenly earning more than some of the biggest names in the game. To keep peace in the locker room NBA general managers paid the equivalent of hush money to their superstars and team leaders. In September Schaus met with the disgruntled Elgin Baylor, who had another year left on his $75,000-per-year contract, and made him a "$100,000 man," then the standard for athletic wealth. Reports circulated that Jerry West and Gail Goodrich wanted more money. And so, the new math went.

Missing from the equation was the other 90 percent of NBA players. Management treated them as though the ABA had never happened and all was business as usual. NBA general managers scribbled out the same take-it-or-leave-it contracts that they had been foisting on players since the days of two-handed set shots. The big difference now was that owners chose to limit pay raises for these mostly rank-and-file veterans, though not to stay solvent, as in the old days, but to control their suddenly hyper-inflating labor costs.

This two-tier, separate-and-unequal player system caused an immediate backlash. An NBA career is brief, and some unsigned veterans didn't want to lock into below-market contracts for a minimum of two seasons (counting the option year) while the NBA-ABA war and salaries would escalate for an undetermined but finite period. Most figured it was in their self-interest to step up to the plate now, ask for an inflated contract, and hope management realized that the days of just-sign-here were over.

For Archie that inflated figure was $35,000. It amounted to a $24,000 raise, or more than triple his rookie contract, and about double the Lakers' current offer of $18,500. As Archie calculated, he had been among the top three rookie guards in the NBA last season. This year's high draft choices hauled in anywhere from $30,000 to $50,000 per season. Why shouldn't he get the same?

When Schaus had heard Archie's $35,000 counteroffer in early August, he'd laughed. Second-year guards didn't get those kinds of raises. Or at least not in the NBA that Schaus had known over the last twenty years as a player, coach, and now general manager. He relayed Archie's displeasure to Mr. Cooke. Then all communication went dead. As far as Archie could tell, Cooke had told Schaus, "Over my dead body."

Archie decided to force the Lakers' hand. In late August he had joined the disgruntled Goodrich in holding out from training camp. After a testy phone call from Schaus, Archie agreed in good faith to join his teammates at Loyola College. But Schaus raised the stakes for Archie and Goodrich: sign or you will be traded. "We have tried to be fair," Schaus explained his side of the story. "But we cannot give them contracts that are out of line with our other contracts."

At home Archie's financial troubles mounted by the day. According to NBA policy, the Lakers had rolled over Archie's rookie contact on October 1 to the option year at 75 percent of its value. If he didn't come to terms with the Lakers, Archie would be stuck dribbling out his option year for a grand total of $8,000. He couldn't live comfortably in Los Angeles on that kind of money.

Swallowing his pride to appease Mr. Cooke was an even worse alternative. Archie knew in the marrow of his bones that he was worth more than $18,500 in today's NBA, and the ultimate Laker insider,

Chick Hearn, had hinted as much last spring. To sign away two years of his career for a minimum wage because Mr. Cooke said so not only would validate an unjust labor system, but it would also cost him cash that his family sorely needed. He couldn't—and wouldn't—do it.

Archie found his emotional release on the basketball court. It was a place where he knew the rules and nobody could con him. Thanks to his offseason workouts with Sauldsberry, Archie had expanded his bag of offensive tricks and, with his extreme quickness, could create his shot at will either with his crossover dribble or an unusual step-back-and-shoot maneuver. Reporters had begun to talk. Clark was going to be a star.

Over the past week, with Goodrich home fighting a bad case of the flu and Jerry West out of the lineup nursing a bum hand, Archie had doubled as the team's playmaker and Baylor's main offensive side-kick. Archie had led the Lakers with twenty-four points last night in Bakersfield against the Bullets. Tonight in Salt Lake City Archie had netted a game-high twenty-eight points when Van Breda Kolff pulled him for the night in the third quarter.

Archie liked the new coach. When he thought of Van Breda Kolff, he heard one word: move. Butch barked this one syllable every few moments at practice like a big-city cop directing traffic. *Moooove.* He wanted everyone to scrap and strain and hustle like there was no tomorrow. Some veterans grumbled about expending so much energy in the preseason. The NBA season wasn't the college campaign. The Lakers had more than one hundred games to scratch off the calendar per year, not twenty-five.

But Van Breda Kolff was as straightforward as a handshake. He spoke his mind, didn't play games or favorites, and was all about winning. When the final buzzer sounded, win, lose, or draw, all was forgotten an hour later over a cigar and pitcher of beer.

There would be little beer poured tonight. The Lakers were in strait-laced Salt Lake City, where the grog was weak by law and most of the after-hours fun took place behind closed doors at private, members-only clubs. It would be an early night. Grab a bite to eat, swap a few stories, and then to bed with sweet dreams of Rupert, Idaho.

LOS ANGELES, OCTOBER 15—Butch Van Breda Kolff kept groaning like he had a toothache. It was two days before the start of the NBA season, and the Lakers were sleepwalking through practice. Yesterday had been even worse. "Move," he had fussed as the Lakers' offense bogged down yet again.

The team was deflated, and Butch knew exactly why: Jerry West's left hand. West had broken blood vessels in the hand in late September and had sat out a few weeks of the preseason. When the swelling persisted into October, West finally had the thing X-rayed. The film showed a clear break in one of the small bones, and the doctor immediately placed the hand in a thick white plaster cast. The Lakers' brightest star would be out of commission up to a month.

"Moooooove."

Watching this disaster of a practice was GM Fred Schaus. He looked like a politician glad-handing everyone in his conservative business suit. But behind his front-office façade, Schaus remained very much a coach. He recalled last year's snap of early season injuries that had put the Lakers in a hole from which the team never recovered. As always Schaus's mind clicked through the basics: the presumed difficulty of the Lakers' early-season schedule, the team's available personnel, and some possible shifts in the lineup to compensate for West's absence.

After practice Schaus appeared in the locker room and asked for a word with Archie. "Do you plan to accompany the team to Chicago?" he asked, referring to the first stop on the Lakers' four-game eastern road trip to start the season.

Archie kept his cool outwardly, but inside his patience was spent. He had played hard all preseason, led the Lakers in scoring at 21.1 points per game, and stepped up his game in West's absence. And yet Schaus continued to wave the same raggedy $18,500 contract at him. Schaus didn't believe in agents, explaining his refusal to call Fred Rosenfeld and work out a deal.

"Not without a contract," Archie replied.

"You have one already waiting to be signed."

"Not without a fair contract."

The conversation continued round and round, with neither side giving an inch. Finally Schaus looked Archie in the eyes and snapped,

"I expect you to make the trip to Chicago." The sternness struck Archie as odd. Why was Schaus so insistent? Then it hit him. Schaus was in trouble.

Think about it. Jerry West was out. With his recent spate of injuries there was no telling when West would be fully healthy. Gail Goodrich was still unsigned, disgruntled, and rounding into shape after a nasty bout of the flu. Top rookie Cliff Anderson had blown out his knee in training camp. And second-year swingman Jerry Chambers was bedridden, probably with Goodrich's flu, and waiting to take an army physical. His draft notice was in the mail.

Without Archie there to stabilize the reed-thin backcourt and assist Baylor in the scoring column, as he had done in the preseason, the Lakers would limp to another slow start through November and into December. The Fabulous Forum, Cooke's personal shrine, would open in late December. The insatiable Cooke fully expected to inaugurate his world-class arena with a world-class basketball team. Rolling out the red carpet for a 5–20 team would rain on Cooke's royal parade, and Schaus knew that he embarrassed his volatile boss at his own professional risk.

Archie consulted with Woody Sauldsberry. They agreed that the tables had been turned on Schaus. Archie could force the situation to his advantage—but only if he was willing to hold out, miss a few regular-season games, and wait for Schaus to panic. Barring a last-minute trade, Schaus would have no option other than to call Fred Rosenfeld, sweeten the pot, and hustle Archie into the lineup before things turned dire in Lakerland.

Archie explained his strategy to his wife Valerie and then called home to his mother to tell her that he planned to hold out. The news soon spread through the projects and onto the playgrounds. Archie Clark wasn't playing for Los Angeles this season.

THE PHONE RANG at Archie's duplex. It was Mr. Bibbs, Archie's long-time mentor in Ecorse. "Archie, what's this I hear about you holding out from the Lakers? Are you sure that's such a good idea? They're paying you good money, and it's no sure thing that that money will be there tomorrow."

Archie laid out his three-month ordeal as straightforwardly as possible. For the first time he could explain to Mr. Bibbs how the NBA worked and how the owners operated.

"Mr. Bibbs, the Lakers are playing games with me. They think that when I run out of money, I'll come begging. Can't do it, Mr. Bibbs."

"How are you going to survive without their money?"

"Mr. Bibbs, I ate my mother's beans for eighteen years, so I can go hungry for a couple of months. I don't need to eat steak."

They turned the conversation to the recent riot in Detroit. The riot was all anybody talked about back home. The cops had raided an after-hours club several weeks ago in a black neighborhood on Detroit's West Side. A bottle was tossed at a police cruiser, the cops charged the crowd, and rioting erupted like a wildfire. For four days and nights the nation's fifth-largest city raged. Forty-one people died, 1,300 buildings turned to rubble, and 2,700 businesses were ransacked.

The charred aftermath pained Mr. Bibbs. He always had worked peacefully from within the system to affect change. In his steadfast, well-mannered way he stood up to power, altered perceptions, and affected incremental change. But the times had changed. A more militant, we're-not-going-to-take-it-anymore spirit simmered in many black neighborhoods. And in white neighborhoods too. While millions of Americans still supported the Vietnam War, others let their hair down, flashed peace signs, and demanded social justice. Not a day passed without news of another protest or prominent critic of U.S. foreign policy. "A time comes when silence is betrayal," the Reverend Martin Luther King had recently informed the congregation in New York's Riverside Church. "That time has come for us in relation to Vietnam."

Archie reflected on his stint in the army, the escalation of the Cold War, and now the daily body counts from Vietnam. A couple hundred GIs had died in combat last week to win the hearts and minds of Vietnamese villagers who didn't know Karl Marx from Adam Smith. Archie wasn't necessarily opposed to the Pentagon and its escalation of the war. He figured the generals had their reasons, and the obedient soldier in him died hard. But he wasn't one to drive around Los Angeles during the day in his Olds with headlights aglow, the

popular show of support for the war. Too           ou
away with deferring their military service,          in
ate number of working-class "boots on the g.
deaths defending God, country, and President .         e
Theory. It wasn't fair, and that's where Archie al

Archie thought about Mr. Bibbs after they hun&
While Detroit smoldered and the world crumbled, ⁄
the good life in California. Folks back home on the
would kill to be in his shoes for just one day. Why wa
all? Because Martin Luther King was correct too. A time
in the NBA, when silence is betrayal.

LOS ANGELES, OCTOBER 16, 1967. The next morning the s
like a torch over the San Gabriel Mountains. The weatherman
for another ninety-degree scorcher. From the northeast the dry S
Ana winds had been howling like banshees for two days, blowi.
away the usual choke of smog from the sky and leaving the sparkl
of a stunning azure morning.

Archie pulled the sports section loose from the morning newspaper. What do you know? The St. Louis Hawks had won again. They
were 2–0 to start the NBA season.

Archie looked in on the baby and then ran a few errands. By early
afternoon the daily medley of feel-good talk and game shows rolled
onto the airwaves. *Art Linkletter's House Party* was on Channel 2,
then came *To Tell The Truth* and *The Match Game*.

Archie glanced at the clock. In a few minutes the Lakers would be
meeting at the airport to board a three o'clock direct flight to Chicago.
Baylor would be in full monologue with Tommy Hawkins or Darrall
Imhoff about wild animals or whatever grabbed him at the moment.
Butch Van Breda Kolff would be yakking it up and puffing a cigar.
Then Frank O'Neill would count heads and ask, "Where's Archie?"
After a quick sweep of the walkways and bathrooms he would alert
Butch. Then Schaus. The boarding call would come, and Archie offi-
cially would be a holdout.

But before that inevitability happened, the phone jolted Archie of his musings. It was Fred Schaus. He wanted to meet Archie his office pronto.

When Archie arrived at the bank in Inglewood where the Lak-rs kept temporary offices until the Forum opened, Schaus did what Lou Mohs and the previous generation of NBA general managers had resisted at all costs: he cried uncle. Schaus had met with Cooke and received approval to meet Archie's contract demands. If Archie caught the next flight to Chicago, Schaus promised to have a one-year, $35,000 contract waiting for him to sign in a week, when the Lakers returned from their eastern road trip. Archie had his word as a man.

The two shook hands, and Archie hustled off to the airport. He'd have to call Valerie and tell her the good news. No more beans. They'd be eating filet mignon in a few days.

## 10

*After I signed my contract, I flew to Chicago for the game. It was Butch's first regular-season contest as an NBA coach, so the players really wanted to get him his first win. And the odds appeared to be stacked in our favor. The Bulls were a second-year team in transition. They'd just moved into Chicago Stadium, where Michael Jordan would make his mark twenty years later. The Chicago Stadium held 18,500 people, making it a great venue when the place was packed. But the Bulls barely drew a crowd back then. They were lucky to fill a third of the seats, and that always made the building a little dreary. But the Bulls always came to play. A lot of that had to do with Jerry Sloan. He only knew one way to approach basketball, and that was all out and in your face. Sloan usually matched up with Jerry West, so I didn't go head to head with him much. But Sloan's teammates always fed off his energy. You could pound the Bulls, bloody them, force them to take a knee. But like Jerry Sloan, the team wouldn't go down easily.*

---

Chicago, October 17, 1967. "Thank you, gentlemen," Butch Van Breda Kolff said in a raspy postgame voice, his tie askew and his shirt soaked through with perspiration. Butch looked like he had been through a car wash with the windows down. He took a deep breath and announced to a crescendo of locker room cheers, "At least I get one [win] before I might get fired."

During his NBA regular-season debut tonight Van Breda Kolff had worked the sidelines like a caged animal—kneeling, leaping, stomping, and snarling at anything in a striped shirt. Between Butch's bark and Elgin Baylor's bite the Lakers staked out a comfortable fourteen-point halftime edge. Then Baylor landed in foul trouble, Van Breda Kolff's new offense stalled, and the Bulls began their inevitable fourth-quarter stampede.

Butch stomped and yelled and looked angry enough to toss his jacket clear into the tenth row. "Sit down right now," Butch hissed after

Bad News Barnes hoisted an ill-advised shot. The hulking Barnes, startled by the coach's bulging insect eyes, sank into the nearest chair and right into Baylor's lap, drawing chuckles from the end of the bench and a get-off-me push from Baylor.

Archie tried to pick up where Baylor had left off and break down his defender for easy mid-range shots. Nothing was falling. But 7-footer Mel Counts hit a clutch shot with eight seconds left, and the Lakers escaped by the skin of their teeth to celebrate Butch's first victory as an NBA coach, 107–105.

"Gonna wear the same tie, Coach?" wisecracked Darrall Imhoff, referring to the habit of NBA coaches to wear the same lucky articles of clothing until they lost a game and broke the spell.

"Same tie, same shirt, same socks," Butch shot back with his wry, toothy grin. "Even the same jacket." The players groaned in unison.

The jacket was a twilled, red-black-gray plaid that looked like something Butch had grabbed from the back of his grandfather's closet. Some joked that the jacket made him look like Fred MacMurray the title character in Disney's *The Absent-Minded Professor*. But that was Butch's weird sartorial style. He truly didn't care what others thought of the plaids in his lucky jacket or the tassels on his karmic shoes. All that mattered was winning.

According to most NBA beat writers, even the luckiest plaid jacket wouldn't save Butch this season. They picked the Lakers to tumble to third place behind San Francisco and St. Louis in the expanded six-team Western Conference. The consensus was that the Lakers' talent was too thin at each position, especially at center, and too prone to injury.

Butch shrugged at such talk. What did a bunch of yellow journalists know anyway? Tonight he was 1–0, the undefeated head coach of the Los Angeles Lakers, and sitting on top of the NBA world. Butch planned to celebrate with a little nightcap. "Little" (hopefully) being the operative word. The Lakers had a flight to catch in the morning. The world-champion 76ers waited in Philadelphia.

PHILADELPHIA, OCTOBER 18. Butch Van Breda Kolff told Archie to buck up and focus on winning basketball games. Archie nodded, but he couldn't shake two thoughts: he still technically wasn't under contract, and what if he got hurt on the road trip? What then? The Lakers would cancel his $35,000 contract and stick him with a minimum-wage deal. Yeah, what then? True, Archie should have stayed in Los Angeles until he had a signed contract in hand. But deep down he didn't want to leave his coach and teammates hanging.

Now he had to live with the consequences for the next week. The right side of his brain told him to be careful. But Archie knew that he couldn't walk on eggshells for the next three games. That's how players got hurt. Butch was correct. His teammates needed him to step up, starting tonight against the world champs.

Assuming, that is, that the Lakers could find the arena. Last night in Chicago they had gotten off to a Keystone Kops start when trainer Frank O'Neill had skidded from cubbyhole to cubbyhole to find the hotel valet to retrieve the team's rental cars. When the Lakers' three-car caravan finally arrived at Chicago Stadium, the no-nonsense parking attendant demanded $1.50 per car up front. No money, no parking. After emptying their pockets for the needed $4.50, the Lakers finally straggled into the old arena, looking very much the worse for wear.

Tonight their three-car convoy would weave through the prolonged honks of Center City Philadelphia to the city's brand-new, $7 million arena, the Spectrum. It was one of several modern arenas that would pop up on the NBA circuit this season. What constituted a modern arena? First, it had to offer creature comforts. Out with the back-breaking metal seats, sweltering temperatures, screeching microphones, filthy bathrooms, long flights of stairs, and lousy sightlines. In with comfortably cushioned seats, air conditioning, computerized scoreboards, booming public address systems, clean bathrooms, step-saving escalators, carpeted lobbies, and not a bad seat in the house.

Second, there had to be privilege on tap. The business classes wanted to ride the elevator up to their own exclusive conspicuous-consumption zones, where they could puff, swill, and close deals in the privacy of their own luxury boxes or reserved tables—in this case at the Spectrum's private Blue Line Club.

Finally, in this age of urban renewal, the arena had to be an architectural showpiece that made residents feel proud and big league. That often translated to supersized facilities, which increased the physical and financial scale of indoor entertainment and featured more grandiose interiors splashed in distinctive mood colors to make everyone feel at home.

For players used to scrapping in old monochromatic, industrial-strength auditoriums, walking into the Spectrum for the first time was like stepping into a Las Vegas wedding chapel. All 15,244 cushioned seats glowed in a jarring red meld of salmon and burgundy. "A person still sitting low and looking up could feel like he's being inundated by a tidal wave of tomato juice," joked a reporter. In each doorway usherettes wore impossible-to-miss candy cane–striped hats, bright blue ties, burnt orange blouses, hot pink miniskirts, and pink leotards.

Against this tidal wave of color Van Breda Kolff's lucky jacket seemed almost conservative. Then again, few in the stands could see him well anyway down on the floor. The architect had goofed and arrayed the overhead lighting to the dimensions of a hockey rink, placing fifteen hundred watts at center court and a good twenty feet past each basket, where the goals would be when the expansion Flyers played.

All points in between were like the set of a bad Boris Karloff movie—all glare and shadows, especially around the baskets. Archie and his teammates struggled during pregame warm-ups to adjust their eyes accordingly. Work crews had labored through the night to install a scoreboard that just wouldn't straighten up and hang right. The large, four-sided orb weighed ten thousand pounds more than planned, forcing management to fly in a specialist from Chicago to offer last-minute advice. He and the workmen finally lashed the eighteen-thousand-pound beast to the ceiling.

Although the modern arena and the NBA ultimately would mesh, their union remained for tonight at least in a difficult honeymoon phase. But in the NBA, like in the Barnum and Bailey circus, the show must go on despite rain, snow, or opening night snafus.

The buzzer sounded, and Dave Zinkoff, the 76ers' public address announcer, growled out the starting lineups as only "the Zink" could do. Each Laker trotted to midcourt, draped in the team's new purple road uniforms, a regal, self-important color heretofore unseen in the NBA. "They look like a bunch of tall eggplants," a grizzled Philadelphia reporter finally grumped.

The eggplants stole the opening tap, and Van Breda Kolff barked for his players to move, move, move. Baylor flashed open and launched an eighteen footer with six seconds left on the shot clock. The shot rattled out into the hands of forward Luke Jackson, and the 76ers were off. Another miss, and another trip downcourt. Finally, the 76ers lobbed the basketball to Chamberlain near the basket. He pivoted and dunked the basketball with two hands. And so it went.

The Lakers literally couldn't find the hoop, and the Sixers found it just enough. "I didn't have the feeling I was watching a great midseason-form basketball game," said 76ers' coach Alex Hannum in the understatement of the year after his team's 103–87 victory. Archie sank just three of ten field-goal attempts in the shadows and glare, finishing with seven points, though not bad for an eggplant.

INGLEWOOD, CALIFORNIA, OCTOBER 22, 1967. Archie caught a ride home from the airport. He dropped his bags and kissed Valerie hello. Most observers had figured the Lakers would be lucky to snag a single win on their four-game tour. But Archie had quarterbacked the team to a 2–2 start, including his twenty-five-point effort last night in a tight victory over New York. More important, he had returned without a serious injury. Now it was Fred Schaus's turn to settle up on the $35,000 contract.

Archie talked with Valerie for a while, but he remained restless after several hours aboard an airplane. He grabbed the keys to his Olds Ninety Eight and ventured out to run an errand. As Archie reached his parking space, he noticed it was empty. He scanned the parking lot. No car. Archie paced back to the duplex, tossing around a bad feeling. He flipped through the stack of mail, and, sure enough, there was a letter from the bank. It had repossessed the car. Archie could feel his blood start to boil. The Lakers had strung him along all summer, and he had skipped a few car payments. Now he had no transportation. All because he had stood up to management and demanded his true market value.

Archie dialed his agent, Fred Rosenfeld, to talk about retrieving the car. Rosenfeld advised Archie not to worry. He had a friend who sold Cadillacs. With the big money that Archie would be making in a few days, he'd give him a deal on a brand-new ride. By the way, Rosenfeld added, the contract signing would take place before the Lakers' home opener in three days.

A year ago Archie would have had to ask Lou Mohs for a cash advance to retrieve his car. But NBA players no longer had to sell their souls to the company store. The arrival of the ABA, the larger contracts, business agents, and the strength of the players' union had begun to change everything.

Three nights later the Lakers thumped Cincinnati, 132–116. Archie finished with twenty-six points and a big smile on his face. His contract dispute was over. He had signed a one-year, $35,000 deal. And the cherry on top was that Archie arrived at the Los Angeles Sports Arena behind the wheel of his brand-new, canary yellow 1967 Cadillac Coupe DeVille with a black vinyl top. This baby he planned to keep for a while.

LOS ANGELES, NOVEMBER 15, 1967. Since the signing of the new contract Archie had proved his worth to the Lakers five times over. Every night he triggered the offense, spearheaded the fast break, launched the full-court press, defended the opponents' top backcourt threat, crashed the boards when needed, and consistently scored twenty points per game. Archie was the backcourt equivalent of a Swiss Army knife. He did it all.

So did Baylor. To the astonishment of most, the man who had built his career on three dribbles and a shot had thrived under Van Breda Kolff's team approach. The astonishment was misplaced. Baylor had grown up in his native Washington DC playing team basketball on the sandlot. Passing and moving without the basketball had always been in his DNA. It just hadn't paid the bills—until now.

Archie, Baylor, and the jump-shooting big man, Mel Counts, had been the main reasons for the Lakers' season-opening 7–5 record. That hardly met Jack Kent Cooke's conquer-the-world standards. But it was a decent start, all things considered, and tonight the Lakers welcomed back Jerry West and his healed left hand against the winless Chicago Bulls.

"I think we're playing very, very well," West told reporters before his debut, a plastic protective shield, wrapped in sponge rubber, slipped over his left hand. "But when I start playing, we'll be more flexible, have more depth."

West struggled in the first half to shake off the rust—and the tenacious, hand-to-hand defense of Jerry Sloan. But Archie and Baylor had the hot hands tonight, propelling the Lakers to a seemingly insurmountable sixteen-point lead early in the fourth quarter. Four minutes later the Bulls had whittled the lead to eight, sending Van Breda Kolff off the bench, snarling like a drill sergeant.

West, after a long, jaw-clenched grumble on the bench about his lackluster debut, finally returned. Over the final ninety seconds—in one of the season's more magical moments—West stopped thinking and let his instincts be in the moment. He took two hard dribbles and lifted into the air as straight as an arrow for his soft jump shot. *Swish.* Then another swish, then another, and then West threaded a pass through the Bulls' defense to the cutting Goodrich for a lay-up.

Game over. Mr. Clutch was back. He and Archie would become the most dangerous backcourt in the NBA.

---

*The games kept coming, and I remember the Lakers flew to Boston to play in a doubleheader. We lost in the final minute to the Celtics in the nightcap, but it was the opening contest that had everyone buzzing. Wilt Chamberlain had put up fifty-two points and thirty-seven rebounds against Seattle. His point total could have been in the seventies, but Wilt missed an NBA record twenty-two free throws. He used a one-handed, tomahawk motion at the free throw line. It wasn't pretty.*

*What was so memorable about Wilt's performance was he hadn't asserted himself offensively all season. He dunked on Bob Rule to start the game—and just kept shooting. And dunking. It was total domination. I mean, Wilt made his last fifteen shots in a row with grown men hanging all over him. Alex Hannum said afterward that "it was real good therapy" for Wilt to work on his offense.*

*There was just one problem. The Lakers were scheduled to be Wilt's next therapy session. Luckily Wilt wasn't quite so offensive-minded against us in Philadelphia. He only scored thirty-five points. He also missed a dunk at the end of regulation, and we surged ahead in overtime. It was a huge win for the Lakers and a real boost for our confidence. We could beat anyone in the NBA.*

*Afterward somebody came up with the hare-brained idea of not washing our uniforms until we lost again. So we rolled, ripe and wrinkled, through Baltimore, Detroit, and San Diego. On the last game of our twelve-day, eight-game trip, Seattle beat us. Or as the headline in the newspaper declared, the Supersonics took us to the cleaners.*

LOS ANGELES, DECEMBER 15, 1967. It was that time of year again: the NBA trade deadline. It was still a few weeks off, but most players spent their down time in airport terminals and late-night diners hashing over the latest lies, damned lies, and NBA trade rumors.

The consensus was that Archie would remain in Los Angeles. He was too valuable to the team to swap. But stranger things had happened. In two weeks Jack Kent Cooke would open his Fabulous Forum, his showpiece arena. He wasn't above trading half of his team to obtain Chamberlain, Oscar Robertson, or another All-Pro to create more buzz around his magical venue.

The more likely scenario was that the third-place Lakers would keep their starting lineup intact and shore up the bench for their playoff run. Butch Van Breda Kolff had confidence in just three reserves—Gail Goodrich, Mel Counts, and Bad News Barnes—and that left him little flexibility to cope with injuries or find a sparkplug on a night when his starters weren't firing.

Walt Hazzard had warned Archie last year that Lakers broadcaster Chick Hearn, the ultimate team insider, always knew which players had fallen out of favor with owner Jack Kent Cooke and/or were on the trading block. Hearn often pounced. He incorporated witty catchphrases into his broadcasts that told his tens of thousands of dedicated listeners that a blacklisted player needed to be replaced. In Hazzard's case, his once good name had become synonymous with

Hearn's "put too much mustard on the bun," which told fans that he was a hot-dog passer, then a serious and tradable offense.

So far Hearn had stuck to his usual superb play-by-play. No verbal kisses of death had passed his lips. But a trade was in the works. Everyone could sense the bad news coming—or going, as Jack Kent Cooke opened the doors to his Fabulous Forum.

INGLEWOOD, CALIFORNIA, JANUARY 10, 1968. Bad News Barnes finally got the bad news. The Lakers had swapped him and a throwaway future draft choice for Chicago's second-year forward/center Erwin Wolfgang Mueller. By coincidence Barnes and Mueller had nearly jumped to the ABA over the summer. Both returned to the NBA in the fall with heftier contracts and then slumped to start the season.

A few days later Archie arrived at practice to another new face. The Lakers had claimed second-year reserve guard Fred Crawford off of waivers. After a hurried flight west Crawford had arrived, living literally out of a suitcase.

"Archie came up to me at practice and said, 'Hey man, where you staying? Why don't you come to my place?" said Crawford, a defensive specialist. "Archie fed me, introduced me to everybody, drove me around town, showed me how to get around Los Angeles. He taught me the ropes."

Archie offered Crawford the same helping hand that Walt Hazzard had given him last season. But Archie's assistance now came with a firm, heartfelt grasp of the big picture. His offseason conversations with Woody Sauldsberry had opened his eyes to the fact that black players had to support each other, a concept that historically had hit some rough spots.

Sauldsberry explained that the lack of black unity arose from a historical double whammy. The first was the NBA's quota system. In the 1950s and into the mid-1960s African American players competed against themselves, not against other white players, to fill and/or retain the three or four available "black" roster spots. Many African American players were forced to think "Me first" to make the cut and fit in with their predominantly white teammates, making calls for race unity impractical and leaving the quota system unchallenged.

The other was the NBA's star system. The NBA had promoted its top black players since the late 1950s, a positive development that inadvertently created a have-and-have-not class system among African American players. The superstars navigated the national spotlight as the NBA's marquee names; everyone else worried about their week-to-week, season-to-season survival in the league. This tale of two career tracks left everyone with many shared experiences but chasing different rainbows.

Archie felt that black players needed to talk more openly. They needed to discuss their contracts, recommend agents, exchange training tips, mentor young black players, share notes on management, and address the barriers that all African American players still faced to varying degrees in the NBA. Archie wasn't an activist; he was a realist. Black players had to have each other's backs; otherwise the NBA system would chew them up and spit them out mostly empty handed.

While Crawford got his bearings in Los Angeles, Archie flew to Crawford's native New York. The NBA had summoned him.

NEW YORK, JANUARY 23, 1968. Butch Van Breda Kolff officially had the night off. He was merely a spectator and member of John Q. Public. But try telling him that. Butch kept leaping from his seat in Madison Square Garden, pointing and blustering to nobody in particular. He finally turned to Dan Hafner, the young Lakers beat reporter for the *Los Angeles Times*, and mugged, "If they're so good, why aren't we in first place?" Van Breda Kolff, now leaping through the 1968 NBA All-Star Game, was referring to his three Lakers representing the Western Division. There were the two perennial All-Pros, Jerry West and Elgin Baylor, and first-time All-Star, Archie Clark.

Archie took his selection to the All-Star team in stride. He'd been battling a foot infection, and his immediate focus was to control the pain and return to full strength. But Archie wasn't surprised. His productivity spoke for itself: twenty points per game, 48 percent field-goal accuracy, second on the Lakers in assists, and playing lockdown defense every night.

But Archie's rise from third-round draft choice to NBA all-star in just eighteen months on the job was nevertheless remarkable. He joined Chicago's Jerry Sloan (1964 third-round draft choice) and Cincinnati's Wayne Embry (1958 third-round draft choice) as the third NBA player to do it. But Archie had done so for an established NBA team that featured two perennial thirty-point-per-game superstars. That had never been done.

Archie pumped in seventeen points in just fifteen minutes on the court. "He belongs with these players," Butch roared from his seat. "Archie is a player. He's my man."

The West All-Stars could have benefitted from a few more Lakers. The East dominated in the second half, sailing to a 144–124 victory. Despite the game's lack of last-minute drama, Commissioner Walter Kennedy walked away pleased with the NBA's premier prime-time television event. The ratings were way up this year, and that gave the league a chance to showcase to the nation some of its exciting young stars.

"I have to be pleased with the way they [the younger All-Stars] played," beamed Kennedy. "We have a lot of young talent coming along ready to step in and take over. It wasn't too long ago that people were saying that players like George Mikan, Jim Pollard, and Bob Cousy would be hard to replace. But each decade seems to produce its own stars like Wilt, Oscar, Russell, and West." Numbered among those future Oscars and Wests was Archie Clark.

# 11

*The Lakers hit their stride after the All-Star break. Everyone suddenly felt comfortable with Butch's offensive and defensive schemes, and we had a little more depth on the bench. That allowed Butch to rest players, fill in better around injuries, and shuffle the lineup to exploit matchups. But we had a lot of ground to make up. We began the second half of the season in third place, six games back of San Francisco and a nine-game eternity behind front-running St. Louis.*

---

Boston, February 11, 1968. Chris Schenkel, the dry-as-a-martini voice of ABC's Sunday afternoon NBA *Game of the Week*, saw his producer flash the signal: time for the first television timeout. Referee Norm Drucker blew his whistle. "Time-out, Boston," Drucker commanded, trying to disguise modern television's necessity as Celtic player-coach Bill Russell's need to regroup. "We'll be right back after this word from our sponsor," Schenkel monotoned. "The score: Boston 11, Los Angeles 10."

As the ABC crew cut away, Archie and his teammates, clad in their purple road jerseys, loped across the parquet floor. All had barely broken a sweat just three minutes into the first quarter. "We can outrun 'em," urged Jerry West.

The Boston Celtics (39–18, in second place in the Eastern Division) remained the same cagey, battle-tested championship machine. But its parts were showing signs of rust. Several Celtics had lost a step. Maybe two. Others coasted through the regular season to save their energy for the team's postseason run for the roses. Conventional NBA wisdom said to run the Celtics at the start of each regular-season game, see whether the old boys with shamrocks on their shorts were too proud to lose or too tired to care.

Butch Van Breda Kolff told everyone to keep running the Celtics. The buzzer sounded, and West thumped, thumped the basketball off the parquet floor, a deep, dull, resonant sound familiar to all basketball fans in the 1960s. He stopped on a dime and laced a jump shot. Baylor thumped, thumped another basket. Then West again. When Drucker whistled the next television time-out, the Lakers had raced to a double-digit lead. As halftime approached, the men with shamrocks on their shorts sat slumped and draped in white towels. They trailed by thirty points.

"This just might be the best Laker team since the organization moved to Los Angeles," raved ABC's Jack Twyman toward the end of the 141–104 Boston massacre, marking the Lakers' thirteenth victory in their last sixteen games.

EVANSVILLE, INDIANA, FEBRUARY 29, 1968. The Lakers remained the hottest team in pro basketball, the operative word being "team." Tonight Archie had finished with eighteen points, Baylor had twenty-seven, and the Lakers had outdistanced Chicago, 117–107. No Jerry West, though. He had pulled a groin muscle a week ago after the Boston game in a blowout of Cincinnati, and the doctors told him to sit out a few games.

Archie returned to his hotel room after the game. The temperature had dipped into the teens and not much was happening on a Thursday night in Evansville, where Chicago had scheduled four games this season. Besides, the Lakers had a Friday morning flight to catch. He clicked on the television and started flipping the dial. The *Tonight Show* with Johnny Carson was on Channel 14. Tonight's guests: actress Joey Heatherton and the spooky Vincent Price.

While the "King of Late Night" deadpanned with the very blonde Heatherton, Archie's mind drifted. The Lakers had departed yesterday for a two-game road swing. Evansville tonight, Philadelphia tomorrow, and then a six-hour trek back to the West Coast. In his second year Archie had grown more attuned to the rhythm of the NBA season. The first four months marched to the beat of opportunity. Words mattered, players believed, and, assuming everyone stayed healthy, championships seemed within reach. By February the words had lost their zing, the players had grown tired and achy, and the losses had usually mounted. Teams either accepted their fate or got stronger for the playoffs.

The Lakers were on the latter course right now. They'd moved into second place, seven games behind front-running St. Louis. Everyone still clamored to overtake the Hawks, whom the Lakers had beaten head to head all season but couldn't seem to catch in the standings.

Archie heard Carson yukking it up with Price. The next thing he heard was the telephone ringing. It was Frank O'Neill and the dreaded morning wake-up call.

The players slammed their bags into their rental cars and headed north along Highway 41 to Evansville's Dress Memorial Airport. By 3:30 p.m. their Eastern Airlines flight had landed in Philadelphia. Then came the bad news: tonight's game was off. A winter storm had blown through Philadelphia that morning and, for the second time in two weeks, had sheared off a large chunk of the Spectrum's roof. The arena was barricaded, and the Sixers couldn't find the basketball floor for the smaller Convention Center, their previous home. The portable floor was tucked away in storage, but nobody knew exactly where.

By 6 p.m. the Lakers were back in the air en route to Los Angeles. When flights got canceled or roofs got blown to Timbuktu, players had their own sarcastic pet catchphrase: "This is the NBA today." It was a play on *This Is the NFL Today* pregame show on CBS, which portrayed pro football as an orderly, highly entertaining corporate entity. The NBA wasn't quite there yet.

About two weeks later Jerry West made his return in a blowout win over San Francisco. He took six shots in fourteen minutes and grumped to the bench, mumbling about his poor conditioning and the lingering pain in his groin. Two nights later in a win over New York West staggered to the bench holding his face. He had taken a wallop from Knicks center Willis Reed. For the eighth time—and the second time at the hands and elbows of Reed—West's nose was broken.

PHILADELPHIA, MARCH 18, 1968. Jack Ramsay, the forty-three-year-old general manager of the Philadelphia 76ers, reached for the telegram and unfolded it. The text read, "Baylor has serious case of influenza. West had corrective nose surgery on Sunday. Cliff Anderson will play tonight. Fred Schaus, general manager."

Ramsay, prematurely bald with owlish eyebrows and the serious demeanor of a college professor, could only shake his head. When the roof had blown off the Spectrum nearly three weeks ago, according to league rules the 76ers had spent $5,000 to send the Lakers home. Both teams were inclined to scrap tonight's make-up game. A win or a loss meant nothing for either team. The Sixers had clinched the Eastern Division championship a week ago, and the Lakers had clinched second place in the Western Division.

But money talked. The Sixers had drawn poorly of late, due largely to the civic embarrassment of the Spectrum disaster. Ramsay figured the star appeal of Baylor and West would pack his smaller backup venue, Convention Hall—and fill his coffers. Instead Ramsay got unsung Philadelphia native Cliff Anderson.

By game time Convention Hall was nearly empty. But those lucky enough to be on hand for the 76ers' thirty-point victory witnessed Wilt Chamberlain at his 7-foot-1 best. He jammed home fifty-three points (making twenty-four of twenty-nine shots), grabbed thirty-four rebounds, and logged fourteen assists. "Every now and then you have to stretch it out and see whether you still have it," Chamberlain shrugged at his monster performance.

Chamberlain wasn't being entirely truthful. As he later explained, "I'd pretty much decided that I'd like to play for the Lakers next season, if possible, and I wanted to show them that I could still score—just in case they had any doubts."

Archie flew back to Los Angeles with his teammates the next morning to close out the season against San Diego. Nobody on the airplane knew about Chamberlain's desire to go west. In about three months it would turn Archie's life upside down.

———————————————————

*The Lakers drew the fourth-place Chicago Bulls to start the playoffs. The series was rough, with lots of jawing among the players that spilled over into a few fistfights. That was playoff basketball back then. Butch Van Breda Kolff and Chicago coach Red Kerr even went toe to toe in the newspapers. Butch said the Bulls played a zone defense, which then was illegal, and Kerr countered that I played man-to-man defense like a Chicago Bear. Again, that was playoff basketball.*

*Despite the bickering we handled the Bulls four games to one to advance to the Western Division championship series. Our opponent was San Francisco, which upset first-place St. Louis in the other opening-round series. It was really our series to lose. The Warriors were banged up at every position, and we swept them in four straight. I hit a twenty-footer in the final seconds to win game four. Afterward we whooped it up in the locker room, popped the champagne corks, and waited over a week to see whether our opponent in the NBA finals would be Boston or Philadelphia. In other words: choose your poison. We got Boston.*

BOSTON, APRIL 20, 1968. Butch Van Breda Kolff belted out over the low rumble of the automobile engine that he knew a thing or two about basketball. He was the coach of the Los Angeles Lakers. The cab driver glanced into his rear-view mirror to see if he recognized his celebrity cargo. Probably not. He finally asked, "What brings you to town?"

Butch, surprised by the question, shot back that the Lakers had come to play the Celtics for the NBA championship. The best-of-seven championship series opened tomorrow afternoon at Boston Garden.

"Isn't it all over?" the cabbie answered, then quickly corrected himself. "Oh, that's right. We still have another series to go, don't we?"

The cabbie's ill-timed memory lapse was forgivable. For the past several seasons the Celtics' success had revolved around one issue: beating the hated Wilt Chamberlain and the Philadelphia 76ers in the NBA playoffs. Everything else came a distant second.

Bill Russell, the Celtics' player-coach, waxed philosophical about the prospects of winning his first NBA championship as a coach. He also offered perfunctory praise of his opponent as a team to fear. Remember how the Lakers had blown out the Celtics on national television in February? Maybe the tables had turned.

But Russell and the C's were hardly quaking in their Converse low tops. The Celtics had faced the Lakers four times in the NBA finals over the past five seasons. They were batting a thousand. Defense ruled in the playoffs, and the Lakers lacked a dominant center to neutralize Russell in the paint. Big Russ would be free to play Goliath, swatting shots and snatching rebounds, unless the Lakers could outrun the older legs and lungs of the Celtics and score the bulk of their points in the unsettled, fast-breaking transition from defense to offense.

"This is the first time in all the years we've met Boston that I honestly feel we've got the better team," said Jerry West, his broken nose surgically mended but still sounding nasally.

They were a better team maybe, but could they topple Celtic Pride in a seven-game battle of wills for all the NBA marbles? That was now the $80,000 question. Whenever Archie entered Boston Garden, nine championship banners greeted him like scalps strung from a fence post. They were part trophy, part psychological ploy. They were warnings like that line from Dante's *Inferno*: "Abandon hope all ye who enter here." Archie was too self-confident to abandon hope, but he respected the Celtics. Boston had earned the right to pound its chest and believe it was the king of the NBA jungle. And into this shamrock jungle the Lakers trotted for games one and two of the 1968 NBA finals. They arrived well rested and, as time would tell, with rust on their wheels.

BOSTON, APRIL 21, 1968. Little known fact: since Bill Russell's arrival twelve years ago, Boston had never lost a playoff series after winning game one. So when the Celtics couldn't miss in the opening minutes, the Celtic faithful, sporting lucky green carnations pinned to their lapels, must have thought happy days were here again. Au contraire. Archie and his teammates shifted into high gear with six minutes gone and left the older Celtics bobbing in their wake. In a flashback to last February's Boston Massacre, the Lakers blitzed the Celtics 52–18 over the remainder of the first half to build a 61–48 advantage at halftime. "We had the game firmly in hand," said Archie. "We just had to keep running them in the third quarter and wait for Bill Russell to throw in the towel."

Down the hallway Russell revised the game plan. He had started the game with forward John Havlicek guarding the stronger Elgin Baylor and then rotated a larger but slower defender onto the Lakers' star every few minutes to mix things up. So far so good. But Russell had an idea. The Celtics would keep rotating larger defenders onto Baylor but shift Havlicek permanently into the backcourt.

The 6-foot-5 Havlicek could post the 6-foot-2 Clark near the basket. It would create a size mismatch in the Celtics' favor and keep Clark trapped in the paint guarding Havlicek, where he would be slower to leak out and trigger the Lakers' fast break.

Boston ran the Havlicek isolation play like an exclamation mark to start the third quarter, and Van Breda Kolff immediately countered. He inserted the taller Freddie Crawford to guard Havlicek and stashed Archie on the bench. Without a true playmaker and their fastest player on the floor, the Lakers' offense downshifted to a pace more to the Celtics' liking, and a Boston rally soon commenced.

Van Breda Kolff countered again. He leather-lunged "E-J," calculating not unreasonably that if the Lakers settled into a slower half-court tempo, Baylor and West were thirty-point-per-game career scorers in the playoffs. He could safely ride their veteran coattails and jump shots to the victory circle.

Instead Van Breda Kolff rode with Baylor and West straight into Boston Harbor. His stars were gassed; their game conditioning presumably had lapsed in the eight days since the end of the San Francisco series. While the Dynamic Duo shot blanks (they made nine of thirty-five shots in the second half), the slower Celtics trotted past the Lakers in true tortoise-and-the-hare fashion. The Celtics snapped off a succession of fast-break baskets to pull into the lead late in the third quarter and ground out a workman-like 107–101 victory.

Butch looked dyspeptic afterward. "As for Clark, it all depends on John Havlicek," Van Breda Kolff bellowed at a second-guessing reporter after the loss. "Archie starts with John in the frontcourt, and then I'll use Fred Crawford when John goes to a backcourt post."

Archie bit his tongue. Havlicek lacked the quickness to guard him, meaning the matchup should have been a wash for both teams. The real issue was that Butch wanted to run the Lakers offense through Baylor and West, as he had done throughout the playoffs. He wasn't inclined to call Archie's number and force the Celtics' hand. As frustrating as Butch's choice was, Archie pushed it aside and moved on to game two, unsure whether he would play long minutes or warm the bench.

One thing Archie knew: the Lakers had nowhere to go but up. As good as Boston's defense could be funneling everything into the middle for Bill Russell to swat, it hadn't stopped the Lakers' attack. The Lakers had stopped themselves, shooting a season-low 27 percent from the field in the second half. Russell may be the king of game ones and championships, but this game one was a fluke. It said nothing about the remainder of the series. As if to hammer home this point, Lakers general manager Fred Schaus suggested an alternative narrative to reporters: "Whoever wins [game two] should take the title," he said.

Schaus seemed like the smartest man in basketball two days later. The rejuvenated Lakers won, 123–113, to tie the series and turn the tables on Boston. Among those smiling in the Los Angeles dressing room was Archie. His bench experiment was short-lived. Archie had logged thirty-eight minutes, and now the Lakers were rolling again.

---

*I thought we had a good chance to take the series. It was tied at one win apiece, and the next two games were in Los Angeles. The odds were in our favor to win both games in the Forum and push Boston to the brink of elimination for a second-straight playoff series. Only this time, we would close them out. We were too fast for the Celtics. They could run with us for a game, maybe two, but not three games in a row.*

*Well, the Celtics quickly dashed that storyline. In game three Boston played its best game of the series to beat us, 127–119, and reclaim the home-court advantage. We regrouped in game four to run past Boston, 119–105, and even the series at two games apiece. Toward the end of the game Jerry collided with John Havlicek going for a loose ball and turned his ankle pretty badly. The speculation was that Jerry was done for the series, and that had everyone nervous. He took a cortisone shot to play in game four in Boston, but we lost a close one in overtime. I remember walking into our locker room afterward, and the place looked like an army MASH unit. Jerry was enveloped in discarded bandages, tape, and ice packs. So was Baylor. Darrall Imhoff, battling a bad back and deep thigh bruise, moved as stiffly as Herman Munster. I thought, "How are we going to keep this series going?"*

INGLEWOOD, CALIFORNIA, MAY 2, 1968. The Lakers succumbed in six. Their passing was swift, as the Celtics, healthy and hell-bent on avoiding that Pandora's box called game seven, jumped out to an early lead and never looked back to thoroughly flatten the Lakers, 124–109.

After congratulating his players on a successful season, Butch Van Breda Kolff wandered into the deserted hallway outside the Lakers' locker room for a smoke. His leather-lunged, drill-sergeant persona was turned off. Butch needed to reflect on a game gone wrong and the cigar smoldering in his right hand. "It's tough, it's tough," he muttered. "When you get behind, only one thing can keep you in the game. That thing is defense, and we certainly didn't have it."

Around the corner the visitors' locker room was awash in champagne. "This has got to rate right up there as one of the greatest titles we've ever won," gushed Bill Russell, keeping an eye out for the next stray spew of white bubbles.

Russell then opened an old wound, although probably unintentionally. In a champagne-soaked attempt to be diplomatic, Russell told a reporter, "The Lakers weren't the most challenging team we've ever beaten, but they had the most heart."

Fred Schaus had heard this same peppy-but-unaccomplished claim for years. "What the hell have you guys ever won out here?" Boston's Red Auerbach once mocked the Lakers. That Russell, as a proxy for his detestable boss Auerbach, could continue to dismiss the Lakers as a spunky but inferior junior-varsity ball club irked Schaus.

Nor did it resonate with his boss. Jack Kent Cooke had too much money invested in the Forum and his burgeoning American sports empire to watch the members of his flagship franchise trot embarrassingly through the paces before a sellout home crowd in the most important game of the season. For the think-big Cooke second place wasn't good enough. The Lakers had to be number one.

# 12

Wilt Chamberlain had once hated Los Angeles. He viewed it as a sprawling suburban oasis, an alien desert world in which bloomed houses, freeways, shopping malls, and swimming pools. Cosmopolitan New York was more his speed. But by the early 1960s Chamberlain said the sunny, carefree ways of the Southland had started to beguile him. The women were prettier in Los Angeles, the racism less overt, and the beach life, like a good massage, melted away the tensions of the NBA's annual eighty-two-game barnstorm. Besides, Chamberlain calculated, maintaining his 7-foot-1 presence in Los Angeles would be a good career move. After basketball he wanted to be an actor.

Chamberlain decided he needed to exit Philadelphia and find an NBA team on the West Coast. In early May Chamberlain met in Los Angeles with Alfred Bloomingdale, the grandson of the department store mogul. The younger Bloomingdale had recently purchased the up-and-coming Fugazy Travel Bureau. Chamberlain wanted to launch a Fugazy franchise of his own and joked to Bloomingdale that their business dealings would be much smoother if he played in Los Angeles.

"Jack Kent Cooke is a good personal friend," Bloomingdale teased. "I'll see what I can do."

"Please do," Chamberlain replied. He wasn't joking.

ALFRED BLOOMINGDALE INFORMED Jack Kent Cooke of his intriguing conversation. Cooke, a week removed from the disappointment of the 1968 NBA finals, immediately called and left an urgent message with Irv Kosloff, owner of the Philadelphia 76ers. On May 17 Kosloff returned Cooke's call. "Would the Lakers be interested in taking over Wilt's contract?" the soft-spoken Kosloff reportedly asked, tipping his hand that he wanted out of Chamberlain's mega contract. "Of course, we would," replied Cooke.

Kosloff explained that Chamberlain was holding out for another raise to push his salary close to $300,000 per season. Assuming Cooke could jump in and reach an agreement with Chamberlain, Kosloff said he would trade him to the Lakers. Kosloff also more than likely threw in another useful tidbit: Seattle's Sam Schulman was interested in obtaining Chamberlain. Cooke hated Schulman—and vice versa.

Cooke scheduled a meeting at his Bel Air mansion with Chamberlain. With a battery of lawyers and accountants in attendance Cooke unveiled a six-figure, multi-year contract with all the fanfare of an executive introducing a new product line. Chamberlain balked. As Chamberlain explained, after playing for Kosloff, whom he didn't like, he wanted to get to know Cooke first and feel comfortable about playing for him. Cooke heeded Chamberlain's wishes and, like a college recruiter, tried to cultivate a friendship.

"I decided that I liked Jack," Chamberlain later recalled of his first night breaking bread with Cooke. "And when I left, he suggested we keep in touch—and that I use a code name ('Mr. Norman,' my middle name) any time I called his office."

Mr. Norman also remained in contact with Schulman. He found the Sonics owner hipper than the "straight-laced" Cooke, and Schulman presented Chamberlain with a whopper of a contract that was 35 percent higher than Cooke's. Chamberlain decided the offer "was just too good to decline." He broke the news to Cooke, taking pains not to rat out Schulman. Cooke called Chamberlain's lawyer and learned of Seattle's generous offer. He matched the offer on the spot.

Chamberlain wanted no part of a bidding war. After some last-minute soul searching, Chamberlain changed his mind. He called Cooke. Goliath would be coming to Los Angeles after all.

Cooke called Kosloff with the news. By the end of May all front-office parties were in agreement. The 76ers would get Archie Clark, Darrall Imhoff, Jerry Chambers, and $250,000. There was just one niggling stipulation holding up the champagne corks. Philadelphia wanted all three, especially Clark, resigned and under contract to avoid any possibility of a holdout and the bad publicity that would follow.

ARCHIE HEARD THE telephone ringing in the kitchen.

"Archie, this is Fred Schaus."

"How you doing, Fred?"

"Fine, thank you. Archie, we need to take care of your contract for next season. We certainly don't want a repeat of last year. I have a one-year, $50,000 contract waiting here for your signature. Come down to the Forum, and we can take care of business."

Archie's mind started to race. Fifty thousand bucks? Archie thought back to the threats and counterthreats last fall to boost his salary to $35,000. Now the Lakers were asking to hand him $50,000 for being a good guy? It had to be a trick. Stall, Archie thought; don't commit to anything.

"Fred, I'm leaving tomorrow to spend some time with my family in Detroit. I'll call you when I return in two weeks."

"Archie, we'd like to take care of this matter as soon as possible."

"Fred, it was a long season, and I just need a break. I'll talk with you when I get back."

Schaus grumbled goodbye, and the phone clicked. Archie took a deep breath and thought, "What was that all about?"

FRED SCHAUS RELAYED the message, and Jack Kent Cooke fussed that he couldn't wait two weeks while Clark lollygagged in Detroit. He needed his signature now.

Schaus tried appeasing the boss. But the frustration in the room was palpable. Cooke instructed Schaus to fly to Detroit and force Clark to sign his new contract. As always, mum was the word about the trade. If Clark caught wind of the deal, he might blow their cover.

"ARCHIE, THIS IS Fred Schaus. We need to take care of your contract. I'll be in Detroit tomorrow on business. Can you meet me at the airport? Let's see if we can get this squared away."

Archie hung up the phone, and his mind raced again. He couldn't shake the image of the burly Schaus lumbering aboard a flight to Detroit. Last year Schaus wouldn't answer Archie's calls. This year Schaus wouldn't leave him alone.

The next day Schaus landed in Detroit and glad-handed Archie into the nearest airport lounge. After a few throwaway comments about the weather Schaus paused and, in a stern, father-knows-best tone, scolded, "Archie, we really need to get this contract done." Archie stared back stone-faced.

"You had a tremendous season for us last season," continued Schaus. "You made the All-Star team and were one of the keys to our play-off success. Mr. Cooke would like to reward you with a one-year, $65,000 contract. I've got the contract in my briefcase. It just needs your signature."

When he heard the new dollar figure, a 30 percent jump from the $50,000 offer of just ten days ago, Archie wasn't sure whether to be thrilled or worried. Something had to be fishy, Archie thought. NBA general managers didn't double player salaries. Nor did they happen to have business in Detroit. Archie trusted his instincts. If Schaus was so anxious to sign him, he might up the ante to $75,000 in another week.

"Fred, I'm on vacation," Archie countered. "I can't sign a contract right now. Look, I'm flying back to Los Angeles on Thursday. Let's talk when I get back!"

Schaus stiffened at the word "Thursday"; it meant waiting three days to finalize the deal. Archie had seen this grumbling, how-dare-you expression many times before while Furnace Fred coached the Lakers. The glare was reserved for a whistle-happy referee who'd gotten under his skin. It warned that Schaus, straining to maintain his composure, was about to blow.

Archie glanced away. He had driven to the airport with a carful of friends from Ecorse who, unbeknown to Schaus, eavesdropped at a nearby table. Archie nodded to them as if to clear his head. Schaus would have to stew. Archie wasn't signing anything. Schaus paid the bill and steamed off to a phone booth. He'd have to break the bad news to Mr. Cooke.

When Archie returned to Ecorse, he called his friend and mentor Woody Sauldsberry in Los Angeles. "A trade must be in the works," Sauldsberry speculated. "The 76ers want to move Wilt. Maybe that's it. Maybe Schaus needs to sign you because you're part of a deal to bring Wilt to the Lakers."

"You think so?" Archie answered.

"When you get back to Los Angeles, I'll call Wilt. I'll get you two on the phone, and he can tell you what's happening."

ARCHIE WALKED INTO his duplex and plopped down his suitcase. He hadn't seen his wife Valerie in two weeks, and she wanted to hear the latest scuttlebutt. Both were reluctant to leave Los Angeles. Archie assured Valerie that the trade was still just a rumor. He'd find out more tomorrow when he talked to Chamberlain. Archie also told her that if the trade rumor was real, Woody Sauldsberry had cooked up a second option to keep them in Los Angeles. Archie would meet next week with the ABA's Los Angeles Stars. If the money was right, he might consider jumping leagues to stay in Southern California.

Archie heard the phone ring. It was Fred Schaus. "Archie, we need to talk about your contract. Please come to the Forum right now for a meeting."

"Fred, I just walked through the front door. I need some time to get myself together. It was a long flight."

"Just a minute," Schaus snapped, and Archie heard a shuffling sound, as though the receiver was being passed from one hand to the next.

"Archie, what do you mean that you can't come and talk to your employer about your contract?"

The stiff, high-pitched voice belonged to Jack Kent Cooke. Archie had never spoken directly to the Lakers' owner, but he recognized the stilted, precise diction that tilted conversations in Cooke's intellectual favor and placed his listeners on the defensive. Archie felt very much on the defensive right now.

"Hello, Mr. Cooke. Of course I have time to speak with you."

"Grand. I'll see you shortly."

Archie put down the telephone and exhaled. He called Woody immediately. He'd know what to do. "Archie, I don't care if the Lakers offer you a million bucks; don't sign anything today," Sauldsberry stressed. "We need to talk to Wilt first."

An hour later Archie entered the reception area of Cooke's spacious office in the Forum. The furniture was ornate and antique. Archie felt as though he was visiting a French monarch.

The secretary ushered him into Mr. Cooke's office and closed the door. Schaus already was seated, and Cooke glanced up from the attention-consuming paperwork on his oversized antique desk. He appeared in no mood for chitchat.

"Archie, you need to sign your contract," Cooke ordered. "I'm offering you $65,000 dollars." He stretched out the dollar figure like a salesman for impact, suggesting that only a fool would walk away from so much loot.

"Mr. Cooke, I just got back into town. . . ."

Cooke cut him off. "Look, I'm going to be candid with you," he said. "We are working on a trade between Boston [not true] and Philadelphia. You're involved. I want this trade. If you interfere, you'll never play professional basketball again. You have my word on that. Do you understand?"

Cooke's venomous tone surprised Archie. He felt a gush of adrenaline, followed by anger. Why was this pale little white man threatening him? Archie told himself to stay calm. To act surprised. Maybe feigned surprise over the trade would bend the conversation toward a more civil tone, where Archie would have room to stall Cooke.

"What? I'm going to be traded? Wow, Mr. Cooke, I can't make a decision about my contract right now. I've got to talk to my wife. We've got a lot to think about."

Cooke glared impatiently. He remembered that Archie had served in the army. "Let's imagine, Archie, that you stood on the firing line holding a rifle," Cooke said. "Are you suggesting to me that you would be unable to render a snap decision on whether or not to pull the trigger?"

The awkward comparison confused Archie. All he could do was shrug off the question. Cooke, sensing the confusion, took a different tack. "You know, Archie, I'm certainly not one to rush decisions either. When I face an important business decision, I make sure to get a good night's sleep. In the morning I take a long, hot shower and let my mind wander aimlessly. Then I turn off the water, reach for the towel, and make my decision. Just like that. Why don't you give it a try? So when can you make a decision?"

"Next Friday."

That was a week off. Archie had calculated on the fly that Friday would give him time to meet with the Los Angeles Stars on Wednesday and another thirty-six hours to make a final decision.

"Why in the world next Friday?" asked Cooke.

"I just need time, Mr. Cooke."

"Listen, Archie, I need a quick decision," Cooke snapped. "Come to my house on Sunday afternoon. That gives you two days to make up your mind. I'll have the contract waiting for your signature."

ARCHIE EXITED THE Forum parking lot and drove his yellow 1968 Coupe DeVille through the late afternoon traffic straight to Woody Sauldsberry's apartment. They called Wilt Chamberlain.

"Archie, I don't like to give advice," Wilt said in his deep, resonant voice. "If people take my advice and things don't work out, they get mad at me."

"Wilt, I'm not like that. I just want to know what's going on between you and the Lakers."

"Well, I'm coming out there to play."

"That's all I needed to know."

ARCHIE ARRIVED, AS ordered, at Cooke's Bel Air mansion. His plan was to continue stalling, though he wasn't exactly sure how. But Archie knew he had to keep his options open. The ABA meeting was in three days.

Cooke's butler shuffled Archie into a library, just off the main vestibule. About ten minutes passed. No sign of Cooke. While Archie nervously scanned the bookcases and practiced the lines in his head for the umpteenth time, Cooke appeared in the doorway. He wore a silk bathrobe and an oversized pair of sunglasses. Archie smelled chlorine on his skin from the swimming pool.

"Have you reached a decision?" the sunglasses interrogated.

"Mr. Cooke, I told you that I wouldn't make up my mind until Friday."

Cooke's jaw tensed. "Alright then," he harrumphed. "Next Friday you tell me what you want." Cooke opened the door to the library and escorted Archie back to the vestibule. Archie shot through the front door and hurried into the sunlight on Cooke's circular driveway. He was free to talk to the ABA. In yet another strange twist to Archie's offseason saga, so was Wilt Chamberlain.

ACCORDING TO WILT Chamberlain, he wanted to "play in the ABA about like I wanted to be a monk." But two days after Chamberlain verbally agreed to join the Lakers, he received a phone call from Bill Sharman, former head coach of the San Francisco Warriors.

Sharman had jumped the NBA two months ago for the Los Angeles Stars. The Stars were under new management and had signed a lease to play in the Los Angeles Sports Arena. To compete head to head against Jerry, Elg, and the Lakers, the Stars' management had high hopes of reeling in a few marquee names, starting with the mighty Chamberlain.

Sharman invited Chamberlain to join him for a conversation with the team's affable owner, James Kirst, and gung-ho general manager Bruce Hardy. Chamberlain said his dance card was full. He was headed to the Lakers. Sharman insisted, and Chamberlain acquiesced. What was one little meeting?

Or so he thought. Chamberlain told the Stars that his asking price was $1 million per season, take it or leave it. Chamberlain imagined that Kirst, woozy from the word "million," would ask the waiter for the check. But Chamberlain rambled on and advised Kirst that he could ask the other ABA owners to help cover his salary.

On Wednesday, July 3, ABA commissioner George Mikan and his staff arranged a secret meeting at the Los Angeles Biltmore Hotel with Chamberlain and his attorney to negotiate pro basketball's first million-dollar contract. Joining them at the table were Kirst, Hardy, and Bill Ringsby, owner of the Denver Rockets, who served as a proxy for his fellow owners.

In the midst of this cloak and dagger, Kirst and Hardy broke for lunch and another appointment. They had a beat on another NBA player. He was the Lakers' young playmaker: Archie Clark.

AS ARCHIE DROVE to the Biltmore Hotel, he hoped that Woody Sauldsberry was right. The Los Angeles Stars would triple or even quadruple his salary. In his heart, though, Archie didn't want to do it. The ABA was too shaky financially. What if the league folded? But like Woody said, nothing ventured, nothing gained.

"Archie, so nice to see you again," beamed Sharman.

Sharman graciously introduced everyone, turned to James Kirst, and, switching from host to head coach, said, "Archie is exactly the type of player that we want." He analyzed Archie's game point by point and concluded, "Archie would be an ideal player to build our team around."

Part of Archie felt like crawling under the table. The Lakers had never placed him on a pedestal. But another part of Archie felt validated. He worked hard at his game, and to hear the highly regarded Sharman sing his praises made those long hours in the gym worth it.

Now it was Kirst's turn to speak, and Archie braced himself. He assumed Kirst, a Los Angeles construction mogul, would now reach into his briefcase and wow him with a breathtaking contract offer. Kirst, preoccupied with the Chamberlain negotiation, cut right to the chase, "How much money do you want?"

Kirst's bluntness jolted Archie, and his mind went blank. He didn't have an answer. But two numbers popped into his head from out of nowhere, and behind his composed façade Archie repeated them to appear prepared for the negotiation: "Around $80,000–$100,000."

"I'm not going to give you that," Kirst smirked. "Look, I know what the Lakers pay you. We're close to signing a really big name [Chamberlain], and let me tell you, you'll want to play with the Stars when he arrives."

The negotiation was over. Archie drove back to his duplex and sat down with Valerie. Archie said he would meet with Jack Kent Cooke on Friday. Start packing. They were moving to Philadelphia.

THE ABA OWNERS were almost unanimous. They would pool their funds to pay Wilt Chamberlain's million-dollar salary. There was one no vote: the Miami Floridians. While Archie met with the Stars, a Floridians spokesperson was on the phone with a *Miami Herald* reporter. He wanted to share a secret. "Chamberlain Negotiating Jump to ABA," screamed the headline in the *Miami Herald* the following day.

Jack Kent Cooke reportedly was apoplectic at the news and called Chamberlain's lawyer for an explanation. Chamberlain, meanwhile, decided to stall Cooke for another day or two. Although he didn't want to play in the ABA, a million dollars was a million dollars.

On Friday Archie still had heard nothing about Chamberlain's secret negotiations with the ABA. He arrived on schedule at Cooke's office, prepared to sign a $65,000 contract. The secretary asked Archie to take a seat in the waiting area. Mr. Cooke would see him shortly.

Moments later Cooke emerged. He looked to be in a foul mood and approached Archie head on and without a hello.

"Well Archie, what do you want?"

The question surprised Archie. He thought Cooke had closed their negotiation at $65,000. The word "want" suggested that wasn't the case. Like yesterday at lunch, his mind raced for a number. One popped into his head. He grabbed it: "I'd like $105,000."

"Okay," Cooke answered. "Have your attorney contact my attorney. They can work out the contract."

Cooke grumped back into his office, and Archie's heart pounded. No counter offer? Cooke, the master negotiator, had caved to a third-year guard from Minnesota. Archie called Fred Rosenfeld. Shortly thereafter Rosenfeld and Cooke's attorney, Clyde Tritt, huddled in the office suite behind closed doors. Archie remained seated in the waiting area, his mind whirling. He was a $100,000 man! He had reached the gold standard of sports wealth. Wait until he told Woody.

The door opened, and both lawyers emerged with furrowed brows.

"We've got a problem," Tritt said.

Archie's heart nearly stopped.

"You will be traded to Philadelphia," announced Tritt. "Philadelphia wants you to sign a standard, one-year NBA contract. But the 76ers are only willing to pay $55,000."

"Oh, no, I can't sign for that," Archie interjected.

"Hold on," Tritt continued. "We can work it out. I'll add an addendum to your $55,000 contract for $50,000, which Mr. Cooke will pay. That puts you at $105,000."

Archie considered the plan and quickly saw the trap. He would earn $105,000 next season, and the 76ers would begin their negotiations the following year at $55,000, a 50 percent pay cut.

"No, I can't do that," said Archie, explaining the dilemma.

"Archie, I think we can solve the problem. If you resign with the

76ers the following season for less than $105,000, Mr. Cooke will personally pay the difference. Do we have a deal?"

Archie thought for a few seconds and answered in the affirmative. Tritt trundled into Cooke's office to share the good news. Clark was in tow. Call Philadelphia.

The following Tuesday Jack Kent Cooke held a press conference at the Fabulous Forum and officially revealed "the worst kept secret in NBA history." Wilt Chamberlain was coming to Los Angeles. Cooke had matched the ABA offer, reportedly committing $1 million to the thirty-one-year-old Chamberlain over the next five years. If we do the math, it looks like Chamberlain may have taken a pay cut. He'd earned $250,000 last season in Philadelphia, a figure that would total $1.25 million over five years. Nevertheless, Chamberlain technically was the first million-dollar man in professional sports.

# 13

*In mid-August 1968 I drove to Philadelphia with Valerie and the baby to start our new life. I tried to keep an open mind about Philadelphia. I had tripled my salary and become one of the highest-paid guards in the NBA, and the Sixers, minus Wilt Chamberlain, still had a boatload of talent. But I enjoyed Los Angeles. I couldn't imagine leaving behind the shorts-and-T-shirt weather for a winter jacket and snow shovel.*

*Today Philadelphia is a vibrant city. That wasn't true in the late 1960s. Philadelphia was pretty gritty. Times were hard, and there was growing dissatisfaction with the Vietnam War and the heavy-handed tactics of the local police, especially in black neighborhoods. This fostered cynicism and social unrest. I remember checking into our motel when we arrived from Los Angeles and seeing young, well-dressed black men milling around everywhere. Some wore baseball-style caps bearing the Black Panther insignia. They were in town to attend the National Conference on Black Power. I remember thinking, "Archie, what in the world have you gotten yourself into?"*

---

Philadelphia, September 2, 1968. The third annual National Conference on Black Power concluded yesterday in a wave of raised-fist salutes. Plans to establish a black nation-state, the conference theme, would have to wait until next year. Archie shrugged at the nation-state idea, though he was sympathetic to the call for social and economic justice. He was a professional basketball player, not a revolutionary. He engaged the system from within—for better or worse.

Right now, it was for worse. Archie, Valerie, and the baby had been stranded at their motel for two days. The 76ers' front office had yet to return their calls and send out the welcome wagon.

Finally, the phone rang. "Archie, welcome to Philadelphia," said an unfamiliar front-office voice.

Archie and Valerie found a three-bedroom rental along a tree-lined street in Germantown, a predominantly black, middle-income neighborhood on Philadelphia's northwest side. The basement would serve as Archie's workout room, from which neighbors could hear the muffled pat, pat, pat of the professional athlete next door practicing his dribbling like a musician running through his scales.

There would be no bouncing in the basement just yet. Training camp started on September 15. The front office instructed Archie, now sporting a moustache and sideburns in a mod 1960s look, to arrive promptly at the Jewish Community Center in a place called Margate City in New Jersey. Archie found New Jersey on the map, and his eyes worked their way south past Atlantic City. He was looking for a saltwater-taffy township, eighty miles from Philadelphia and a world away from the palm trees of Los Angeles.

MARGATE CITY, NEW Jersey, September 15, 1968. Archie had met Jack Ramsay, the general manager of the 76ers, two months ago. The balding, forty-three-year-old with the striking owlish eyebrows had materialized in Los Angeles shortly after "The Trade" to welcome Archie into the Philadelphia fold. Ramsay surprised no one with his next move. He would pull double duty and also serve as the team's head coach.

Today Ramsay opened his first training camp as an NBA coach in this lazy seaside town. Running the 76ers through the paces in this nondescript gymnasium brought Ramsay full circle in his strange personal odyssey. Two years ago, in his eleventh season as the successful head men's basketball coach at St. Joseph's College, Ramsay had lost sight in his right eye. Doctors diagnosed retinal swelling and attributed it to extreme stress. They advised Ramsey to relax. His vision would return. But he had to quit coaching. The stress was too much for him.

Ramsay convinced family and friends that his coaching hiatus had taught him to relax. He could handle the NBA and its now eighty-two-game grind, no problem. To prove it Ramsay had arrived last week for rookie training camp suntanned and speaking in an exaggerated, shoulder-shrugging, easy-does-it mumble.

"Call me Coach. Or by my first name, Jack. Whichever is more comfortable," he mumbled. "I prefer you don't call me Mister. And Doctor is even worse."

Archie of course had been down this college-to-pros road before with Butch Van Breda Kolff. Whereas Butch was an eastern-style basketball purist, Ramsay hit the court as the quintessential "modern coach." The term described a first wave of college coaches in the 1950s and 1960s whose strategic thinking had evolved beyond the regional styles that had dominated the game prior to World War II. Modern coaches were eclectic theorists who mixed the best from all regions to concoct their own winning formulas. Ergo Ramsey. He had a PhD in education and published his own coaching manifesto titled *Pressure Basketball*.

To implement pressure basketball in the pros Ramsay turned to three of the NBA's premier defensive guards in Archie, the tenacious Wally Jones, and the pass-snatching Hal Greer. Ramsay would play the trio for a quarter or two each game as the 1960s NBA equivalent of a SWAT team. The threesome would hustle, tussle, and otherwise spook the opposition at the front end of his signature 3-1-1 college zone press. It would be, as a Philadelphia columnist called the tactic, "Pro Basketball—College Style."

At St. Joseph's Dr. Jack had built his 3-1-1 zone from mostly white, God-fearing Catholic kids. Staring back at him in training camp was a demographically mixed bag of white and black men who, in keeping with the changing times, increasingly sported facial hair, smoked in the locker room, dressed in loud colors and psychedelic patterns off court, discussed war and peace, and listened to Motown music. Dr. Jack didn't have a chapter in his book on Motown and the modern player. But as a can-do modern coach, he would be busy pondering one.

MARGATE CITY, NEW Jersey, September 19, 1968. The mumbling, easy-going coach of two weeks ago was gone. "Chill" Ramsay had morphed into an intense, whistle-blowing, order-enunciating, one-more-time-with-gusto choreographer. As the brains behind the show, Ramsay battled one single-minded and at times manic obsession: perfection. He strove for the perfect defensive rotation. The perfect pass. The perfect fast break. Anything less was weakness. For Ramsay those who weren't wholeheartedly chasing perfection weren't necessarily against him. They just weren't his type of player.

Despite his hard-driving demeanor, Ramsay-the-Modern-Coach remained almost paradoxically open-minded to suggestions. He mulled his players' what-ifs and tried to incorporate them like a chef would a secret Chinese herb.

Today Ramsay's exotic ingredient was Motown. Make that Wally Jones's high-fidelity record player. Jones, always hip to the latest hits, now balanced a record album on the spindle, flicked the start button, and the big, Gospel-laden voice of Aretha Franklin filled the Jewish Community Center gymnasium like the sweet Holy Ghost: "Baby, baby, sweet baby / I didn't mean to run you away."

Archie danced along at one of the baskets. Luke Jackson, the 6-foot-9 bruiser who would slide over to center to fill Wilt Chamberlain's shoes, did the Boogaloo. Jackson had arrived for training camp at a blubbery 272 pounds and needed the extra motion to melt away the tire around his waist.

"This is dunkin' music," Darrall Imhoff said of the novelty of practicing to Motown. "You play that, and you have to start dunkin'."

Even Ramsay, who didn't know the Queen of Soul from Martha and the Vandellas, clapped his hands to the beat. When the album stopped and the needle clicked back to its cradle, Ramsay called to trainer, Al Domenico, in a telling, unhip gaffe, "Let's get some [more] noise, Al."

"Tell him it's music," Jones grumbled.

Despite Ramsay's gaffe Jones respected the new coach. During a recent playoff run Ramsay had singled out Jones as Philadelphia's most valuable player for his "perfect" playmaking and defense. Jones never forgot the compliment. But he'd arrived for training camp flustered. If Ramsay thought so highly of him, why trade for Archie Clark, one of the league's top young playmakers? "I'm prepared to battle anyone for my job, a position that I held when the season closed," warned the Philadelphia native.

But the competition struck an unpredictable snag. Archie and "Wally Wonder," as Jones was nicknamed, hit it off immediately. After practice, over games of one-on-one, they bantered like teenagers on the playground.

"You can't stop this."

"Watch me."

Archie, as was his nature, carefully observed Jones. On defense Jones was a whirling dervish. His arms held aloft, rotating like propeller blades, while his feet skittered in lockstep with those of the man whom he guarded. On offense Jones possessed a jump shot like no other. According to one sportswriter, Jones's signature shot was "like trying to explain a Jackson Pollock painting to somebody over the phone." He wrote, "Wally jumps, cranks, hitch kicks, and flutters, and the next thing you know, the ball is going through the basket—if he's on one of his hot streaks." The key word was "if."

Above all Archie admired Jones's heart and playmaking ability. Man, could he run the team! Toward the end of training camp Ramsay told Archie that he was on the fence about whom to start at the playmaker position.

"I told Jack not to worry," said Archie. "I volunteered to be the team's sixth man. I'd decided that Wally could run Jack's offense better than me. He'd already developed a rapport with the guys over the last couple seasons."

"Coming off the bench was a bad career move," he continued. "But at the time, taking on the sixth-man role was the right move for the team. More than personal accolades, I wanted to win in Philadelphia."

Ramsay seemed to have assembled a true team. Jones ran the show. Archie was the catalyst off the bench. Luke Jackson, Darrall Imhoff, and presumably Chet Walker crashed the boards. The go-to scorers were Hal Greer and the new offensive focal point, Billy Cunningham, formerly the team's fleet-footed sixth man.

And therein lay Ramsay's first miscalculation as an NBA coach. He handed the ball—and the team's marquee billing—to a young white player at the expense of the high-scoring Walker and an equally talented core of black veterans. The team's black players rolled their eyes and assumed that Ramsay was conducting 1960s NBA business as usual: when in doubt, boost the white guy to sell tickets.

"Nothing against Billy," said Archie. "He's a tremendous person and could play with the best of them. But so could Hal, Chet, Luke, and Wally. For Jack to feature Billy and consign future stars and Hall of Famers to supportive roles just wasn't making the most of the team's full potential. It amounted to a rookie mistake."

It was a rookie mistake that sowed the seeds of discord between Ramsay and his black players. "He told me my new job was to rebound and defend. I was speechless," said Walker, a three-time NBA All-Star and a seven-year veteran known for his scoring punch. "There was absolutely no doubt in my mind why he was handing the ball to Billy."

The NBA had embarked upon an expansion movement, adding five teams in three seasons and extending its national network to fifteen cities. Milwaukee and Phoenix were the latest to join the fold. In this watered-down NBA the new-look 76ers were almost assured of a winning season. They would play a quarter of their games against expansion teams. The larger question was whether Ramsay could whip his veteran talent into a championship contender minus the dominant Wilt Chamberlain inside.

NBA wisdom said no. The thinking was the 76ers' small frontline couldn't rebound consistently against the Wilts and Russells or, for that matter, the Willis Reeds and Zelmo Beatys. No rebounds meant no run and intelligently gun. No rebounds also meant the 76ers would have to jumpstart their offense each night with ball-hawking front-court pressure to create steals and go-the-other-way lay-ups. As quick and as pesky as Archie, Jones, and Greer could be, the experts were certain that no 1960s NBA team could run sprints for twenty or thirty minutes per night. The season was too long, knees and ankles too brittle, and sports medicine still too rudimentary.

PHILADELPHIA, OCTOBER 16, 1968. In another of life's stranger-than-fiction moments, the 76ers tipped off the 1968–69 season against Wilt Chamberlain and the Los Angeles Lakers. "I have nothing to prove at all," Chamberlain sniffed after landing in town. "It is just one game to me that I'd like to get on the left-handed [win] side."

Archie shared the same sentiments. He had no score to settle with his former teammates. Tonight was just one out of eighty-two regular-season games. Try telling that to Jack Ramsay. Dr. Jack wanted desperately to get the season off on the right foot and, wearing his general manager hat, send the loud promotional message that his 76ers were more exciting and capable without Wilt. He expected Archie and crew would vehemently second that emotion.

Lucky for Ramsay, his pressure basketball caught the Lakers flat-footed and yawning from their long flight east. The 76ers were up by seventeen at the end of the first quarter and cruised thereafter to an eighteen-point victory. What about The Trade? Archie finished with twenty points, and Chamberlain pumped in a tepid fifteen.

NEW YORK, OCTOBER 22, 1968. The 76ers had started the season with two straight wins. Tonight Ramsay wanted the trifecta in the worst way against the New York Knicks. "[Ramsay] seemed to be right out of central casting, playing perfectly the role of the enemy incarnated," recalled author David Halberstam, seated in the stands. "There he was, face flushed, arguing what seemed like an endless series of calls. So I did what any well-brought-up New York boy would do in a situation like that: I booed him."

With 6:30 to play and the Knicks coasting by eleven points, the flush-faced Ramsay gestured for Wally Jones to punch the ball inside to Billy Cunningham, isolated on the smaller Bill Bradley, not known for his defense. Billy C snagged the entry pass, leaned into Bradley, and hoisted the ball toward the hoop. His shot rattled out, and Ramsay waited for the referee's whistle to signify that Bradley had hacked him. Nothing. Ramsay, beside himself at the no call, leapt to his feet, paced behind the 76ers' bench with head bowed as if counting to ten, and finally stomped his foot. Referee Norm Drucker heard the stomp, turned, and popped Ramsay with his first NBA technical foul.

"Norm, what's the matter with you?" Ramsay gasped.

Drucker smacked his hands into the form of another "T," jerked his thumb in the direction of the locker room, and growled his best "Yer outta here."

Archie had seen this stunt before. Rookie coaches were supposed to behave. Show up a referee and risk ejection. Last season Van Breda Kolff had popped off to a reporter in Chicago about NBA officiating—or the lack thereof. He spent the rest of the season ducking technicals.

After Ramsay's untimely exit the 76ers roared back from fifteen down, only to succumb to three twenty-foot bombs from Knicks forward Cazzie Russell in the closing minutes. "[Ramsay will] be thrown out a lot the way he is," mumbled Knicks coach Red Holzman afterward, taking Ramsay and his attention-sucking behavior to task. "He's got to be. He's so intense, and he gets so wrapped up. We all make idiots out of ourselves."

"I think a coach is entitled to stand up," Ramsay countered. "It's ridiculous." Ramsay paused, much like the bewildered Van Breda Kolff a year ago trying to avoid another $250 fine for conduct detrimental to the league. "I can't say it's ridiculous," he corrected. It was step one in the taming of another rookie coach right out of central casting.

PHILADELPHIA, NOVEMBER 9, 1968. Jack Ramsay's pressure basketball was batting under .500. Then, like a bolt out of the blue, everything clicked. The bolt came on what appeared to be a yawn of a play in a close but sloppy game with Seattle. Opposing center Bob Rule bumped into position, called for the ball, and lofted up a shot. Jumping Johnny Green, the 76ers' high-octane backup, slid over and hurled the ball back at Rule. The Golden Rule tried again. Same result. A tussle ensued between Rule and Green, and order was quickly restored.

But the Sixers were riled now. Archie made two steals, and Philadelphia started playing as one within Ramsay's system—running, scrapping, rotating, and mostly getting the ball to Cunningham and Greer. When the final horn sounded on the 76ers' victory, Ramsay scanned the box score. "I think we're going," he smiled to a pack of reporters. "We've got it started. . . . Everybody contributed. Now I look for this team to get into contention [for the Eastern Division title]"

PHILADELPHIA, NOVEMBER 23, 1968. The 76ers were going all right. Since Jumping Johnny's rejections the 76ers had won six straight with a win tonight over Baltimore. Archie shushed his way home after midnight. He didn't want to wake the baby or Valerie, who was four months pregnant with their second child. About five hours later the alarm clock buzzed. Archie rolled out of bed, gathered his bags, and hurried off at dawn to the airport. Per NBA rules the 76ers had to catch the day's first available flight to Cincinnati.

As the plane lifted into the air and the Philadelphia skyline disappeared behind a veil of clouds, Archie settled in for the roughly ninety-minute flight. He was glad to escape Philadelphia. The City of Brotherly Love wasn't working for him. It just wasn't Los Angeles. If the Lakers hadn't traded him, he'd have made the All-Star team for a second season. Instead he struggled to make sense of his sixth-man role and, like a relief pitcher in baseball, the nightly call to give his team a brief lift. When Archie loosened up and found his rhythm on the court, Ramsay often yanked him for Jones or Greer. It was hard. He had been a starter since grade school and (his rookie season excluded) had always played a starter's thirty or forty minutes per night. But Archie swallowed hard. The team was winning, and he had given Ramsay his word to come off the bench.

Archie thought about Cincinnati—the Queen City, wiener schnitzel, sauerkraut, and chili galore. He and his teammates would have to kill Saturday afternoon palling around downtown and pulling up a corner table at Empress Chili to jaw over women, the Vietnam War, and the latest trade rumors. Always trade rumors. The other option was to kick back at the hotel, catch the Ohio State–Michigan football game on television. Maybe grab a nap. Archie sometimes thought that if he had a dollar for every wasted hour on the NBA road, he could afford a brand-new Cadillac every offseason.

By 7 p.m. it was showtime at Cincinnati Gardens, the aging home of the NBA Royals (12–5). Archie already ached at the thought of guarding superstar Oscar Robertson. The Big O pounded his large frame into the chest and ribs of defenders, knocking them off balance, and dribbling a few feet forward. Guarding the Big O was like riding a rodeo bull. The best that a defender could do was absorb the pounding, hang on as long as possible, and hope the shot clock blew—or, better yet, hope the Big O was nursing an injury.

Luck was on Archie's side. Robertson had received treatment for a pulled leg muscle and likely would need the first half to get loose. Ramsay repeated to his players to attack the Royals from the starting whistle. Archie watched the starting five meet the challenge, hit shot after big shot, and grab the early lead. When Ramsay called Archie's number, his job tonight was strictly to quarterback. Keep feeding Cunningham and Greer. Keep the 76ers machine rolling while Wally Jones caught his breath.

With six minutes left in the game, Philadelphia held a seemingly comfortable thirteen-point lead. But Robertson, his bad leg now loose, had started to beat the zone press and draw a few fouls. Luckily it was too little too late. The 76ers toughened up and coasted to a 120–105 victory.

By daylight Archie and his bleary-eyed teammates straggled through Cincinnati's Lunken Airport in search of their departure gate. Thirty minutes later they were in the air and off to the next city to deliver their next performance of Ramsay Ball.

# 14

Philadelphia, December 12, 1968. The expansion Phoenix Suns limped into the Spectrum tonight, "limped" being the operative word. The Suns had dropped sixteen of their last seventeen contests and were on pace to lose an estimated $750,000 in their first season.

And yet these were giddy times for the Suns. Each loss pushed them closer to the fateful coin flip for the first pick in the 1969 NBA college draft. If the Suns guessed right, they would win the rights to UCLA's 7-foot-1 Lew Alcindor, (later Kareem Abdul-Jabbar). Alcindor, the most celebrated college player of the decade, could turn Phoenix into an instant championship contender and a money-making machine—that is, assuming Phoenix could outmuscle the ABA to sign him. ABA commissioner George Mikan had hinted that the ABA planned to tender Alcindor the first million-dollar rookie contract offer in pro sports.

A million bucks. The words shouted like a headline from *Ripley's Believe It Not*. All had played for peanuts in Philadelphia for the past several seasons under the guise that Wilt Chamberlain, the team's headliner, had dibs on the big bucks. "I kept telling them, 'Well, Wilt's not here anymore,'" said Archie. "'Go in and talk with Jack.' But they wouldn't do it."

The topic of take-home pay remained too jock inappropriate, like discussing the latest in the *Wall Street Journal*. Most of the 76ers still had yet to hire agents, and few knew the first thing about how to negotiate with management.

Archie told his teammates, much like a labor organizer would on a factory floor, that they remained woefully underpaid. The days of the penny-pinching arena owners and minimum-wage player contracts were over. The millionaires had arrived in the NBA, and 76ers' paper mogul owner Irving Kosloff was one of them. As Jack Kent Cooke had once quipped, "Irving needs money like he needs leprosy."

"Archie was progressive; he wasn't a radical," said Chet Walker. "He knew things that we didn't know, and he shared his information. He challenged us to see the basketball business in a different light."

"I remember Archie telling me that I shouldn't play when I was hurt," said Wally Jones. "He said it would affect my productivity, and that would limit my bargaining power at the end of the season. That was a revelation to me. Management always told us that come rain or shine or sprained ankle, we had to play. Their attitude was, 'If you don't play, we'll find somebody else.' Nobody wanted to lose his job and be thrown out of the NBA. So we hobbled along with the game plan to our own peril."

Peril hobbled along again tonight. Not far from Archie's locker stood Luke Jackson. He wasn't sure he could go against the Suns. It was his left foot again. The Achilles tendon felt like a five-alarm fire. As Jackson later recalled, Ramsay told him that he must play. A cortisone-filled syringe was produced. The pain numbed.

Fourteen points and nine rebounds later, Jackson trotted to midcourt. The Suns had unveiled their crude version of Ramsay's zone press in a last-ditch effort to mount a rally. The ball inbounded and pinged into Jackson's hands. He pivoted and glanced toward the 76ers' basket. In the 1960s coaches frowned on big men dribbling in the open court and tempting smaller, quicker players to steal the ball. But Jackson's foot felt okay, and he saw an open lane to the basket with just Phoenix center George Wilson to beat.

Jackson lumbered forward and, by about the third dribble, fell to the court with a grimace and a thud. He winced himself upright. But Jackson could place no weight on his left foot. His Achilles tendon had ripped in two. "We don't know why it happens," said the team's orthopedic consultant, Dr. Charles Parsons, either repeating the state of the 1960s science or just avoiding the obvious.

---

*Darrall Imhoff stepped in for Luke, and we won our next five games. No surprise there. Darrall was a real pro. He passed well, set solid screens, and even blocked a few shots on defense. Here's the rub: Darrall was no match physically for Bill Russell and the other top centers in the Eastern Division, and our backup center was the 6-foot-5 Johnny Green.*

*That had Jack perplexed. So in January, Jack traded for rebounding help. He sent Jerry Chambers [still in the army] to Phoenix for backup center George Wilson. It was a bad trade. If Jerry could have landed on the right NBA team to showcase his talents, he could have been an All-Star. He was that good of a shooter and scorer.*

*But Jack wanted to win NOW. Somebody wrote once that Jack "goes after each game so intensely you would think a win means an income tax deduction." I just wish that he hadn't written off Jerry. He could have helped us.*

ATLANTA, JANUARY 26, 1969. The 76ers had won four in a row. Tonight's 119–115 victims were the formerly St. Louis and now Atlanta Hawks, the NBA's first outpost in the American South. Afterward a sportswriter wrote, "Ramsay did a most unusual thing. Returning to his room [after the game], he got off the elevator on the sixth floor of the Marriott Motor Hotel, took two or three steps and bellowed— yes, bellowed is the word—down the corridor, 'The Hawk is dead.'"

PHILADELPHIA, JANUARY 29, 1969. "THE HAWK IS DEAD" flashed the overhead scoreboard in the Spectrum. The 76ers (36–15) had done it again to their fine feathered friends, 119–96. The win pulled Philadelphia to within one game of first-place Baltimore, with thirty-two games left in the season to catch them.

ATLANTA, MARCH 6, 1969. What an endless road trip it had been— fourteen days and an eleven-city NBA tour. It tipped off in Seattle, dribbled to San Francisco then Los Angeles, jumped to Cincinnati, detoured to Philadelphia, zigzagged through five stops in the Midwest, and screeched to a halt tonight in Atlanta, where the Hawk remained very much alive.

So far the 76ers had won nine of ten, the lone defeat coming two nights ago in a five-point heartbreaker to Chicago. The loss left the second-place 76ers three games behind Baltimore and a game and a half ahead of the red-hot New York Knicks, with ten contests remaining in the regular season. Boston was six and a half games behind

Philadelphia in fourth place, with Cincinnati, Detroit, and Milwaukee out of playoff contention.

"If we play well, we have a chance of finishing first," Ramsay advised his players at a team meeting before practice. "We have an excellent chance of finishing second, and it would appear that we can't finish worse than third."

Ramsay called the meeting to rally his players and, more important, to ease the tension that had surfaced recently over playing time. That tension involved Archie. Ramsay had noticed on a few occasions that Archie had cast incredulous, who-me stares in his direction when pulled from the game. Rather than let the tension fester, Ramsay decided to meet it head on.

"Archie was always a professional on the court," said Ramsay. "He was skilled and played extremely hard. But Archie was tough to coach because he always wanted more—more minutes, more shots. I had three outstanding guards on the team, counting Archie. So it was hard to give him the minutes that he wanted."

"It was more about fairness than minutes," said Archie. "Like they say in the NBA, go with the hot hand. There would be games where I had the hot hand, and I would be doing the NBA equivalent of storming the beaches of Normandy to bring the team back from a big deficit—and the next thing I knew, the buzzer sounded and Jack had me on the bench. I'm a competitor. I just wanted to finish the job that I had started."

The tension defused soon thereafter in a romp of basketball and the ribbing of Billy Cunningham about a story in this morning's *Atlanta Constitution*. It declared him "the best white man currently playing basketball."

"Isn't that a hell of a thing to write?" Cunningham grumped.

"Yeah, especially when Jerry West is the best white player," drilled Darrall Imhoff.

On the next court Archie had just rolled a few teammates in a series of *mano a mano* games of horse that matched jump shot against jump shot.

"I sent Chet to the showers," Archie laughed.

"I burned Shay [rookie Shaler Halimon] and George [Wilson] and Chet," countered Wally Jones.

"I got Georgie too," Archie added.

"Are you ready for me?" Ramsay said, stepping up for some action.

The road weary 76ers weren't ready the next day for the Hawks, risen from the dead after recently scrapping their traditional half-court offense for a pressing, fast-breaking knockoff of Ramsay Ball. The Hawks blasted the original Ramsay Ballers, greatest white player and all, 138–99. It was never close.

"We've got nine left and six at home," Ramsay said after the massacre. "We gotta regroup and get ready. We don't have much time . . . but this team has always done it. They always come up with games they have to win, and I expect they'll do it again."

PHILADELPHIA, MARCH 9, 1969. Remember Wally Jones and his Jackson Pollack jump shot? On ABC's Sunday afternoon NBA *Game of the Week* Jones jumped, cranked, hitched, kicked, and fluttered the sluggish 76ers back into the ballgame in the fourth quarter, and his teammates snapped to down the home stretch to stun the New York Knicks, 110–101.

The win, coupled with a Bullets loss, pulled the 76ers (51–24) to within one game of first place with seven games left. "Can it be done?" Ramsay asked afterward of a first-place finish. "Pessimistic attitudes of the writers to the contrary, some members of the 76ers say yes."

Even the pessimistic writers suddenly were feeling the love. One wrote, "The 76ers have been pronounced dead more often than Middle East peace." Maybe, just maybe, Ramsay's team was one of destiny.

BOSTON, MARCH 12, 1969. Destiny lasted exactly three days. After the Sixers fell to the Knicks last night in a rematch and dropped two games out of first place, Ramsay summoned another team meeting before the Celtics game to talk strategy. When things apparently turned heated, Ramsay sent word to the officials. He needed to delay the start of tonight's game for seven minutes.

"It was a good meeting," Hal Greer said afterward. "It brought a lot of things out in the open."

"What kind of things?"

"A lot of private things."

Despite the pregame heat and twenty-five points from Archie, the Celtics triumphed, 126–117, sending Philadelphia to an untimely fourth loss in six games. To borrow a phrase from baseball, the 76ers now were down to their last out.

BALTIMORE, MARCH 23, 1969. And then the race was over.

Last night in Chicago Baltimore clinched its first NBA division title in a spray of champagne and forty-one points from the amazing Earl Monroe. Baltimore's championship now forced the 76ers to turn their attention to the third-place New York Knicks. With two regular-season contests remaining the 76ers were one game up on the Knicks and badly needed to beat the Bullets today to clinch second place and home-court advantage in the first round of the playoffs against the fourth-place Boston Celtics.

The Bullets were happy to accommodate. Bullets coach Gene Shue rested his weary starters for the playoffs, and Ramsay Ball clinched second place in the division. Dr. Jack's reward: a first-round death march against the defending-champion Boston Celtics, who had famously loafed through the regular season to a misleading fourth-place finish.

---

*The Celtics were a real tough matchup for us. Their guards handled our zone press without a hiccough, and Bill Russell still could dominate the paint when needed. The million-dollar question was: How were we going to generate our offense without steals and rebounds to trigger our running game?*

*Boston rolled us in game one to take the home-court advantage. The next thing we knew the Celtics had a three games to nothing advantage, leaving us one game from elimination. The Celtics just knew how to win in the playoffs. We didn't.*

*We also didn't have any miracles in us. Billy [Cunningham] was getting cortisone shots before games to ease his back spasms, and Chet Walker was down for the count with a bad knee.*

*Jack rejiggered our lineup on the fly for game four, and I scored twenty-nine points playing as a starter and hit the winning shot to*

*extend the series. Our stay of execution was brief. Boston drilled us in*
*game five. Season over.*

*After game three Valerie had given birth to our son, Archie Jr. He*
*weighed seven pounds, one ounce, the same numbers as Wilt Cham-*
*berlain's height. A reporter joked that I couldn't get away from "The*
*Trade." But if I had my way, I remember thinking that maybe I would.*
*I liked my teammates. But I was tired of Philadelphia, and I didn't like*
*the direction that the team was headed.*

# 15

*The summer of 1969 brought the first rumors of an NBA-ABA merger. I had no idea what they meant, and neither did anyone else. But the rumors put us on alert that our window of financial opportunity might slam shut. That got more mid- and late-career players comparing notes and exchanging the names of agents.*

*I wouldn't say that players rebelled against that old taboo about players discussing contracts. It was more that events in the summer of 1969 overtook the taboo. Players stopped going along and started worrying on their own about moving up the pay ladder while they still could, and this shift spawned the entrepreneurial mindset that is dominant today.*

*The other major factor was the collective mood in 1960s America. Think of the revolution in music and fashion. Think of the rise in civil disobedience. The Civil Rights Movement, the anti-war protests, women's liberation, the sexual revolution, the ecology movement. What began as unruly ideas had coalesced into a more hip, mainstream American mindset that championed social justice and personal freedom. To champion these values you had to question authority. Well, NBA veterans are products of society too, and they felt wronged by the NBA system. The owners had pleaded poverty and lowball contracts for years, and they now handed million-dollar deals to gangly college kids but were slow to renegotiate our contracts to match the money that the rookies were getting. It was a real slap in the face.*

*What I didn't realize that summer is how fast this liberated mindset took hold. My teammates started digging in their heels at the bargaining table. They said, in essence, if Jack Ramsay and Irv Kosloff wouldn't pay them the going rate, they would find a way to take their talents elsewhere. That just didn't happen a year earlier.*

---

I n late summer 1969 Billy Cunningham drove to Ramsay's home on the Jersey shore to deliver the news before the story broke: he was jumping to the ABA. Ramsay, an avid surfer, thanked Cunningham for telling him, then disappeared into the ocean with his board to ride the breakers and curse the ABA.

The next day Cunningham flew to Greensboro to make the big announcement. He'd signed a multi-year contract with the ABA Carolina Cougars. "It was a big decision which my wife and I made," he answered in his thick New York accent. "We weighed the pros and cons and decided it would be better if I played in Carolina. I want to spend the rest of my life here."

As flashbulbs popped, a reporter quizzed the assembled parties on the likelihood that Billy C would ever play in the ABA. "It's on paper, and a contract is a contract," interrupted Cunningham's new agent, Sheldon Bendit. "We're very confident of our legal position."

In Philadelphia Ramsay also played to the cameras to deflate the story and its embarrassing implications. Cunningham couldn't go anywhere, he said, because every NBA player agrees in his contract to a reserve clause, not an option year. Ergo the 76ers owned the rights to Cunningham as long as he played basketball. Only Irv Kosloff had the authority to transfer those reserve rights to another team, and he wasn't feeling especially generous toward the ABA at the moment.

A reporter asked Ramsay about Rick Barry's successful leap to the ABA. Hadn't a precedent already been set? "Franklin Mieuli GAVE Barry an option, but that is not in the terms of an NBA contract," Ramsay clarified.

Cunningham, meanwhile, just wanted to play ball. His face was omnipresent on the 76ers' preseason promotional materials, and Cunningham vowed to forget red, white, and blue basketballs for the time being. "I think the fans realize that when I play basketball, I give my all," he told an NBA reporter. "I'll do the same thing for the next two years" in Philadelphia. Or until Cunningham was free to do something finer in Carolina. For a proud and ruthless sports town like Philadelphia, losing its star basketball attraction to the ABA felt like a blow to the midsection. If Cunningham had no loyalty to the 76ers, why should fans?

FOR JACK RAMSAY life would go on with or without Billy Cunningham. Pressure basketball was greater than any one player. As if to emphasize that point, Ramsay began pruning his roster to eliminate the deadwood that didn't fit his hard-pressing style. Second-year prospect Shaler Halimon, whom Ramsay had once called another Earl Monroe: gone. He was lacking defensively. Veteran forward Johnny Green: gone. He was too old to play pressure basketball.

Ramsay's analytical mind also reached another vital conclusion: Chet Walker didn't fit his system. Chester, as he called him, wasn't fast, wasn't stout defensively, and, at 6 feet 6 inches, he lacked the size and athleticism to control the backboards. So Ramsay traded his All-Pro to Chicago for fifth-year, diamond-in-the-rough Jim Washington. The 6-foot-6 Washington ran like a deer, jumped out of the gym, dunked with fury, swatted shots, and could, in theory, dominate the backboards. In Ramsay's mind Washington's athleticism was exactly what his 76ers had lacked last season.

Ramsay knew his stuff, and he could make these roster moves sound exciting, brilliant even—that is, unless you were an NBA player.

WHEN ARCHIE HEARD about Billy Cunningham's pending defection, he winced. When he heard that Shaler Halimon and Johnny Green were let go, he felt bad for them. Halimon had never been given a chance to showcase his talent, and Green had just been thrown away. But when Archie heard that Ramsay had unloaded Chet Walker for Jim Washington, his jaw dropped. Washington was known around the league as a nice guy, tremendous athlete, and a perpetual offensive work in progress. Walker was one of the NBA's elite forwards. "I had worked out a lot with Chet over the summer," recalled Archie. "So I knew how irreplaceable he was. Chet could back down his defender and get whatever shot he wanted whenever we needed a basket. He was amazing."

From Archie's perspective the pro game ran on talent first, philosophy second. Ramsay had inherited the NBA equivalent of a straight royal flush, and he had opined, overanalyzed, and foolishly discarded his premier talent in the vain hope of assembling a combination of cards more to his personal liking and style. Wilt Chamberlain, Jerry Chambers, Chet Walker—all discarded. Even Billy Cunningham had been shown the door to save a few bucks. But the Walker giveaway was the final straw. To unload a proven All-Pro for an unproven role player was self-defeating.

Archie was now convinced that Ramsay's hubris as one of the NBA's enlightened basketball strategists had doomed the 76ers. The 76ers opened training camp in less than two weeks. He had a plan. Archie pulled his wife Valerie aside. Remember how Bill Sharman, coach of the ABA's Los Angeles Stars, had been so complimentary last summer? Archie would fly to Southern California next week, reconnect with Sharman, and hopefully land a contract offer from the Stars. He told Valerie to expect a phone call from Ramsay while he was away. Ramsay would want to schedule another meeting to discuss Archie's contract for next season. "Tell Jack that I'm out of town and haven't checked in yet with a telephone number to reach me," Archie told her. "That will buy me a couple of extra days, and, hopefully, we'll be headed back to California."

BILL SHARMAN HAD no patience for players who arrived for training camp fat and out of shape. For Sharman the extra pounds were unfair to the team and, if they involved key players, guaranteed a sluggish start to the season. To prevent twenty-pound tires from forming around key waistlines, Sharman sponsored an open gym once or twice per week during the summer for his Stars and any interested free agents. Attendance was optional, but the hyper-organized Sharman always hovered along the sidelines to take an unofficial roll call.

His latest roll call brought a big NBA surprise. Archie Clark was on the court in practice gear. Archie explained that he was vacationing in Los Angeles for a few weeks and needed a good place to work out to prepare for training camp with the 76ers. Sharman welcomed him like an old friend before fading back into the shadows to continue his silent evaluation of the talent. Archie cranked up his NBA All-Star skills and let Sharman's imagination kick into gear.

The ball now was in Sharman's court. Archie had made it clear last summer that he was open to joining the Stars. This summer Wilt Chamberlain was no longer in the picture, much to the crosstown detriment of Sharman's ball club. The trio of Chamberlain, Jerry West, and Elgin Baylor had given Jack Kent Cooke and the rival NBA

Lakers a lock on the pro basketball market in celebrity-worshipping Los Angeles. The lesser Stars couldn't give away tickets to games in the Sports Arena. Why not sign a former Laker to lend credibility to the team?

Archie reappeared a few more times at the Stars' open gym, and Sharman finally broached the subject. What about playing for the Stars? Archie pulled up a chair, but their conversation stalled over two issues. The first was Archie's then hefty $105,000-per-season salary. With Merv Jackson and Mack Calvin, two good young backcourt players already on the Stars' roster, Sharman would face stiff resistance from his owner to invest most of the team's limited resources in another guard. The second issue was that a still nameless NBA star had beaten Archie to those limited resources. Nothing had been finalized, Sharman said, but it was a prominent NBA center (Atlanta's Zelmo Beaty). They shook hands. Archie shrugged and thought to himself, "Well, it was worth a try."

The 76ers still were doomed to disaster in his mind. But Archie was out of options for now. His one-year contract would expire in a few weeks, and Ramsay held all the cards and financial leverage. Or so Archie thought. Except three thousand miles away Luke Jackson had just signed with the ABA's Carolina Cougars, courtesy of Sheldon Bendit, Billy Cunningham's agent. It would turn the 76ers' front office upside down.

ARCHIE GRABBED THE PHONE. It was Valerie in Philadelphia.

"Jack Ramsay just called."

"What did you tell him?"

She replayed the brief Friday morning conversation. Nothing out of the ordinary was said, but Ramsay seemed anxious to talk.

"The ABA offer didn't work out," Archie said. "Call Jack back and give him my telephone number. I need to hear what he has to say. I'll be home on Sunday. If I can get my contract worked out, training camp opens on Monday in New Jersey."

The phone rang a few minutes later. It was Ramsay.

"Archie, we need to talk about your contract." Ramsay had used roughly the same phrase about two months ago when they had first met in person to hammer out a quick deal. Ramsay had produced a one-page standard NBA contract for him to sign. Archie saw typed neatly above the dotted line a salary of $60,000 per season, which included a $5,000 raise.

"Jack, I can't sign this," Archie said. "I'd be taking a huge pay cut."

Ramsay's Mad Hatter eyebrows glared back. Archie explained that Jack Kent Cooke, in his haste to complete last season's Chamberlain trade, had agreed to kick in an additional $50,000 per season, boosting his salary to $105,000. The glare turned blank. Ramsay seemed to have no idea that Archie was the highest-paid player on his team. Nor did he seem to know anything about Cooke's secret agreement with Archie. Ramsay broke off the meeting. He had to make a few phone calls. He would be back in touch.

Now Ramsay was finally going to deliver his counter-offer. Archie braced. If he heard $60,000, Archie would have to threaten to hold out.

"What do you have in mind?" Archie answered, trying to sound calm.

The first words he heard were "three seasons," instead of the usual one-year deal. Bad sign. Management had begun to push multi-year contracts under the guise that they offered players better job security than the traditional one-year deal. But better job security was really a Trojan horse that served management's interests in two ways. First, the multi-year contracts allowed NBA teams to lock in their best players just long enough for the ABA presumably to wither and die. Second, although players were legally bound to fulfill their contracts, NBA teams weren't. Teams refused to guarantee them, with a few seven-foot exceptions. If Archie blew out his knee after one season, the 76ers were free to terminate the contract.

Ramsay continued reading the contract's basic terms and conditions to Archie over the phone and finally came to the money. "The first season pays $115,000," he said. "The second season increases to $125,000, and the third season tops out at $135,000."

Archie felt his shoulders loosen and a smile cross his lips. The multi-year format actually worked in his favor to keep his salary edging upward. Ramsay didn't mention Jack Kent Cooke, but the Lakers' owner wouldn't have agreed to pay half of Archie's salary. No, this had to be Kosloff's doing. But why? A month ago Kosloff wouldn't give a well-deserved raise to his designated superstar Billy Cunningham (precipitating his jump to the ABA); now Kosloff had agreed to give Archie one of the more lucrative contracts in the league. He must have heard that Archie had been in Los Angeles talking to the ABA.

Archie wondered whether he should press for more and see how far Ramsay was willing to bend to get him under contract and into training camp. What about a signing bonus? Fine. Archie said he had been considering making a few investments and paying a few bills. What if Mr. Kosloff advanced him a $75,000 loan on his salary? Ramsay said he'd give Archie a call back. The phone rang a few minutes later. Yes, the loan would be fine.

Archie landed in Philadelphia on Saturday evening and drove to Kosloff's home in Merion the following afternoon to finalize everything. Kosloff, thin, gray-haired, and always calm and a little aloof, tried to be upbeat and welcoming. But it had been a long night. Around 2 a.m. he had convinced his renegade center Luke Jackson to resign with the 76ers, the ABA be damned.

"Luke Jackson has been our property, never ceased being our property, and he remains our property," his sidekick Ramsay declared afterward. For his misbehavior Jackson got a guaranteed three-year, likely $350,000 contract, and a job with the 76ers' front office upon his retirement. Next on Kosloff's goodwill tour were Wally Jones and reconciliation with Billy Cunningham.

Without further ado Archie scribbled his name on the contract, exchanged an obligatory handshake with Kosloff, and parroted the usual clichés for another successful season. As he drove back to his rented house in Germantown, Archie laughed at the irony of it all. The Lakers had paid him handsomely to go away, and the 76ers had done the same ostensibly to make him stay. Archie wanted to live in Los Angeles. He had no desire to be in Philadelphia. But here he was stuck to play another doomed season of Ramsay Ball.

# 16

**M**argate, New Jersey, September 15, 1969. The horn section stabbed ahead in short, staccato bursts, followed by the slow, crooning vocals of the Chicago Transit Authority, or just plain "Chicago" to rock 'n' roll fans. Ramsay's record player, which he brought this year from home, was spinning their hit song, "Does Anybody Really Know What Time It Is?"

Archie, in white gym pants and red T-shirt with the white letters "Phila 76ers" across the front, knew exactly what time it was. Opening day of training camp at the Margate Jewish Community Center. Time to push aside the chaotic summer, recommit to another NBA season, and hope for a magical team that made the nightly aches all worthwhile.

"We've got to get better music; that stuff was awful," Ramsay quipped to trainer Al Domenico as the arm of the record player clicked to a halt and a cacophonous thud of bouncing basketballs filled the void. Domenico suggested the soulful Aretha Franklin. Ramsay shrugged. He wasn't sold on her either.

Ramsay eased across the gym floor to call practice and the 1969–70 season to order. Ramsay wore a casual T-shirt with a psychedelic orange, green, and purple butterfly tattooed across the back, making him resemble a wind-chapped surfer dude more than a hard-edged pro basketball drill sergeant. But Archie already knew the drill from last season. Give Ramsay a few days, and his manic transformation into Dr. Jack would be complete.

MARGATE, NEW JERSEY, SEPTEMBER 22, 1969. Dr. Jack pulled Archie aside a week into training camp. Archie's days as the team's sixth man were over. Wally Jones would come off the bench this season.

Archie thanked Ramsay for the vote of confidence. Or was it a vote of appeasement? Either way Archie welcomed his expanded role and chance to put his career back on its rightful All-Star track after a year in undeserved limbo.

PHILADELPHIA, OCTOBER 16,1969. First his friends had tried on the nickname "Dippy" for size. The young Wilt Chamberlain dipped his tall head to pass through most doorways. "Dippy" later morphed to the metaphorical "Big Dipper." Then came the newspaper smart alecks interjecting "Wilt the Stilt" and "Goliath." For most, though, Wilt said it all. The name was spoken with familiarity and slight bemusement, like speaking of Miles, Trane, or another too-cool-for-two-names jazz icon.

All of the verbal gymnastics missed the inner Wilt, a man of fast cars and sartorial statement. Chamberlain had recently brought his unflinching sartorial eye to the basketball court to solve a chronic problem. Beads of sweat constantly dribbled off his forehead and into his eyes. His solution, which broke with the starched and staid gym-class conventions of traditional basketball attire, was to wear a thick red, white, and blue headband on the court to soak up the perspiration. Confused onlookers weren't sure whether Chamberlain was making an anti-war statement, had attended Woodstock, or had taken up karate.

Al Meltzer, the television voice of the 76ers, suggested a fourth option today while emceeing the annual 76ers' Booster Club luncheon to tip off the new season. Meltzer said Wilt looked this season like he'd joined an Indian tribe. Forget "Dippy" and "Wilt the Stilt." Those monikers were so passé. Chamberlain's new nickname: Chief Dunk-a-Bucket. The room erupted.

Archie, sitting on the podium beside teammate Darrall Imhoff, joined in the momentary mirth. The corny line captured the giddy sense of possibility that greeted the new NBA season. With Bill Russell's retirement the Boston dynasty seemed a thing of the past. Bring on Los Angeles with Jerry West, Elgin Baylor, and the mighty Chief Dunk-a-Bucket. Baltimore featured Earl the Pearl, Wes Unseld, and Gus Johnson. Milwaukee had super rookie Lew Alcindor. New York flashed outstanding team chemistry. Philadelphia touted pressure basketball.

At NBA headquarters Commissioner Walter Kennedy had distilled this tremendous sense of possibility into three words: The New NBA. The tagline wasn't quite Madison Avenue tested, but it was a start.

Meltzer turned to Archie and asked, "Where will the 76ers finish this season in the new Eastern Division?" Archie, still quietly convinced that Ramsay was headed in the wrong direction, offered his honest appraisal of "[somewhere] in the top four." Imhoff smiled and gave the 76er faithful the answer they wanted. "Heck," he said, the 76ers will "go all the way."

Eight hours later Imhoff seemed like a savant. The 76ers, ten players strong and forty points wiser from the timeless Hal Greer, defeated the Los Angeles Lakers, 131–126, in the season opener at the Spectrum. "I feel the team can do it," declared Ramsay in his usual postgame mumble. "We'll be near the top—at or near the top."

That is, assuming Luke Jackson could remain healthy for longer than one quarter. About twelve minutes into tonight's contest Jackson gave Chief Dunk-a-Bucket a hard bump near the basket to push him out of position. Chamberlain, ripped a right elbow of warning into Luke's chest. The blunt force partially collapsed one of his lungs. Jackson was ruled out for at least two weeks.

PHILADELPHIA, NOVEMBER 1, 1969. "Ladies and gentleman, may I have your attention, please." The crowd pricked up its ears for The Voice. Who didn't love The Voice? It boomed; it confided; it carried on in the tragicomic self-parody of a circus barker. The Voice belonged to the little gray-haired public address man, Dave Zinkoff, or just Zink. He sat tucked away somewhere along courtside, his thick glasses sliding down his nose and the mount of a microphone obscuring his face. "May I have your attention, PLEASE. Will the owner of the silver Cadillac . . . Pennsylvania license plate 123456. . . ."

Eyes rolled. Here we go again. The bogus announcement was part of his nightly schtick. "Your car is parked with its lights on, motor running, and doors locked."

Zink's mirth might have been the highlight of the evening. The 76ers' battery was as dead tonight as the one in Zink's phantom silver Cadillac. Against Boston Ramsay's zone press didn't produce a single turnover in the first half, nor did his running game yield a single fast break bucket until the third quarter. By then many in attendance had pulled on their overcoats and headed for the exits under the opinion that after three straight home losses, something was terribly amiss in Sixerland.

Archie didn't have much to say afterward. Despite the loss he had played well, scoring twenty-nine points and dishing out six assists. Archie, in fact, had played extremely well in five of the seven games thus far. The team's problem wasn't in the backcourt. Heck, NBA great Bob Cousy called the 76ers' backcourt the best in the league. The problem remained Ramsay and his best intentions. He still insisted on calling Billy Cunningham's number early and often to establish him as the team's go-to guy. By force-feeding Cunningham, Ramsay often asked Archie and crew to go without the ball early in the game, and that impeded an easy, five-man offensive rhythm.

As an often-stagnant offense spilled over into a stagnant defense, Ramsay reverted to his zone press like a doctor ordering an adrenaline shot. And therein resided the latest rub. Ramsay's zone press was no longer the NBA equivalent of a stun gun that subdued the opposition. Most teams had rolled out copycat zone presses during training camp and were better drilled to pass here, cut there, and beat the pressure. With the opposition often one pass ahead and capable of stretching holes in the Philadelphia defense, Ramsay needed a Bill Russell–type shot blocker to protect the basket. He had none. Jim Washington was undersized, Darrall Imhoff tended to foul, and Luke Jackson reacted a step too slowly on his bad foot.

All of the above translated to frequent double-digit deficits. That meant Ramsay had to double down on the press, insert extra speed, and hope an all-out, ball-pressure blitz would generate quick turnovers. Sometimes the extra energy and desperation worked; other times, as the Boston game showed, the Sixers fell short or just plain flat.

Ramsay was a smart guy and a decent person. But he was a rookie NBA coach hell-bent on riding "pro basketball—college style" into the winner's circle. Archie wondered whether Ramsay saw the built-in conflict that bedeviled his team. In one corner was the coach's mind-over-matter idealism and conceptual clarity. In the other corner stood reality. There was no way Ramsay could coach his way out of Jackson's bum left foot or the disheartening Walker trade or the questionable draft choices at the end of the bench. Nor could Archie and his teammates do more every night with less to compensate for Ramsay's bad judgment.

"I remember Jack taking me out of a game once after I'd had the hot hand," said Archie. "Jack said, 'Archie, how can I get you more shots?' I said, 'Jack, I can get my shot any time I want.' But that was the problem right there. Jack thought that the burden was on him to engineer a forty-point night for me or Billy. It wasn't. Sometimes he just had to step aside."

PHILADELPHIA, NOVEMBER 8, 1969. Archie navigated his yellow Cadillac through the gathering darkness and pulled into a space in the still mostly empty Spectrum parking lot. He grabbed his gym bag and hurried ahead as best he could. His back was killing him. It was just a tweak, but still. Jack Ramsay had called a team meeting for 6:30 to thrash out the latest in the team's string of losses. Thereafter Archie and crew would begin dressing for tonight's fray with Seattle. The third-year Supersonics, just for the record, had never beaten the 76ers.

Ramsay, always calm but very much in control standing before his players, said the team had to start the game with more offensive punch. Ramsay wanted to try a more offensive-minded look tonight. Fred Hetzel and Luke Jackson would replace Jim Washington and Darrall Imhoff in the starting lineup. Wally Jones would fill in for Archie. His back willing, he'd play limited minutes tonight.

Ramsay's best intentions went nowhere. Seattle, known for its failure to win consistently on the road, snapped off a 10–0 lead without missing a shot, and Ramsay's more offensive-minded frontline couldn't hit the broad side of a barn. When Seattle extended the lead to sixteen points with just seven minutes gone, Ramsay cried uncle. Archie, Washington, and Imhoff checked into the game, and the zone pressing commenced.

Seattle kept pounding the ball inside to center Bob Rule, who would bang his large body into position near the basket, turn, and loft his soft, left-handed hook shot over the outstretched arms of Imhoff. With five minutes left in the game and Seattle in control, Ramsay signaled for the zone press again. Ramsay got nothing but whistles and more aggravation. His players couldn't stop fouling. Fourteen Seattle free-throw attempts later, the 76ers had sunk to their fifth-straight home loss.

A distraught Ramsay called another closed-door team meeting immediately after the game. About thirty minutes later, his tie askew and face flushed, Ramsey emerged from behind the closed door.

A reporter asked him about tonight's loss. "I don't know," Ramsay mumbled. "We're not getting the job done." Ramsay started to enumerate all of the shortcomings yet again. He could have saved his breath. Journalism is the fine art of summary, and the reporters already had boiled down Ramsay's musings to one sentence: the 76ers were in trouble.

"Sometimes players quit on their coach," said Archie. "That wasn't the case here. Jack was a gentleman. He was well organized and knew his stuff, and I think most everybody liked him. Yes, I had serious reservations about the direction that he had taken the team. But when the season started, I tried to push that aside. All I wanted was to win. The question for all of us was how to do it. Jack's game plan just wasn't working."

PHILADELPHIA, NOVEMBER 19, 1969. Late last night the 76ers had arrived home to close their first western road trip of the season: eight nights, five cities, one win, and a broken defense. The NBA record for defensive ineptitude was 125.1 points per game. The 76ers now were bleeding 124.5 points per game. "The 76ers are dying," the *Philadelphia Inquirer* declared this morning. "Maybe they're already dead. Sometimes it's hard to tell."

Jack Ramsay ordered an emergency team meeting before tonight's game against the San Diego Rockets. His message: Enough talk. Let's turn the season around starting tonight. Right here, right now. Heads nodded.

Then nothing happened. Ramsay's pressure defense generated just one steal in the first half, and Philadelphia failed again, 125–116. The

76ers had dropped four straight, ten of their last twelve games, and six in a row on their home floor. It was now official. The 76ers (6–11) had hit rock bottom.

---

*Don't ask me what happened next. But we finally started playing as a team and winning. Heck, we flew up to Boston and beat the Celtics by twenty points. Now that game was memorable because Wally Jones and [Boston's] Larry Siegfried got into it during an inbounds pass. I think Wally wrestled Larry to the floor, and they had each other in headlocks. Referees are supposed to break up fights, but they were stuck in place. One of them said to Fred Hetzel, "You think I'm crazy?" So Gene Conley, a 6-foot-8 former Celtic who was sitting courtside, lumbered onto the floor. He separated the combatants, double technical fouls were issued, and Conley lumbered back to his seat.*

*But Conley's emergency rescue was nothing compared to what happened nine days later on our next trip to Boston. We were losing to the Celtics, 104–101, with ten seconds left. Keep in mind there is no three-point shot in the NBA. It's a two-possession game. So we need a miracle. Well, Hal cuts to the basket, and I hit him for a lay-up with seven seconds left. Celtics 104, 76ers 103. Larry Siegfried inbounds the ball, and John Havlicek passes it right back to him before he steps onto the court. Or so says referee Jack Madden. He blows his whistle and awards the ball to the 76ers with three seconds left. Remember, referees aren't supposed to blow their whistles at the end of the game. Boston Garden goes nuts. They'd been robbed. The ball is inbounded to me, and I get it to Billy at the top of the key. He stumbles and crashes into Havlicek. The clock is ticking. Fast. Billy tries to fling the ball at the hoop but sees Hal at the last second standing alone in the paint. Basket. Buzzer. Game. 76ers 105, Celtics 104.*

*Fans storm the court to get a piece of that good-for-nothing Madden. There's this one Celtic fan on the court holding a small child in his right arm, and he somehow makes it over to Madden. Denny from Dorchester we called him. Denny tries awkwardly to shift his child to his left arm so he can clobber Madden with a right cross. But a group of coaches, players, and Celtics officials jump in to save Madden. Leading the rescue party is Ed McHugh, Boston's beloved sixty-year-old public relations man. The next thing I know the circle of people shifts, [Celt-ics' reserve] Bailey Howell is holding the child, and McHugh tries to shove Denny away from Madden. McHugh misses Denny but follows through and whacks Madden on the head. Madden didn't know what to do. It was pure Keystone Kops.*

PHOENIX, DECEMBER 16, 1969. Archie didn't think the exchange was such a big deal. But the security at the Arizona Veterans' Memorial Coliseum wasn't taking any chances.

The 76ers just had beaten the Phoenix Suns, 141–119, and Archie took the victory walk back to the visitors' dressing room with a big smile on his face. He had sparked a first-half run from which the Suns never recovered, closing out the night with twenty-five points and helping the 76ers to their fourth straight win.

"What you laughin' for?" asked a man in street clothes standing in the walkway.

"Because I'm happy," Archie answered quizzically.

"You'll be happy if I put a bullet in you?" he sneered, his right hand stuffed suspiciously in the pocket of his work jacket.

Archie stared back. Was that a threat?

The man glared, "If you think I'm kidding, you'll get it when you come outside."

Archie proceeded into the locker room, but 76ers trainer Al Domenico, having overhead the clipped exchange, called arena security. An Arizona state patrolman arrived shortly thereafter and asked Archie to step outside the locker room and point out the would-be gunman. Sure enough, he was lingering near the walkway. "Oh, not him again," nodded the patrolman. The perp previously had threatened to shoot NBA referees. The patrolman ambled over and shooed off the man and the lump of nothing in his pocket. "If we can ever get somebody to sign a complaint, we could grab hold of him," the patrolman said.

But Archie already had returned to the locker room and the catcalls of his teammates. They wanted to know if Archie needed a bodyguard.

"I'll get Rock," laughed Archie, referring to the rail-thin Matt Goukas, who had come to blows with one of the Suns tonight. "Hey Rocky," Archie yelled across the room to Goukas. He grabbed Cunningham by the arm and goofed, "I'm taking somebody [down] with me. Where's my boy, Wally?"

Outside the locker room the patrolman and his large black sheriff's hat stood watch just in case, prompting the familiar muttered refrain, "Only in the NBA." The mutter was delivered with an exasperated shake of the head meant to elicit the zany images of the NBA's bush league past. Only in the NBA was Benny the Boob in St. Louis; luggage-laden players lumbering through the snow like the Russian infantry to reach Fort Wayne, fans in the cheap seats tossing heated, red-hot coins onto the court in New York; and the attack of the killer horse flies in San Francisco.

While the past still blew like tumbleweeds through the league, such as the other night in Boston and tonight in Phoenix, the New NBA was nevertheless more than just a passing slogan. A short list of teams was indeed in full jostle this season to fill the void left by the passing of the Celtics empire, and New York finally had an NBA winner.

The New NBA's emerging wild card was the New Player. He was more athletic, sometimes flamboyant, more likely African American, commanded larger salaries, and could be outspoken about social and political issues. To garble a Bible verse, the New Player was in the NBA but certainly not of it and its bush-league past.

Many owners continued to fear that the New Player would be more marketing bane than blessing. And their instincts weren't totally wrong. Traditional fans, their values molded in the peanuts-and-crackerjacks 1950s, grumped at the New Player for being culturally out of frame. Sports critic Leonard Shecter explained, "It is comforting to believe that athletes are kind, upright, gentle and truthful, and sports writers have learned that the image they project of the athlete that will be believed is the one the public wants to believe."

But in these countercultural times, the younger minds valued truth over comfort. They wanted the same free expression in sports that thumped on their turntables and concert halls. Race was worthy of exploring and, in fact, fed into the larger contemporary issues of civil rights and social justice.

"What books have you read lately?" a reporter asked Archie three days later aboard the 76ers' late-night flight from Seattle to San Francisco.

"*Soul on Ice*," he answered, referring to black activist Eldridge Cleaver's book of philosophical and political essays on race in America. "I would recommend the book to everybody . . . to see some of the realities and truths in life, to see somebody else's viewpoint."

Wally Jones' booklist? *Psycho-Cybernetics*, *The Glorious Ages of Africa*, and *Before the Mayflower*.

When the flight landed in San Francisco, Archie and Wally Wonder proceeded down the gangway decked out in matching bowler hats and tight, bright, and funky sixties threads. No need to be square in San Francisco. High fashion, though certainly not embraced by all players, had hit the NBA with all the energy of a new dance craze. It arrived in a riot of bell bottoms, a shout of pastel shirts, a swish of Edwardian jackets, and, as one commentator put it, "neckties as wide as the Jersey turnpike."

## 17

*Not only did I dress well and keep up on current events, but I was also Philadelphia's representative on the NBA Players Association. It was kind of a pro forma thing. But somebody had to do it and do it at some personal risk. Management branded player reps as agitators in the house or, (the term it preferred) "locker-room lawyers." But you know what? That was fine with me. Old Joe Hill was right. There is power in a union.*

*The union reps always met during the All-Star break, and we got to hear the latest union struggles straight from the horse's mouth. The horse, in this case, was the union's attorney, Larry Fleisher. He was a brilliant New York labor lawyer whom most NBA owners loved to hate. But Larry persevered and eventually got the owners to agree to the first player pensions and a collective bargaining process. So Larry was on a roll, and at the 1970 All-Star game Larry shared with us the union's next battle: blocking the NBA-ABA merger.*

*In just three seasons the ABA had so destabilized pro basketball that the NBA was ready to negotiate a merger. Larry literally planned to make a federal case of the merger. He argued that the merger would create a pro basketball monopoly in open violation of federal laws for free trade. But Larry went a step further. He linked the anticipated free-trade violations to the NBA's existing labor system, the so-called reserve system. This blankety-blank system made every NBA player of my generation the exclusive property of an owner for the duration of his career. That's slavery! The owners had gotten away with it for twenty-five years because nobody had the resources or the guts to challenge them in court.*

*That is, until Larry. He would make the merger contingent on eliminating the reserve system and granting players the right to free agency. Larry's brainstorm would result a few months later in what people today call the "Oscar Robertson case." Oscar, as the union leader, was actually the lead litigant. Larry insisted, in a show of solidarity, that each player rep be a named litigant on the case, and that included me.*

Philadelphia, February 10, 1970. January had been a mostly winning month. Then the 76ers dropped four in a row, five of their last seven. As much as this midseason swoon frustrated him, Jack Ramsay kept his eye on a silver lining. The 76ers, as the likely fourth and final seed in the Eastern Division, would face the second-place Milwaukee Bucks in the first round, not the first-place New York Knicks. The 76ers had yet to beat the Knicks. But they already had downed the Bucks two out of four.

Ramsay may have wanted to reconsider that silver lining five minutes into tonight's game. The Bucks kept lobbing the ball inside to Lew Alcindor, no longer the overwhelmed rookie he had been earlier in the season. He was too tall, too quick, and too skilled for Darrell Imhoff to defend alone. So Ramsay sent a double team into the post. Alcindor, a skilled passer, merely dished the ball to an open teammate cutting to the basket or flipped it to one of the long-range bombers waiting along the perimeter.

After the loss Ramsay tried to remain upbeat. But it was tough. Ten days ago a local headline had screamed, "The 76ers a Team with Problems and Bleak Future." These words stated for the record what now passed for common knowledge in Philadelphia. Ramsay had ruined a young team with a once bright future, and attendance had dropped about 20 percent from last season.

Ramsay had to get out of this season on a high note for the good of the franchise and his reputation as a can-do coach. That meant first and foremost solving his team's defensive woes. No more breakdowns. He had to have everyone sharp, committed, and playing Ramsay Ball. Seize the tempo. Set the tone. In Ramsay's mind it was the only logical way out.

CHICAGO, FEBRUARY 20, 1970. Archie had taken a hard knee to his lower back the other night, courtesy of Walt Frazier. The knot had finally loosened, and Archie again felt like his old shaking-and-baking self. He'd already popped in twenty-four points to keep tonight's game close against Chet Walker and the Chicago Bulls.

Then, to start the fourth quarter, Jack Ramsay signaled for Archie and crew to fall into an illegal zone defense to rest their legs. Bulls coach Dick Motta wasn't stupid. Motta countered by bellowing the play "twenty-one," which dropped guard Clem Haskins into the zone's soft spot in the corner. Haskins merely waited for a pass, set his feet, and fired away like it was target practice. "In that lousy zone Ramsay is playing, it's easy to get those shots," Motta sniped after Chicago's zone-busting 126–119 win.

"First of all, I can't be concerned with any criticism that Motta makes of our team," Ramsay countered. "We don't like to give up any good shot." Ramsay thumped his finger on the postgame stat sheet to offer an alternative theory of defeat. "That's the game right there." His finger rested on the numbers fifty-seven and thirty-eight in the rebounding column. Advantage Bulls.

In the locker room trainer Al Domenico reminded everyone to shower quickly. They had a red-eye flight to Detroit. Ninety minutes later the team was in the air, the concentrated aerial glitter of Chicagoland replaced by the dead of night and the dull background hum of the airplane's engines. Ramsay spread the word to his players. After they landed in Detroit and checked into the Hotel Pontchartrain, he wanted to see everybody in his room. No excuses.

JACK RAMSAY WAS in room 710. Archie glanced at the number on the hotel door. The left side was the even numbers. He proceeded further down the hallway, his back throbbing. What possibly could be so pressing to call a team meeting at two in the morning, midway through a four-games-in-four-nights road trip?

Archie entered Ramsay's room and squeezed in with the other long faces. Ramsay acknowledged the obligatory happy-birthday wishes. As of two hours ago he was forty-five years old. The birthday boy turned serious, promising to keep this brief. Ramsay said he would borrow an idea from the Atlanta Hawks. For the remainder of the regular season the 76ers would have a system of "penalties and incentives."

The players exchanged glances. Did that translate to fines and bonuses? Ramsay said the system worked like this:

- Let your man jump over you for an offensive rebound, $15 penalty.

- If your man shoots and grabs his own rebound, $25 penalty.

- Gather an offensive rebound, $10 incentive.

One of the team's scouts (whom the players quickly dubbed Ramsay's bookkeeper) would maintain a running tally during games of each player's penalties versus incentives. He would hand the tally to Ramsay after each game. Any questions?

Eighteen hours later the 76ers eked out a 112–110 victory over Detroit. The two-point win was but prelude. The night's real drama came when Ramsay's rumpled bookkeeper presented his findings in the locker room.

"My man did NOT get a rebound off his own shot, not one time," Archie protested, reading over Ramsay's shoulder.

"No way," Fred Hetzel protested like a convict reading his rap sheet.

But Ramsay was pleased with the first results of his experiment. The 76ers had outrebounded the Pistons by sixteen.

BALTIMORE, MARCH 1, 1970. A reporter glanced at the latest penalties/incentives sheet. "Where does the money go?" he asked.

"A fund for old, retired, lame sportswriters," Ramsay wisecracked.

The old sportswriters' fund swelled two nights later in Milwaukee, much to Ramsay's chagrin. The Bucks savaged the Sixers for a second straight time, dominating the glass from start to finish and exposing the folly of Ramsay's penalties/incentives experiment. Increased effort wasn't the problem. His team hustled. The problem was, as it had been all season, Ramsay's gifted but physically underwhelming frontline. Jim Washington (minus $85), Billy Cunningham (minus $50), and Darrall Imhoff (minus $40) battled gamely on the boards all night.

Ten games remained in the regular season. The 76ers (37–35) would meet Milwaukee in the first round of the playoffs. Ramsay had two weeks to build a better mousetrap for Alcindor. Or, as the *Philadelphia Inquirer*'s Mark Heisler joked, the 76ers could get a jump on the off-season and its usual intrigues of "mowing lawns and jumping leagues."

NEW YORK, MARCH 8, 1970. The American Broadcasting Corporation had recently made the NBA's day and next three years. ABC Sports finalized a reported $17.5 million contract to televise seventeen regular-season games, the All-Star Game, and seven playoff contests through the 1972–73 season. The NBA's current one-year pact with ABC Sports, set to expire at the end of the season, brought in $1.5 million. The new contract nearly quadrupled that to $5.6 million per year and would pay out a total of $1 million to each team over the three years.

"To me, this new contract indicates that pro basketball has reached the status of pro football," bragged the thirty-eight-year-old president of ABC Sports, Roone Arledge, during a press conference at the popular Gallagher's Restaurant in Manhattan.

NBA commissioner Walter Kennedy, sitting next to Arledge, looked like he had swallowed a worm. "If I thought you really believed that pro basketball had reached the stature of pro football," Kennedy bantered, "I certainly wouldn't have signed for the figures we agreed to. Can we renegotiate?"

The room erupted with glee. But Arledge wasn't necessarily pandering to Kennedy and the roughly one hundred people in attendance. Arledge had spent the 1960s championing the idea that television must give America's living rooms the best seats and live vantage point at football and baseball games. That meant liberating the mounted, box-like television cameras (the RCA TK 41s), from their traditional haunts in the nosebleed seats and wheeling them like blinking steel robots as close to the action as possible.

That's where the NBA had an advantage over the NFL. Its indoor arenas were more compact than the NFL's vast, weather-soaked, seventy-five-thousand-seat stadiums. The RCA TK 41s could more readily capture the magical ambiance of Madison Square Garden, from the "Good evening, ladies and gentlemen" of public address announcer John Condon to the squeaking sneakers on the court to the organ in the background rhythmically bleating out fight songs. Arledge felt ABC could convince millions each Sunday that they had actually spent the afternoon in the Garden, seated next to guys named Vinnie and Saul from Yonkers.

Today ABC Sports got the 76ers and Knicks. Three minutes into the game Knicks coach Red Holzman motioned for a word with referee Richie Powers. The television camera under the 76ers' basket was way too close for comfort. Powers turned and calculated. The camera appeared to be twelve feet back behind the endline and directly under the basket. Violation. "You'll have to move your camera back and away," Powers barked to cameraman Stan Majdanski.

Majdanski's young assistant started gathering up the loose cable in preparation to move the camera. Majdanski waved him off. He wasn't budging. ABC Sports had paid a lot of money to broadcast the game.

Less than a minute later the basketball landed in Archie's hands with a clear path to the hoop. The Knicks' Walt Frazier gave chase and caught Archie in midair. Frazier leaned into Archie and, out of Powers's view, gave him a swift belated nudge to foil the lay-up. The ball trickled through the hoop, but Archie's momentum sent him sprawling into the camera, hands and hips first, like a bird thumping into a windowpane. "I'd never felt pain like that," said Archie, who slumped to the floor, his hand bleeding and his hip throbbing.

Archie told himself to get up. He couldn't move. The right side of his body felt broken. A stretcher was wheeled out, and Archie found himself suddenly strapped into the back of an ambulance, siren wailing, en route to St. Clare Hospital in nearby Hell's Kitchen.

The X-rays proved negative, and Archie got the okay to return to the Garden. He limped stiffly to the end of the bench just in time to see the 76ers pull off the upset. Afterward Ramsay seethed when asked about the ABC camera's 2–0 record this afternoon. Majdanski had also KO'ed the Knicks' reserve center Nate Bowman in the second quarter.

"It's an occupational hazard," a New York reporter cut him off.

"Like hell it is," Ramsay answered. "They have no business being there."

"Then why are they there?"

"Because the NBA kowtows to the network."

PHILADELPHIA, MARCH 9, 1970. Archie awoke in the morning feeling like he had been struck by a Peterbilt truck. Irv Kosloff had threatened publicly to sue ABC for willful negligence. The likelihood of Kosloff's following through and biting the hand that now partially fed all of the NBA owners fell somewhere between laughable and zero.

Jack Ramsay wasn't laughing, however. The magic number for Philadelphia (39–36) to clinch a playoff spot was one, with seven games remaining. Ramsay, anxious to get that one big win in the bag, wanted Archie on the court tonight in neutral Houston against last-place San Diego. Archie shrugged. He was in no shape to play. Wally Jones would have to pull double duty.

Double duty lasted exactly nine minutes. A stray elbow felled Wally Wonder in the first quarter and fractured his nose. Hal Greer moved into the unfamiliar lead guard position against San Diego's younger quicksilver guards and somehow made it work. Boy, did he make it work. Greer scored thirty-eight points, including fourteen in the decisive fourth quarter, to propel the 76ers into the playoffs against—who else?—Milwaukee.

---

*We opened the series pressing, Hal, Wally, and me. We were flying over the court like there was no tomorrow. The Bucks handled it. Jack forgot about Guy Rodgers. He was in his final season and sitting there at the end of the bench. Guy remained one of the all-time great ball handlers, and he came off the bench with his veteran presence to defuse the pressure. That allowed the Bucks to get back to dumping the ball inside to Kareem and killing us on the boards. We lost the opener, 125–118. But you know what? I saw the glass half full. Billy had a subpar game, Hal was good but not great, and I had scored twenty-one points in my first game back. That was something to build on in game two.*

*Well, Jack being Jack had another one of his brainstorms. He sent me to the bench for game two. All I could figure was he wanted to keep Wally in the starting lineup on principal because I'd missed two weeks. That burned me. Last season, when Wally returned from an injury, Jack inserted him right back into the starting lineup. No questions asked. I'd been a starter all year, and Jack buries me on the bench. I didn't think it was right. In game two I played twenty minutes, or about half of my usual time on the floor, and I sat there fuming. I'm a competitor. What do you expect?*

*Jack mentioned this moment thirty years later in his book, Dr. Jack's Leadership Lessons.*

*Jack recalled coming into the locker room after the 76ers had pulled off the upset in game two, and he heard me ranting, "You can trade me. You can just trade me now." That's not how it went down, not even close. Jack came into the locker room and saw me sitting there quietly but clearly fuming. Instead of letting it go and addressing the matter later in private, he called me out in front of everybody. He said, "Oh, look at Archie. We win the biggest game of the year, and he's pouting." That was like pouring gasoline on the situation. I lit into Jack, and he lit into me. Emotions run high in the playoffs, and we very nearly came to blows.*

*Afterward Jack settled down and fell back into his usual cordial ways. For Jack our disagreement became a conceptual challenge to his authority, and that is how he liked to view things: in the abstract. So what did Jack do? He called another team meeting to smooth things over in theory. But the damage was personal and already done. As Jack wrote in his book, "The team's high spirit was deflated, and the Bucks blew us away in Game 3, then won the next two to end our season." That's all true.*

*I mention this story not so much to set the record straight, although I've certainly done that. I do so more to give you an idea of the bad taste that the Milwaukee series left in my mouth. I cleared out my locker at the Spectrum and exited into a bittersweet offseason. On the positive side, I didn't have to renew my contract for the first time in my career. I was making good money, and I'd had a pretty good season. On the negative side, I was the exclusive property of a team that was headed nowhere. Jack wanted to prove himself as an NBA coach—and he was failing. His failures now became mine. This is nothing new in the NBA. Players today face the same boxed-in situations, except they have free agency looming on the horizon. I didn't.*

## 18

*In the summer of 1970 the Philadelphia 76ers had a player payroll of nearly $850,000. That was a mind-blowing figure back then. Nobody could believe our owner, Irv Kosloff, was in that deep. Heck, in the early 1960s Eddie Gottlieb, the founder of Philadelphia's original NBA franchise, had a payroll of well under $50,000.*

*Kosloff, not a real big spender, wanted to dump a few contracts. So by early summer I was on the trading block. His timing wasn't ideal—I'd just purchased a house in suburban New Jersey. But I was cool with it. The rumor was Milwaukee would be my next stop, and I would have gone there in a heartbeat to play for an NBA championship with Kareem. It would have been a defining moment in my career.*

*But the trade never happened. You're going to laugh when I tell you why: we didn't have a general manager for four months! Jack Ramsay, our former general manager, had resigned under pressure after the season to concentrate on coaching. When Milwaukee called in midsummer to inquire about my availability, no GM was in place to negotiate the trade. So the Bucks went elsewhere and worked out a deal for Oscar Robertson. The rest is NBA history.*

---

Philadelphia, August 4, 1970. Bob Vetrone, the 76ers' publicity director, had leaked the name of the team's new general manager two days ago. But protocol was protocol, so the front office had scheduled today's press conference at the swishy Blue Line Restaurant to make it official. The 76ers had hired Don DeJardin, the former general manager of the ABA's Carolina Cougars, the same team suing for Billy Cunningham's services.

"In the very beginning, it was a detriment," Irv Kosloff admitted of DeJardin's ABA pedigree. But Kosloff had to let bygones be bygones. He desperately needed a general manager, and the thirty-four-year-old DeJardin accepted a modest $30,000-per-year salary to get his foot in the NBA door. More important, Kosloff also viewed DeJardin, a West Point graduate, as the right man to declare war on his runaway player salaries.

CHERRY HILL, NEW Jersey, September 13, 1970. Archie deposited his bags in the trunk of the car and said his goodbyes to Valerie, the kids, and now the German shepherd. He'd be home in ten days, when training camp ended. Archie started the car and, after a final wave goodbye down the driveway, was en route to Margate, the little Jewish enclave and NBA training camp by the sea.

When Archie pulled into the team motel, Wally Jones, now sporting a full beard and Afro, bantered with Billy Cunningham about his big payday. Wasn't the ABA beautiful, he said? The conversation hushed when the topic turned to Darrall Imhoff and trusted reserve Matt Goukas. The new guy DeJardin had lowballed them on their new contracts. Both had refused to sign, and DeJardin had suspended them for failing to report to training camp.

"When I first heard about it, I thought somebody was pulling my leg," said Archie. "Darrall and Mattie were as clean cut as boy scouts. They were the last two that I would have ever thought would land in hot water with management."

Archie, as he was wont to do, pondered the possibility of life without Imhoff. The 76ers had nobody else. Luke Jackson had missed most of the last two seasons and, as his cranky Achilles tendon and the long crater in the back of his surgically repaired leg attested, remained a question mark. That left rookie Al Henry. Archie snickered.

Last March Ramsay had attempted a high-tech NBA first to ace the college draft. Ramsay had rented time on an IBM mainframe for $3,000 and performed his own pre-draft analysis to determine the best college prospects in the land. Garbage in, garbage out. Among the first names spit out: Al Henry, a 6-foot-9 forward from the University of Wisconsin. Confident modern science and technology had his back, Dr. Jack selected the unheralded Henry in the first round, describing him as a defensive stopper.

"Al Who?" muttered the 76er faithful. Al Who quickly became R. U. Kidding when reporters discovered that the future of the franchise had been a part-time starter on a mediocre Big Ten team. The city's basketball aficionados sniggered when the rail-thin Henry and his awkward jump shot debuted in Philadelphia's summer Baker League several weeks later. Most figured he'd be lucky even to make the 76ers roster. That is, had Ramsay not signed him to a three-year, no-cut contract.

Ramsay, meanwhile, had yet to speak up publicly on behalf of Imhoff or Goukas, the latter having starred for him in college. Dr. Jack seemed once again convinced that his system trumped talent. If DeJardin chose to trade them, so be it. Dr. Jack would still X and O and, like a movie director, inspire brilliance from whatever cast of characters walked onto the set.

"I liked Jack," said Imhoff. "He was personable, had a wicked sense of humor, and was just a great teacher of the game. But he had absolutely no loyalty to his players, and I don't know why."

PHILADELPHIA, OCTOBER 14, 1970. The house lights dipped, and public address announcer Dave Zinkoff leaned forward into the long silver microphone to welcome everyone to the Spectrum for tonight's season opener between the Chicago Bulls and the Philadelphia 76ers. Zink, keeping with Spectrum protocol, announced Chicago's starting five with complete disinterest.

Then Zink stretched out the phrase, "And noooow." It was his trademark transition before introducing the good guys. "And noooow, here are the Philadelphia 76ers."

Tradition dictated that for the home opener Zink would introduce the team's full roster to the Philadelphia faithful, like Marvel rolling out its latest line of comic book superheroes. Save for Wally Wonder, a.k.a. Wally Jones, little "super" or "heroic" would be sitting on the bench this season. Gone were most of last season's familiar subs. In their place stood unfamiliar last names stitched to the backs of warm-up jackets. Henry. Ogden. Awtrey. Former Celtics scrapper Bailey Howell was the lone familiar newcomer. But after eleven seasons of running the NBA floorboards, this superhero was tired.

Matt Goukas was back in uniform, having halted his holdout two weeks ago. DeJardin had inched up his offer to a two-year, $60,000 contract. Goukas relented, and DeJardin told him not to get too comfortable. A trade was in the works.

"And here are your starters. From Minnesota, number twenty-one, Ar-cheeee CLARK."

Archie jogged to center court, serenaded by the three-second vamp of the arena's pipe organ. *Dun, dun, dun, da, dah*. He glanced into the stands. The 76ers' staff had dotted the arena with their signs, featuring a William Penn-like cartoon figure, a basketball, and the season's official promotional theme: the Year of Hoopla. Don DeJardin strikes again. DeJardin had hired a marketing firm to upgrade the team's sagging public image.

"From Marshall, number fifteen, Hal Greer." *Dah, Dah*.

Bulldog slapped hands with Archie. He wore bulky white braces over each knee, making him look like he had just escaped from the local surgical ward. Greer still could score in bunches like few others in the league. But after twelve NBA seasons the mileage was piling up fast.

"Out of Pan American, number fifty-four, Loooo-scious Jackson." *Dun, dun, dun, da, dah*.

Big Luke had looked good in the preseason. But could he last eighty-two games?

"From Villanova. Number twelve. Jimm-eeee Washington." *Dah, dah*.

"Wash" jogged to center court and slapped three hands with his teammates. This would be his final full season in Philadelphia. Jack Ramsay, forever tweaking his lineup, would decide that Wash's skill set didn't translate to the NBA and would ship him to Atlanta.

"From North Carolina, number thirty two, Bill-eeee Cun-NING-ham."

Cunningham now wanted to stay in Philadelphia. Last winter he had agreed verbally to a new five-year deal with the 76ers worth $1.1 million. But the agreement remained all verbal. Cunningham and his lawyers still had to figure out a way to cancel the ABA contract.

The pipe organ threw in a final flourish for good measure, and the 76ers reassembled around Ramsay for a final "don't forget" pre-game shout. The starters pulled off their warm-ups, unveiling the team's hoopla-friendly new uniforms. "The 76ers have these new white home uniforms that look as though they were designed by kids doing homework for Sesame Street," someone at press row panned the louder look. "Seventy-Sixers is spelled out across their chests in the kind of shaky script you see in kidnap messages."

As in seasons past Ramsay's team was simply better drilled for opening night than its cobwebbed opponent. Archie and crew trapped the step-slow Bulls on defense, found the open man on offense, and made William Penn seem like a very wise man. The 76ers had a nineteen-point edge midway through the third quarter, and, faster than both coaches could clear their benches and say "hoopla," the Bulls' Walker found his inner jet in the fourth quarter. Chet the Jet dropped fifteen points in rapid succession, pulling the Bulls to within three. Thankfully time expired, and Philadelphia checked off the 110–107 victory.

Ramsay reviewed the stat sheet afterward and focused on the positives. The 76ers had five double-figure scorers, easily outrebounded Chicago, and had played the stifling team defense that Ramsay loved. The bigger news was Jackson's return. After spending most of the last two seasons on the mend, Jackson logged thirty-five productive minutes, knocking down his mid-range shot and outworking Chicago's man mountain of a 7-footer, Tom Boerwinkle. Ramsay put down the stat sheet and concluded hopefully, "We're going to be in the thick of it."

PHILADELPHIA, OCTOBER 16, 1970. Day thirty-one of the Darrall Imhoff holdout. When last Imhoff had spoken with DeJardin, warm and fuzzy was nowhere to be found.

"We've reached an impasse," said DeJardin. "Maybe you ought to ask to be traded."

"I'm not going to ask that," Imhoff fired back. "I want to play here."

"I've got nothing else to say."

This morning Irv Kosloff had met privately with Imhoff's recently hired agent, Fred Rosenfeld, who announced his client would sign for $60,000 after all. "Before the ink even was dry on the paper, DeJardin had me traded to Cincinnati," said Imhoff. However, Rosenfeld inserted a key clause into Imhoff's contract. If traded, Imhoff's salary would jump to $80,000, giving the veteran center the raise that he'd wanted all along.

In return Philadelphia got reserve swingman Fred Foster and the thirty-four-year-old backup center Connie Dierking. Long time 76er fans remembered "Shirking" Dierking, having booed him out of town early in his career for his poor play. Rather than submit to more boos and uproot his Cincinnati business interests, Dierking announced his retirement.

CINCINNATI, OCTOBER 17, 1970. As fans spilled through the turnstiles into the 1950s-quaint, red-brick foyer of the Cincinnati Gardens, they were greeted with a familiar, take-me-out-to-the-ballgame bark, "Programs. Programs here." The cover of tonight's playbill featured a photo collage of this season's Royals, including the smiling Shirking Dierking. "The closest Connie Dierking got to the Cincinnati Gardens last night was the cover of the souvenir program," lampooned a reporter.

Even with no Dierking on their bench the 76ers claimed their third-straight victory, 123–104, as Archie picked up his offensive pace. He had been given a green light this season to look for his shot with more defenses double-teaming Billy Cunningham. As an onlooker wrote of his shake-and-bake move, "Archie Clark fakes west, dribbles east, stops, fidgets, starts again, jerks his head, shakes his shoulders, jiggles his feet, changes gears and directions three or four more times, and suddenly he has a free shot inside. Invariably it is a good shot. Archie Clark can go a month without taking a bad shot."

Earlier in the day Ramsay had visited Dierking to play the good cop. "Don DeJardin came next, and I met with him in my basement," said Dierking. "He offered me a lot more money than I was making with the Royals. It was a one-year deal for $80,000." Or precisely the amount that Imhoff had wanted all along. Dierking unretired on the spot.

SAN BRUNO, CALIFORNIA, October 27, 1970. Jack Ramsay had been polite but firm. No more pirouettes. Instructor Marci Robb needed to wrap up her beginning ballet class for tots. The Philadelphia 76ers had reserved the San Bruno War Memorial Recreation Center for practice at 4:30 p.m. sharp. Rules are rules.

Robb, having run several minutes over her allotted time, objected to the big rush. "Kicking out little kids so a bunch of seven-foot giants can play basketball," muttered Robb as she exited the large community center near the San Francisco airport with her ballerinas in training.

Only in the 1970s NBA. Teams practiced wherever they could, especially on the road. Archie, although dressed for practice, planned to do as little running as possible. He had rolled his left ankle three nights ago and, multiple ice bags later, felt a tad better. He just needed to take it easy in preparation for tomorrow night's game against the San Francisco Warriors.

The next night Ramsay looked like he had picked up a few new moves from Robb. He hopped and twirled and even picked up another technical foul. But it was just one of those *Nights of the NBA Living Dead*. The arena was seemingly empty, and Ramsay's hobbled and road-weary troops were a step slow on defense and settling for bad shots instead of making the extra pass.

Just when all seemed lost, Hal Greer found his midrange jump shot and brought the 76ers charging back to within seven points of the Warriors to end the third quarter. Ramsay implored his players to fight through the fatigue. Win this game. No regrets. But San Francisco's lanky Joe Ellis intercepted a regrettable pass to start the fourth quarter, dribbled ahead, and, as the Warriors announcer Bill King often alliterated during his broadcasts, "twinkled the twine" to push the lead to nine.

Over the next few minutes Warriors coach Al Attles called out in his husky, foghorn voice to get the ball inside to center Nate Thurmond. A year ago Nate the Great would have used his long arms and legs to dominate board and basket, à la Wilt and Alcindor. But now those legs ached. Thurmond had a pulled muscle in one and had a bulky gauze bandage over the other to protect the now surgically repaired knee that had nearly ended his career last season. "Diving is out of the question," he told a reporter about the new list of dos and don'ts to help him, at age twenty-nine, scrape out a few more seasons in the NBA.

As Thurmond banged inside for position, the surgically repaired Luke Jackson matched him bump for bump. God only knows how many injections and incisions they had between them. Nate the Great, out of shape and out of sorts after nine months on the mend and forty-plus minutes of action tonight, twinkled very little twine. But his shots smacked iron—lots of iron—and the San Francisco offense stalled. The 76ers, misfiring plenty, inched ahead tortoise-like to claim the victory by a hair, 111–108.

For Ramsay an ugly win was still a win, and he told his team that their mind-over-matter effort had pushed the 76ers into first place in the NBA's four-team Atlantic Division. Actually it had pushed Philadelphia to within a half game of first-place New York. Ramsay was undeterred when informed of the mistake. "They can't run away from us forever."

PHILADELPHIA, NOVEMBER 6, 1970. The Atlanta Hawks (2–6) rolled into Philadelphia tonight toting an expensive Pistol named Pete. Following in the promotional footsteps of baseball's Charlie Finley and his yellow-shirted, white-shoed Oakland Athletics, Atlanta had unveiled nontraditional uniforms this season to position the Hawks as the NBA's most progressive franchise and add to Pete Maravich's mystique as a trend-setting showman. The "New Hawks" took the floor in warm-up pants that were candy-striped in artichoke green, royal blue, and oyster-shell white. The game jerseys were pure artichoke overlaid on the left-hand side with competing white and royal blue linear squiggles that resembled a subway map.

But the Hawks' polyester fashion statement remained for now mere window dressing. Maravich continued to struggle to find his rhythm in the twenty-four-second NBA, especially playing for the first time in his career without the ball in his hands to create shots; nor could he remember all of the plays. That had forced coach Richie Guerin to toss out two-thirds of the playbook last week in favor of a half dozen bread-and-butter sets. It had also forced Guerin to start games with his Pistol holstered on the bench to let the veterans find their rhythm.

That's where Maravich started the game tonight and logged just nine minutes in the first half, much to the chagrin of William Penn and the Year of Hoopla. On second thought, the crowd of 9,871 might not have been too crestfallen. A banner hung in the Spectrum that asked, "HEY, PISTOL PETE, WHY DO HOT DOGS COST TWO MILLION DOLLARS IN ATLANTA AND ONLY 35 CENTS IN PHILADELPHIA?"

Guerin started his hot dog in the second half, and he sank nine quick points midway through the third quarter. Jack Ramsay rushed his defensive stopper Wally Jones into the game. Maravich didn't score another basket. "When he's standing out there doing his tricks, four other guys are just standing around," Jones critiqued the rookie.

The same could have been said about the 76ers tonight. Ramsay was back to calling plays for Cunningham. He had Archie get the ball to Billy C at the top of the key and set a screen for him. The Hawks switched on screens, and that gave Ramsay the matchups that he wanted: Cunningham one-on-one against a smaller guard.

By midway through the fourth quarter Cunningham had rung up the Hawks for thirty-eight-points. But the 76ers couldn't quite shake their visitors. Remember that hole in the middle of the 76ers' defense? Hawks forward Bill Bridges began maneuvering inside as though he were Wilt Chamberlain. But Archie quarterbacked the team through the final two minutes without Cunningham, who'd fouled out late, and the 76ers escaped with a 118–112 victory.

"It's just blown out of proportion," Maravich rambled to a mob of reporters about his transition to the pro game. "I was loose out there. I wish I'd been tight."

Away from the media mob Archie bantered in private with his old friend Walt Hazzard. Archie had expended much of his energy on defense this evening, in part because Hazzard kept yo-yoing the basketball and looking for his shot. That wasn't his game. But, as Hazzard joked about his twenty-two shot attempts, he was auditioning for a trade. His days were numbered in Atlanta. The franchise belonged to an expensive Pistol named Pete.

NEW YORK, NOVEMBER 14, 1970. "Dee-fense, dee-fense." The sellout crowd in Madison Square Garden thundered those two syllables like a proclamation, and time spiraled back to game seven of last season's NBA championship against the Los Angeles Lakers.

But the Liberty Bellers, as the 76ers were derisively nicknamed in New York, had done little in the second half to merit the collective call to action. The Knicks were comfortably ahead, 125–94, and the game had entered its final minute of garbage time. So why the late-game "dee-fense" chant? Many in the crowd, anxious to collect on side bets, needed the Knicks reserves to hold the 76ers scrubs to under one hundred points.

When the final buzzer sounded and the crowd heaved a lucrative sigh of relief, Jack Ramsay steamed to the dressing room. "They are the infallible Knicks," he said, blaming the refs for the loss. "They can't commit a foul. They can get away with all kinds of pushing and grabbing."

As Ramsay singled out forward Bill Bradley as the grabbiest of the Knicks, 76er reserve Al Henry pulled on his slacks about thirty feet away, reached into his pockets, and drew a blank. Where was his wallet? Archie checked his pants. One hundred and sixty dollars—gone. A burglar had padded into the 76ers' dressing room during their disastrous second half. He had disappeared $1,142 richer.

But the 76ers had lost more than money in New York. Wally Jones, complaining about a constant pain in his right knee, went to have it checked out the next day. The doctor told him he had a bone chip in the knee. Wally Wonder needed surgery and would be out of action for about six weeks. The timing couldn't have been worse. The Sixers played seven games in eight nights.

---

*After Don DeJardin banished Matt Goukas, he and Jack Ramsay decided to keep three guards on the roster. So when Wally went down, Hal Greer and I were the last backcourt men standing until DeJardin finally signed my good friend Fred Crawford.*

*The roster turmoil, all of it predictable in training camp, sent Jack into full fix-it mode. He tinkered with the lineup for about two weeks to settle on his best five-man combinations and safest substitution patterns. When Jack finished his chemistry experiment, Connie Dierking had landed at the end of the bench, where he remained, and Luke Jackson went into a funk. He suddenly couldn't put anything in the basket, and his legs clearly were hurting him. Jack's solution was to forge full steam ahead with our other rookie center, Dennis Awtrey. We called him Harpo because of his curly blondish hair and quiet disposition, à la Harpo Marx. Jack thought he was ready to log big minutes. He wasn't. By mid-December our record had dipped below .500, and the Philadelphia newspapers began writing our obituary. It turned out to be premature.*

OAKLAND, DECEMBER 19, 1970. Referees Don Murphy and Manny Gomes weren't, shall we say, at the top of their officiating games. Both teams stomped and moaned over their flip-flopping whistles, and it was only a matter of time before the men in striped shirts returned the harsh feelings. Archie picked up his technical midway through the first quarter, Billy Cunningham got his in the second quarter, and Jack Ramsay received a cheap one in the third stanza.

Despite the game within a game the 76ers kept their poise. Cunningham waited for the double team and found the open teammate. Hal Greer topped the scoring parade with thirty-three points, Archie was next with twenty-one, and Philadelphia notched its third win in a row, 108–99.

As the team prepared for its moonlight drive over the Bay Bridge to the San Francisco Peninsula and its San Bruno hotel, trainer Al Domenico told everyone to be ready for an early-morning wake-up call. They had another early flight to catch. The 76ers were headed to Portland for their maiden game against the expansion Trail Blazers. The next night, in the City of Roses, the 76ers made it four in a row.

# 19

Philadelphia, January 15, 1971. When Archie had arrived in Philadelphia two seasons ago, he and Wally Jones had spent untold hours balancing suitcases through airports and hotels while debating the pros and cons of NBA life. Archie opened Jones's eyes to a new reality: NBA players didn't have to play while injured, contrary to management's traditional play-or-perish edict.

Archie's message hit home—a little too well. Before last night's five-point loss in Chicago, Wally Wonder had practiced at full speed for the first time since his knee surgery. No, he said, the knee wasn't ready. Jones disappeared into the locker room and reemerged dressed in a flowing, African-inspired dashiki shirt that, along with his ample Afro and full beard, made him look more like a militant than a basketball player. Jack Ramsay grumbled, less about the look than the inconvenience. He had expected his third super guard back in uniform two weeks ago.

For Archie pulling double duty the past two months had been a mixed bag. The fierce competitor in him wanted to be on the court, and the extra time had him at the top of his game in this Year of Hoopla. The downside was that Archie could never drop his guard. Ramsay depended on him to stay aggressive at all times. Although Archie felt healthy with a few minor dings, the extra minutes were adding up as the 76ers (27–21) started their second-half run for the Atlantic Division title.

LOS ANGELES, JANUARY 18, 1971. Time to send a box of fine cigars to NBA scheduler Eddie Gottlieb. After subjecting the 76ers to four games in four nights, "the Mogul" granted the team two days off before facing the Lakers to enjoy the short-sleeve weather of Los Angeles.

Archie visited his Aunt Ruby, the relative who had so kindly opened her home to him as a rookie. Archie's father, Houston, was there visiting with everybody and encouraging his son to stick it to the Lakers.

Archie felt no animosity toward his former team. Besides, all anybody cared to talk about anymore was the aftermath of "The Trade." With Darrall Imhoff and Jerry Chambers now at the end of their NBA careers, Archie was known as the guard traded for arguably the greatest basketball player of all time. According to the experts, that equaled the worst trade in NBA history. Wilt would always be Wilt, and Jack Ramsay had won zip in the playoffs with Clark.

True, but "the Trade" seemed far more lopsided that it really was, largely because of Ramsay's miscalculation early in his career that coaching trumped talent in the NBA. It didn't. Archie was one of the NBA's most talented guards. If Ramsay had given him the green light, Archie could have shaked and baked his way onto magazine covers as one of the NBA's most electrifying scorers and elite playmakers. Sure, Wilt would always be Wilt, but Archie would always be Archie. And that Archie, unleashed, might have helped Ramsay notch a playoff series or two.

Tonight, as if to illustrate all of the above, Archie got the green light with Billy Cunningham's ankle on the mend. It came early in the third quarter with the Lakers ahead and Ramsay furious at the refs. He told Archie to step up his game a notch. The 76ers made a few steals, sending Archie on the offensive. He shoulder-faked his former teammates Goodrich and West, crossed over his dribble to create space, and sank one pull-up jump shot after the next.

The Lakers lead was eight as the third quarter wound down, and Ramsay, often more logical than intuitive, buzzed Hal Greer into the ballgame. Ramsay reasoned that Archie and his red-hot right hand needed a rest. Archie went along with Ramsay's miscalculation. When he reentered the game in the fourth quarter, the Lakers controlled the tempo, allowing Wilt, Baylor, and West to dominate and carry their team to victory. Archie finished with a loud thirty-eight points on a night that he could have netted fifty.

Archie's green light turned yellow in the next game against Phoenix. Cunningham carried the offensive load, and Archie quarterbacked the 76ers to a one-point victory. The next morning the 76ers (31–22) flew to Seattle and the mother of all NBA scandals. The Supersonics had recently signed ABA superstar Spencer Haywood to a fat contract. Though the ABA allowed Haywood to turn pro early as a "hardship case" in need of money, his college class had yet to graduate. The NBA, wedded to its four-year rule, treated Haywood as though he was still in college. Seattle begged to differ, and the lawyers were getting rich.

---

*I was there when Spencer Haywood got the idea to jump to the NBA. In fact I might have been the one who planted the idea. The previous summer he and I were on an American All-Star team that played seven exhibition games in Panama. We had a lot of down time between games, and all the American players hung out and talked about everything under the sun, including our pro contracts.*

*Spencer started bragging about his latest ABA deal. I heard him out and said, "Your contract isn't so great. Read the fine print real closely; most of your money is deferred." Spencer had no assurance that he'd get paid in twenty years and, with inflation, how much that money would be worth. I told Spencer that my base salary was more than double his take-home pay. That got his attention, and I remember advising him to jump to the NBA as soon as his college class graduated.*

*Spencer filed away the conversation, and it wasn't long before he voiced his dissatisfaction with the ABA contract. Then in late December 1970 Spencer didn't wait. He signed with the Seattle Supersonics, got a preliminary court injunction against the NBA challenging his contract, and played immediately.*

SEATTLE, JANUARY 24, 1971. The 76ers looked like NBA champions tonight. They played Dr. Jack's swarming defense to perfection while connecting on 61 percent of their shots. Every time Seattle tried to tighten the defensive screws, according to a reporter seated at courtside, "the 76ers were too nifty, too solid, too quick, and too clever."

In the third quarter, however, the sublime devolved into the theater of the NBA absurd when the 76ers trainer Al Domenico padded to the scorekeeper's table and submitted a pre-written sheet of paper. It read that Philadelphia hereby protested its best game of the season on the grounds that the ineligible Spencer Haywood had dressed, sat on the bench, and played for Seattle.

The public address announcer dutifully announced the protest, the thirteenth we're-mad-as-hell filing since Haywood had joined Seattle three weeks ago. The fans booed the visitors' bad manners, and the game dribbled on into the fourth quarter without further controversy.

Domenico had no choice. The protest put Philadelphia owner Irv Kosloff on record as opposing Seattle owner Sam Schulman, and, by morning Kosloff's show of solidarity was dutifully forwarded to the league office in New York. There it would join twelve previous calls for Schulman's head. All were strictly in the hands of the lawyers.

Assuming the game and the victory stood, Sixers fans back home could do the math on their fingers: two in a row, four out of five on the latest road trip, and eight out of their last ten. The Sixers were the hottest team in pro basketball.

BOSTON, JANUARY 31, 1971. When Archie turned pro in 1966, Boston Garden already was one of the NBA's lower-end arenas. Five years and a boom of multi-million-dollar showpiece arenas later, Boston Garden had become just plain old and cranky, with its perma-popcorn smell, old-fashioned checkerboard floor (dead zones and all), view-obstructing poles in the stands, and the dry Yankee intonations of the public address announcer whenever Archie scored: "Occhie Clock."

Tonight a Garden employee shuffled "Occhie Clock" and the 76ers along a disorienting wend to a little-used visitors' locker room that could have doubled as a dungeon. The windowless concrete chamber consisted of a single exposed, tell-me-your-secrets light bulb in the middle of the room, a row of standard metal lockers, and two dripping showers. An unlined, industrial-sized barrel stood near the door as a communal garbage can. That's also where the Celtics' staff would deliver the obligatory postgame case of beer and soda.

In this disorienting drip-drip of time and locker-room space Ramsay gathered everyone and stated the obvious: this was a big game. A win tonight, coupled with a victory two nights hence in their rematch in Philadelphia, would put the second-place 76ers six games ahead of Boston. With roughly a month left in the regular season, six games might be enough of a cushion for the 76ers to cinch a playoff spot.

But trainer (and travel agent) Al Domenico had a second, now-hear-this request. In another of GM Don DeJardin's run of cost-cutting measures the 76ers would fly back to Philadelphia immediately after the game to avoid incurring an extra hotel bill. The game tipped off at 7:30 p.m., and the team was booked on the last commercial flight of the day to Philadelphia at 10:30. Domenico barked for everyone to be prepared to make a quick getaway. By his calculations the game would end no later than 9:50. After a dash to the locker room, they'd have thirty minutes max to pile into the backs of yellow cabs, navigate the three miles to the airport, zip through the terminal, and board their flight.

The 76ers got off to a flying start, connecting on fourteen of their first sixteen shots to take an early nineteen-point advantage. The Celtics chipped away at the lead early in the second quarter, but before Ramsay could call a time-out to regroup, Boston Garden malfunctioned. The ancient twenty-four-second clock, originally used in the 1930s to time bull riders when the arena hosted rodeos, bucked one last time and died. Referees Mendy Rudolph and Paul Mihalik signaled both benches. Garden staff were looking into the matter, but this might take a while.

A staff member ventured deep into the catacombs of this forty-three-year-old building to rummage for an even-lower-budget portable clock that somebody seemed to remember might still be back there. Jackpot! After a lengthy delay the game continued without further technical difficulties until Rudolph halted play again at the end of the third quarter. The twenty-four-second clock and the overhead scoreboard, purchased for hockey matches and not basketball games, were out of sync. This might take a while.

After the wires had been jiggled and rejiggled, Boston Garden creaked ahead into the nine o'clock hour and a tight fourth quarter. With 2:30 left and Philadelphia leading by one, Ramsay called a play for Archie, who had a game-high thirty-two points. His teammates cleared out for him, and Archie jab-stepped Boston guard Don Chaney, quickly gained a step on him, and angled hard on the dribble toward the baseline. The octopus-armed Chaney reached behind

Archie, whacking the ball like a stray balloon into the tentative hands of the 76ers' Fred Crawford. He lobbed the balloon back for Archie to restart his move. But Chaney anticipated the return pass and took the ball the other way. Two made free throws later, Chaney gave Boston a one-point lead. The time: ten o'clock.

At exactly 10:17 Boston had secured the win, 132–126. "Disappointed," Ramsay nodded to a reporter as he hastened to the mystery locker room while Domenico dashed to the nearest telephone booth to plead with the airline to hold the flight. They'd be at Logan in fifteen minutes. Make that thirty minutes. When the last 76er buckled into his seat, the pilot's voice crackled over the intercom, "We couldn't leave Boston without the Sixers."

PHILADELPHIA, FEBRUARY 2, 1971. Jack Ramsay arrived early at the Spectrum for tonight's rematch with the Boston Celtics. Wally Jones already had been out on the floor testing his surgically repaired right knee. Not yet, Jones told Ramsay; the leg remained too weak for the wear and tear of an NBA game.

Ramsay, tired of waiting, grumped for the first time that Jones should risk playing at less than 100 percent. The team needed him tonight. Within minutes Jones had been summoned to the 76ers' front office in another part of the arena to meet with Ramsay and Don DeJardin. The latter, always four-star officious in keeping with his West Point pedigree, formally charged Jones with "malingering." He advised Jones that the team physician had cleared him to play a month ago, and the terms of his contract were crystal clear. If the team physician considered him to be in satisfactory health, he must play. Unless Jones returned to action, DeJardin warned, he would be forced to start the paperwork to suspend him without pay. "Do you understand?"

Jones nodded behind his thick tangle of facial hair and processed a cold realization. DeJardin, sitting across from him, buttoned down and as cool as a cucumber, had just threatened him. Suspension without pay? For having a bad knee?

Jones reluctantly agreed to join the team on its upcoming road trip to Chicago. But he put his foot down. Playing tonight was out of the question. "Nobody can make you do anything," he vented to a reporter afterward. "I'm not a slave."

By 8 p.m. DeJardin had taken his place at courtside, and the red-seated Spectrum transformed itself into "America's Showplace," narrated by the incomparable public-address shtick of Dave Zinkoff and the zany Year of Hoopla antics of the PR firm Sonder, Levitt, and Sagorsky. The latter, in cahoots with 76ers staff, had hijacked the message board on the scoreboard in one of the NBA's earliest attempts to turn technology into fan-friendly entertainment. "Mr. Wonderful," the scoreboard flashed whenever Billy Cunningham scored. "The Tower of Strength" heralded a Luke Jackson rebound.

Bob Ryan of the *Boston Globe*, ignoring the scoreboard pyrotechnics, was smitten with the sneaker-squeaking intensity of it all: "The faces may change, but the Celtics and 76ers will, apparently, always provide us with the same show." But Ryan admitted in the next breath that tonight's installment hardly ranked as a rip-roaring artistic success. The game had brought forty-one mostly unforced turnovers, sixty-one fouls, a near fistfight, and a brief wrestling match, and (as one attendee complained) "both coaches spent practically the whole game shouting uncomplimentary remarks at the referees."

And yet the final minute delivered a classic NBA nail biter. The Celtics' Jo Jo White blew an uncontested lay-up that would have cut the 76ers' lead to two, and the ensuing rebound and point-blank shot bubbled out. The Celtics, forced to foul to stop the clock, put the tried-and-true Hal Greer on the line for two freebies. Check and mate. The 76ers sealed the victory, 108–105, and regained a four-game lead in the standings over the Celtics.

After the game was in the books, Wally Jones went home to ponder DeJardin's threat and the dull ache in his right knee. He talked with Archie, his friend and union representative, about whether to play or stand his ground. Archie said there was a middle ground. By rejoining the team for the Chicago game, Jones would suffer no damage to his name or wallet. But he could still protect his knee from further injury. The trick was to keep his minutes down. Jones had two days to make a decision.

Two days later Al Domenico woke up everyone with the bad news.

Chicago was fogged in, and O'Hare Airport was closed. The 76ers would need to take the train to ensure their arrival for their next game against the Bulls. The change in plans was quickly relayed, and a few hours later, standing among the players huddled on the platform at Philadelphia's Thirtieth Street Station, was Wally Jones. After forty-two games on the sidelines Wally Wonder planned to take the next twenty-three for the team in small doses.

PHILADELPHIA, FEBRUARY 7, 1971. Wally Jones remained in one piece after playing twelve minutes in Chicago (loss) and nineteen minutes in Cincinnati (win). It was his teammates who worried him. Billy Cunningham had strained a back muscle. Jim Washington had caught a finger in the eye. Bailey Howell had dislocated and torn a ligament in a finger. Fred Foster had dislocated his thumb. Hal Greer had a pulled hamstring, and Luke Jackson kept complaining about the hairline fracture of his right index finger. "It looks like a meat hook," groaned Jackson. "I thought there was someone in the stands sticking pins into dolls," joked Al Domenico of the voodoo-like raft of injuries.

With bad mojo and muscle ointment wafting through the 76ers locker room, tonight's must-win game against the New York Knicks couldn't have popped up on the schedule at a worse time. Or had it? Down the hall Red Holtzman and crew were preparing for their third game in three nights. The previous two had ended in defeat, and center Willis Reed, battling tendonitis in his knee, could barely move. He needed another cortisone shot, but according to protocol, would need to wait a few more days before the next stick.

With Reed, the Knicks' defensive anchor, lumbering at half speed, the usually aggressive Knicks struggled out of the gate. After about four minutes, the Knicks had yet to grab a rebound. Three minutes later they were down by eleven points. The Knicks rallied briefly, but the 76ers just kept running. Archie was the prime Knick slayer tonight. He "methodically dissected" All-Star Walt Frazier, holding him to twelve points and racking up thirty-three (shooting fourteen-for-twenty from the field).

"THREE AND A HALF GAME LEAD AND DWINDLING," blinked the Spectrum scoreboard after the home team finalized the 127–99 blowout. Oh, what a Year of Hoopla!

CHERRY HILL, NEW Jersey, March 14, 1971. Archie reached for the gym bag, checked his pockets for the car keys, and stepped out the front door. A chill hung in the air, and the sun had begun to set in the west. It was a metaphor for the state of his marriage. He and Valerie were having problems.

Archie drove through the first stoplight and continued on his usual route to the expressway. Maybe he should look for an apartment in Philadelphia. His thoughts drifted from the tensions at home to those last night at the arena. The 76ers had dribbled out a lousy game in Atlanta, though Archie had dropped twenty-nine points on rookie Pete Maravich. After the Atlanta victory Maravich confessed to the ever-present mob of reporters that he was pleased with his defensive effort. It was his eight-for-twenty-one shooting from the field that got his goat. The reporters scribbled it all down, as though Paul McCartney were dishing on his life as a member of the Beatles. Up was down, and down was up.

As the Philadelphia skyline rose along the horizon like pieces on a chessboard, Archie considered tonight's rematch with Maravich and the Hawks. Jack Ramsay should have been as tense as a bowstring about clinching a playoff spot. But the third-place Celtics had eased Ramsay's blood pressure two nights ago. They had eliminated themselves from the playoff race with an untimely loss, handing the 76ers second place (they weren't going to catch the Knicks) and a first-round playoff date with the Baltimore Bullets. Playoff tickets would go on sale in two days for $5 and $7 a pop.

After Archie and his teammates had changed into their uniforms, Ramsay repeated his locker-room plea from last night. He reminded everyone that the team's goal during training camp wasn't to make the playoffs. The goal was to avoid a first-round knockout and advance to the championship rounds. Was everyone still in agreement? Ramsay asked his players to commit to beating Baltimore. That commitment started tonight with a defensively dominant team victory over the Atlanta Hawks.

All hands joined into a huddle. One, two, three. Archie and eleven other voices repeated the same willful, monosyllabic vow of strength. That strength propelled them to an eighteen-point lead midway through the second quarter. That should have been the ballgame right there. As Hawks coach Richie Guerin admitted, his team might have had trouble on some nights stopping a good church-league team.

Enter Archie's college teammate Lou Hudson. With Maravich missing his shots more often than not, the ball started sticking in Sweet Lou's hands. He knocked down a jump shot, then another, and Guerin decided to run the offense through His Sweetness. Why not? Billy Cunningham remained a little under the weather and Jim Washington was inactive; that meant overmatched reserve Fred Foster was the next man up to wave a hand in Hudson's face. When Foster faltered, Ramsay countered with the slow-footed veteran moxie of Bailey Howell. That only made matters worse. By the final buzzer Hudson had forty-three points, and the Hawks had a 130–125 victory. "One of our worst performances in months," Ramsay complained.

Ramsay stood face to face with a perpetual NBA problem. He had a good, not great, team that felt worse for the eighty-two-game NBA wear. How could Ramsay breathe a second wind into a worn-out, injury-plagued band of brothers for the playoffs?

---

*Jack huffed and puffed, but we didn't find a second wind. The Bullets beat us in seven games. I had a productive series, but let me tell you, it was tough for me mentally because my thoughts were riveted on Valerie, the kids, and what to do next. I remember Billy Cunningham coming over to me in the locker room at halftime of game six and asking, "What's wrong, Archie? Come on, let's go!" Everything was all bottled up in my head. I had to sort it out.*

*So did Jack Ramsay after the Baltimore series. Ramsay Ball had failed to win a playoff series for the third straight year, and Jack's pressing defenses were almost old hat. Teams were better prepared to break the press, and they just didn't turn the ball over that much anymore. But come rain or shine, Jack still had us pressing every night, and the* wear and tear had left me and everyone else on the team worn down. The tired looks became a real problem against the better teams because our bench was so short.

Several years later Jack would move on to Portland and win an NBA title with center Bill Walton as his star. The title would secure his reputation as a Hall of Fame coach and vindicate his basketball philosophy. But minus a dominant center like Walton and a hard-nosed enforcer like Maurice Lucas, Ramsay Ball was in serious trouble.

# 20

*Valerie and I decided over the summer to split up. She got the kids and the house in Cherry Hill, and I moved into an apartment in Philadelphia's Center City. If all went well, I wouldn't be there long. I needed to make a clean break, and that meant leaving the 76ers.*

*I decided to force the issue via Sonny Hill, the color commentator on the 76ers' radio broadcasts. He was a trusted friend who was also on good terms with Jack Ramsay. I told Sonny to let it slip to Jack that I wouldn't be opposed to a trade. So sure enough, Sonny dropped the hint, and I crossed my fingers that a trade would be forthcoming.*

*Playing for Jack was like my other bad marriage. It was just a bad match. Jack was like a high school coach who demanded complete trust from his players to let him run the show and dazzle them with his command of the game. Well, I was a thirty-year-old pro. This was business, and I wanted to win. While I certainly wasn't out to rock the boat, if I saw something questionable or unfair happening, I'd speak up about it. That's always been my nature. My directness made me expendable. I wasn't Jack's kind of guy.*

---

Philadelphia, September 11, 1971. GM Don DeJardin had been floating Archie's name around the NBA as possible trade bait. No deal so far. That meant Archie would depart tomorrow for training camp and the start of year four in Philadelphia.

Archie was told to arrive bright and early with the other sixteen roster hopefuls at Temple University Hospital for physical examinations. After the just-say-ahs, a charter bus would transport everyone to the Poconos, where training camp would open at the University of Scranton. Five days later the 76ers would relocate to the beaches of Fort Pierce, Florida, for a week. Stealing a page from Major League Baseball, Philadelphia and Atlanta had decided to hold training camp this year in balmy Florida, where they could scrimmage and try out an inaugural two-team Grapefruit League.

The good news was that Billy Cunningham would be in Scranton. Whether Cunningham would be among the Grapefruit Leaguers, nobody knew except the Honorable Judge Edwin Stanley. He would render his verdict shortly on whether Cunningham must honor his contract with the ABA's Carolina Cougars. In Sixerland folks weren't holding their breath.

WEST PALM BEACH, Florida, September 23, 1971. Still no trade.

Archie's twenty-points-per-game talent should have been highly coveted. But his large contract was proving difficult to move. Unlike Jerry West and Walt Frazier, Archie had never been on the cover of *Sports Illustrated* or endorsed a pair of sneakers. Prospective teams worried that bringing a top-tier but underrated guard to town wouldn't spike ticket sales, and most general managers believed any veteran bearing a $135,000-per-year price tag had to deliver lots of box office bang for his big bucks.

Archie kept the faith. The preseason was still young. But he couldn't help but scan the lay-up line and wonder about the woeful state of the Sixers. Veterans Bailey Howell and Connie Dierking had retired; reserve forward Bud Ogden had been waived a few days ago; and regulars Hal Greer, Jimmy Washington, and Wally Jones remained holdouts.

A collision of rookies competed for the open roster spots, led by first rounder Dana Lewis of Tulsa. Drafted as a big-bodied clone of Baltimore's Wes Unseld, Lewis was handed the job of starting center in training camp, and veteran Luke Jackson shifted to forward. A week later Jackson shifted back into the post, and Lewis landed on the team's third unit. Only time would tell if the 76ers had blown another first-round draft choice.

"The overall pool of talent was so depleted from when I had arrived in Philadelphia four years ago," said Archie. "I looked around and had to pinch myself sometimes. The practice gear and logo were the same. But it was like preparing to go to battle with new enlistees. Something had to give."

A few hours later it finally did. Hal Greer rolled into the team hotel signed, sealed, and looking relieved to start his fourteenth season as

Mr. 76er. The next day brought more good news. Judge Edwin Stanley had unexpectedly thrown out the ABA's lawsuit against Billy Cunningham. The boy from Brooklyn would remain in Philadelphia.

TRENTON, NEW JERSEY, OCTOBER 8, 1971. Hal Greer, now doubling as an assistant coach, held a clinic tonight on the art of the mid-range jump shot, popping in ten of thirteen tries during the 76ers' next-to-last preseason game against Atlanta. Less appreciated was the clinic that Atlanta forward Jim Davis held on the art of the rebound. After another seemingly uncontested rebound and score from Davis, a red-faced Jack Ramsay signaled referee Don Murphy for a time-out and looked like he was ready to explode as Philadelphia center Dennis Awtrey ambled to the sideline. "Knock somebody down!" Ramsay lit into Awtrey. "Kill 'em! You can't let 'em push you all over the floor."

After the game reporters inquired about the team's continued troubles inside. Ramsay seemed taken aback. "My evaluation right now is that our center situation should be better than last year," Ramsay intoned. "We have the same people, and I would anticipate they'd improve."

The reporters looked quizzically at each other. All recognized that Awtrey had been awful in the preseason; the injury-riddled Luke Jackson was a shadow of his former self; and the team's top rookie, Dana Lewis, might lose his roster spot to last season's first-round bust Al Henry. Was Ramsay being disingenuous? Or could he no longer see the NBA forest from the trees?

Philadelphia's notoriously tough press corps had been critical of Ramsay in the past. But none dared to question his credibility as a basketball coach. He was, after all, Dr. Jack. In year four of the Ramsay Era questioning Dr. Jack's credibility as an NBA coach suddenly became fair game. The city's cynics with pens eyed the 76ers' dismal roster and saw what Archie had seen all along. Dr. Jack had a serious blind spot for the game-changing utility of one-on-one NBA talent.

"For years [Ramsay] was a master tactician at St. Joseph's College, where he took players with a minimum of talent and molded them into formidable teams," wrote the *Philadelphia Evening Bulletin*'s Al Richman. "He would kneel on the sidelines at the Palestra and direct his players with the precision of a youngster sending toy soldiers into battle." Richman continued: "Ramsay came to the NBA, where he saw the Celtics and the Knicks and finally the Bucks win championships with great team play. He intends to build up an organization in Philadelphia that will produce the ultimate in team play. His 76ers will be an extension of the Ramsay personality, which is warm to the team player but ice cold to the individualist of the NBA."

Richman may have overstated his case. Ramsay certainly allowed his players to improvise within the offense at times. But like an alarm clock, Ramsay would tick, tick, tick and finally ring out instructions that reasserted the snap and precision that marched in his head—or an isolation play for Cunningham.

In the meantime the bad decisions continued. Baltimore had recently offered to swap Earl Monroe straight up for Archie. The 76ers declined. Although Monroe and his arthritic knees likely could have met Ramsay Ball halfway, Dr. Jack had no interest in adapting his coaching philosophy to suit the skills of one of Philadelphia's most beloved sports figures. In typical Ramsay fashion he passed up an All-Pro, future Hall of Famer and potentially huge box-office draw to inquire about the availability of Monroe's backup, Fred Carter. He was a better defender.

HOUSTON, OCTOBER 14, 1971. Archie felt the tightening, then came the familiar burning sensation. There went his hamstring. Archie stopped in mid-stride and pulled up limping and grabbing the back of his thigh. In the distance the figure of Al Domenico continued to run like a little monkey. Archie had bet the wisecracking Domenico after today's practice that he could let him get halfway across the floor and still beat him in a footrace out of the gym.

Domenico huffed back to declare himself the fastest man in the universe and reached into his leather bag for an ace bandage to keep any swelling down. But it was no use. The hamstring remained tight overnight. After scoring twenty-nine points last night and lifting the 76ers to a season-opening road win over Chicago, Archie would have to miss tomorrow night's game against the now Houston Rockets to put his hamstring back together again.

PHILADELPHIA, OCTOBER 18, 1971. Though the pulled hamstring remained cranky, Archie assured Jack Ramsay that he would be ready to play in the next game against Seattle. Ramsay nodded but seemed strangely aloof, almost indifferent. That wasn't like the coach. Archie didn't want to overanalyze the encounter, but did Ramsay know something that he didn't know?

Archie got his answer late that evening, when the phone rang unexpectedly. He picked up the receiver, and an unfamiliar, overly sedate voice announced, "I'm Jerry Sachs, the general manager of the Baltimore Bullets. I wanted to be the first to let you know we just finalized a trade with the 76ers. You are now a member of the Baltimore Bullets."

After two weeks of on-again, off-again trade discussions Don DeJardin had finally squeezed the trigger. In exchange for Archie, an undisclosed amount of cash, and the 76ers' second-round selection in the 1973 NBA draft, the Baltimore Bullets unloaded guards Fred Carter and Kevin Loughery. Ramsay would applaud the two-for-one deal as solidifying his backcourt, and DeJardin would pat himself on the back for lopping off about $50,000 from the payroll and parting with a player who wanted out.

In truth it was another silly 76er giveaway. The Bullets parted with two good backcourt men to get a higher value, top-tier NBA guard. Archie would pair with fellow top-tier guard Earl Monroe. Baltimore now featured the most dynamic backcourt in the league. Archie had originated the hard crossover and step-back moves in the NBA, while Monroe had popularized the spin move and an assortment of double-clutch shots released from odd angles. As the 1970s NBA continued its slow evolution toward a more athletic, one-on-one style of play, hardcore NBA fans could look to the future in Baltimore and just sit back and say, "Wow."

Maybe that's why Sachs wanted to be the first to tell Archie about the trade. As the Bullets' general manager bounced from point to point, Archie punctuated the conversation with brief answers to his occasional questions. "The hamstring is fine. . . . Yes, I'm looking forward to playing with Earl."

Although Archie was thrilled to start his career anew with a contender, business was still business. He had to speak his mind. "We all know it's the last year of my contract," Archie remembers saying. "I'd really like to get my new contract worked out."

"What we'll do is when you get to Baltimore, we'll tear up your current contract. We'll start a new one and get everything squared away."

"Before I start playing?" Archie asked.

"Yes."

## 21

*Before I left for Baltimore, I called my old agent, Fred Rosenfeld, and asked him to negotiate my new contract. Fred said sure, he'd fly to Baltimore. I related my conversations with Jerry Sachs, and that was that.*

*The Bullets put me up in the new Holiday Inn downtown until I found a place to live. I hadn't been there more than a day when the phone rang. It was Fred. He said he'd met with Sachs and not to worry. Everything was fine. But Fred shocked me when he said he was flying back to Los Angeles. I said, "What about my contract? The agreement was I would have a new contract in place before I started playing for the Bullets. I thought you were going to handle it." Fred said there was nothing to handle. Sachs told him the contract would have to wait a few days. [Owner] Abe Pollin was out of town.*

*Now I'm as mad as a hornet. I'm angry with Fred for being wishy-washy, and I'm ticked off at Sachs for lying to me. From my perspective we had a deal. My big concern was that once I reported to the Bullets and became their "property," they gained the upper hand. The Bullets could just name their price and tell me to take it or leave it. I had to get the contract squared away while the trade remained in the headlines. That was my only leverage. I hung up the phone with Fred and started thinking about the situation. I decided that I needed to talk to Earl [Monroe] about a few things before I made my next move.*

---

**B**altimore, October 20, 1971. Earl "the Pearl" Monroe popped open the driver's side door of his silver-blue Cadillac El Dorado, reached across the console, and opened the lock on the passenger's side. The passenger door immediately swung open, and into the seat angled Phil Chenier, a quiet rookie from the University of California.

Chenier settled into the leather seat and pulled the car door shut. He was living the dream. Not only had the twenty-year-old just turned pro, but an NBA great had also befriended him. Every morning the

Pearl and his tail-finned El Dorado breezed in front of his hotel to drive him to practice. And tonight the Pearl had swung by to take him out to dinner. How cool was that?

Monroe slipped the car into gear, and they rolled through the darkness past abandoned storefronts and the tired urban grit that was 1970s Baltimore as wisps of white steam vented cauldron-like from street grates. "I've got to stop and see a buddy of mine," said Monroe. "You might know him. Archie Clark. He just got traded to the team."

"I don't know Archie, but I know who he is," Chenier answered.

"We need to talk about something. We'll just go by there for a minute."

A moment later Chenier found himself standing in front of a hotel door. Monroe knocked. The door clicked, and Archie greeted Monroe like an old army buddy. In a way, they were. The two had teamed over the summer to conquer Philadelphia's Baker League.

Archie shot a puzzled glance at the light-skinned figure that accompanied Monroe. "This is Phil," Monroe jumped in to dampen the confusion. "He's one of the rookies on the team. I'm trying to show him the ropes."

"Nice meeting you," Archie softened, sticking out his hand in welcome. After the exchange of a few more perfunctory comments, Archie's demeanor hardened, as though returning to an unpleasant thought.

"Look Phil, we're about to talk some business," Archie said. "Why don't you go down to the lobby and wait."

The door clicked shut, and Archie launched into the details of the last twenty-four hours. He explained how Jerry Sachs had promised him a new contract, and Baltimore owner Abe Pollin was nowhere to be found to keep the promise. Here the Bullets were one signature away from securing the most dynamic backcourt in the NBA, and rumor had it that Pollin was in Oregon attending his niece's bat mitzvah. A bat mitzvah?

Archie remembered something else. In the middle of today's press conference to introduce him as the newest member of the Bullets, a journalist asked for his thoughts on Monroe's pending trade. Archie knew the twenty-seven-year-old Monroe wasn't fond of Baltimore, but a trade? Now? Archie played it cool with the reporter. "I wouldn't have wanted to come here without Earl," he replied. "Maybe my coming will help him decide to stay."

Now Archie needed to know the truth. Monroe answered that he wasn't quite sure of his plans. He said the Bullets had sweet-talked him into a lowball rookie contract and underpaid him on his current deal. His knees hurt every day, reminding him that his career could end tomorrow. He needed to make some money.

"Why don't you take time off from the game and get your knees right?" Archie encouraged.

Monroe didn't answer—and with good reason. There was more to the story than Monroe was telling. In this new age when unhappy NBA players lawyered up to air their grievances, Larry Fleisher, the attorney for the then NBA Players Association who doubled as Monroe's agent, had arrived in Pollin's office a month ago with the Pearl in tow. Fleisher had informed Pollin that his client would no longer play in Baltimore and requested a trade to one of the following teams: Philadelphia, New York, Los Angeles, or Chicago.

Pollin, a gangly man in his late forties, with short black hair combed over a high, narrow forehead and eyes that alternated between doleful and penetrating, took the news hard. Pollin liked to think that he formed strong personal bonds with his players, and Monroe in particular was like a member of his family. After mulling his options, Pollin finally advised his staff to make a few exploratory phone calls. The reported asking price: $250,000 to get Monroe, plus two name players. Chicago balked. Philadelphia wanted reserve guard Fred Carter, not Monroe.

At Pollin's request Monroe had agreed in good faith to start the season in Baltimore while a trade was brokered. No hard feelings. Yesterday another of Pollin's proposed trade deadlines had passed without news, and Monroe was getting antsy.

All of the above was a little overwhelming, and Monroe, nicknamed "Clam" by Baltimore reporters for his propensity to clam up in interviews, seemed unsure of how or even what to confide in Archie. As much as he wanted to play with Archie, events had overtaken that possibility.

Monroe rose from his seat, explaining he and Chenier needed to grab dinner. As Monroe reached for the door, he reminded Archie that the Bullets had practice tomorrow afternoon. Monroe chuckled that Archie would face his own boot camp of sorts. Gene Shue, a former NBA player and incurable gym rat, would be waiting to play Archie one on one. That was how he welcomed new additions to the team.

FORT MEADE, MARYLAND, October 21, 1971. Archie stood dribbling the basketball at the top of the key. Staring back at him in a crouched defensive stance was Gene Shue. Archie unleashed a quick series of head and shoulder fakes. Shue scuttled crab-like backward. Archie gave a hard feint right and crossed over his dribble to the left. Shue scuttled forward, but it was too late. *Swish.*

Shue, though an All-Pro eleven years ago, was pushing forty and in no shape to chase NBA jackrabbits. He called it a game and clapped practice to order. If Jack Ramsay was Dr. Jack, Shue was just plain Gene. He was a happy-go-lucky guy from working-class Baltimore who believed in the power of positive thinking to win friends and influence basketball games. His Dale Carnegie approach (and the trio of Earl Monroe, Gus Johnson, and Wes Unseld) had helped turn around this once woeful franchise, and Shue had earned NBA Coach of the Year two seasons ago for his trouble. But Shue could claim another remarkable NBA distinction. He held down a second job selling life insurance for the Penn Mutual Company. Shue tended to his phone calls and paperwork on most mornings before trundling off to practice.

If Dr. Jack placed his system before his talent, Gene was the consummate players' coach who patiently, resourcefully, and of course positively molded his strategy around his available talent.

Shue clapped for everyone's attention and asked his players to walk through a few more of the team's set plays for Archie. Later Shue paired his players for shooting drills, and Archie found himself toeing the free-throw line with Monroe.

"I've got to get my contract straight," Archie confided. "I'm not showing up for tomorrow night's game." Archie was referring to Baltimore's rematch of last season's Eastern Division championship series with the arch-rival New York Knicks.

"Neither am I," nodded Monroe.

After practice Archie called Fred Rosenfeld for an update. Rosenfeld said Baltimore's numbers were disappointing. Archie told Rosenfeld to make another phone call tomorrow afternoon. Tell Sachs thanks but no thanks.

BALTIMORE, OCTOBER 12, 1971. The special announcement reached the anxious hands of Johnny Dark, the public address announcer for the Bullets. Dark, better known around town for his day job as the hip voice on "the Big Sixty" WCAO-AM, grabbed the big metal microphone. The clock overhead read 8:10—or five minutes before tipoff. "Ladies and gentlemen. May I have your attention please."

As the 7,700 fans complied by degrees, Dark read from the sheet of paper: "The Bullets regret to announce that neither Earl Monroe nor Archie Clark are in uniform tonight. When they failed to report for tonight's game, the Bullets announced that they are placing both of them under suspension."

The usual jeers and catcalls followed, but Dark persevered. He said the Bullets were sorry for the inconvenience—so much so that everyone in the house could receive free admission to the Chicago game in early November. Some cheered; most grumped.

Jerry Sachs stood off to the side absorbing the moment. It had been one of his longest days since joining the Bullets. Fred Rosenfeld had called him at noon. Rosenfeld said that unless the Bullets tore up Archie's current contract and offered him a suitable new one, he would look into voiding the trade. At 3:00 Larry Fleisher called Sachs. Fleisher told him his client's career with the Bullets was over. Baltimore must trade Monroe immediately, he said, or the Pearl would sit out the season or, if the price was right, jump to the ABA.

Sachs called Abe Pollin in Oregon and said something comparable to, "Are you sitting down?" Pollin approved the suspensions without pay. That was standard NBA policy when players refused to play. But in this era of agents and growing labor unrest neither Sachs nor Pollin knew exactly what to do next.

Pollin told his general manager that he had no intention of racing back to Baltimore two days early. Pacify the fans, he said. Stall the media. Pollin said he would consult with NBA commissioner Walter Kennedy to iron out his options. In the meantime he had a bat mitzvah to attend.

Dark's public-address announcement took care of the fans. Sachs and Gene Shue took care of the press. Puzzled reporters asked why Archie would go AWOL after practicing with the team yesterday afternoon. It's just a big misunderstanding, they answered. "As far as Clark is concerned, he's satisfied with his present contract but wants to extend it," fibbed Shue. "We're willing to do that, but we're waiting for Mr. Pollin to return from Portland."

---

*My holdout lasted exactly two games. While waiting for Abe Pollin to return, Jerry Sachs told me about Larry Fleisher's latest phone call and how Earl was pretty much out of the picture in Baltimore. I was shocked.*

*Although my preference was to play with Earl, his departure made me see my situation in a new light. I was the only veteran guard in Baltimore, and Gene Shue had nobody but me to run the team. After three seasons on a fairly tight leash in Philadelphia, I would have total freedom to play basketball. You know, that was very appealing to me to test my talents and see how good I could be in the NBA when given the chance.*

*Sachs said he wanted me on the floor ASAP. But he warned that it might take a couple of weeks to finalize the new contract. I said okay, and Sachs assured me that the contract would get done. I took him at his word and ended my holdout. The Bullets issued a make-believe statement from me that falsely threw Fred Rosenfeld under the bus for staging the contract dispute. The front-office propaganda was that agents were bad for pro basketball.*

MILWAUKEE, OCTOBER 25, 1971. "Good evening, [this is the] Downtowner Motor Inn. How may I direct your call?"

"Room 418."

Gene Shue heard the click of the motel operator transferring his telephone call, then the familiar, deep-throated "hello" of Charles McGeehan in Room 418. McGeehan covered the Bullets for the *Baltimore News American*.

"Archie Clark will be here tomorrow," Shue said. "That's all I can tell you right now. Except not only is this terrific, but it's fabulous."

The following morning Shue and the Bullets' young trainer, Skip Feldman, were all smiles when Archie arrived at Milwaukee's Timmerman Airport. Shue must have told Archie five times on the drive to the motel that he was thrilled to have him in uniform for tonight's game.

The reasons were obvious. The defending Eastern Division champions were in disarray. Gone were guards Kevin Loughery, Fred Carter, and Earl Monroe. Perennial All-Star Gus Johnson was recovering from knee surgery, and Wes Unseld, the team's 6-foot-7 linchpin, was listed game to game following his offseason knee surgery and now chronic problems with his ankles.

That left holdover Jack Marin and five new additions to log the majority of minutes, and Baltimore's patchwork lineup wasn't working. "We played our best the other night against Cleveland, and we still got beat," admitted Shue.

Shue considered that Archie brought the veteran leadership and toughness that was lacking. He told Archie not to worry about memorizing the plays. Just play ball. Think of tonight as a dry run of better things to come.

And dry the run certainly was. The Bullets, with zero team chemistry, shot a dismal 34 percent from the field for the game, while the defending world-champion Bucks couldn't miss. Milwaukee built a thirteen-point first quarter lead, extended it to nineteen at halftime, and never looked back.

Afterward in the locker room Archie looked like a basketball player on loan. He wore a loud, unfamiliar orange uniform with the equally unfamiliar number forty-four and no name stitched on the back. Archie's dry run continued tomorrow night at home against the struggling Detroit Pistons.

BALTIMORE, OCTOBER 27, 1971. The Bullets' locker room ranked above average in the NBA for space and comfort. Where it scored poorly was logistics. Tucked away like a custodian's closet on the second floor of the Baltimore Civic Center, it presented no obvious route for the uninitiated to arrive downstairs onto the court.

Archie, as the new addition, had been advised not to trust the freight elevator. What goes up doesn't always come down. The safer bet was to find the stairwell, scamper down two flights of stairs, and exit onto the back of a darkened performance stage, where all of the day's most popular musical acts had shouted their "Hello, Baltimore's" at one time or another. Archie was told to keep moving across the wooden stage and trot down to the walkway that led to the polyurethane sheen of the basketball court.

As Archie stepped onto the polyurethane tonight for his home debut as a Bullet, he scanned the Civic Center's odd three-sided design. To the north, south, and west rows of white upholstered seats terraced from the floor up to the ceiling like any big-league arena. But to the east, behind the other basket, a pleated cement wall extended like a giant ceramic kilt straight up toward the roof. Below the pleats at ground level stood the performance stage, veiled by a set of temporary bleachers.

The Bullets always ranked near the bottom of NBA attendance, and for tonight's contest against the Detroit Pistons the turnstiles clicked in at a measly 3,718 paying customers. The reasons for the empty seats ran the sociological gamut. Baltimore was a football town, and its neighborhoods were extremely working class and often tight for money. But most of all, Baltimore was in the midst of a mass middle-class exodus to the suburbs. Coaxing moms and dads back at night to a ho-hum arena with spotty sightlines was tough. So was combating public perception of Baltimore's rampant after-hours crime and still rollicking red-light district, known simply as "the Block." In this devil's half-acre, backlit and popping like the Midway, burlesque shows whooped and hollered into the wee hours, and the barkers outside sold the got-to-see-it-to-believe-it charms of Irma the Body, Tempest Storm, Princess Domay, and of course the beautiful Blaze Starr.

Jerry Sachs rolled out all of the tried-and-true promotional stunts, from frequent fan handouts and hosting NBA doubleheaders to tonight's "Nickel Beer Night," sure to send the harder drinking souls stumbling to the Block afterward for a nightcap.

But Archie was convinced that the Bullets were better than their record. He had watched forward Jack Marin position himself in the corner during yesterday's shoot-around and knock down one twenty-foot jump shot after another. Rookie Phil Chenier wasn't far behind Marin in his marksmanship. For Archie that was something to work with as a playmaker. He could fake his defender out of position, drive to the basket, and pitch the ball back out to Marin or Chenier. Maybe it would work to build some offensive rhythm.

Tonight it did against Detroit. Marin knocked down six straight long jump shots to start the game, and the nameless number forty-four found the open man all night to give the Pistons a chemistry lesson. Butch Van Breda Kolff, the basketball purist in his second season with the Pistons, stood speechless. He needed a nickel beer.

BALTIMORE, NOVEMBER 11, 1971. The hydraulic whirr stuttered, and then Bullets PR man Jim Henneman felt the elevator groan to an abrupt, bone-jarring halt. Henneman jabbed the button for the lobby. Nothing. He punched again and took a deep, God-help-me breath.

Henneman had just mimeographed this morning's big announcement and flown out of the Bullets' office suite on the fourth floor of the Civic Center. Why he kept pressing the button for the freight elevator instead of taking the stairs, he didn't know. But now Henneman hung suspended in a metal box somewhere between the first and second floors, clutching this afternoon's read-all-about-it: "Bullets Trade Earl Monroe to New York."

Abe Pollin had called with the news last night from Phoenix, where he was attending the latest two-day NBA Board of Governors pow-wow. Pollin said he had just finalized a trade that sent Monroe to New York for reserve forward Dave Stallworth, injured swingman Mike Riordan, and $450,000 in cash. Henneman, a former newspaper reporter, had hammered out the press release embargoed for noon. Jerry Sachs waited impatiently downstairs for Henneman to hand him the magic words.

Ten tense minutes later the elevator jolted, and the hydraulic whirr continued its programmed descent and found the ground floor. The double doors thankfully scraped open, and Henneman darted off to the media room.

"Where have you been?" Sachs whispered.

"I got stuck in the elevator."

Sachs spilled the news to the assembled throng, and a few hours later the headline dribbled out onto the radio and into the afternoon edition of the *Baltimore Sun*. The Monroe era was officially over. Now it was time for Baltimore to shake and bake.

BALTIMORE, NOVEMBER 13, 1971. There was a new Rave in town. Dave "the Rave" Stallworth arrived as the newest active member of the Baltimore Bullets. The former Knicks' sixth man, who was known for his versatility, took the injured Gus Johnson's job. The 6-foot-7 Stallworth also arrived with another intangible. "I already knew all of Baltimore's regular plays," he explained, having faced the Bullets and their same generic numbered half-court sets so often during his five NBA seasons.

Gene Shue offered Bullets fans a promise: "We're going to be a different team now," he said, explaining that Stallworth plugged the final hole in his starting lineup. His New Bullets were built to play tight defense, run the floor even more aggressively, and find the open man on offense.

The engine in the middle that would make it all go was center Wes Unseld, now back in uniform. Big Wes, built like a pro football lineman—only wider, with "thighs like Greek columns" and calves "so thick that they look[ed] like they should have bark on them"— squeezed rebounds and, as Shue envisioned, snapped his two-handed slingshot to Archie near midcourt well ahead of the pack. If teams cheated and dropped players back to protect their basket, Archie had two of the NBA's better stop-and-pop shooters in Jack Marin and Phil Chenier in his wake. "Watch us win all over again," Shue crowed. "Not immediately though."

Shue's point was that the New Bullets would spend the next several weeks putting their own house in working order. That house, he calculated, would be sturdy enough to win the four-team Central Division (Baltimore, Atlanta, Cincinnati, and Cleveland) and give the archrival New York Knicks or defending champion Milwaukee Bucks a run for the roses in the Eastern Division playoffs.

Tonight the New Bullets would try to get it right against none other than the Philadelphia 76ers (9–4). Archie certainly bore no ill will to his former teammates. He had parted on good terms with everyone, except possibly Jack Ramsay. But he had nothing to say to Dr. Jack. Archie's newfound freedom and more able supporting cast would do all the talking. And sure enough, Philadelphia's perennially weak frontline was no match for Unseld on one of his more mobile nights.

Down big early in the fourth quarter, Ramsay finally threw every zone press in the book at the Bullets. The extra pressure made things interesting for a while. But Unseld kept outletting the ball to half court, and Archie (twenty-seven points and eleven assists) kept finding the open man to thwart the Philadelphia comeback.

When Archie dribbled out the clock, the overhead scoreboard flashed in orange: Bullets 111, 76ers 105. Make that New Bullets 1, NBA 0.

NEW YORK, NOVEMBER 20, 1971. When Archie had last seen Earl Monroe, the two were preparing to walk out on the Bullets. Tonight they reunited before the Bullets-Knicks game, six weeks the wiser and pondering the same question: had their jousts with management been worth it financially?

For Archie the answer was a frustrated "Who knows?" Jerry Sachs of course had promised a new contract. Unbeknown to Archie, Abe Pollin had no intention of fulfilling Sachs's promise. Pollin, upset that Monroe had broken his contract and alarmed by the agent-driven, anything-goes culture that seemed to have the NBA by the throat, refused to humor Archie's request. For Pollin right was still right, a deal was still a deal, and a contract was still a binding agreement. Archie had to fulfill the terms of his current contract. Then they could talk.

Caught between a promise and a hard place, Sachs seemed to take the easy way out. He strung Archie along, telling him that the new contract would be ready soon but never committing to a deadline. Archie, nobody's fool, grew ever more distrustful of Sachs. But Archie decided not to push too hard. He was off to the best season in his NBA career. He ranked among the NBA leaders in scoring and assists, his turnovers were low, his shooting percentage was high, and his defensive prowess was unquestioned. As Archie told himself, all of the numbers tipped in his favor. Sachs would have to live up to his promise in the end.

Monroe had signed a two-year, $300,000 deal that paid him real money up front. The problem was that Monroe's transition from being the NBA's Godfather of One on One to being a consummate team player was off to a choppy start. Monroe had totaled just nineteen points off the bench in three games with the Knicks and continued to contend with painful bone spurs in his left foot, which had him assigned to limited duty tonight against the Bullets.

Monroe and his bum foot creaked through just five spotty minutes of action to be exact. But the veteran Knicks made the extra pass, clamped down defensively, and played by far their best game in weeks. When the Knicks wrapped up the 125–114 shellacking, Gene Shue looked like he needed to dive into the shower with his players. It was just one of those crappy NBA nights.

FORT MEADE, MARYLAND, November 25, 1971. The New Bullets suddenly had dropped three in a row. As Gene Shue knew, the NBA talked. Boy, did it talk. The word was out that to scuttle the Baltimore fast break, stifle Wes Unseld's outlet passes.

Shue, shooting baskets per usual after practice, had no brilliant countermove up his sleeve to keep the New Bullets firing from all chambers. His bench was thin; his options were few to help the ailing Unseld. Dave Stallworth wasn't quite the answer after all. The injured Gus Johnson, who had teamed with Unseld in seasons past to pick the backboards clean, had dressed for practice today. Shue watched him carefully. His former All-Star still could barely jump or move laterally. It was sad to watch such a superhuman athlete reduced to a mere mortal. If only that mere mortal could give him a solid, twenty-five minutes per night of rebounding moxie, the New Bullets would be back in business.

Shue noticed swingman Mike Riordan, a bulky white plaster cast covering his broken left wrist, running sprints to stay in shape. "Up for a game of one on one?" Shue asked. Riordan nodded.

The two immediately started jostling full court. Shue dribbled the ball in place like he was pounding a drum and bumped Riordan backward to inch his way closer and closer to the basket. Riordan retaliated by thumping his coach with his cast. The 6-foot-4 Riordan, scheduled to join the Bullets in a week, was as tough and cagey as NBA veterans come. He also ran the floor like he'd been shot out of a cannon. That begged another question for Shue: could he possibly rebound?

# 22

Los Angeles, January 17, 1972. The pilot stuck the landing, and the big commercial jet rumbled along the runway for several seconds before decelerating to ground speed. Bells dinged, and Muzak infused the cabin with good cheer. "Ladies and gentlemen, welcome to Los Angeles International Airport, where the local time is. . . ." Archie, traveling from Phoenix with teammates Jack Marin and Wes Unseld, unbuckled the seatbelt and inched his way toward the exit with all of the other carry-on-laden passengers in coach.

The three Bullets would represent the Eastern Conference the next day at the NBA All-Star Game at the Forum. Marin was thrilled to appear in his first All-Star game. Big Wes felt duty bound to appear, although he would have preferred to be home resting his aching knees and ankles. Archie, meanwhile, wasn't sure what to make of his second All-Star appearance. It was the "been named" part that rankled. Archie should have been voted by the media as a starter ahead of New York's Walt Frazier. The numbers didn't lie. "I can play with anybody," Archie had explained before departing Phoenix. "You look back and check the games I played this year against Walt Frazier—or anybody. In terms of production, I outplayed them. That's all, I'm saying."

For Archie the slight was more of a ding to his business plans than his ego. Being recognized as one of the top two guards in the Eastern Conference would have bolstered his case for a healthy raise whenever he finally met with Jerry Sachs to negotiate a new contract. But the league continued to let the twenty-six newspaper beat reporters vote on the first seven roster spots for each conference, and that meant a landslide of tired ballots for Frazier, Kareem Abdul-Jabbar, and the league's established superstars. Archie had to wait on the coaches to fill out their final roster spots.

Archie grabbed his suitcase and caught a ride from the airport to Century City, headquarters for this year's All-Star game and the fashionable new business district in West Los Angeles. Century City had risen over the past decade from 178 acres of backlot movie sets plowed asunder in a real-estate fire sale that kept Twentieth Century Fox from bankruptcy on a bad motion picture deal. Where plywood western saloons once stood, red convertibles now cruised along the tony Avenue of the Stars with its ultramodern high-rise office and apartment towers laid out in "the geometry and the gee-whiz of an erector set." This is where the ultra-rich from neighboring Beverly Hills came for fine dining and Hollywood moguls worked the phones in their offices negotiating motion picture deals.

Archie scanned the new high-rise buildings along the Avenue of the Stars. Most of the gleam overhead had been under construction when he played for the Lakers. So Archie had no idea where he was until he felt the car suddenly turn into a long entranceway that led to the front door of the crescent-shaped, twenty-story Century Plaza Hotel, with its low-rumbling bank of water fountains and porters in red beefeater costumes who greeted all like visiting English royalty.

It was precisely this pomp and circumstance that the aristocratic Jack Kent Cooke, host of this year's All-Star bash, hoped to impress upon his many splendored friends: his record-setting Lakers and the NBA equaled world-class entertainment. From all indications Cooke's high-class offensive would face no embarrassing disruptions. Sam Schulman, last year's cancer on the league, was in remission. The ABA had been on its best behavior, and the union man, Larry Fleisher, hadn't organized any last-minute player strikes. In fact jolly was the mood downstairs in the lobby. "Every five feet, you trip over an NBA coach," quipped a reporter, "most of whom even shaved for the occasion."

Tonight all would eat, drink, and be merry. For tomorrow night ABC would preempt its regular programming to bring American living rooms what amounted to a two-hour, prime-time pro basketball infomercial with some of Hollywood's brightest stars conspicuously dotting the crowd.

Archie lugged his suitcase off the elevator and followed the numbers to his hotel room. When he unlocked the door, he noticed that the wait staff had placed a chocolate mint on his pillow in a show of hospitality. And that was just the start. In what constituted high-class lodging in early 1970s America, all of the rooms in the Century Plaza featured a color television set (as opposed to the usual black-and-white boob tube), brocade toilet paper, two varieties of scented soap, bath oil, an alarm clock (to replace wake-up calls), a retractable clothes line, and even a small roll of Life Savers.

The only thing missing was a steamed-and-pressed men's suit waiting in the closet. Archie had forgotten to pack one, and he needed one to look smashing for tonight's All-Star banquet, a $25-a-plate roast beef dinner and a chance for fifteen hundred basketball junkies to mix socially with the game's brightest stars. NBA commissioner Walter Kennedy already had spread the word to the All-Stars. Attendance was mandatory.

ARCHIE ARRIVED FASHIONABLY late for the banquet. Assembling his wardrobe had taken longer than expected. But once the ensemble was complete, Archie looked dapper enough to run for mayor of Century City. "They're sharp threads all right," Archie answered a nod of approval as he passed into the banquet hall. "But they're rented."

The late entry into the banquet hall drew anxious stares and renewed the buzz over two still unfilled seats at the head table. Wilt Chamberlain and Kareem Abdul-Jabbar, the biggest names in pro basketball, remained conspicuous no shows. Chamberlain had filmed a television commercial that morning and sent his last-minute apologies that he was too tired to attend. Jabbar, meanwhile, was in a bind. He had imported a Mercedes for his mother that had finally arrived at the Port of Los Angeles, and Jabbar needed to hire someone to drive it cross-country to her in New York. Or so the story went. The wicked (false) rumor working the banquet hall was that Chamberlain had skipped tonight's event to throw his own bash, and Jabbar had joined him.

As Archie settled into his seat, middle-aged white men in black ties waxed on at the podium in forced, back-slapping hilarity. Actor Lorne Greene—oh, he of the Shakespearian voice—commanded the microphone for the presentation of a special plaque to the newly retired Elgin Baylor. Greene already had dragged on in his grandiloquence two minutes too long, determined to roast Baylor with a string of really bad one-liners. "Elgin has scored more than Richard Burton and handled more passes than Raquel Welch."

Greene ended with an obligatory dumb-blonde joke and returned the microphone to Chick Hearn, the trusted voice of the Lakers and tonight's toastmaster. It was Hearn's turn to make the rounds and banter with each All-Star for about thirty seconds without drawing too much attention to the missing 7-footers. He teased Walt Frazier about his exotic elephant-skin jacket, praised Billy Cunningham, and bantered with Wes Unseld.

"What about Gus Johnson?" asked Hearn.

"What about him?"

"Are his knees going to be okay?"

"Gus is getting old," Unseld deadpanned.

Laughter.

Hearn sidled over to Archie and ribbed him like an old friend that All-Stars usually stick with one team. Archie had played for three. "I'll probably move again next year," Archie interjected, drawing more laughs.

ARCHIE LOGGED TWENTY-ONE minutes in the All-Star game as the first guard off the bench. He'd played against Jerry West and Gail Goodrich too many times to count. All that was different were the crowd's giddy oohs and ahhs at beholding the best of the best assembled on one floor. Archie dribbled past All-Star Jimmy Walker. The crowd oohed. Boston's Dave Cowens rattled in his soft left-handed jumper. The crowd ahhed. But with the game on the line late in the fourth quarter, Archie sat uncomfortably on the bench with Jack Marin and Wes Unseld. Crunch time belonged to the starters.

That was just dandy for Jack Kent Cooke, sitting courtside in his designated seat with his mother and sister down from his native Canada. Cooke let everybody know a little too adamantly that he was having the time of this life. NBA basketball was fabulous, and so was the Forum.

Not if you were a reporter. Cooke had banished the Fourth Estate far from the floor in a ten-row cluster starting at row thirty-two. With less than three minutes to play and the outcome still undecided, NBA publicity man Nick Curran hurried to row thirty-two to collect the votes for the game's most valuable player from eighty or so reporters. Curran trudged back downstairs with less than two minutes to play, found a semi-private place to tally the votes, and scratched his head. Dave Cowens and league icon Jerry West had tied for top honors.

Curran faced a logistical nightmare. He needed to race back to row thirty-two for a run-off ballot that would take at least twenty minutes to tally a second time. He didn't have that kind of time. The West Coast ABC affiliates would scream bloody murder if the game ran over into the eleven o'clock time slot, which was reserved for the news and lots of local advertising dollars. Just then West came around a screen to drill the game winner. Curran made an executive decision. Jerry West it was.

## 23

*The Bullets remained in first place in the Central Division with a losing record. People asked, "How can a loser be a winner?" Let me put it like this. The pieces were there for an upper echelon team, but we had a gaping hole. Gene Shue had hoped Dave Stallworth could play power forward. He couldn't. Dave relied on finesse. He was no more a power forward than I was. By default that made Gus Johnson our savior. Once Gus got healthy, we would be a winner.*

---

C ollege Park, Maryland, January 22, 1972. For the first time this season Gene Shue had all his big guns in uniform for today's win over Portland. The parts equaled an impressive NBA whole in Cole Field House, the Bullets' second home this season in preparation for their move to Washington.

There was Gus Johnson back, "grunting like his old self on the defensive boards." He and Wes Unseld vacuumed up most of the misses, and Archie sailed ahead on the fast break with Jack Marin and Phil Chenier filling the lanes. "Clark penetrates and simply because he does, when he passes the ball, there's always something you can do with it," observed a courtside reporter.

Shue liked what he saw—that is, if Johnson could remain his grunting, growling veteran self, if even part time. Shue, the positive thinker, wanted to believe he could, but Johnson's lateral movement remained pained. He had no cartilage in his left knee and almost none in the right one. How could two bone-on-bone knees endure the strain of thirty-four more regular-season games? But for one night the Baltimore Bullets were back at full strength. Though his knees were packed down in ice to prevent them from swelling, Johnson and his booming bass voice animated the locker room. "I was getting up real high and colliding with Wes in midair," he boomed. "It was like old times again."

COLLEGE PARK, MARYLAND, January 30, 1972. Exactly seven years ago today the former Lewis Ferdinand Alcindor had visited Cole Field House and lost the only game of his storied prep career to Washington DC powerhouse DeMatha Catholic. "I don't want to say anything about my first visit," snapped the current Kareem Abdul-Jabbar upon entering the doorway to a bad memory.

Inside the ABC broadcast duo of Keith Jackson and Bill Russell stood backlit at half court. Jackson welcomed viewers to Cole Field House and set up the storyline for today's NBA *Game of the Week.* America would see a midseason clash between the hottest two teams in pro basketball. The world champion Bucks (42–11) looked at times unbeatable, while the resurgent Bullets (24–26) had claimed four straight and eleven of their last fifteen games.

It was the Bullets that looked unbeatable in the first half, thanks to the defensive muscle and sheer will of Wes Unseld. Big Wes consciously hurried down the floor and planted his double-wide frame, sumo wrestler–like, on the exact spot where Jabbar liked to operate with his back to the basket or, in basketball vernacular, in the post. Jabbar, forced to waste valuable time and energy trying to uproot this 6-foot-7 tree trunk of a man, jostled himself out of rhythm and breath and either passed the ball back outside to a guard or settled for a rushed, slightly out-of-range sky hook.

On each sky hook Unseld leaned on Jabbar's non-shooting lead arm to upset his balance, pivoted toward the rim, and rose into the air with his legs spread wide in a "V" and elbows bowed to fend off other rebounders. Unseld more often than not squeezed the miss in his large hands, sending Archie and the now healthy Mike Riordan sprinting to the other end of the floor. As the two sailed in for one uncontested lay-up after the other, the Milwaukee guards finally got smart and cheated back on defense. No problem. Archie went one on one to create a seam to the basket and either broke free to the rim or fed Jack Marin waiting on the perimeter for an open jump shot.

The Bucks, trailing by thirteen at the half and tired of contending with Messrs. Clark and Unseld, decided to commit the NBA equivalent of a misdemeanor: play a zone defense. Each Buck would guard a designated area of the floor, not opposing players as the league rules clearly stipulated. The zone would sag in the middle like a bad mattress, keeping three Bucks near the basket at all times to outnumber Unseld and stifle Archie's game-changing penetration.

Many NBA referees preferred to look the other way on zone defenses. Blowing the whistle only led to heated sideline debates over a complicated and utterly subjective calculation of defensive time, space, and rotation.

"Milwaukee's in a zone," Shue wailed at lead referee Ed Rush. Rush ignored him.

So did the crowd. New to NBA basketball and with no allegiance to a team from Baltimore, the Washington crowd cheered for Jabbar, as he started lofting his poetic sky hooks into the bottom of the net. With 3:10 left in the third quarter the Bucks took the lead on a Lucius Allen free throw. Seven seconds later Rush blew his whistle and, like a bad joke, paraded to the scorer's table and barked a belated warning to Bucks coach Larry Costello: "Quit the zone."

Costello complied, more or less, and the NBA *Game of the Week* turned into a fourth-quarter thriller. With thirty second left and Milwaukee up by two, the ball batted into Archie's hands, with Oscar Robertson and Jon McGlocklin to beat. Archie faked, whirled between them, and felt McGlocklin bump him hard with his hip. The bump, coming in mid-whirl, sent Archie contorting in all directions, like he was free-falling down an elevator shaft. He somehow semi-righted himself to scoop a shot that kissed the rim once, twice, and fell out.

"That was a foul," stomped Shue.

The Bucks rebounded Archie's miss, and tic-tac-toed the ball to the waiting Jabbar for the game-winning dunk. Take that, DeMatha Catholic!

COLLEGE PARK, MARYLAND, February 13, 1972. A cast now encased Wes Unseld's severely sprained left ankle, hurt in last week's game against Chicago. Without him the Bullets seemingly couldn't beat a CYO team. They dropped all four games on the latest West Coast trip, and the bad times continued this afternoon against the Los Angeles

Lakers in the nationally televised NBA *Game of the Week*. The losing streak now stood at eight.

Archie departed Cole Field House soon after the game, driving through a downpour along Interstate 95 to Baltimore and his room at the Holiday Inn. He'd played like an All-Star out west, racking up big numbers and carrying the team on his travel-weary back. But Archie was stuck in the same problem that had hounded his NBA career from day one. He kept landing on teams that, because of injuries or bad choices, struggled with weakened frontlines and couldn't win consistently.

According to Shue, the best was yet to come. He'd assembled his New Bullets and introduced everyone to his system, heavy on defensive pressure and the fast break. Now, as the third phase, the New Bullets had to learn to pull together and win the close ballgames. Archie hoped for the best. He just wanted to win.

Archie was thinking about buying a condominium in one of the unfamiliar names on the green exit signs that kept blurring in and out of his line of vision: Columbia; Cockeysville; Catonsville. The rumor was that Abe Pollin was hell-bent on moving to Washington as soon as humanly possible, and Archie wanted to hedge his geographic bets by getting a place somewhere equidistant between the two cities.

The new contract of course still hung like a cloud over Archie's head. Jerry Sachs kept promising a fair contract but kicking it like a can another month down the road. Archie humored him, mostly because his productivity remained high. As Archie kept repeating, the Bullets would have to pay him sooner or later. He was one of the top three guards in the league.

BALTIMORE, FEBRUARY 15, 1972. Wes Unseld had the plaster cast sawed off his ankle, and he returned to the Bullets' starting lineup tonight against the struggling Houston Rockets. With tighter defense and Unseld and Gus Johnson vacuuming up the misses, Archie (twenty-nine points) was off to the races again, either slashing to the hoop or kicking out passes to forward Jack Marin, whose jump shot was lights out all night. By the third period, the Bullets leading by twenty-five points, the only drama left was pugilistic. Houston's middleweight, Mike Newlin, and Phil Chenier came to blows. But all drama ceased when the heavyweight Johnson, bad knees and all, raked a right cross in the direction of Newlin. Newell dropped his mitts. He wanted no piece of Big Gus.

The Bullets (25–34) remained the best team in the losing Central Division. Reporters dubbed it the Losers' Division, the Subtraction Division, and the Last Chance Saloon. "If you remember . . . a lot of people were making jokes about us winning the division [last season] with a record of 42–40," Shue rebutted. "But we went all the way to the championship finals."

BALTIMORE, FEBRUARY 21, 1972. By noon another winter squall had dumped four inches of snow over Baltimore, ensuring a light turnout for today's nationally televised rematch between the Bullets and 76ers. But the show would go on. A production truck bearing the black-and-white corporate logo of ABC Sports had pulled up to the Civic Center hours ago to begin the slow installation of three mounted banks of overhead lights, the latest technological advance to illuminate the NBA *Game of the Week*.

With the flick of a switch the hot white lights bathed the basketball court and temporarily blinded the players. Archie missed his first three shots looking into that God-awful glare. But pupils adjusted, and all went well until about three minutes left. The heavy electrical draw finally blew a fuse, and the bank of lights went black and took the overhead scoreboard offline with it.

After workmen finally restored power, the game seesawed to a Baltimore time-out with twenty-five seconds left. Philadelphia 101, Bullets 100. Archie got the ball, with rookie Dave Wohl waiting in a defensive crouch. Archie immediately motored right on the dribble, rubbing the rookie into the brick wall named Wes Unseld. Archie came open off the screen while two 76ers raced over to slap a hand in his face. Too little, too late. Archie launched a soft eighteen-footer from the right corner.

Lost somewhere in the archives of ABC Sports is one wicked "woe Nellie" from the NBA *Game of the Week*'s play-by-play man, Keith

Jackson. Archie's game winner gave Baltimore a four-and-a-half-game advantage in the race for the Central Division title. Gene Shue wasn't quite ready to pass out victory cigars, but the skies momentarily were blue again. After their early February swoon the Bullets had rebounded to win three of their last four games. Maybe Shue was a genius. But was phase three working?

BALTIMORE, FEBRUARY 23, 1972. Gene Shue ordered the doors to the locker room closed. No reporters allowed. The Genius, ecstatic two days ago, now felt that familiar gnaw of exasperation. He needed everybody's attention. Eying his players, he asked in so many words: Why can't we win the close games? Of Baltimore's thirty-seven losses this season twenty were by eight points or less. Among the missed opportunities was tonight's predictable fourth-quarter collapse to the Milwaukee Bucks. The Bullets had led from the opening tap until the final 2:29, when Kareem Abdul-Jabbar and the Bucks' bigger front-line muffled the Bullets to win by eight.

Shue announced he'd done all that he could. It was now up to the players to work harder and finish this season strong and playing as one.

Archie listened to Shue's breakdown of the last-minute collapses as attentively as a graduate student in a lecture hall. He'd always been one to speak up in Philadelphia if Dr. Jack's lecture overlooked a key fact. Archie's comments were always analytical, never personal. Right now his new professor in Baltimore seemed to be contradicting himself, calling for the Bullets to share the basketball and work for better shots in the final minutes of the game. Shue had given Archie the green light months ago to take the game-winning shot in close games. Archie asked for clarification. Did the final shot still belong to him? Or was it now open to all comers?

Shue's mind seemed to go blank. He stammered for an answer that started with the word "team" and ended pragmatically in Archie's indeed taking the final shot. Archie posed another question. Other voices chimed in, and Shue stepped back to stay above the fray.

Outside the heavy metal doors ears strained to decipher the muffled voices inside. The muffle rose to a few competing, inaudible shouts, and the reporters pressed their ears to the doors to capture some telling word or phrase. No luck. After thirty minutes of this Shue finally emerged and assured everyone outside that all was well inside the locker room. "We just talked things out," he said. "Everyone talked. But it wasn't what you'd call a team meeting. We've been losing a lot of close games, and I wanted to find out the reasons why."

All was indeed okay in the Bullets' locker room. Despite a little heat-of-the-moment tough-guy talk, the criticism remained constructive. Everyone seemed to stand on common ground, agreeing to sweat the details and, above all, solve the nightly rebounding woes. Gus Johnson, all could now agree, wouldn't be their late-season savior. Shue was right. Phase three was up to them.

LOS ANGELES, MARCH 5, 1972. Hallelujah! The New Bullets strafed Wilt Chamberlain, Jerry West, and the Los Angeles Lakers, 108–94, holding the best team in basketball to under one hundred points for the first time this season while shooting over 60 percent from the field. Phase three, though still wrapped in far too much gauze and tape, was complete.

"We did just about everything right," beamed Jack Marin about the hot shooting. "Archie set things up beautiful, but Gene [Shue] has gotten through to us on that. It's now flexible, but disciplined."

"You could sense [the Lakers'] apprehension," Archie said. "We were sustaining the pressure on them like we haven't on other good clubs."

Shue's *It's a Wonderful Life* moment of beating—no, embarrassing—the Lakers continued as word reached the locker room that Atlanta had lost tonight. The Bullets' lead now stood at four games. They had the Central Division title in the bag.

SEATTLE, MARCH 7, 1972. Gene Shue had never looked happier all season. The Bullets jumped all over the Seattle Supersonics tonight, 105–98, to sweep their four-game West Coast March of Death. The now hottest team in basketball had extended its lead over Atlanta to four and a half games with ten regular-season contests left. "Unbelievable, this is unbelievable," Shue repeated. "Do you realize we held four West Coast teams under 100 points in four games? Beating them all is one thing, but our defense is something else again. It's twice as unbelievable."

The Bullets now had three whole days to kick back until their next game, and Archie (nineteen points and eight assists) needed the rest. Woody Sauldsberry had advised him long ago that it wasn't in an NBA player's best interest to suit up while sick or injured. But Archie had pushed Sauldsberry's words and his stomach flu aside on this road trip. His shooting percentage had suffered, but Archie's sacrifice and heady veteran play may have just turned around the Bullets' season.

The operative word was "may." The Bullets boarded their flight home the next morning with starters Phil Chenier and Jack Marin on crutches. Both had slipped during the game and sprained their left ankles in the same exact spot on the basketball court. The floor was dry, though oddly the slippery spot was near where the facility's leaky roof had brought down Spencer Haywood a few days ago. While the litigious Supersonics prepared to sue the city for failing to repair the roof of the Seattle Center Coliseum, the Bullets prepared to have the injuries evaluated more carefully once they landed in Baltimore.

BOSTON, MARCH 19, 1972. Boston's radio announcer, Johnny Most, sounding as raspy as a three-pack-a-day longshoreman, repeated today's final score before signing off for the evening: Bullets 125, Celtics 112. What Most didn't mention was that he'd mostly wasted his breath on this one. The Bullets came, they saw, and they conquered a tired Celtics crew to claim the Central Division title once and for all in mostly non-dramatic fashion.

"It's a tribute to Gene [Shue]," Archie (twenty-two points) told reporters afterward. "We've had some rough days this season and some losing steaks. When you lose, you can have an attitude problem. But this team has come together, and now we're really streaking at just the right time."

There were no cases of champagne stacked and waiting in the locker room this afternoon for a wet postgame celebration. Just the usual postgame six packs of soda and beer stuffed into the metal garbage can near the locker room door, compliments of Red Auerbach and the Celtics. Shue's sentiment was that the Bullets had achieved nothing just yet. Beat the Knicks in the playoffs, and the champagne would flow like the healing waters of Bethesda.

---

*We split our first two games against the Knicks. For game three in Baltimore I made an adjustment. Part of my strength was going right because if you didn't stop me going right, I'd go all the way to the basket and lay it up on both sides of the rim. But if you stopped me from going right, I had a crossover going to the middle. Nobody wanted me to cross over. So good teams like the Knicks forced me from the time that I got the ball [on the inbounds pass] to dribble up the left side of the floor. That was fine with me. I'd already worked it out. From the left side I'd kill you with my jump shot. That's why I say that I could play with anybody. Because all you had to do was show me what you were going to do, and I could adjust and do something different.*

*I had thirty-five points and nine assists in game three, which the Baltimore* Sun *raved afterward "will be talked about as long as one little kid is dribbling a basketball in Baltimore." It was just one of those NBA playoff classics. The lead seesawed back and forth, and then with about two minutes left Earl [Monroe] missed a breakaway lay-up. I hauled in the rebound, and Frazier landed on my back. I made both free throws to put us up for good, and, a pretty good fistfight later between Jack Marin and Phil Jackson, we ran out the final twenty-one seconds in a five-man game of keep-away that had the Civic Center on its feet in a loud roar that had been missing all season in Baltimore.*

*But the Knicks made a few adjustments and closed out this hard-fought series in six games. Afterward a photographer took a picture of me slumped at my locker, still in uniform, head in hands, and looking like I'd just finished the Boston Marathon. That picture said it all. I'd given everything I had in the playoffs and really all season to make this franchise successful. In the end the Knicks weren't necessarily better, just more cohesive and experienced.*

# 24

*The Bullets traded Gus Johnson and his bad knees to Phoenix for a second-round draft choice. With nobody on the roster ready to fill his shoes, that told us that the Bullets were shopping for his replacement.*

*Meanwhile, Jerry Sachs got the green light from Abe Pollin to get started on my new contract. He stopped telling me that we'd talk soon and started floating actual dates and times for our discussion. It was as though Abe was trying to get me to understand a few things: One, he ran the show. Two, his players were going to behave civilly to him. Three, I had to trust him to do the right thing on my behalf financially. In Abe's mind he'd earned that trust by being fair to his players.*

*Well look, I grew up in the projects. Life had taught me to be wary of authority and white middle-aged men who want to do you a favor. In my mind Abe already had broken his promise last November to set-tle my contract, and that made it hard to trust him. So I wasn't going to kowtow to Abe. Time would prove my instincts to be correct.*

---

Archie still could get steamed about last November. All that agent Fred Rosenfeld had had to do was deliver Archie's untimely ultimatum: give my client a new contract, as promised, or I'll advise him to hold out. Instead Rosenfeld had breezed into Baltimore, schmoozed with Jerry Sachs, and let the Bullets off the hook.

Archie decided then and there that he needed a new agent, and he settled on a guy in New York with a rising reputation: Irwin Weiner. He had gotten Knicks guard Walt Frazier a big contract. Maybe he could do the same for him.

The two talked by phone, and Archie told Weiner about a scheduled meeting in Baltimore with Sachs to launch the negotiation. Archie stressed that the trick would be to focus on his productivity last season. Archie's numbers didn't lie. He'd finished as the league's ninth-leading scorer and the fourth best assist man and had earned second team All-NBA honors.

"Whaddya makin' now?" asked Weiner in his thick Bronx accent.

"I made $135,000 last season."

"Whaddya askin'?"

Archie didn't really have a number in mind. But he was at the peak of his career, and this would likely be his last big NBA contract. Archie wanted to make the most of it. A number popped into his head, and he thought why not? It's always best to start a negotiation with an inflated demand to keep the final number high. "I want $375,000 a year."

WHEN ARCHIE MET Irwin Weiner, he imagined himself shaking hands with the popular comedian Red Buttons. Weiner and Buttons shared the same facial features, pasty complexion, and shout of red hair. But Weiner's shout was louder and longer, and the gold chains draped around his neck with his open collar and the tight polyester everything made him look like Buttons caricaturing a big-city hustler. Or a gangster.

Weiner squinted like a bag of nails. The narrowed eyes weren't a conscious effort to project an up-from-the-streets toughness. The man who chauffeured Walt Frazier around town had had cataracts since childhood. Weiner told his friends that his lifelong difficulty with reading had forced him to drop out of school. His brain was sharp as a tack, he assured, just not his vision.

This admission, punctuated with a crazy-as-a-fox wink and a puff from the ever-present cigar in his right hand, was but a rare detour in Weiner's otherwise bantering, high-energy, watch-me-go torrent of words and wisdom. Some found Weiner's shtick charming; others found it cloying. Right now Archie leaned toward the latter.

"I've got endorsements waitin' for you, magazine covers, the whole works," said Weiner, slightly whistling his S's in his stoic, flat, authoritative affect.

"Irwin, I'm not worrying about endorsements right now. I need a contract. Look, I can play with anybody in the NBA, but I didn't come into the league as a big star. So don't try to sell me like I'm Oscar Robertson. You've got to sell them on my productivity. The numbers speak for themselves."

Archie wasn't sure whether the man sitting in the passenger's seat had heard a single word. Weiner merely deflected their conversation back to his bustling life, his wonderful partnership with Walt Frazier, and now with Julius Erving. "The Doctor is sensational," Weiner repeated like a slogan.

Archie backed into a parking spot near the Civic Center, and the two entered through a side door where the elevator waited a few steps away to lift them upstairs to the Bullets' front office.

"Irwin, remember: productivity."

The elevator dinged, and Weiner squinted full steam ahead to charm and conquer.

"Jerry, how nice to meet you finally."

Jerry Sachs, dark-haired, conservatively dressed, and incurably upbeat, thanked Weiner for making the trip down from New York and transitioned into an apology. He hadn't had time to draw up a formal contract offer for today's meeting. Sachs explained he'd been working around the clock to beat the tight application deadline for Abe Pollin's latest foray into professional sports: a National Hockey League expansion franchise. The hockey moguls would decide in early June whether to place a team in Washington, and their yes or no balanced on whether Pollin could win formal approval to construct an arena, as he now intended, to expand his footprint in Washington sports. In April he'd purchased the lease on a sixty-acre swath of parkland near Washington in rural Prince George's County, Maryland, and he'd already started digging in the dirt to pour the foundation for his proposed seventeen-thousand-seat Capital Centre.

Sachs gushed a little more about the arena to come until Weiner bumped the topic aside to wax prosaic about the many splendors of New York, taking an odd ethnic detour to sausages. Weiner apparently loved kielbasa and bratwurst, chiding himself for not packing something smoked as a treat for everyone. Just wait, Weiner promised, he'd make everyone's mouth water on his next visit to Baltimore.

"I just sat there boiling," recalled Archie. "Here I am all business, and Irwin won't stop talking about sausage."

The meeting ended a while later with everyone hungry for dinner and having made no real progress on the contract.

"What were you doing?" Archie steamed.

"Archie, you can't go in there, put out your hand, and ask for money," Weiner rambled. "That's not how these guys operate. You've got to chat them up first, make them feel comfortable, and then go for the kill shot."

If Archie hadn't been so frustrated with Weiner, he probably would have burst out laughing. Pollin was a hard-nosed businessman, not a gourmand. Handing out smoked sausage wouldn't sway him.

Archie drove Weiner to Baltimore's Penn Station to catch his train back to New York. As Weiner stepped out of the car, Archie wished him well and silently thought, "What in the world have I gotten myself into?"

ARCHIE HEARD THE phone ring, picked up the receiver, and heard the baritone voice of Charlie Scott, the ABA expat now with the Phoenix Suns. The two had met a few years ago and remained friends.

"Archie, I just wanted to let you know that Irwin Weiner is putting your business in the street."

"What are you talking about?"

Scott recounted that he'd decided to look for a new agent, and a former ABA teammate had suggested Weiner. A meeting was arranged in New York, and Weiner drove Scott to Walt Frazier's plush Manhattan apartment to schmooze with him. In between puffs on his cigar Weiner mentioned that Archie was one of his clients and then snidely dismissed him as "a clubhouse lawyer." Weiner, in his opinionated but cocksure way, claimed that Archie didn't understand how to negotiate an NBA contract, and that was why he was having trouble finding common ground with the Bullets.

"He told me that you're asking for $375,000," said Scott.

"Oh yeah?"

Archie finished up with Scott and immediately dialed Weiner.

"Howz things, Archie?"

"Irwin, what are you doing telling everybody about my business?"

Weiner hemmed and hawed and tried to charm his way out of admitting to breaking a cardinal rule of agents: Thou shalt not weaken a client's bargaining position by telling the world his asking price.

Archie hung up on Weiner in mid-sentence. He booked a flight to New York and the next day stood face to face with Weiner in his office, calm but determined. "Irwin, we're done. I want you to release me from our contract right now."

Weiner glared back, partly squinting but clearly irked at the intrusion on his day. He typed out a release, snatched the sheet of paper from the typewriter, and handed it to Archie. Done!

JERRY SACHS WELCOMED the usual clatter of local reporters to the Civic Center press room on this sweltering Friday afternoon in late June. Sachs, sounding upbeat, explained that the Baltimore Bullets had hastily arranged today's press conference in order to deliver a major announcement: they had Gus Johnson's replacement.

Sachs continued through his pleasant meander of words before finally confirming everyone's suspicion: Jack Marin had been traded to Houston. It was the "in return for" part that nobody in the press corps could have imagined. The Bullets had just acquired NBA superstar Elvin Hayes.

The room immediately grasped the irony. In the lead up to the 1968 college draft the Bullets had famously called "heads" during the coin flip for the first pick and a shot at Hayes. "It's tails," announced Commissioner Walter Kennedy, and the Bullets settled for the second pick and the then inferior Unseld. Now the Bullets had effectively traveled back in time and called both sides of Kennedy's shiny silver dollar, snapping up Hayes and keeping their anchor, Unseld.

This big boil of a trade had started simmering last month at the NBA leadership conference in Phoenix, when Gene Shue had bumped into Houston general manager Ray Patterson. While swapping the usual NBA war stories, Patterson admitted that Hayes, the Big E, had worn out his welcome in Houston for feuding with teammates and delivering far below everyone's high expectations. Shue, long enamored with Hayes's versatility for a big man, eventually got the okay from Pollin to dangle Marin, one of the owner's fair-haired personal favorites, as trade bait.

Yesterday Patterson had packed up his troubles with Hayes and sent them COD to Baltimore. Al Ross, Hayes's controversial new agent, had been prepping to meet with Patterson when news of the trade broke. "The Baltimore Bullets?" Ross exclaimed. Patterson hadn't said boo about a trade yesterday during their meeting. Ross eventually let go of his surprise and thought strategically of the possible business opportunities presented by the trade. Archie Clark! Ross dialed a mutual acquaintance, scribbled down a telephone number, and cold-called Archie, with whom he'd never spoken.

"Archie, I represent Elvin," Ross said. "What would you say about working together on your contract? You and Elvin could negotiate like Koufax and Drysdale," referring to the then famous one-two pitching duo of the Los Angeles Dodgers.

Archie recognized immediately that this was just the leverage that he needed. Pollin's arena deal reportedly was on the rocks. Community activists in Prince George's County opposed having the monstrosity in their backyard, and the squabble seemed headed for the courts. That meant Pollin's newly awarded NHL hockey team now faced homelessness, and the last thing that Pollin needed was for his basketball team to implode. With Ross driving his usual hard bargain—and assuming Hayes dug in his heels for more money—Pollin would be backed into a corner of bad options. The easiest way out would be to swallow hard, entertain their inflated salary demands, and get back to fighting for his new arena.

"Where's Elvin?" Archie asked at the end of Ross's sales pitch.

"He's sitting right next to me."

"Let me talk to him for a minute."

"How're you doing Archie?" Hayes said.

"Elvin, are we going to do this thing together?"

"Yeah."

"Are you sure?"

"Yes."

"Well okay, tell Al that we have a deal."

Ross called Sachs and passed along the news that Clark was now his client. Ross also dropped a bomb: Hayes's contract would need to be renegotiated based on his new asking price of $300,000 per year—up from the $188,000 that he had reportedly earned last season—and he floated the then diabolical possibility that free agency—and an expensive legal battle—would be Hayes's next course of action.

Sachs relayed the bad news to Pollin, seven months removed and still smarting from getting his clock cleaned by agent Larry Fleisher in the Earl Monroe trade. He wasn't about to let another agent back him into a corner. Pollin called the Washington law firm of Arent Fox Kintner Plotzkin and Kahn. Yes, he wanted to take Hayes to court. A lawyer with the firm called back a few days later with good news. A hearing was scheduled for Tuesday afternoon, July 18, in the U.S. District Court in Houston.

THE BAILIFF, A six-shooter strapped to his side, called the next case: the Baltimore Bullets Basketball Club, Inc. vs. Elvin Ernest Hayes, the Honorable Allan Hannay presiding. Hannay, still mentally sharp but pushing a tired eighty years old, fumbled through the papers before him and in his soft Texas drawl asked the lawyers for the plaintiff to proceed. "Thank you, Your Honor," answered Pollin's attorney, Michael Jaffe.

Jaffe laid out the basic, indisputable set of facts and your-honored ahead to the highly disputable. He said Hayes had declared his intention to break his contract, pursue free agency, and visit tremendous financial hardship upon the Baltimore Bullets. Jaffe asked the court to consider ruling his existing contract "valid and binding" and, in the meantime, approve a temporary injunction that prohibited Hayes from discussing employment with or playing for any other professional basketball team.

Hannay scheduled another hearing for September and signed the temporary injunction, contingent upon the Bullets' posting of a $50,000 bond. Pollin, sitting near Jaffe, agreed to the bond, although he'd never need to post it.

About thirty minutes before today's hearing Pollin had asked to have a word in private with Hayes, leaving Jaffe to chat with Ross and his high-powered legal gun du jour, Leon Jaworski, soon to be of Watergate fame. Pollin repeated the same heartfelt message that Hayes had been hearing from his family for the past several days: quit listening to your agent and just play ball. Pollin then looked Hayes in the eyes and promised to give him a new contract. Hayes stared back, touched by Pollin's candor. Hayes nodded his head. They had a deal.

ARCHIE WAS THUNDERSTRUCK when he heard the news: Elvin Hayes had signed a million-dollar contract with the Baltimore Bullets. Al Ross had even attended the press conference. What happened to Ross's promised package deal? More important, why hadn't Archie been consulted about any of this?

Archie called Ross in Los Angeles. "Al, I thought we were going to do this thing together?"

"I'm not particularly happy about the latest turn of events either, but Elvin needed the money."

"Oh man," Archie exclaimed. "You tell me one thing, and then you go out and do another."

The conversation went downhill from there, and Archie hung up miffed and unsure of his next move. Spencer Haywood, Charlie Scott, and others swore by Ross as an agent who took no guff from management. But Archie no longer trusted him for squandering their golden bargaining position. What's more, with Hayes now signed, sealed, and delivered to team with Wes Unseld and Phil Chenier, Pollin had a relatively young, solid core of rising stars to move to Washington. Signing their aging All-Pro just became a need, not a necessity.

Strained though their relationship was, Ross continued to represent Archie through August, September, and into October. Sachs had flatly rejected Archie's asking price of $375,000 and—a key point to come—countered with a $135,000 offer that allowed the Bullets to exercise their option year on Archie's contract. Ross said he'd look into arranging a trade. Sachs said fine.

In Ecorse, where Archie closed out the summer, the frustration mounted. Irwin Weiner had fumbled the ball, Ross couldn't seem to run to daylight, and Pollin and Sachs were in a prevent defense. If Pollin and Sachs could string out the negotiation until September 12, the start of training camp, the pressure would be squarely on Archie to take the $135,000 and get on the court with Hayes, Unseld, Chenier, and a ball club that former NBA great Bill Russell said might just have the right stuff to win an NBA championship.

EVEN THOUGH ARCHIE still hadn't worked out a new contract for next season, he had managed to negotiate the purchase of a condo in the Baltimore suburb of Cockeysville. His new place was a short drive down I-83 to Towson State College, where the Bullets opened their preseason training camp in a small gym called Burdick Hall. But Archie wouldn't be joining his teammates for breakfast on the first day. He was in Ecorse. Frustrated by the Bullets' unwillingness to take seriously his $375,000 salary request, Archie decided to force the issue. He wouldn't report to training camp.

"Where's Archie Clark?" a reporter asked a few hours later in Burdick Hall. Gene Shue said he wasn't sure. By mid-morning Jerry Sachs admitted that Archie's no-show was related to his contract dispute. "I can't tell you how," vowed Sachs. "But I'm certain at this point that somehow, some way, all of this will be resolved, and Archie will be playing ball for the Bullets this season."

THE HOLDOUT HAD reached nearly three weeks. Abe Pollin stood firm on his $135,000 offer, and Jerry Sachs warned Archie that he would be fined a then pretty stiff $350 for each day of training camp missed. The missed days now totaled about $5,000.

Al Ross decided that the best strategy was to fight fire with fire and verbal hand grenades. "Every day they fine him, Archie's demand will go up another $1,000," Ross warned. "It's his constitutional right to stay home if he doesn't want to work."

For all his incendiary rhetoric Ross had succeeded only in torching all lines of communication with the Bullets. On October 3 Archie finally decided that he'd had enough. He picked up the phone and called Larry Fleisher, lead counsel for the NBA Players Association.

"Larry, I need to part ways with Al Ross. How would I fire an agent?"
"Just send him a letter."
"But what do I write in the letter?"
Fleisher thought a moment and rattled off the following:

Dear Al, This is to inform that I, Archie. L. Clark, am no longer in need of your services to represent me in contract negotiations. As of this date, October 3rd 1972, I am requesting that you discontinue any and all relationships on contract negotiations with any and all teams in the National Basketball Association and the American Basketball Association on my behalf. Please send me a bill for the services rendered.

Archie read the words back, and Fleisher said they would do the trick. Fleisher inquired about the holdout, and Archie confided that he was unsure of his next move. Ross had wanted him to drop his asking price, and Archie was still considering it. But he wasn't quite sure how low to go at the risk of leaving money on the table.

"Archie, I already know what everybody is making," Fleisher said, referring to a perk of being the attorney for the players association. "Why don't you let me represent you? I'm already working on contracts for Willis Reed, Lenny Wilkens, Paul Silas, and John Havlicek. I'll get you what you deserve."

"You want to do this for me?"

"Sure, I'll represent you."

Fleisher, Archie, and Sachs met a few days later in Baltimore, and the standstill took its first lurch forward in weeks. Fleisher, sticking to NBA salaries and player statistics, told Sachs that Archie ranked within the very top tier of NBA guards. Jerry West, now thirty-four years old, had just resigned with Los Angeles for $300,000 per year. Archie's numbers were on par with West's output last season, and he was three years younger.

Sachs scoffed at the analysis. But he did so knowing that Fleisher, unlike Ross and Weiner, had the front-office connections to pull another "Monroe" and move their All-Pro elsewhere.

"I'll tell you what we should do," Fleisher finally said. "Since you don't think Archie's value is where he says it is, let me go out and check a couple of teams and see what they're willing to pay him." Fleisher called Sachs a few days later with quotes of $300,000 per year from Buffalo and Seattle.

"Sachs shrugged off Larry's quotes," said Archie. "That's when I got another idea. The Bullets had offered me my former salary of $135,000 to exercise the reserve clause. But they'd forgotten to add in the signing bonus and loan that the 76ers also gave me and averaged them out over the course of the contract. They'd shorted me. I should be free to sign with another team."

Archie picked up the phone and called Fleisher.

"I think we've got them," Fleisher answered.

Fleisher called Sachs and explained the Bullets' blunder. "You've tendered a contract that wasn't prorated," he said. "So technically Archie's already a free agent. Why not sign Archie at a fair market price or just let him go?"

Sachs relayed the conversation to Pollin, who no doubt didn't take it lightly. A year ago Fleisher had forced his hand on Earl Monroe. Now Pollin's nemesis was about to strike again.

A FEW DAYS later Archie answered the phone.

"Hi Archie, Irwin here. How ya doin' today?"

The two hadn't spoken in months, and hearing his flat, just-listen-to-me-kid New York affect brought back a flood of unpleasant memories for Archie and immediately put him a little on edge. What in the world did Irwin want now?

"Whaddya think about playin' in the ABA? If you're interested, I can get ya close to what yer askin' from the Virginia Squires."

Archie's mind froze at the words "Virginia Squires." Weiner had walked off with Julius Erving, the prize possession of Virginia owner Earl Foreman. Why was Foreman still talking to him? More important, why were the two letting bygones be bygones over him? Weiner had to know that the low-budget Foreman couldn't come close to affording Archie's $375,000-a-year salary.

Archie pondered Weiner's offer. His new contract wasn't moving fast enough, and ABA offers came in handy at contract time to scare NBA front offices into action. Why not, he thought?

"Irwin, that's not really what I'm looking for. But I've always said that I'm open to any and all offers. If you want to have the Squires call me, I'll certainly talk to them. I'll talk to anybody."

Weiner said he'd be in touch, and Archie hung up with a shrug. Nothing would come of the phone call, he figured. Irwin was just being Irwin. Or was it that simple?

"ALL RISE," THE bailiff boomed. "The United States District Court for the District of Maryland is now in session, the Honorable C. Stanley Blair presiding." A door opened and into the courtroom stepped a tall, thin white man in a pleated black robe. He appeared to be in his early forties with an unusually long, oversized head extending above the robe, his black hair slicked carefully back.

Blair nodded down from the bench to begin the preliminary hearing, and the Bullets' legal team, led by the young attorney Michael Jaffe, launched into a tale of pro basketball woe. Jaffe said the Bullets had offered Archie Clark a contract extension in June worth $135,000 per season, which fully matched his previous salary and represented one of the team's highest contracts. He refused to sign. Jaffe pointed out that by offering to match—not cut—Clark's salary, the Bullets had visited no financial hardship upon him and therefore had every legal right to exercise the one-year option clause that was clearly stated in his contract.

Jaffe informed the court that the Bullets had credible evidence that Clark had not only refused to report to training camp and honor his team's legal right to an option year, but also that he was now planning to jump to the ABA's Virginia Squires. If Clark were allowed to walk out on his contract, the Bullets would receive no compensation and lose considerable revenue from fielding a lesser team through no error of their own. Also implied in Jaffe's statement was that the Bullets were in a race against time to stop Clark from jumping to the ABA and were fully justified in requesting today's emergency *ex parte* hearing (meaning in the absence of the other party). Archie wasn't in the courtroom and in fact still had no idea that the Bullets had taken legal action against him.

Had Blair, the former chief of staff for Vice President Spiro Agnew, known his basketball, he might have chuckled at the maudlin allegations. But Blair simply took them at face value and, pending a $50,000 bond from the Bullets to show their earnestness in this matter, granted a temporary restraining order that prohibited Archie from negotiating with the Squires or any other pro basketball team. Blair then set a hearing for October 24 to take a closer look at Archie's contract and the option clause.

By evening the Baltimore television and radio stations reported as fact the allegations presented at this one-sided hearing. Given Archie's holdout and the then almost unfathomable $375,000-per-year salary request, public opinion sided swiftly—and erroneously—behind Abe Pollin and the Bullets. Archie now was assumed guilty in the sports pages until proven innocent.

LARRY FLEISHER CALLED Archie with the bad news. The Bullets had slapped an injunction on him.

"For what?" Archie asked.

"To prevent you from jumping to the ABA."

Archie drew a blank. He hadn't been in contact with any ABA teams. Then he remembered his conversation with Irwin Weiner. His first thought was that Weiner had been running his mouth again, and somebody had alerted the Bullets. His second thought was that Weiner's phone call had been a setup. Maybe Abe Pollin or Jerry Sachs had put him up to it for an excuse to drag Archie, like Elvin Hayes, into court and gain the upper hand. These were only guesses, but that's all that Archie had to steady himself. He hung up with Fleisher and stewed for a moment about Weiner and the trouble that always seemed to follow him.

# 25

*When Abe Pollin threw me into court, it didn't intimidate me. It made me more determined to stand up for my rights. Now I was either going to get the money that I deserved or declare my free agency immediately and without playing an option year. With the help of Larry Fleisher I was ready to challenge the NBA's reserve system.*

---

**B**altimore, November 13, 1972. Peter Gruenberger glanced at his watch. He was due in federal court in an hour, and his flight kept circling Baltimore's Friendship Airport, stuck above an impossibly dense gauze of early morning fog that had closed all runways. Gruenberger signaled the stewardess and explained his predicament. She swished ahead to the cockpit, and the pilot radioed Gruenberger's SOS to the airport tower. One of the voices down below rogered and overed, promising to phone the court and ask its indulgence in delaying the start of Case 72–1050: the Baltimore Bullets Basketball Club, Inc. vs. Archie Clark.

When Gruenberger finally emerged from the fog and stepped into the hard glare of the courtroom, Archie and local attorney Franklin Goldstein, an old law school buddy of Gruenberger's, welcomed him to Baltimore. Gruenberger, a New York–based trial attorney in his mid-thirties with the A-list firm of Weil, Gotshal, and Manges, had litigated the NBA Players Association's recently filed antitrust case to block the NBA-ABA merger. At the request of Larry Fleisher, Gruenberger would represent Archie.

"All rise," the bailiff bellowed, rousing everyone to their feet.

Judge Edward Northrop, pinch-hitting today for Judge C. Stanley Blair and best known for his reactionary views on the Vietnam War, strode into place and bid a belated welcome to Gruenberger. As Gruenberger sat behind the defense table listening to Northrop deliver his introductory remarks for this non-jury civil trial, he formed two snap judgments about the man behind the gavel: a pleasant chap who doesn't know a thing about antitrust law.

Judge Northrop called for opening arguments, and the defense got its first opportunity to respond to the *ex parte* hearing and the public perception that the Bullets were the victims in this dispute. Gruenberger headed straight for the reserve clause. He didn't dispute that the Bullets had offered Archie $135,000 to play out his option year. Gruenberger said he questioned the math. Archie's previous contract included a $20,000 advance and $75,000 bank loan. If the sums were averaged over the life of the three-year contract, Archie had made more than $141,000 last season. That meant the Bullets, having miscalculated his salary, were underpaying him in his option year. Moreover, the $135,000 offer mistakenly—or perhaps cleverly—dropped the no-cut clause from Archie's previous contract, a sneaky way to cut Archie without owing him a penny.

Michael Jaffe, lead attorney for the Bullets, disputed all of the above. He argued that the option clause could indeed be invoked and that the solution to the contract dispute was staring them right in the face: arbitration. The aforementioned collective-bargaining agreement mandated that NBA players and owners must first attempt to resolve their contract disputes through arbitration before moving on to the courts.

Gruenberger objected that arbitration wasn't applicable. He reminded Judge Northrop that the Bullets may have offered Archie a contract on July 26, but they had dragged their feet on filing a grievance with the NBA, a first step toward arbitration, until November 2. A delay of a month? Maybe. But three months? What's more, by jumping straight to federal court, the Bullets had bypassed the arbitration process and forfeited their opportunity to use it.

Judge Northrop thanked the attorneys. Ten minutes later he returned to the bench, leaned into his microphone, and said, "Now I am going to render a short oral opinion in this case. . . . Is that agreeable to you, gentlemen?"

"Yes, Your Honor."

Judge Northrop then proceeded to reject Gruenberger's arguments one by one, stating that arbitration was clearly indicated in NBA contracts to solve salary disputes and that the Bullets had "exercised their right to arbitrate in a timely manner."

Gruenberger bit his tongue. "It was no secret why the owners liked arbitration," he said later. "You get compromises that you don't have to explain. There were no appeals, and the owners figured that they'd have the economic clout to keep appellate courts away."

With his preamble now concluded, Judge Northrup delivered his decision: "This court is of the opinion that this issue is not one properly before the Court, in that [Clark] has failed to exhaust the grievance and arbitration procedures available to him under the collective bargaining agreement between the National Basketball Association and Players Association," he said. "Have we had a preliminary injunction in this order?"

"A temporary restraining order," answered Jaffe.

Northrop nodded and immediately ruled, "The temporary restraining order is dissolved. A preliminary injunction is granted, and counsel for plaintiff will draft a proper order to be presented to me for my signature."

As Pollin exited the courtroom, he paused as if recognizing that Judge Northrop had just dealt him a winning hand and said, "Archie, call me at the office if you want to talk things over."

Archie nodded uncertainly and said, "I want to take two or three days to think things over."

Standing nearby were Gruenberger and Larry Fleisher. They were polite with Pollin, but they didn't particularly trust him. "Pollin loved his reputation as a philanthropist," said Gruenberger. "But behind the scenes he was very, very difficult. Pollin never gave an inch. He was always on the NBA committees that voted for the harshest penalties against players who tried to break with the reserve clause."

Gruenberger and Fleisher recognized the tough fight ahead with Pollin. Fleisher had already outmaneuvered him once with Earl Monroe. Could he do it again with Archie?

ECORSE, MICHIGAN, NOVEMBER 18, 1972. Several days had passed since Judge Northrop had rendered his decision, and Archie had reached a few heartfelt decisions. First, he wouldn't call Abe Pollin. As Archie saw it, he hadn't done anything wrong. Pro basketball was a business, and he'd merely tried to negotiate a contract as one businessman to another. Pollin had created the legal mountain out of a molehill and then cried victim. That wasn't fighting fairly, and Archie, harkening back to the sense of fairness that had always guided him, couldn't let Pollin get away with it.

Second, come what may, Archie vowed to see arbitration through to the end. What distinguished Archie from most of his NBA brethren was his ability to see the big picture on labor issues and take the long view. The big picture told him that he was "a well-paid slave," baseball star Curt Flood's description of pro athletes, and the long view beckoned free agency. The challenge was getting there. Nobody had succeeded, at least publicly, in baseball, football, hockey, or basketball. Flood had tried at great personal sacrifice, going the distance with baseball's reserve clause but losing his appeal for free agency last summer in U.S. Supreme Court.

Larry Fleisher would be there to help Archie through arbitration. But like Flood, Archie would stand mostly alone. His teammates, though now anxious to sign big contracts, still tended to defer to management to avoid conflict and the career-killing labels of "troublemaker" and "locker room lawyer."

Archie had a different view. Right was right, and underpaying one's employees was wrong. "What they're [the Bullets] offering me may seem like a substantial raise to them, but it's not in line with what the top players are commanding today," Archie clarified his position. "I know Baltimore isn't New York or Los Angeles. But a player should be paid for what he produces no matter what city he plays in."

But Baltimoreans weren't especially sympathetic to Archie's cause. The Bullets went public with their claim that Archie had rejected their latest verbal offer of $200,000 per year, which came to roughly $2,400 per game. Most Baltimore factory workers didn't bring home that kind of money in two months.

The longer Archie held out, the more mean-spirited grew the public resentment. The 1972–73 NBA season was now a month old, and the "New" New Bullets were carrying on without him. The word on the

Baltimore street was that the Bullets (8–9) may have happened onto Archie's low-cost replacement in unheralded rookie Kevin Porter.

Fortunately Archie wasn't around to hear any of it. He was hunkered down in Ecorse with his family, trying his best to keep his eye on the big picture and avoid the same unfulfilled fate as Curt Flood.

ECORSE, MICHIGAN, DECEMBER 14, 1972. Where was Abe Pollin? He hadn't floated a counteroffer in weeks. Nor apparently did Pollin feel the need to do so. Arbitration takes months, not days, and the NBA season moves quickly. The pressure was on Archie not to crack under the growing financial and professional strain to get back in uniform.

Today the strain ratcheted upward a notch when the NBA owners rejected Archie's request for immediate free agency. Larry Fleisher had filed the request with the NBA Labor Relations Committee, claiming the Baltimore Bullets had exercised the option clause improperly. The grievance admittedly was a shot in the dark. It drew a cursory hearing, and the Labor Relations Committee had reached the Soviet-style, one-line decision soon thereafter: the Baltimore Bullets had exercised the option clause correctly. No explanation included.

A few days later Pollin finally reemerged to re-offer Archie $200,000 to play out the remainder of the option year and a $1.2 million insurance policy should he suffer a career-ending injury. The Bullets also offered him the too-good-to-be-true promise of free agency at the end of the season. But maybe the promise wasn't so outlandish. Fleisher would intervene to ensure Pollin didn't blackball him. Maybe Archie could be the first "open" NBA free agent. As Pollin told him, "Only the lawyers win when you go to court. We need to settle."

Archie thought about it. He was dog tired of holding out. But Archie decided no. Right was right, and somebody had to take a stand against the owners. His true value, based on his production last season, was over $300,000 per season. So Pollin did what most savvy NBA owners would have done to break a player. He kept postponing the arbitration hearing. Pollin claimed to have scheduling conflicts while building his new arena.

BALTIMORE, JANUARY 4, 1973. After last night's cakewalk against the lowly Cleveland Cavaliers, Gene Shue rewarded his team for a job well done. Tomorrow's scheduled practice, he said, would be optional. That's why Shue wasn't surprised today to see just eight players straggle into their practice gym at the University of Baltimore. What dropped his jaw was the sight of Archie, dressed in his practice gear, entering the dumpy little facility a few minutes later.

"It was a complete surprise to me," said Shue. "He just showed up." Shue welcomed his absentee playmaker and rotated him into the four-on-four scrimmage. What was Archie doing there? "The holdout had kind of beaten me down," he explained, noting that he'd started tuning in regularly to Bullets games on television and radio. "I just wanted to get back out on the basketball court."

Archie worked up a good sweat but exited a while later back onto Charles Street to find his car. Beaten down though he was four months into his holdout—then the longest in NBA history—Archie wasn't quite ready to cave. Right was right, and he owed it to himself and the other players to challenge the system, like Curt Flood had done, and see this thing through to arbitration in two days.

NEW YORK, JANUARY 6, 1973. Archie arrived in New York to see the Seitz. That would be Peter Seitz, the wise legal mind that the NBA Labor Relations Committee and the NBA Players Association (namely, Larry Fleisher) had agreed should serve as the league's arbitrator. Both sides knew Seitz and respected his body of work as an arbitrator over two decades, most recently with the New York City Office of Collective Bargaining, which enforced the collective bargaining agreement between the city and its labor unions.

Archie, joined by Fleisher, squeezed out of the yellow cab that had pulled to the curb near 2 Pennsylvania Plaza, where today's arbitration hearing would be held in the NBA's office suite on the twenty-third floor. The two had hashed out the merits of their case in the cab, agreeing that there was reason to believe Archie could win this one. Abe Pollin and the Bullets had gotten a little sloppy in meeting the terms and conditions of Archie's option year, and Seitz, as a labor expert, "had a heart" for David and his union lawyers, not Goliath and his company men in Brooks Brothers suits.

But Fleisher recognized a possible complicating factor. Seitz might be especially inclined today to make nice with Goliath. This was Seitz's first sports arbitration, and he was savvy enough to know that it would be his last if he turned the sports world upside down by approving NBA free agency.

"Arbitrators are on a contract," Peter Gruenberger explained a point that Fleisher knew well. "They like to split [cases] and keep their own scorecards so that they don't get fired. Peter wasn't above doing that. Everybody understood that. It's a game that's played with arbitration."

When he stepped into the conference room for today's closed-door hearing, Archie exchanged a clipped hello with Pollin and Jerry Sachs. A few minutes later the door clicked, and Seitz entered the room, drawing the rapt attention paid to royalty. But Seitz was no King Olaf. He was a slightly built man in his late sixties, with a long, angular face dominated by droopy cheeks and gold oversized wire-framed glasses that magnified a pair of tired, slightly rheumy eyes belonging to a mere mortal.

This mere-mortal visage surprised Archie when its voice sounded so full of life. Seitz entered into a zippy round of hellos delivered with the urbanity of a gentleman and punctuated with the comedic turn of phrase of the vaudeville stage. The chuckles "at Peter being Peter" made Archie feel more at ease and in the moment. But his stomach remained twisted in a knot. Why all the lightheartedness? His NBA career was hanging in the balance.

Peter and his puns finally paused, and Seitz called the arbitration to order. Both sides reiterated the same arguments made last November in federal court before Judge Northrop. Fleisher, representing Archie today on behalf of the players' union, submitted a comprehensive, twenty-four-page brief to Seitz that detailed the reserve clause, the parameters for arbitration in the collective bargaining agreement, and the Bullets' clear muddling of both.

The Bullets' attorneys scoffed. Referring to their eleven-page brief and its alternative view of history, they told Seitz that the Bullets were faultless. They'd made Clark a timely, good-faith offer as stipulated by Paragraph 22 in the NBA's uniform player contract, the source of the option clause. Clark was the one who kept switching agents and refusing to state his intentions in what should have been an open-and-shut negotiation.

After Seitz asked for clarifications in his self-described, quasi-judicial role "to interpret and apply the agreements and understandings of the parties," the hearing dead-ended into an abrupt thank you. Seitz promised to deliver his decision within two weeks. Archie rose from his chair and exited the office suite to catch the elevator downstairs with Fleisher. His heart told him that he'd just won the arbitration. But a voice in his head reminded Archie to expect the unexpected. Nothing had been straightforward with this contract negotiation. Little did that voice know that the unexpected would come not from the crafty Abe Pollin but from the crafty man standing beside him in the elevator.

---

*The day before Peter Seitz was supposed to rule, I got a call from Larry Fleisher. Larry said he'd just spoken with Seitz, who told him that if he had to rule today, I would lose the arbitration.*

*I asked, "What did you tell Seitz?"*

*Larry answered, "I asked Peter whether he'd been in contact with the Bullets, and he said no."*

*Larry could be sneaky to get ahead, and he told Seitz, "Why don't you call the Bullets and tell them what you're telling us—but flip it the other way. Tell them that if you ruled today, they would lose." In other words, tell Abe Pollin that I was a few days away from becoming the first "open" NBA free agent and creating a gigantic, paradigm-shifting problem for professional sports. Seitz could claim that out of respect for Pollin, he was just giving the Bullets time to prepare for the decision.*

*According to Larry, that's what Seitz did. I wasn't in Baltimore to watch Abe Pollin and Jerry Sachs leap into action. But the next thing I knew Larry and Abe were talking. The negotiation that had been stalled for a year suddenly couldn't move fast enough, and I agreed to the terms of a three-year contract that very day. The Bullets prorated the half year that I was off. The second year was for $200,000. And then the last year was for $300,000. Best of all, it had no option clause.*

# 26

*After signing the contract, I flew to Los Angeles to join the Bullets on their West Coast trip. I remember sitting aboard that airplane and wondering whether the holdout had been worth it. Yes, I'd gotten the salary that I was demanding. And yes, I'd helped to show players that they could stand their ground and ask for a fair salary in line with what the market would bear. Owners couldn't arbitrarily dictate a player's worth, as had always been the case. But you know what? I didn't succeed in changing the NBA's labor system and becoming the first open free agent.*

*Forty-something years later I still ask myself sometimes whether the holdout was worth it. I had total freedom in Baltimore to play my game for the first time in my NBA career. Had I not held out, I could have had a second breakout season and shown what I was capable of doing when given the chance. But the holdout cost me forty-two games or roughly half of the NBA season.*

---

Los Angeles, January 16, 1973. Archie stepped out of the airport into a downpour. Rain had been falling for two days straight over the City of Angels. His teammates told him the rain was par for the course on this miserable West Coast trip. After the Bullets had landed in Portland a week ago, a super storm had howled with wind gusts in excess of fifty miles per hour. In Seattle there was a near Biblical deluge of rain. The weather was tame in Phoenix, the third stop, but the team's departing flight was delayed for four hours after its jet blew two tires.

The good news was that, rain or shine, the Bullets were on a roll. They'd won all four games, including this afternoon's impressive eight-point upset of the defending world-champion Lakers. "Biggest win of the season for us," beamed Elvin Hayes to Baltimore reporter Chuck McGeehan.

McGeehan finished up with Hayes and inched over to Archie to make nice. He'd been critical of the holdout, and McGeehan needed a quote for tomorrow's story. "How's it feel to be back?"

Archie glanced up, and McGeehan saw the excitement in his eyes. "I got a little winded and didn't have control of the ball, but I'm going to get back as fast as possible," Archie critiqued his twenty-four-minute season debut. "But, man, we are some kind of strong. We are going to challenge them all."

They exchanged thoughts on "some kind of strong." Rookie guard Kevin Porter was a real find. Phil Chenier was the most improved player in the league. "Iron" Mike Riordan was playing the best basketball of his career, and the tandem of Hayes and center Wes Unseld was an NBA match made in heaven. The team-first Unseld took care of the dirty work inside, freeing Hayes to be the Big E and show just how talented he was.

The Bullets (27–17) had won fifteen of their last twenty games, good enough for first place in the NBA's Central Division. The $300,000 question: how would Shue fold Archie's twenty-five points per game into a starting lineup?

On the return flight to Baltimore McGeehan asked Shue for his take on the $300,000 question. "We're not going to change our style because of Archie," Shue explained. "He's come back with the idea of fitting in with our style. But, at the same time, we're going to try and utilize his great offensive ability."

For further elaboration of "great offensive ability" the two just had to ask swingman Mike Riordan. "Whenever Archie comes into the game," said Riordan, "he lets it be known right away, 'Hey look, I can handle this. Trust me.' And we did. We called him the General. Archie was comfortable giving orders, and we were comfortable following them." Three days later against Philadelphia the General came off the bench in the second half with the veteran leadership that Porter, the rookie, lacked to get Riordan and crew to buckle down and stick to Shue's game plan.

Watching from press row, in what would be an easy win for the Bullets, was Peter Carry of *Sports Illustrated*. "Last week, when the roster of the new Bullets was finally completed by the return of hold-out guard Archie Clark, it only made a hot team hotter," noted Carry. "The old Bullets were good enough to win games, lots of them, but the new ones are better. They are capable of winning championships."

Shue was even more to the point. "We had the pieces in place to become the next NBA dynasty." The Bullets? Dynasty?

Yes, Shue's Bullets were young and built to last. Elvin Hayes and Mike Riordan were twenty-seven years old, Wes Unseld was twenty-six, and Phil Chenier and Kevin Porter were twenty-two. With Archie, one of the NBA's elite veteran guards, no other NBA team had more upside. The Los Angeles Lakers were aging fast. So were the New York Knicks, and Oscar Robertson was on his last legs with the Milwaukee Bucks.

These whispers of NBA dynasty meant that Archie had to adjust his game yet again. In Los Angeles he'd broken into the league as a defensive ace and then learned how to play without the ball as an All-Star second guard. In Philadelphia he'd transitioned to a sixth man, playmaker, defensive ace, and whatever role struck Jack Ramsay's tightly wound fancy. In Baltimore Archie had embraced his new-found freedom last season to become an offensive machine and All-Pro. Now he would need to dial down his scoring from the twenties to the teens, bump up his assists, and help mold this young talent into an NBA monster.

COLLEGE PARK, MARYLAND, January 20, 1973. The hardwood floor at the University of Maryland's Cole Field House, laid out over cement, had absolutely no give to it when one was jumping or cutting to the basket. Archie's knees already ached just at the thought of playing there tonight against the Seattle Supersonics. The good news was that his knees would be partially spared. For a third straight game Archie would come off the bench to spell Kevin Porter. "I'm going to keep on starting Porter as long as we keep winning," Shue vowed.

Sure enough, Porter pushed the Bullets to a lead in the first quarter, and the General took care of business in the second quarter. Seattle gained ground in the third stanza, and Archie triggered a 20–4 run in the fourth period that ended in a Baltimore blowout win. These eight minutes didn't quite rise to the level of career high-lights, but they were sweet just the same with a quick steal, a driving hook shot for two, another steal, and a no-look pass to Mike Rior-dan for an easy lay-in. When the fourth-quarter blitz was over, the General had racked up ten points, five rebounds and three assists and had had a hand in forcing the Sonics into ten turnovers. "It's just like old times, almost natural," said Phil Chenier afterward of teaming with Archie.

A few minutes later Alan Goldstein of the *Baltimore Sun* took a first stab at the lead paragraph for his story on the game. What popped into his head was nothing short of poetic justice for Archie: "After watching Clark the last two nights, you get the feeling that perhaps Archie priced himself too low."

BALTIMORE, JANUARY 21, 1973. Archie decided to call it an eve-ning. He pulled his car out of its parking space, wove his way through downtown Baltimore, and finally merged into traffic on I-83 north-bound. Destination: his townhouse in Cockeysville.

As Archie stared ahead through the white glow of his headlights, he reflected on today's easy win over Philadelphia. He'd come off the bench again to notch seven points and dish out six assists. It wasn't his most memorable outing for sure, but it did not need to be. The sinking ship that Archie had feared while playing in Philadelphia had now capsized and was sinking to the bottom of the NBA record book.

As Archie kept telling people, he was ready to sacrifice his offense to win an NBA championship. At age thirty-one what else was left? Archie already had proved himself on the court against the best that the league had to offer. He had a giant contract to show for it. Now he needed a giant championship ring.

Archie's sacrifice came with a built-in conflict. Although Archie and Gene Shue were at heart gym rats who played to win, they often approached the path to victory differently. Their tactical differences had been apparent to Archie from day one, when Shue had pulled him aside and asked where on the floor he liked to shoot the ball. Archie navigated the floor—the whole floor—as a prototype of the more modern athletic players to come, relying on his time-tested instincts to carve up defenses and create openings for himself or his teammates.

Shue, meanwhile, roamed the sidelines, still very much a player's coach. He valued talent and, unlike Jack Ramsay, still used it as his starting point to inform his game plan. But, like Ramsay and the new breed of modern NBA coaches, Shue could pull up a cup of coffee and talk Xs and Os for hours. So single minded was Shue toward managing his talent and allowing it to succeed that he had a habit of sketching out new plays in his head for Hayes or Chenier while mowing the lawn or driving around town. He jotted down the best ones in a three-ring binder. During games Shue stood obsessively flipping through the binder, hardwired in his head, to engineer the perfect two points or a defensive stop.

For Archie, Shue's playbook was fine. Coaches called plays. But some of Shue's late-game brainstorms were frustrating. "If it ain't broke, why fix it?" Archie would think to himself upon seeing a late-game substitution waiting at the scorer's table.

Not one to keep quiet, Archie spoke up in the locker room after games to rehash the problematic play calls and substitutions. Shue would go head to head with Archie, in part because he considered one of his coaching strengths to be his intuitive feel for the game. Too often coach and floor leader agreed to disagree. For the team to excel Archie and Shue would need to work out their sometimes competing feels for the game.

They also needed to hammer out a timeline for Archie's return to the starting lineup. Although Archie had played well coming off the bench, he needed more action to get his legs fully under him and catch up to a league that was in peak midseason form. Archie was the first to admit that he had gotten winded chasing Gail Goodrich in Los Angeles and Fred Carter tonight. The momentary huffing and puffing had him reacting to—not attacking—the opposition. With fans now expecting big things from Archie for his big dollars, that wasn't good for him or the Bullets.

Archie took the exit for Cockeysville and a few minutes later turned onto Hogarth Circle. His townhouse was 19C, just ahead. A year ago Archie was preparing to play in the NBA All-Star game. This year his four-game body of work qualified him for a few days off and a chance to prepare for what promised to be an exciting second half of the season.

CLEVELAND, JANUARY 28, 1973. Gene Shue had been chewing for days on the imperfect state of his backcourt. He realized that the success or failure of all NBA seasons boiled down to a team's being hot for the playoffs. Porter was an untested rookie. Archie had averaged nearly twenty-seven points and eight assists per game against the New York Knicks last season in the playoffs.

The decision was a no brainer. Two games after the All-Star break Archie moved into the starting lineup, helping to put away the Cleveland Cavaliers, 102–93. The next night he notched twenty-four points and eleven assists in a romp over visiting Golden State. Archie wasn't all the way back just yet, but he had the Bullets looking sharper than ever.

BUFFALO, FEBRUARY 9, 1973. Whenever NBA players arrived in Buffalo for a night game with the Braves, they often killed a quiet afternoon milling among the masses downtown in the Main Place Shopping Mall or hoofing the half mile over the Peace Bridge into Canada.

But Archie wasn't in a mood to explore "the Niagara Frontier" today. The thermometer mounted outside the window read seventeen degrees. Gusts of wind shook trees and rattled street signs, while occasional flurries dusted the already snow-banked downtown streets in a fresh shade of winter white.

That's why Archie was hibernating in the eight-story Holiday Inn Downtown this afternoon. Several in the Bullets contingent sufficed with gathering downstairs in the lobby. Somebody bought a copy of the *Buffalo Evening News* and flipped ahead to page thirty-eight, where a three-column story offered a brief preview of tonight's game. The article dead-ended into a recap of yesterday's NBA Board of Governors meeting in New York, where the owners announced a reshuffling of the league's playoff format.

Effective immediately, the article stated, the NBA's Eastern and Western Conferences would seed playoff teams based on their winning percentage, not their order of finish within each conference's two divisions. In other words, the Knicks, currently in second place in the Atlantic Division with the second-best record in the Eastern Conference, had just leapfrogged the Central Division–leading Bullets into the second seed and home court for their presumed opening-round playoff series.

In the lobby of the Holiday Inn the dismay was palpable. All wanted the answer to one question (expletives deleted): How could the owners change the playoff format fifty-five games into the regular season?

Alan Goldstein of the *Baltimore Sun* called Bullets owner Abe Pollin for an explanation. Pollin, who'd missed the meeting, said he was unaware of the change. Goldstein called Walter Kennedy in New York. The Commish explained his good friend Pollin was mistaken. The change had actually been approved by a 13–4 count a year ago, with Pollin voting for the minority. Goldstein asked Kennedy why the NBA had waited a full year to announce the change. Kennedy offered no explanation.

"I knew New York was fighting for the change," Shue filled in the blanks, after the bitter Bullets took out their frustration on the blundering Braves. "They were sore last year about having a better record than us and not having the home-court advantage."

PHILADELPHIA, FEBRUARY 28, 1973. Archie agreed that the Bullets had notched some impressive wins earlier in the month. But look at the letdown since: a nine-point embarrassment to Phoenix; a two-point disaster in Detroit. The Bullets had lost three of the last five games to some of the least of their NBA brothers, including tonight's improbable six-point defeat at the hands of the woeful Philadelphia 76ers, last season the worst team in NBA history.

Championship teams took care of business every night, and Archie felt that the last several outings had proved the Bullets still lacked the machine-like mindset needed to throttle through the playoffs. He raised the issue with Shue: the Bullets needed more precision, not plays. Ever the optimist, Shue assured Archie that the team had plenty of time to lock in that machine-like mindset.

But Archie kept noticing things within Shue's system that needed an immediate hammer or wrench. The latest involved Wes Unseld. Last season Archie had spent most games running fly patterns and hauling in Unseld's perfect outlet passes. Lately Archie noticed that Unseld often faked the outlet pass to him and hurled the ball to Chenier. Archie suspected the sleight was intentional, a sign that Unseld wasn't pleased with Archie's lengthy holdout and big contract.

"Oh no, not Wes Unseld," Shue gasped when Archie raised the issue. Implied in the reply was a cardinal tenet not only of Shue and his assistants, but also of Pollin and every member of the Bullets front office: Unseld was the perfect teammate—talented, humble, strong, selfless, disciplined, charitable, and, above all, committed to winning. "If you couldn't get along with Wes, you needed to make an adjustment," said publicity director Jim Henneman. "Wes played the game hard, played the game right, and he lived right."

Archie didn't dispute most of the above. Unseld was an outstanding teammate and a good person. But Shue's refusal to consider that Unseld had his less-than-perfect moments reminded Archie just how provincial the Bullets front office could be. If new players didn't subscribe to the front-office dogma—which included the unassailable character not only of Unseld, but also of Abe Pollin—they weren't going to fit in with the team. Something was wrong with them.

Archie, having challenged the Holy Trinity of Pollin, Shue, and now Unseld, was in the final throes of wearing out his welcome in Baltimore. The front office had lost its ability to forgive Archie, and none seemed interested in trying to understand him or his blunt brand of constructive criticism.

"Why don't you tell Archie to keep quiet?" trainer Skip Feldman would ask Shue.

"I can't do that," Shue would answer. "I need Archie. We can't win without him."

So Shue kept the peace. He also kept the faith that winning a few ballgames would be the best remedy for his team's late-season funk.

BALTIMORE, MARCH 28, 1973. The Bullets had clinched their third-straight Central Division title two days ago. Now, with Fan Appreciation Night, it was time for the Bullets to begin saying their good-byes to Baltimore after nine seasons in town. Among the prizes: a five-day vacation for two in Puerto Rico, one hundred gallons of gasoline to ease the global oil crisis, a week at the Wes Unseld Basketball Camp, and a palm reading by Brother Richard.

Brother Richard no doubt had a few things to say about the upcoming Knicks-Bullets playoff series. Sadly none were recorded for posterity. Posterity, however, did jot down the musings of Atlanta Hawks coach Cotton Fitzsimmons. He had the Bullets defeating the Knicks: "The first time I saw the Bullets, even without Archie Clark, I knew they were going to be tough. Clark gives them another dimension, and you give credit to Gene Shue for the way Clark is in their picture."

Shue wasn't making any postseason predictions. He was too much of a gentleman for that. But there was no doubt that Shue believed his monster of a team would scare the Knicks to death in seven games or less. Let the 1970s Bullets dynasty begin!

---

*The Bullets dynasty pretty much crumbled against the Knicks. They beat us four games to one in our best of seven series and of course went on to win the 1973 NBA title.*

*I could give you a game-by-game rundown of the series, but there's really no point. What happened was pretty simple. The Knicks were a veteran ball club that had been together for about five seasons. We were still a young ball club and had been together for all of three months. The Knicks came at us in the first two games in the Garden, and we buckled—and broke. It's what I was trying to tell Gene during the regular season. We had to be mentally tough for the playoffs to fight through the adversity, and we just weren't ready for it.*

*The rumor was I couldn't get along with Phil [Chenier]. That wasn't true. But NBA rumors can take on a cruel life of their own, and it wasn't long before the blame for our playoff crash fell at my feet. People complained that I controlled the basketball. I was too "individualistic." Hey, I was just the veteran playmaker trying to hold together a young ball club that was suddenly coming apart at the seams.*

*People said Gene and I were at odds. Now that might have been true, you know, sort of in the moment. I say that because I met with Gene right after the Knicks series. The defeat wasn't sitting well with him. He was convinced that his lineup had to be partially rebuilt to beat the Knicks next season. Gene didn't come right out and say it. But he implied strongly that the Bullets planned to trade me.*

*I wouldn't say it was a shock. I'd learned long ago that the NBA is a business, and decisions get made that are out of your control. From Gene's perspective the cornerstones of the franchise were solidly in place for the next six or seven seasons—Wes, Elvin, and Phil. He just had to fill in the pieces around them with willing role players. Well, I wasn't a role player. Not with my skills, not with my big contract. I'd received the talk that almost every NBA player, if he sticks around long enough, eventually gets: You don't fit into our future plans.*

## 27

*The Bullets tried to trade me to Golden State for Cazzie Russell. No luck. Bob Ferry, our former assistant coach-turned-general manager, thought that my services were too valuable for next season's championship run. He was counting on me.*

*But life doesn't always go as planned. On August 29, 1973—I still remember the date—I was playing in a full-court pickup game at a little community center in Ecorse just to stay in shape. A high school kid snuck up, blocked my shot, and scooted the other way for a lay-up. Well, I couldn't let that go. I chased him down, and as I leapt at full speed to block his shot, my hand smacked the backboard. The force threw me off balance and flailing in the air in one of those slow-motion, think quick, "Oh-no-what-did-I-just-do?" moments. All I knew was I needed to break my fall to avoid landing on my head, so I stuck out my right arm. As it hit the floor, I felt my right shoulder give, followed by a sharp pain.*

*Some friends got me to the hospital, and the doctors said I'd separated my right shoulder. They wanted to operate to reattach the ligaments severed in the fall. I said, "No, you can't do that. I'm a pro basketball player. I've got to talk to my team first."*

*I went home that night and called Bob Ferry. Bob clearly wasn't happy, but he agreed that the team's orthopedic surgeon, Dr. Stanford Lavine, needed to take a look. Per Bob's instructions I flew to Washington the next day to meet with Dr. Lavine, and I'll never forget getting off the airplane with my arm in a sling and wincing into the airport terminal. I kept looking around for Bob or just somebody from the Bullets' front office to greet me. They'd want to make sure that I got to Dr. Lavine's office in one piece, right?*

*Wrong. The Bullets stood me up. I guess they wanted to let me know that they were ticked about the injury. Where much money is given, much is expected.*

*So I winced over to a telephone booth and called Dr. Lavine from the airport. After a bumpy cab ride to his office and a brief examina-*

*tion, he stated the obvious: I needed surgery to reattach the ligaments. Dr. Lavine told me to take another cab to the Washington Hospital Center. The next morning a nurse rolled me into the operating room.*

*Dr. Lavine, the go-to orthopedic sports surgeon in Washington, is credited with saving a number of football and basketball careers, including those of Wes Unseld and Rick Barry. In my case things didn't go so smoothly. Dr. Lavine reattached the ligaments to the clavicle bone in a way that made my shoulder, and really the whole joint, as tight as a drum. The surgery left me with no flexibility in my right arm, and it took me weeks to loosen up my shoulder even a little bit.*

*Not being able to extend my right arm threw off my ability to put up different kinds of shots. My jump shot was a mess. I couldn't shoot the ball from behind my head, like I'd done before. Even with my cross-over move I couldn't extend my arm real far like I used to and snap the ball back. The combination of the injury and surgery just really devastated my whole game.*

---

L aurel, Maryland, October 30, 1973. Two months after severing ligaments in his right shoulder, Archie resumed practicing with the Bullets today at Laurel High School, where the team often worked out between games. Archie rotated in with the second unit, but his main item of business was the slow process of loosening the ligaments in his surgically repaired shoulder.

Watching him short-arm his jump shots was a now mostly Washington press corps. With the team renamed the Capital Bullets and waiting to move into the brand-new Capital Centre in Landover in December, owner Abe Pollin had severed his Baltimore connections. But the old team gossip remained fair game, and the Washington reporters wasted little time in peppering Archie with tough questions. Do you get along with Phil Chenier? (Yes.) Are you too critical of your teammates? (No.) How quickly will you unseat Kevin Porter as the team's point guard? (Not my decision.)

One tough question crossed off the list was Archie's rumored strained relationship with Gene Shue, his former coach. Yes, former. Shue had resigned last spring, explaining, "My contract was up, and I wasn't getting good vibes about resigning from Abe." To avoid the inevitable Shue signed to coach Philadelphia.

Pollin then hired retired Boston Celtic KC Jones, his first black coach. But Pollin wasn't necessarily trying to be progressive. He was trying to be big league. His well-known new hire had helped to hoist eight championship banners in Boston and a ninth in Los Angeles as an assistant coach. Maybe Jones could hoist a tenth banner in Pollin's expensive new arena to inaugurate it in style. That was Pollin's hope, no doubt planted by Jones's former coach, Red Auerbach, a longtime Washington resident. Auerbach was Pollin's tennis buddy.

Archie didn't know KC well. But the two sat down in Washington over the summer to get better acquainted. KC kicked back in his chair, slightly whistling the letter "s" and regaling Archie in a blurt of pointed sentence fragments about the good old days, when the Celtics had battled the 76ers and Lakers for NBA superiority.

For KC, basketball was all about chemistry, and it started five men at a time on defense. After studying the Bullets on film, he and his African American assistant coach, Bernie Bickerstaff, concluded it was defense that had ailed the Bullets last season. To build better defensive chemistry Jones had rolled out "the Green Wave" in training camp.

The Wave was the full-court pressure scheme of KC's championship years in Boston. It was more of a mindset than a Dr. Jack choreography. His guards would menace their covers from end line to end line. His big men had to protect the lanes around the basket and swat shots like Bill Russell. Above all KC wanted everyone talking on defense, having each other's backs, and running the floor hard whenever the ball changed hands.

All of the above had Archie confident that good things would happen in Washington. Maybe he even stood poised for another breakout All-Pro season. Now if only his shoulder would cooperate.

ATLANTA, NOVEMBER 17, 1973. Tonight Archie got his first taste of NBA action this season against division rival Atlanta. KC had wanted to work Archie into the game slowly, limiting him to fifteen minutes max. But Kevin Porter hacked and grabbed his way into early foul trouble and was done for the evening midway through the third quarter, leaving Archie to pull the team out of a nineteen-point hole.

For Archie running the Bullets offense was like riding a bicycle. Instinct took hold, and he got the team quickly into plays and delivered the ball to the hot hand. That was Elvin Hayes. While the Big E found the bottom of the net, the Bullets defense stiffened. Atlanta's nineteen-point lead magically dwindled to nine and then one.

Hawks star Pete Maravich, who had thirty-three points through three quarters, suddenly turned butterfingered. Phil Chenier stripped him of the ball and found Hayes for an eighteen-footer that put the Bullets ahead midway through the fourth quarter. The Bullets never looked back as Hayes, who had found Jesus over the offseason, finished with a miraculous forty-three points and thirty-two rebounds.

Afterward Archie (thirteen points, nine assists) sat by his locker a little gassed. He couldn't shake the tightness in his right shoulder. It grabbed all night when he extended his arm on his jump shot. It gripped sometimes when he dribbled, and it locked when he swung his arm on his Shake-and-Bake crossover move.

He glanced at the hulking figure sitting a lazy chest pass away. Wes Unseld had just completed his second game back from the injured list. His cranky left knee looked awful. Archie thought of all the surgeries and horse shots that it took to keep Unseld on the court. Was that his future too?

Amid this crackle of ice bags and the cloying scent of wintergreen lineaments everybody was upbeat about the Bullets returning to full strength one month into the regular season—at least on paper. Would this core group now begin its rise as one of the NBA's great teams of the 1970s, as Gene Shue had envisioned last season? Or would the Bullets remain just a good team comprised of exceptional individual talent?

The answer would depend on KC's favorite basketball term: chemistry. Although KC had the Bullets playing his kind of reactive Celtics defense, the offense still had more fizzle than fizz. So much fizzle, in fact, that the Bullets ranked dead last in the league in field goal percentage. Now Archie and Unseld, with their veteran moxie and ability to create good shots for their teammates, would bring back the fizz.

"When will Wes and Archie return to the starting lineup?" a reporter asked.

"Wes and Archie know they have to earn their way back into the starting lineup," snapped Bernie Bickerstaff.

The real answer was whenever Wes and Archie said they were ready to return to the starting lineup.

BOSTON, NOVEMBER 28, 1973. For Wes Unseld "ready" had become a relative term. He said his left knee wasn't "really feeling any better, but it's not getting any worse either." So Unseld, wearing a protective knee brace approaching the size of a catcher's shin guard, told KC Jones to pencil him into the starting lineup against the surging Celtics, winners of eleven in a row.

Archie wouldn't be far behind him. Kevin Porter wouldn't be thrilled about coming off the bench, and KC would have to talk him through the transition. But there was no arguing about Archie's productivity. In his five games back Archie had averaged a solid ten points and five assists in just twenty minutes per game. More important, the Bullets (10–8) were winning again with him in the lineup.

The Celtics jumped to an early lead and quickly doubled it to sixteen by the second quarter. KC motioned for Archie to get in there. He tugged off his warm-ups and, channeling the General, took charge of his old team. Phil Chenier drilled a few shots. Archie did the same, and the visitors were back in business.

But the Celtics roared right back. Unseld, who had adjusted his bulky knee brace several times to improve his mobility, couldn't keep up with Boston center Dave Cowens. The gritty Cowens would outmaneuver Unseld for defensive rebounds, then sprint the other way to give Boston a three-on-two advantage and lots of easy shots.

On one of those sprints Boston's big forward Paul Silas took a pass and rumbled uncontested to the rim. Archie wrapped him up for the intentional foul, but Silas bulled forward, shedding Archie and sending him crashing to the floor on his right elbow. Archie took a seat on the bench in excruciating pain. He was done for the night, and so were the Bullets as their deficit grew to twenty-three to start the fourth quarter.

In the morning Archie felt the usual tug and pain in his right shoulder and now a terrible throb in his swollen right elbow. Archie took a deep breath. How would he play with one arm?

Archie called Larry Fleisher, his agent, with the latest setback. He'd landed on his elbow, and the small bursar's sacs that lubricate the joint had burst on impact. Fleisher advised Archie, for God's sake, to sit out a few games and get healthy. It was the same advice that Woody Sauldsberry had passed along six years ago in Los Angeles. It was the same advice that Archie had faithfully passed along to his injured teammates ever since: if you don't feel well, sit out the game to keep your productivity and next contract high.

But in his heart Archie knew that the advice no longer applied to him. At age thirty-two he wasn't playing for a big contract. He already had one. All that was left was his pride as one of the league's top performers. It was the fuel that drove Archie to fight every morning through the pain in his shoulder. He'd taken two steps forward since his shoulder surgery. Why take three steps back?

HOUSTON, DECEMBER 5, 1973. KC Jones reminded everyone this was just one bad game. Tomorrow would be a new day. KC, always disarmingly calm, didn't have much more to offer.

Privately KC and Bickerstaff shook their heads with exasperation and disbelief. Neither had seen this 119–99 blowout loss coming in Houston. The Rockets (9–17) had played like lightweights a month ago. Now the Rockets had grown into NBA heavyweights. In fact, if this had been a boxing match, the game would have been stopped a few minutes into the third quarter. That's when Wes Unseld had started struggling up and down the floor on his bum left knee. KC shook his head. What was he going to do about Big Wes? His knee didn't look good. The Bullets, winners of eleven of their last fifteen games and on a roll until tonight, were just getting started on a nearly two-week western jaunt that took them to Phoenix tomorrow, working their way from there up the Pacific Coast.

PHOENIX, DECEMBER 7, 1973. Nick Weatherspoon, better known as "Spoon" to his teammates, glanced at the two cards that he'd just been dealt. The Bullets rookie forward, now off the injured list, wasn't much of a blackjack player, the team's preferred card game. Spoon seemed to think he had to hit twenty-one on the nose to win each hand and reportedly would call for a card even when he was sitting pretty at nineteen or even twenty.

"Hit me, man."

A card skidded in his direction, and the rookie took a glance.

"Oh shit, I'm busted."

And so were the Bullets for a second straight night against Phoenix, 114–92. Their defense went bust in the second half, and the Bullets never got started with Kevin Porter at quarterback. So far on this road trip the second-year pro couldn't keep from dribbling and whizzing passes into the third row. His bad passes turned contagious. By the final buzzer the Bullets had coughed up the basketball a season-high thirty times.

For KC Jones, it was time to have a private chat with Archie. Was he ready physically to return to the starting lineup and whip this underachieving offense into shape?

LOS ANGELES, DECEMBER 8, 1973. Archie leveled with KC. The inflammation in his elbow had worsened, and the tightness in his shoulder remained. But his legs and lungs were fine. He was ready to run this team. KC said he'd relay the news to Kevin Porter.

On his way back to the hotel Archie thought about breaking into the NBA with the Lakers seven years ago. Like Porter, Archie had been single-minded about making the final cut. But not once had Archie tried to show up Jerry West, Gail Goodrich, or Walt Hazzard in practice. Not once had he complained about his reserve role. Archie was just happy to be in the league, and when his chance came, he made the most of it. That's how the league worked.

Not anymore. Whatever Porter was after—be it fame or pre-merger fortune—he clearly viewed Archie as an impediment. For the past two-plus months in practice Porter had gone out of his way to challenge Archie and prove to KC and all onlookers that he deserved to be the one running the team. The lack of respect bugged Archie. When he snapped back to put the youngster in his place, sparks flew. Members of the press, hearing about those sparks in practice, started to whisper among themselves in hot pursuit of the wrong conclusion: clearly Clark doesn't get along with his teammates.

Two young Washington reporters were tagging along with the Bullets on the road trip. Archie knew their eyebrows would arch when tomorrow's starting lineup was announced. So be it. They would eventually grasp that Archie had the skills and postseason body of work to help guide Abe Pollin's team into the winner's circle in May. Porter didn't. He needed to wait his turn.

LOS ANGELES, DECEMBER 9, 1973. By the fourth quarter most of the announced crowd of 12,958 had departed for various and sundry better things to do. The Los Angeles Lakers, NBA champions two years ago under coach Bill Sharman, looked awful yet again. Good thing Jack Kent Cooke, recovering from a heart attack and under doctor's orders to avoid too much excitement, wasn't there. But he could still read the reviews of his team, and they were scathing. According to one courtside critic, "Their offense is shoddy, they fastbreak at a snail's pace, they throw as many passes into the $11.50 seats as they do into teammates' hands, their rebounding is ineffective, and their defense is practically non-existent."

Down the hall in the Bullets locker room the Washington reporters were interested in Clark. Why was he back in the starting lineup? "It had to come sometime, and I felt that now Archie was physically capable of playing like he wanted to," shrugged Jones in his usual low-key affect.

Going with the veteran for forty minutes tonight produced just eleven points. But Archie got the offense rolling, protected the basketball, and, with the Lakers unwilling to double-team Hayes, milked the mismatch all game. The Bullets now had a few days off before departing for Portland.

PORTLAND, DECEMBER 11, 1973. The Bullets had grown a little tired of dragging their luggage from city to city. Anticipating the physical drain late in the road trip, KC Jones had been trying to engage the minds of his players. "Think," he kept admonishing them in Los

Angeles, pointing to his temples for emphasis. His message: a smart team can win anywhere.

But KC's smart team looked remedial at the opening whistle against Portland. The often bickering home team kept getting the matchup that it wanted on offense: the mobile Sidney Wicks on the immobile Wes Unseld. Big Wes committed three fouls in just over a minute and took a reluctant seat on the bench beside KC and Kevin Porter.

Without Big Wes to set the screens and open the driving lanes, the Bullets set offense looked out of sync. Normally Archie would have improvised off the dribble to create shots for his teammates, but his aching arm wouldn't let him. He took a seat on the bench for the second quarter and watched the Bullets offense, shooting an anemic 38 percent, turn to mush. The Blazers, growing more confident with each passing twenty-four seconds, extended their lead to eleven at halftime.

"Think," KC implored. So the Bullets clamped down on Wicks inside and dared Portland to beat them from outside. It wasn't complicated stuff. But it worked. The fourth quarter belonged to Archie. With the Bullets trailing by a half dozen, Archie stepped into the moment, bad arm be damned, and started dropping in midrange jump shots, sailed through the lane for a sweet left-handed hook shot, and clinched the five-point victory by putting on a dribbling clinic and, when intentionally fouled, making six straight free throws in the final 1:30.

The following day a Portland newspaper credited the win to Archie's domination of the fourth quarter, declaring "the grand old man of the Capital Bullets was back." Grand old man? That was a first.

The Bullets would close out the road trip with a three-game lead in the Central Division. KC still had everyone believing that the best was yet to come. The team had just moved into its new digs in the state-of-the-art Capital Centre, and the energized fan base was ready to root in style for a winner. The bad news was that Archie and Unseld remained big ifs returning home. KC desperately needed both healthy and back in the lineup full time. The second half of the season depended on it.

# 28

*There was a joke making the rounds among NBA players. Question: What does "NBA" really stand for? Answer: Nothing but airports. We passed through so many airports, it could be hard to keep the cities straight. But the airports themselves didn't bother me so much. It was some of the airplanes.*

---

Landover, Maryland, January 17, 1974. The Bullets' new trainer, Bill Ford, repeated the same two lines: "Grab your bags. We've got a plane to catch."

Standing beside his locker in the Bullets' dressing room, Archie struggled to stuff his stiff right arm into his winter coat. He couldn't stop thinking about tonight's near collapse to last-place Cleveland to open the second half of the NBA season. What was that all about? But the Bullets had tightened things up and walked away with a 101–86 win. It was the latter number that had everyone slapping palms. The defensive-minded Bullets had now held the opposition to under one hundred points in twenty-six of their forty-three games.

"Grab your bags. We've got a plane to catch." Was there time to eat? No. "Grab your bags. We've got a plane to catch."

After some zigzagging through the usual knot of Thursday night traffic, Ford, in his mid-forties, paunchy, and with an any-which-way receding hairline, stood in the observation deck at Baltimore's Friendship International Airport with its jumble of display cases and model airplanes. He took a head count and realized a few players remained stuck in traffic. Thank God, the Bullets were flying charter, the latest infrequent wrinkle in NBA travel. Ford notified the crew of the delay. An hour passed, and the stragglers finally arrived, suitcases in hand. The time approached midnight.

Ford led everyone out to a small airplane. Despite the white-collar cachet of "ExecAir," painted on the side, this twin-engine plane wasn't more than a puddle jumper. As Archie ducked his head through the doorway and boarded into the cabin, he did a double take. There were a total of nineteen seats, all sized to fit the elbows and knees of undersized businessmen, not an NBA team of gangly seven 7-footers.

"Please fill all of the seats in the front," instructed Doris the Stewardess. "We need it for balance."

The little jet finally lifted into the air after midnight. The ascent was brief as the plane leveled off in the darkness at a mere six thousand feet and settled in at a cruising speed of just two hundred miles per hour. A commercial airliner traveled at thirty-five thousand feet and six hundred miles per hour.

"Will you be serving anything during the flight?" a ravenous player asked.

"There's plenty of beer," answered Doris, transitioning to the tired punch line of an old army joke. "But there's no bathroom."

The small airplane hit a patch of turbulence and bumped along for a few minutes like a toboggan, the back end shimmying left then right. "I don't care if we have blankets," one player was overheard telling another. "Where are the parachutes?"

"Hey, there's a draft back here," called out Elvin Hayes, feeling a cold, steady wind blowing through his hair.

"That crack is supposed to be by the door," Doris replied.

Hayes yanked his leather jacket over his head and delivered himself to the power of prayer.

When the charter landed, thankfully without incident, at Buffalo Niagara International Airport, the time was well past 2 a.m., and there were no taxis to be had. Ford made a few calls, and several yellow vehicles screeched to a halt about twenty minutes later at the cab stand. The temperature: six degrees.

Around 3 a.m. the Bullets shivered into the Holiday Inn, the rookies lugging in all of the bags from the cold, per NBA tradition. The veterans made a beeline for food, only to discover that the motel coffee shop was closed. Now, five hours after beating the Cleveland Cavaliers before sixteen thousand fans in the NBA's most modern-and-suddenly-hopping arena, Archie and his teammates gathered around a vending machine to grab something to eat. Their choices: crackers, candy, and chewing gum. "Here we are third in the league in attendance," somebody had muttered aboard the flight to Buffalo. "Wonder how the lousy-drawing teams travel?"

BUFFALO, JANUARY 18, 1974. The massive black scoreboard suspended from the roof of the Buffalo Auditorium showed 4:50 left in the ballgame. Braves 88, Bullets 87. At press row the critics had begun to mutter. KC Jones was cutting it close. If the Bullets wanted to get out of Buffalo with a win, he had to send in Archie and fellow starters Phil Chenier and Mike Riordan.

Another awkward minute passed. Then came more mutters, when KC sent backup center Manny Leaks into the game for Wes Unseld. Victory now belonged in the unfamiliar hands of Leaks, Kevin Porter, rookie reserves Nick Weatherspoon and Louie Nelson, and All-Star Elvin Hayes.

Was KC dumping the game? Not exactly. KC was miffed at the usually mild-mannered Chenier for blowing his top at the referees and playing his worst game of the season. KC remembered his old days with the Celtics, when Red Auerbach would sometimes bench a slumping starter for sulking so as to send the message: everyone is replaceable. Tonight KC had resurrected Auerbach's tough love, though without most of the bark.

KC's more pressing problem was a left knee. Unseld had been fighting a losing battle to control the inflammation. In mid-December, right after the team had returned from the West Coast, he immobilized the left leg in a walking cast. By New Year's Unseld had limped back into the lineup, only to bow out again for another week of R & R in a walking cast. Unseld's status remained game to game, and KC had noticed his big man lumbering tonight. He wasn't taking any chances.

Archie's right arm wasn't any better. Dr. Lavine, the surgeon who had messed up his shoulder, had drained his elbow a few weeks ago, and the troublesome bump already had swollen back to the size of a plum. Lavine's instructions to Archie: keep taking the pills that he'd prescribed. They would knock out the inflammation.

Archie followed the doctor's orders and waited. Nothing happened. Out of desperation Archie wrapped the elbow in an ace bandage for games, but he kept whacking it on arms and floorboards, and the pain was beyond excruciating. Archie had even tried playing with an elbow pad for extra protection. That only further limited the flexibility in his right arm.

Archie now glanced at the scoreboard. Forty seconds left. Bullets 92, Braves 94. Archie hated sitting on the bench like a potted plant. He kept watching, analyzing, instinctively seeing plays before they developed. Like now. Buffalo's Ernie DiGregorio dribbled the ball up the floor, and Kevin Porter kept slapping at him with each thump of the basketball. Porter needed to back off. He had five fouls, or one shy of disqualification. He reached again, and the referee's whistle blew. Porter was done for the night and, worse, he'd sent Ernie D to the free-throw line, where he was automatic.

KC motioned for Archie to replace Porter. He entered the game with one thought in mind. As adept as Ernie D was with the basketball on offense, he was slow on defense. Time to take him to the hoop.

After making both free throws, Ernie D trotted back on defense. Archie called for the ball, and Braves coach Jack Ramsay called for someone to help his rookie. Archie, veteran that he was, worked quickly.

Braves 96, Bullets 94. Twenty-four seconds left. KC and Bernie Bickerstaff stomped and gestured. Play tight defense; force a steal; send the game into overtime. Don't foul DiGregorio. But little-used rookies will be little-used rookies, and Louie Nelson promptly hacked Ernie D. Two free throws later, that was the ballgame.

"Grab your bags. We've got a plane to catch."

Their nineteen-seat "scare in the air" was waiting to fly the Bullets back to Friendship International. Most would have preferred a seat aboard the next Greyhound bus, plenty of beer, and a bathroom.

BALTIMORE, JANUARY 21, 1974. Archie glanced at the departure board on the wall. Flight 63. Destination: San Francisco. On time.

Perfect! Archie wended his way through Friendship International to his departure gate, grateful to be flying commercial again. Most of his teammates were already waiting. Although it was a miserably cold Monday morning, everyone seemed to be in decent spirits. After all, the Bullets had returned home from Buffalo to play their best basketball of the season in beating Golden State and Houston last night.

While the Bullets' defense remained one of the NBA's best, the big news was the fast break of seasons past was suddenly back. Its return made no medical sense. Wes Unseld, listed as game to game, had bounced back in top form. With Unseld snagging rebounds and firing off the best outlet pass in the game's history, the Bullets got to witness a second medical mystery. Archie, though badly favoring his right arm, had grimaced through the pain to make all the right plays.

"If we can keep this up, there's not much that you can improve upon now, except little things," forward Mike Riordan sized up the state of his team. "We're covering every area now—the running game, the pattern game, the defense, the defensive rebounding. Up to now, we just didn't have the running game going."

The boarding call came for Flight 63. As the Bullets prepared to board the airplane, they did so with the second-best record in the Eastern Division at 27–19. Overtaking Boston (33–10) for the best record in the East wasn't out of the question.

As this three-game West Coast swing would soon show, NBA seasons can turn on a dime. And not always as expected.

OAKLAND, JANUARY 22, 1974. Oakland was home to Tower of Power, the funk band that was all over AM radio in the Bay Area with its single "So Very Hard to Go." But tonight it was the Bullets that found it, literally, so very hard to go against the Golden State Warriors. They arrived jet lagged and with nothing in the tank in the first half. Twenty-plus turnovers later, the Bullets were back in gear by midway through the third quarter, playing their trademark aggressive defense and scrapping to within four points of Golden State to start the final quarter.

The Warriors, equally jet-lagged after a long East Coast trip that had featured multiple travel glitches, seemed more than willing to quit under the heavy barrage of Bullets. They went scoreless over the final 3:26 of the game. But luck was on their side. Make that the referees. They whistled the Bullets for two backbreaking violations in the final minute to hand the Warriors a two-point win.

In the visitors' locker room Archie needed to find two bags of ice ASAP to quiet the loud throbs in his elbow and shoulder. He had experimented tonight with playing minus the bulky bandage around his elbow. It hadn't made a bit of difference. He'd struggled early in the game like everyone else, gutting out the team's rash of turnovers to finish with a respectable twenty-two points.

Archie didn't want to let down his teammates, but he was a realist. His right arm had never felt worse. He couldn't possibly keep up this pace for thirty-six more games, plus the playoffs, with this thing from outer space on his elbow growing larger and more painful every day. He couldn't keep swallowing the pills prescribed by Dr. Lavine. They weren't working.

Nearby a tired Wes Unseld scrolled through roughly the same bleak thoughts while icing down his troublesome knee. It was in real bad shape—again—after Wes had played five games in six nights, and he'd struggled mightily tonight. Should he risk playing through the pain? Unseld decided to take two aspirin and call Dr. Lavine in the morning.

LOS ANGELES, JANUARY 25, 1974. Thanks to the kindness—or more likely necessity—of NBA scheduler Eddie Gottlieb, the Bullets had four days off in sunny Los Angeles before their next game against the Lakers.

"Where you guys from?" the hotel clerk asked, not sure where to place the generic name of "Capital."

Although the daily team practices poked a two-hour hole in the middle of the day, the players and coaches planned to relax in the seventy-degree weather as much as possible. Some had managed to schedule tee times at their favorite golf courses.

Wes Unseld wouldn't be joining them with his nine iron. Big Wes had flown back to "Capital" after the Golden State loss for more medical attention. His return to action: to be determined.

The medical news wasn't good for Archie either. He'd used the extra down time to get a second opinion on his elbow. The doctor, examining a set of X-rays of the damaged limb, speculated that calcium chips might be floating around in there. Archie asked if he needed surgery. Possibly.

Surgery? It would shut him down for the rest of the season. And what if the surgeon screwed up his elbow too? Between a surgically ruined shoulder and elbow, his career would be over with two seasons left on his contract.

With all of the above now weighing heavily on his mind, Archie dressed for practice each day. As always Kevin Porter was waiting. Archie would eventually lose his patience with Porter's one-upmanship, and tempers would flare. After practice Porter would stick around to work tirelessly on his game, running from spot to spot to attempt fifty jump shots in a row without a dribble to improve his outside shooting. Nobody doubted his dedication. Nobody doubted that it would pay off. The question was when—and it couldn't be soon enough for Porter.

PHOENIX, JANUARY 27, 1974. The door to the Bullets' locker room had slammed shut. "Nobody's allowed inside," a voice grumped.

The whispered explanation from others waiting in the concrete hallway was that the Bullets' coach had called an impromptu team meeting. Call it crisis management after Capital had taken another whack on the chin tonight to the last-place Phoenix Suns. "I considered it serious; that's why we had a meeting," KC Jones explained calmly but firmly soon after the locker-room door finally opened about ten minutes later.

The "it" was the team's suddenly wayward defense, which had yielded 143 points the other night in the loss to the Lakers and now 127 big ones to the Suns. Above all, the forever-hustling Bullets prided themselves on holding opponents to under one hundred points. "Our defense has fallen apart here," was KC's blunt assessment. "We were damn near the best in the league until we started this trip."

All season the team's defensive strategy had been to funnel opposing players into the middle and straight into Unseld's barrel chest. That allowed Elvin Hayes to roam freely inside the key to slide over and block shots or rebound the misses. Two games and a shocking 270 points surrendered minus Unseld, KC had concluded that his team was in deep trouble. With Archie ailing too, the Bullets were in a full-blown crisis.

OKLAHOMA CITY, JANUARY 31, 1974. Archie hung up the phone and continued waiting at the boarding gate. What else could he do? His flight to Cleveland had been delayed for a few hours, and he'd never make it in time for tonight's game against the Cavaliers. Not that he was in any shape to play of course. Archie had banged his elbow so badly before the Chicago game last night that he had sat out the loss—Capital's fourth in a row—and his agent, Larry Fleisher, finally intervened. Fleisher arranged for Archie to fly to Oklahoma City today to be examined by Dr. Donald Horatio O'Donoghue, an orthopedic surgeon and the so-called Father of Sports Medicine.

The good news was that the trek to Oklahoma City had been worth it. Dr. O'Donoghue confirmed the painful buildup of calcium chips in Archie's elbow. O'Donoghue advised Archie to have the bursar sacs in his right elbow drained yet again in Washington to eliminate the calcium chips. This time, he told Archie, have the arm immobilized in a cast. If all went well, Archie should be back on the court in three weeks, just about as good as new, the chronic tightness and ache in his shoulder excluded.

At long last the boarding call came for Archie's flight. It got him into Cleveland too late to see the Bullets snap their four-game losing streak. The next morning Archie was surprised to see Wes Unseld at the Marriott Hotel, free of the walking cast. He prepared to rejoin the team for Sunday's nationally televised game against the Boston Celtics.

BOSTON, FEBRUARY 3, 1974. The large commercial jet departed Cleveland's Hopkins International Airport on time. The plane should have landed in Boston before noon. But a winter snowstorm had enveloped the Massachusetts coastline, and Boston's Logan Airport had closed temporarily. After the monotony of circling Boston for well over an hour waiting to receive permission to land, the flight was finally diverted to Hartford, Connecticut, where Bullets trainer Bill Ford had to think fast. He chartered a bus that slip-slided the one hundred miles along the interstate between Hartford and Boston and reached the Sheraton-Prudential Center in Boston's Back Bay as darkness fell.

By morning the sun had risen on an urban winter wonderland. After a late breakfast the Bullets taxied to the Boston Garden, where somebody in a suit led them to the dungeon called the visitors' locker room. Within minutes a few Bullets had straggled onto the parquet floor to be reminded of the locations of its bad bounces, while the CBS crew mounted television lights for today's broadcast.

The NBA *Game of the Week* continued to struggle in the ratings. But the playoffs were fast approaching, and basketball junkies were tuning in for the more heated late-season battles. That included this afternoon's spirited contest. The injury-plagued Bullets left their aches behind to outrun the Celtics for four quarters, 112–99.

The star of the game was the flamboyant Kevin Porter, filling in for Archie for a third straight game. He was everywhere, pestering everyone in his path on defense and orchestrating the Bullets' offense with equal parts poise and pizzazz, especially in the second half. An unfamiliar reporter with a Boston accent inched up to Archie and asked an unfamiliar question: "How about that Kevin Porter?"

Archie praised Porter, not as an emerging NBA star but as a member of an outstanding three-man backcourt. It was an honest assessment. Archie wished Porter no ill. What he struggled with every day in practice was Porter's boundless ambition. In three days Archie would have his elbow drained and placed in a cast. That gave Porter three weeks to build his case for taking Archie's job.

DETROIT, FEBRUARY 22, 1974. Archie had had the cast removed from his right arm yesterday. The elbow still looked puffy. But the swelling was down, and Archie got the pro forma thumbs up from Dr. Lavine to return to the court. Feeling hopeful, Archie packed his bags this morning and flew to Detroit for tonight's game.

Archie rejoined a ball club that looked like a hospital ward. "Everybody's doubtful," joked KC Jones about the injury report. Phil Chenier had pulled a hamstring last week and had missed the last three games. Nick Weatherspoon had just taken a finger to the eye, and backup center Manny Leaks was out of action with a deep thigh bruise. His loss was significant because Wes Unseld, though in and out of the lineup, had started losing patience with his wobbly knee. "I figured that I'd play and it would get better," Unseld said. "But now, to be honest, I don't know. I have my doubts as to whether I can come back. There are some things, basic things—like jumping and moving to my left—that I can't do properly and may not be able to do again."

Despite the wobble in the franchise's cornerstone player, the Bullets had beaten the odds in February, trotting out a makeshift starting lineup that featured little-used rookie Tom Kozelko in Unseld's stead. Most of KC's wing-and-a-prayer maneuvering had paid off with wins in nine of thirteen games this month, including a second victory over Boston. In fact going into tonight's game, the Bullets (36–26) remained atop the Central Division by a comfortable nine games and held the third-best record in the Eastern Conference behind Boston (43–17) and New York (39–26).

The glue holding together the team was none other than Kevin Porter. He had cut down his turnovers dramatically and upped his scoring and assists per game to a level comparable to Archie's former production when healthy. He also had great newfound chemistry with his teammates.

Archie watched in street clothes as Porter (twenty points, eleven assists) piloted the Bullets to a thirteen-point lead midway through the third quarter. Porter, known for taking risks on defense, took a bad one and was whistled for a disqualifying sixth foul. With Porter gone, the Bullets stopped beating Detroit down the floor for easy baskets, and the Pistons fell back into an illegal zone defense designed to collapse on Elvin Hayes every time he touched the ball. A harried Hayes kept passing the ball back out to the perimeter, where the Bullets' makeshift backcourt of rookie Louie Nelson and Mike Riordan couldn't buy a bucket.

The Pistons pulled ahead in the fourth quarter and held on, zone defense and all, for a one-point victory. "I don't know what the league is going to do about it," complained Hayes afterward, referring to the zone. "You keep mentioning it and mentioning it, and nothing happens."

LANDOVER, MARYLAND, FEBRUARY 24, 1974. Referee Manny Sokol, a whistle propped in his mouth, was about to receive another loud helpful hint from the Bullets' bench in tonight's rematch with Detroit: "Zone! Zone!"

Accusatory fingers from the Bullets' bench poked toward Bob Lanier and the other Detroit Pistons encircling Elvin Hayes yet again after he'd caught the ball in scoring position. There was no doubt that the Pistons were running an illegal zone defense, and Sokol, who had refereed the game in Detroit, knew it. But the coaches and referees had worked out an unwritten gentleman's agreement about zone defenses that remained ingrained in NBA culture. As long as teams weren't so blatant about it that they made the refs look bad, no technical fouls would be forthcoming. "Zone! Zone!"

One of those full throats on the Bullets' bench belonged to Archie, finally back in uniform after a three-week convalescence. His elbow, though hardly perfect, felt better—or good enough in theory for him to gut out the final seventeen games of the regular season and the playoffs. His shoulder was another story, but he'd deal with that chronic pain in the offseason.

Already Archie had spelled rookie Louie Nelson for a few minutes in the first half and was on call to play, if absolutely needed, to close out the game. Kevin Porter sat on the bench in street clothes, having sprained his ankle in Capital's loss to Cleveland last night, and Nelson had his hands full keeping up with Detroit's perennial All-Pro Dave Bing.

Archie and Phil Chenier, also returning tonight from a pulled hamstring, finally got the call late in the third quarter. The SOS caught Archie by surprise. But his instincts kicked into gear quickly, and Capital, playing with its projected preseason starting lineup for the first time since early February, picked up the pace on both ends of the floor before another loud, sellout crowd in the ultra-modern Capital Centre.

With seven minutes to play Archie shadowed Detroit's Bing as he dribbled the ball up the floor. The score deadlocked at seventy-two. Bing looked inside to Bob Lanier, who seemed to have Wes Unseld pinned behind him for position to take an easy, close-in shot attempt.

As Bing's pass sailed inside, Unseld reached around Lanier's 270-pound frame and deflected the ball on a bounce to Archie.

Now came the fun. Archie spun the other way on the dribble en route to the Pistons' basket, Bing backpedaling in the center of the court about two steps ahead. Out of the corner of his eye Archie spotted Phil Chenier on the run to his left and sensed Mike Riordan thump-thump-thumping a step behind the play to the right. As Archie approached the free throw line, he stutter-stepped his way past Bing and snaked ahead to another waiting Piston defender, arms raised. Archie flipped the ball back outside to Riordan, now spotting up twenty feet away. To repeat the signature line of Bullets' radio announcer Jim Karvelis: Bingo!

The final six minutes was one bingo after another, most of them coming from Chenier and Elvin Hayes. Hayes found room to maneuver offensively early in the fourth quarter, when Sokol caved to the hoots of the Bullets' bench and whistled a technical foul on Detroit for playing a zone defense. The Pistons' bench seethed at the tattletales on the home team, and the seething turned to a full-blown hiss when Riordan admitted in a postgame interview with Karvelis, "We play a lot of [zone] too."

Back in the Bullets' locker room following the 94–84 win, showers splashed and a boisterous, self-gratulatory confidence filled the steamy air for the first time in weeks. The team was healthy again—or so it seemed—with the playoffs just around the corner and a likely first-round matchup against—who else?—the New York Knicks.

"There's nothing like having those starters in there," interjected KC Jones, his fashionable wide tie loosened, a beer in one hand and a cigarette smoldering in the other. "Makeshift lineups can hold on only so long."

Archie was more circumspect. "It felt strange," Archie summarized his first action in a month. "But when the time came, I just did what felt natural."

A few lockers down Wes Unseld sat stoically. He had played all forty-eight minutes, barrel-chesting Lanier in the lane and corralling a quiet six rebounds. He wasn't saying anything, but his knee was killing him.

NEW YORK, FEBRUARY 26, 1974. Nobody saw this one coming. The confident Bullets of two nights ago arrived in New York carrying a bag of bricks. They shot just 37 percent from the field. So jarring was the outside shooting—ironically on a mostly ho-hum night for the Knicks' defense—that KC Jones offered this one-line postgame assessment after the 85–71 loss that said it all: "That shooting—whew!"

The "whew" started when Wes Unseld pulled up lame in the first quarter. No Unseld, no Bullets' fast break. That left orchestrating the Bullets' half-court offense to Kevin Porter, who had rushed back into the lineup after the Detroit game on a bad ankle. His poor mobility against the Knicks' usual defensive pressure prevented the Bullets from getting into their offense quickly, and that had everyone standing around and out of rhythm. Even Archie, who was the only Bullet to bring a reliable shooting eye to Madison Square Garden, couldn't jump start the offense when he entered the game. Whew!

The rotten shooting wasn't KC's only world of trouble, however. After the game Wes Unseld sat staring at the ice pack propped on his swollen left knee. The stare seemed a million miles away.

A *Washington Post* reporter saw the ice pack and asked Unseld for an update, letting the medical record show that the knee had been injected with drugs, drained multiple times, and immobilized three times in a walking cast over the past two months. Nothing had worked, and Unseld even admitted that his wife had been gently floating the idea that, at age twenty-eight, his best option might be to retire while he could still walk. "The operation is a definite," Unseld answered. "When is the question."

Unseld then uttered a sentence that caught the reporter off guard. He would make his decision within the week on whether to have surgery *immediately*. Unseld said he didn't want to dim the Bullets' championship hopes, but he needed to do something about his knee. It was that bad. The reporter thanked Big Wes for his candor—and for giving him a scoop.

LANDOVER, MARYLAND, FEBRUARY 27, 1974. By morning the *Washington Post* sports section had run with the breaking news that Wes Unseld might be done for the season. His consideration of immediate surgery seemed to have snuck up on the Bullets' front office. It shouldn't have. Unseld had lost patience several weeks ago with the Bullets' medical team, taking the highly uncharacteristic step of going public with his frustration. "I want to know where I stand, but they won't tell me," he'd said. "I ask what chance I have of surgery helping me, and I can't get an answer. I'd like to know—I can take it. If my chances of being helped by surgery are 90–10 or 50–50, I want to know. But they won't tell me."

Big Wes sure had everyone's attention now. After tonight's four-point win over Seattle Unseld sat in the locker room ringed by Bullets owner Abe Pollin, Dr. Stanford Lavine, and two Capital Centre executives. The foursome presented Unseld with a new medical option: fly to Toronto tomorrow and have the knee examined by Dr. Robert W. Jackson. Dr. Jackson's name was synonymous with a cutting-edge surgical technique called arthroscopy. It allowed surgeons to place a small, camera-bearing probe inside a joint and for the first time image the actual extent of the pathology in the bone and cartilage, removing a lot of the guesswork from sports medicine.

Pollin then popped the question upon which the Bullets' season now seemed to hinge: if the arthroscope showed the knee was structurally sound and thus no threat to his career, would Unseld finish out the season? Though frustrated, Unseld remained profoundly loyal to Pollin and the Bullets. He answered yes.

Hearing of Unseld's trek to Toronto, Archie cycled through his own frustrations with the team's medical staff. Had it not been for Larry Fleisher's intervention, Archie would be in the same boat as Unseld right now—contemplating retirement. Instead Archie felt okay physically for the first time this season. His elbow was almost back to normal, and his shoulder had loosened by degrees. There were still another twenty-five degrees to go, but Archie had made peace with the fact that his shoulder might never be the same. He'd learned to compensate for the chinks in his one-on-one play with veteran smarts, as he had done tonight: instead of crossing over his defender one on one whenever possible (as in seasons past), Archie had read the defense to maneuver in and around the screens set by

Unseld and create space for his shot. He'd drilled seven out of eleven from the field playing two quarters.

It was the two quarters—twenty-five minutes—that now had Archie thinking. Kevin Porter, for all of his second-year spunk, had earned the trust of the team over the past month. It was the classic NBA story of "next man up" and making the most of one's opportunity when it knocked. Porter's opportunistic play had staked him a thirty-minute-per-game claim in KC's three-guard backcourt rotation. What had Archie a little pensive was that most of those minutes came at his expense.

Pensive wasn't petulant, though. As Archie had stated from day one with the Bullets, "All I wanted was to win." If that meant adapting to a diminished role in this season of injuries, so be it. Archie didn't dislike Porter, despite their tussles in practice. He didn't understand him. Archie also remained convinced that KC, more than any coach in his eight-year pro career, knew how to win an NBA championship. That's why he would go along with his two quarters of work, come what may, for the greater good of the team.

LANDOVER, MARYLAND, MARCH 5, 1974. Modern medicine had spoken. Wes Unseld's knee, terribly inflamed though it was, appeared structurally sound and capable of grinding on for many years to come. A relieved Unseld canceled the surgery. He would finish out the season. "I'm still not in good shape," he explained. "To me, being in shape doesn't mean being able to run. Hell, I never run if I can help it. What I mean about being in shape is my reaction on defense and my jumping and timing. I'm still not throwing the outlet pass like I want, but it's coming. It takes time."

Tonight Unseld had received forty-four minutes of duty in a 103–89 win over the Atlanta Hawks. A reinvigorated Unseld, his knee feeling loose from the week off, had bumped and pushed Atlanta's Walt Bellamy out of the way all night to control the action inside. With Unseld, Elvin Hayes, and Mike Riordan combining to snatch forty-nine rebounds, the Bullets' backcourt took care of the rest, running past an openly feuding Hawks team that was dying to call it a season.

The good news was that the Bullets were now one victory away from clinching another Central Division title. The bad news was that while Unseld traveled to Toronto to have his knee scoped, the Bullets had dropped another one to the New York Knicks. The Bullets were down to twelve games in the regular season, and the Knicks held a four-game lead over them to clinch the home-court advantage in their first-round playoff series.

LANDOVER, MARYLAND, MARCH 9, 1974. Portland's Geoff Petrie had jacked up twenty-six shot attempts tonight. Good for the Bullets, he had missed fifteen of them. That included a short jump shot with ten seconds left that would have sent the game to overtime.

With this narrow escape the Bullets officially clinched the Central Division championship. Although no champagne chilled in the locker room, hoots and handshakes there were all around over the usual ice-cold bottle of beer. It had been a long, injury-filled season. "The way injuries kept cropping up this year, there were times we didn't think we'd make it to the playoffs," said KC Jones. "Now there are encouraging signs. The way things stand we could go all the way."

---

*Go all the way? Heck, we didn't even get past the first round. The Knicks beat us in six games. I sprained my ankle in the opening game. Not bad enough to sideline me for the series but enough to limit my availability for a few games.*

*As difficult as it was to lose again to the Knicks, the mood of those in the Bullets' front office was surprisingly upbeat. As they saw it, KC had introduced a championship style of basketball in Washington, and their roster was set. If Wes Unseld could stay healthy—and that was the big "if"—they had an outstanding frontcourt with him, Elvin [Hayes], and Mike Riordan. In the backcourt Kevin looked like he was ready to man the point, and Phil [Chenier] had outplayed Walt Frazier.*

*Reading between the lines, I was suddenly expendable as a thirty-something-year-old NBA veteran whose best days were thought to be behind him. So when I went home to Ecorse for the offseason, I was*

*under no delusions about returning to Washington in the fall for train-*
*ing camp. And that was okay with me. Let 'em trade me.*

*The bigger issue was my physical condition. My elbow was fine, but*
*the range of motion in my shoulder remained poor. If my future was*
*to step onto the court each night with a physical handicap, did I really*
*want to keep playing? I didn't know the answer.*

## 29

*To retire or not to retire? In the end the decision came down to money. There was still a season to go on my contract for $300,000, and I figured that I could gut it out one more year for that kind of cash. The question was where? The Bullets wanted to trade me, and I kept waiting for the phone to ring. As the weeks stretched to months, it became clear that something was amiss. Teams were wary of bringing in a thirty-three-year-old guard with a bum shoulder and big contract.*

*The exception was Seattle. Bill Russell, the NBA great who now coached the Supersonics, had traded his starting guard and badly needed a veteran playmaker to stabilize his young ball club. Bill called his old friend KC Jones to see about a trade. Because the Bullets were so anxious to make a deal, Bill lowballed them with a bench player named Dick Gibbs and asked Abe Pollin to keep paying half of my salary.*

*The Bullets took the bait. Pollin wanted to lock Phil Chenier into a multi-year, million-dollar contract. By trading me and getting Seattle to pay half my salary, Pollin could free up some cash to pay Phil. So, in the strange calculus of NBA front offices, the Bullets would come out ahead by accepting Russell's one-sided offer. So in mid-August the phone call finally came. I was now a member of the Seattle Supersonics.*

---

**D**etroit, September 15, 1974. The big commercial jet rumbled along the runway and lifted through the clouds with a few awkward sways left and right. Looking out of the port windows, passengers watched ten thousand feet below as the tree-lined neighborhoods in the Detroit suburbs gave way to vast square parcels of farmland. Once the plane had leveled off on its cruising altitude to Seattle, a beverage cart clattered into view, followed by the pleasant voice of a stewardess asking Archie if he cared for something to drink. She scooped some ice cubes into a cup and handed him something wet.

Archie took a sip and swallowed the words "Seattle" and "Supersonics." His new team. Would the return to the West Coast revive his NBA career? Or would Seattle be the end of the line? The ache in his surgically repaired shoulder suggested the latter. The shoulder remained God-awfully tight one year post surgery, and the lack of mobility in his right arm kept him performing below his former All-Pro self. The good news was that Bill Russell didn't expect Archie to turn back the NBA clock. Russell just needed Archie to carry himself like a seasoned pro in Seattle—show the youngsters how to commit to a defense-first mentality, be Russell's veteran eyes and ears on the floor.

That Archie could do, especially since Russell didn't expect him to log forty minutes a night through the regular season. Russell needed to work a high-energy young guard into the rotation named Donald Watts, a.k.a. Slick, for his then unusual shaved head. Watts, a skinny, 6-foot eternal underdog from small-town Mississippi and beloved fan favorite, would also surely prove to be a more respectful understudy than Kevin Porter. According to Slick, Archie had been one of his boyhood idols.

Archie of course knew all about the pre-Russell drama in Seattle. Four years ago owner Sam Schulman had declared war on the NBA bylaws to get superstar-in-the-making Spencer Haywood. Schulman had spent a couple million more to get ABA refugees Jim McDaniels and John Brisker. Schulman, who knew little about judging basketball talent, had been assured that his millions had been well spent. The one-two-three punch of Haywood, McDaniels, and Brisker would dominate pro basketball into the 1980s.

Hardly. Two seasons ago the Supersonics had mustered just twenty-two wins and likely had thrown a game to get their disciplinarian coach fired. Schulman hired Russell to save his investment, granting him total control over the franchise and a then absurdly inflated salary of $150,000 per year to coach and run the front office.

Russell arrived in Seattle with a hero's welcome befitting Winston Churchill as the greatest winner in the history of American sports. Even bad-boy forward John Brisker threw a welcome party to hip, hip, hooray Russell. Brisker and his teammates believed there was no way that they could lose with the mighty Russell at the helm. Everything the man touched turned to gold—gold medals, gold rings, and gold NBA championship trophies. If only it had been that simple.

IN THE WEEKS following his arrival Bill Russell talked regularly with Sam Schulman about *their* $6.6 million player payroll, second highest in the NBA, behind New York. To put Seattle's payroll into perspective, let us note that Jim McDaniels made more than football god Joe Namath; Spencer Haywood made more than home run king Hank Aaron; John Brisker made more than baseball's Pete Rose; and the now-departed top draft choice, Isaac "Bud" Stallworth, pocketed more than NFL superstar O. J. Simpson.

Russell promised to make things right for Schulman. Reassuring his boss was a strange role for Russell, one that he'd never had to fill with the cocksure basketball man Red Auerbach, the architect of the Boston Celtics dynasty as coach and now general manager. Auerbach had famously declared, "Basketball is a dictatorship, not a democracy."

But Auerbach was eight seasons removed from coaching, and almost all of the familiar faces of Russell's NBA era had now passed the baton to the Baby Boomers, the rising generation born from 1946 to 1964. The Boomers came of age opposing the Vietnam War, joining in the churn of the Civil Rights Movement, and throwing peace signs up in the air like they just didn't care. America's Boomers took to the basketball court generally looking hipper and, depending on their skill set, anxious to express themselves as individuals outside the conformity of the team, a trend that would stick like glue to the game and drive its evolution.

The Baby Boomers bit their tongues at first at Russell's old-fashioned get-with-the-team scare tactics. Who were they to question an all-time great? But it soon became apparent that Russell lacked the tact—and above all the patience—to communicate with his Baby Boomers. Within days they started grumbling among themselves. In Russell's day the grumbling was called bellyaching. In the here and now of the Baby Boomers it was called standing up for one's rights. Granted, none had the nerve to challenge their famous coach, but out of his earshot they dribbled ahead with mixed emotions about the Seattle Celtics.

THE "FASTEN SEATBELT" icon dinged overhead. Archie reached reflexively for the belt buckle and felt the plane skid left then right on patches of turbulent air. His shoulder had stiffened from sitting so long. The airplane couldn't land soon enough in Seattle.

As a player, Bill Russell had been above all else a keen student of the game. His extreme court smarts had allowed him to anticipate plays, spot tendencies, and, with his then supreme quickness and agility for a big man, come flying to the rescue like a comic book hero to swat shots, snatch rebounds, and trigger Boston's unrelenting "Green Wave" fast break. His otherworldly defensive skills had made his teammates better and had turned the sum of the Celtics' veteran parts into a usually unbeatable championship machine.

For Russell it was as though the NBA had mutated since his glory years. His current team of mostly black Baby Boomers had mastered the game one flashy playground move at a time. All they wanted was the ball in their hands, isolated on their defender to dribble, bump, dribble, bump, spin, pump fake, score "and one!"

That so many of the current generation could reach the pros without mastering the fundamentals shocked Russell. Their reluctance to play team basketball also flabbergasted him. But Russell viewed both as fixable with time and the strength of his dictatorial will. What left him cold was that some of his main contributors seemed to lack the pride in team that had been the lifeblood of his former Boston dynasty. Nor did they handle themselves like professionals off the court. Russell would get calls in the middle of the night informing him that one of his players had been busted. "Oh shit, who's in jail now?" the team lawyer would answer when Russell called and roused him out of bed. The lawyer would quietly cover the bail and whisk the latest oops out a side door without anyone, except those in the Supersonics' front office, being the wiser.

Russell's response to all of the above was to get even tougher with his players to teach them discipline and focus. For every minute late to practice, players owed him $100. For every point that the opponent scored in the previous night's game, the team owed him a lap at the start of the next practice. "You bunch of gutless wonders," he bellowed repeatedly, his Louisville slugger always in sight, a symbol of his generation's tough love.

His young gutless wonders now wore their fragile egos on their sleeves, and they tipped from resentful to borderline rebellious of Russell's barbed personal attacks. They still respected Russell's resume, but some began to question the man behind the legend. They found Russell to be arrogant, petty at times, exasperatingly aloof, condescending, and addicted to playing imponderable mind games calculated to assert his absolute control over the team.

Russell kept up the tough love, and his "gutless wonders," through a mix of respect and fear, had played better basketball in the second half of last season, winning about half of their games. "When you're going bad, the hardest thing to do is put the brakes on," critiqued Russell. "But we're almost a basketball team now."

Now Archie was descending through the cumulous clouds suspended over Puget Sound into the great unknown called Bill Russell's second season. Archie's mission: help this "almost a basketball team" qualify for the NBA playoffs for the first time in franchise history.

BELLEVUE, WASHINGTON, OCTOBER 12, 1974. When Archie awoke this morning, he heard the steady patter of rain outside. He shut his eyes as if in silent protest. "Not again." Since he had arrived four weeks ago in Washington State, it had rained every single morning. Archie made his way down the hallway, heartened by another local weather fact: the sun poked through the thick canopy of clouds every day around noon to drip dry one of the most beautiful places on the planet.

Archie now occupied his own soggy patch of the Washington dream. He'd moved into a comfortable, multi-bedroom rental in the suburban boomtown of Bellevue, just east across Lake Washington from Seattle on Interstate 405. Outside his window Archie stared up at tall stands of Douglas firs and western white pines. Brown creepers, dark-eyed juncos, and God knows what other birds often flitted there from branch to branch. Driving around town in his brand-new Mercedes, Archie caught glimpses of the snow-capped Cascade Mountains framing the horizon. He'd truly come a long way from the smokestacks of downriver Detroit.

Beautiful though it was, Archie wasn't quite ready to settle permanently in the Pacific Northwest. His family remained rooted in Detroit, and he'd made several business investments there. The good news was that Archie felt comfortable in Seattle. The young players looked up to him as an established NBA star—the father of the step-back jump shot, the greatest crossover move in the game's history, and a proven winner who had made the playoffs every season. "You got to remember, I'd grown up watching Archie and Earl Monroe playing against each other on television," said Talvin Skinner, a rookie from the University of Maryland Eastern Shore. "So having Archie there was a real stabilizing influence on us."

Bill Russell had also been fairly collegial thus far. He seemed to view Archie as an old-school veteran whom he could trust. They shared an internal encyclopedia of past players and coaches that most of the younger players didn't. Four years ago Gene Shue had handed Archie the basketball. Now Russell handed him his hard-earned respect.

What bothered Archie, as the team's designated veteran leader, was the team's stinky preseason. Despite the injuries to Spencer Haywood and the team's other mainstays, Seattle still had enough impressive young talent in Leonard Gray, Tommy Burleson, and especially John Brisker to compete and build the pride in team that Russell wanted.

But Russell had curiously buried Brisker and his hot hand on the bench. Big mistake. Archie had known Brisker for years. Archie took pains to tell people that Brisker was profoundly misunderstood. Befriend him in the casual argot of the streets, and he opened up like a book. That book was laid back, funny, philosophical, and endlessly curious about popular culture and current events. Cross Brisker, and you had reason to fear him.

As Archie saw it, Russell had been blatantly crossing Brisker for weeks. While Brisker had enough restraint to avoid clocking his famous coach and suffer the career-ending repercussions, Archie thought making Brisker miserable wasn't just divisive in the locker room, but was also terrible for the team.

"Bill, why aren't you playing John?" Archie finally piped up. "He can help us. Everybody in the NBA is afraid of him."

Russell stared past Archie.

"Bill, nobody wants to guard John, and nobody wants John guarding them."

Russell finally shook his head. "Archie, John can't play."

"What are you talking about?"

"John can't play."

Afterward Archie parsed Russell's cryptic comment. Of course John could play. It was on Russell's watch last season that Brisker, when given a chance, had lit up Kansas City–Omaha for forty-seven points.

Archie remembered hearing whispers last season about a feud between Russell and Brisker. It had started in training camp and culminated at midseason, when Russell demoted Brisker to the Eastern League, the NBA's unofficial minor league, with orders to "work on his defense." Russell, using his bully pulpit as one of the game's all-time greats, then declared in the press, like a kiss of death, that Brisker was a flawed basketball player who wasn't worthy of his big contract.

Behind the scenes Brisker was apoplectic. He had a baby on the way in Seattle, and suddenly Brisker needed an apartment in New Jersey. Brisker wasn't stupid. Nobody played defense in the Eastern League. Russell wanted him gone.

Suddenly Russell's words made sense to Archie. When Russell said, "John can't play," he meant the words literally. John wasn't allowed to play while Russell plotted his exit.

SEATTLE, OCTOBER 18, 1974. The spotlight in Seattle Center Coliseum trained on the familiar face of actor William Shatner, leaving over eight thousand spectators to wonder whether "Scotty" had just beamed him down from the deck of the Starship Enterprise in squiggles of yellow light. Then again, maybe not. Shatner, six years removed from playing Captain James T. Kirk in the television series *Star Trek*, had fallen on hard financial times. Hollywood wasn't interested in casting "Captain Kirk" in traditional terrestrial roles, and financial necessity now dictated that he make glad-handing personal appearances at banquets, shopping malls, and sporting events. Tonight, for the home opener of the Seattle Supersonics' 1974–75 season, the Canadian-born Shatner agreed to deliver a thespian reading of the National Anthem, heavy on a dry, nightly-news intonation and leavened with joltingly placed inflections: "Oh say can you see, through-hhh the dawn's early light."

Archie stood at attention with his teammates in their brand-new white home uniforms with green and gold trim. Near him stood John Brisker. Archie didn't know the details, but Bill Russell had blinked on cutting Brisker. Seattle still owed a then substantial $800,000 on Brisker's no-cut contract. Unless Russell could lower that amount substantially, owner Sam Schulman wouldn't agree to make Brisker a rich man for no services rendered. On financial matters Schulman could be pushed only so far.

Last night in Seattle's predictably discombobulated season-opening 114–97 loss in Phoenix, Brisker was the only Sonic who didn't play. Tonight against the Detroit Pistons more of Russell's cold shoulder awaited him. But Archie couldn't worry about the Russell-Brisker feud. He had a discombobulated team to run. Against Phoenix, Archie and Fred Brown had combined to net twenty-three of twenty-nine shots from the field to keep Seattle in the game most of the night. The problem was that Spencer Haywood and his sidekick Kennedy McIntosh had been on the shelf with preseason injuries and weren't ready to play.

"O'er the land of the free. And the ho-ome of the-eeeee brave." Shatner glanced upward at the white tiled ceiling (was he saying, "Beam me up, Scotty"?), and the opening-night crowd roared to welcome the start of season two of the Russell era. The Sonics kept everybody cheering through three quarters, primarily running Russell's Celtics offense. It had Archie slicing to the basket, Freddie Brown knocking down his long jump shots, and rookie center Tom Burleson diving for every loose ball like he was still in college. But in the fourth quarter all of the diving landed the Sonics in foul trouble, and the Pistons fired their way back into the ballgame behind the always explosive veteran Dave Bing, whose right sneaker was two sizes too big to accommodate a badly inflamed toenail.

The Pistons finally pulled ahead, and, with about thirty seconds left, the lead was four. Russell called for a play to get the ball to Haywood. Dribble, bump, dribble, bump, shot. When it bounced out, the rebound ricocheted into Burleson's inexperienced hands. As the tallest player on the court, Burleson could have easily kept the ball overhead and flicked it through the hoop. But Burleson gathered himself and brought the ball down to his waist, drawing an immediate upward slap from burly Bob Lanier and a downward whack from the big-shoed Bing. The ball squirted into Detroit hands, and that was all she wrote for the Sonics.

SEATTLE, OCTOBER 20, 1974. And the third time was the charm. The Seattle Supersonics held on tonight to defeat the visiting Cleveland Cavaliers, 100–93, for their first victory in three tries. Afterward all agreed that the Sonics still at times looked discombobulated, but the team was now showing the first signs of clicking. Archie and Fred Brown were a tight fit. Spencer Haywood, though still hobbled, had shown signs of his old All-NBA self. Helping him crash the boards was a rotation of crafty veterans—Jim Fox, Kennedy McIntosh, and John Hummer—and high-energy rookies Tom Burleson, Leonard Gray, and Talvin Skinner.

"Since I've been coaching Detroit, this is the best Seattle team I've ever played," Pistons coach Ray Scott had commented the other night. "I mean crashing the boards, never giving up, playing both offense and defense." The compliment was intended for Russell. But the kind words belonged mostly to assistant coach Bob "Hoppy" Hopkins, Russell's cousin who ran most of the practices. He had everyone playing hard, except Brisker, who had yet to get off the bench.

Brisker's inactivity led to the young season's first confrontation. Brisker, tamping down his resentment, greeted Russell and cut right to the chase. He wanted a chance to play. "I'm willing to do anything, just tell me what it is you want."

Russell glared back: "Just keep the fuck out of my face!"

On the streets of Detroit those would have been fighting words. But in Seattle the NBA's most feared fighter had no choice but to ask his tormentor to please stop bullying him.

SEATTLE, OCTOBER 23, 1974. To most Americans Bill Russell was the personable black sports personality known for his clever comments and jolly, full-throated, chest-heaving laughter. Out of the public eye Russell was known for his glower, his chin usually cocked slightly forward and his eyes often dark and impenetrable. He glowered his way onto elevators. He glowered his way onto airplanes. This fixed scowl, like a mask, made him appear invulnerable, as though he stood in eternal judgment of the vertically challenged humans below.

"If you can get close enough to Bill, don't let him down, and don't go around talking about him, you know, and keep to yourself; he's an amazing guy and you can be a lifelong friend," said the team's assistant general manager Bob Walsh. "But if something happens, and he turns against you for some reason, you're finished."

Russell should have been thrilled about tonight's 107–97 victory over Portland. In his first matchup with the NBA's next presumed dominant center, Bill Walton, Tom Burleson had held his own. A sign of good things to come in Seattle. But Russell's smiles had turned to a glower. He wanted to be finished with these stupid postgame questions. "Bill, what made you play John Brisker tonight?" asked a reporter.

"Oh, John and I had a talk the other night, and he said all he wanted was a chance to show me he could play the way I wanted him to play," answered the Glower.

As hard as he tried, Archie couldn't quite wrap his mind around the Russell-Brisker feud. Everybody had a pet theory. A woman. Jealousy. Ego. Power. All accounts made the beef deeply personal, and all may have been correct to varying degrees. Brisker came with that chip on his shoulder, and Russell held grudges. Just ask Archie's friend Woody Sauldsberry, whose career Russell helped to ruin in a fit of jealousy over a woman. But the NBA was a business, and Brisker could help Seattle win, and that's what mattered most to Russell. Winning fueled his national celebrity and allowed him to stretch out his light-hearted public alter ego and cackle heart-felt truth to power in ways that proud African American males, like Russell, never could in years past. Why cut off your nose to spite your legendary face?

While Russell would slip in occasional digs to the press about Brisker's deficiencies on the court (an old Red Auerbach stunt to get under a player's skin and into his head), he never overtly attacked his nemesis. That wasn't his style. "Bill never really badmouths his enemies," explained Walsh. "He just goes about his business as though they don't exist."

For Russell handling the Brisker affair was more like a poker game. There was no need to yell and scream. He maintained his poker face, his glower, and went about his business of waiting out Brisker. As the team's coach and general manager, Russell already held the winning hand, having total control over the roster and Brisker's playing time. He just needed to play the right card—the Eastern League, the disabled list, a quote in the newspaper—to get Brisker to slip up and discard his ace in the hole, the no-cut contract.

"People say Russell is moody, but I think that's the wrong word," said Blaine Johnson, who covered the Sonics for the *Seattle Post-Intelligencer*. "The better word is disciplined. He has this incredible ability to focus until he gets what he wants."

SEATTLE, OCTOBER 30, 1974. Archie remembered the first time he had played against Spencer Haywood. Haywood, then in his late teens, always soared to the basket a little higher and floated a little longer than everyone else. Now twenty-five years old, Haywood had endured a rash of leg injuries that had let some of the air out of his breathtaking athleticism. But pass the ball to Haywood on a clear out along the baseline, and on his good nights he still possessed the explosiveness—that extra God-given gear—to blow past most NBA forwards and soar to the rim.

Tonight was one of those good nights. Haywood, having been prodded and injected with needles during a recent doctor visit, felt no pain or numbness en route to his first dominating performance of the young season in a 117–97 smackdown of the Los Angeles Lakers. Nearly as exciting, in his second pro start, rookie forward Leonard Gray played like a beast. Make that like a dancing bear. "We called Leonard the Dancing Bear," said Slick Watts. "For such a bear of a man, Leonard was incredibly light on his feet."

The Dancing Bear and the Flying Haywood combined for sixty-four points, twenty-one rebounds, five blocked shots, and eight assists. Throw in 7-foot-2 Tom Burleson, "the Needle," and Seattle now had the makings of a physically dominant young frontline and trouble for the rest of the Pacific Division.

SEATTLE, NOVEMBER 14, 1974. The Seattle-Tacoma Airport had wrapped up its $175 million expansion last year and now ranked among the classier airports in the country. And yet the tinny, pre-renovation microphones and garbled boarding calls remained the same. A loud click and, garbled somewhere in the shrieking dissonance, the magic words, "8:30 a.m.," "boarding call," "United Airlines," and "flight to Chicago."

Time to roll. Archie grabbed his carry-on bag and joined his teammates on a trek outside to the tarmac, up a metal ramp, and into the brand-new DC-10, Boeing's modern wide-body jet that every tall basketball player loved for its roominess. The commercial jet would fly the friendly skies to Chicago O'Hare, where the team had a connecting flight to Detroit. Tomorrow night the Supersonics would face the Pistons on the first leg of the team's first eastern road trip of the season. It was an eight-day jaunt with additional stops in New York, Atlanta, and the brand-new NBA city of New Orleans.

Towering over Archie on his way into the airplane was Tom Burleson. Everywhere the Needle loped, heads turned in jaw-dropping wonder at his freakish height.

Archie found his assigned seat and glanced across the aisle. Spencer Haywood, per usual, was dressed to the nines: gray slacks, plaid sports coat, and a cool hat. Veteran center Jim Fox, a.k.a. Foxy, wore a brown pinstriped suit that made him look like he was running for mayor—or tax collector. Though complaints about the enigmatic Russell still circulated among the players, this was one happy basketball team at the moment. Russell's mostly twenty-somethings kept things loose off the court, but everyone fought like a band of brothers on the court. This one-for-all vibe had tightened up the team's defense to approach the high standards of Hopkins and Russell, pushing the Sonics to eight wins in their last ten games, including a current four-game win streak.

"Here you go, Archie," greeted the team's trainer, Frank Furtado. Before the plane took off, Furtado doled out an envelope to each player that was filled with travel money. Archie didn't need to count the dough. The NBA allotted $19 a day. For eight days that came to $152 to eat, drink, and survive on the road.

Furtado, a broad-shouldered former college wrestler in his early fifties, balding, with dark, bushy eyebrows, moved on to the next row, and Slick Watts shot him a wide, welcoming grin: "Frank, Frank, Frank." Watts, on a minimum-wage first contract, needed the cash.

Furtado distributed all of the envelopes but two. Where were Leonard Gray and Wardell Jackson? Right on cue, the rookies scooted aboard the airplane. "Some food problems at the restaurant," Jackson tried to explain.

Just after 9 a.m. the DC-10 thump-thump-thumped down the runway and lifted into the air, Puget Sound undulating royal blue below until it vanished beneath a gauze of clouds. The stewardesses looked like young beauty queens in their stylish blue uniforms with their long tresses pulled up under their caps. "My name is Dawn, as in morning," one coquettishly informed handsome reserve forward John Hummer.

Haywood, Fred Brown, and John Brisker pulled out a deck of cards to help pass the time. Yes, Brisker was back on the active roster after his two-week banishment to the injured list. Try as he may, Russell couldn't pass the kidney stone that was Brisker's no-cut contract. With Brisker in, Kennedy McIntosh was the odd man out in Seattle. Literally. Nicknamed "East Star" for his at times cosmic train of thought, the 6-foot-7 McIntosh was famous around the league for once having held onto the basketball in the middle of a play and staring transfixed into the nosebleed seats. After the twenty-four-second clock expired, McIntosh gasped, "I've just seen God. He's right up there."

Archie didn't know McIntosh well, though East Star also hailed from Detroit. But the release of this former first-round draft choice prompted Archie to ponder yet again about how brief an NBA career really was, especially for those "oddballs" who viewed the world—and, in McIntosh's case, the universe—a little differently.

As Brisker now shuffled the cards, he seemed relieved to have one more chance to salvage his NBA career. This much Archie knew: the cards would never fall in Brisker's favor in Seattle. Russell's memory was too long. Brisker thought he had an ace in the hole in his old friend Haywood, who'd bonded with Russell (or so he and most of the players thought). Brisker kept asking "Wood," as he was known, to talk to Russell and straighten things out for him.

But Haywood had no desire to get mixed up in the feud. Haywood truly believed that Russell, his beloved boyhood hero, was building something big in Seattle. He wanted not only to be a part of it, but also to be viewed forevermore as its cornerstone. Russell shrewdly pumped Haywood's ego, telling him that the franchise would rise or fall with his development as a dominant NBA player.

The flight's intercom system suddenly dinged. It was the captain. He wanted to welcome everyone aboard and to share some chilling travel news: the current temperature in Chicago was 29 degrees.

For the next three hours Archie and several other Supersonics tried to catch up on their sleep. Just as Archie's shoulder started tightening up, the captain dinged again over the intercom: "We'll be starting our descent soon into Chicago O'Hare." Thank God, thought Archie.

Once on the ground, Furtado motioned for Archie and the rest of the Seattle contingent to step it up. Their connecting flight was already boarding. By 3:30 p.m. Furtado and his charges had landed in Detroit, where five inches of snow awaited and seven pieces of team luggage had been lost in transit. While Furtado trekked to the baggage claim office, onlookers poked one another at the sight of the giant Burleson: "He must be eight feet tall!"

DETROIT, NOVEMBER 16, 1974. Seattle's four-game winning streak came to a screeching halt last night against the Detroit Pistons. It was never close, and if Bob Hopkins had been handing out grades, the Supersonics likely would have gotten a big, fat "D" for effort. "There's nothing that I can say about that game, except it was a fanny whipping with a chair on it," he said in his down-home Louisiana drawl, stretching out the words in a mix of humor and brutal honesty.

Of course Hopkins had plenty to say about the failing performance. As the team's X's and O's guy, he'd been too upset to sleep and too anxious to stay cooped in his room in the Hotel Pontchartrain. So in the still of Saturday morning with daybreak an hour away, Hoppy rode the elevator down to the lobby, hoping to find a sympathetic ear to bend.

Luck was with him. Center Jim Fox couldn't sleep either, and neither could the Seattle newspaper reporters traveling with the team. The group gathered in the coffee shop to jaw over cups of coffee and the aroma of bacon about last night's blot on an otherwise outstand-

ing week. The Pistons had shrewdly ignored Haywood and the Seattle frontline, recognizing that Archie and Fred Brown were the keys
to the Seattle offense. Everywhere Archie dribbled, he had two and
three bodies switching onto him, chests out and arms waving and
grabbing. The same went for Brown.

The sun had now risen, and upstairs Archie heard the dreaded
wake-up call. Trainer Frank Furtado said a bus was en route to transport the team to the airport for its flight to New York. "Be downstairs
no later than 9:30." Archie and John Brisker, his roommate for the
road trip, packed their suitcases, joining everyone in the lobby a few
minutes ahead of schedule. Outside a large bus idled near a snow
bank, sending a noxious white plume spiraling upward into the icy
morning air. The temperature: 22 degrees.

"Put your own bags in the luggage racks," barked the bus driver.

Per NBA custom the rookies stepped forward to tend to the suitcases. Archie boarded the bus feeling an unusual twinge of regret
about leaving Detroit. The team wouldn't return until mid-December,
and he'd miss seeing his family.

By 11:30 the team was in the air en route to La Guardia International Airport. "Will this be the first time that you play in the [Madi-
son Square] Garden?" Archie asked Tom Burleson seated next to him.

Burleson nodded yes.

"Remember, it's just another court," said Archie, channeling his
role as the team's calming, battle-tested elder statesman.

Up in first class Bill Russell had done his level best to forget the
Friday night massacre. "It was like jet lag or something," he'd told
reporters after the game, sloughing off the "fanny whipping" as a
fluke. He'd already met with Hoppy. The Supersonics would be back
on the rise tonight against the Knicks. Just wait and see.

NEW YORK, NOVEMBER 16, 1974. The scoreboard said it all: Knicks
50, Seattle 19. For a second straight night there was nothing super
about the Supersonics.

A wise guy heckled between organ vamps, "Russell, your team looks
like a prison team." That would be a team that had shot a criminal 24
percent from the field and whose swarming defense of the last few

weeks had gone on the lam. Nobody was jumping out on screens or making the right switches, allowing the Knicks to work the basketball to the open man for uncontested shots.

Russell, following the psychological playbook of his mentor Red Auerbach, yanked his starting backcourt halfway through the second quarter. In went hustling reserves Slick Watts and Tal Skinner, come what may. What came was a blistering Sonics press that forced the Knicks into a turnover-filled second half and flipped this laughable game into a fourth-quarter nail-biter until Earl Monroe took over in a flashback to his pirouetting, double-clutching, you-can't-stop-me days in Baltimore.

Afterward Russell spewed fire and brimstone at his starters behind closed locker room doors for nine heated minutes. ("It was a damn basketball clinic out there," he kept repeating.) Had Russell gone a minute longer, it would have cost him a $1,000 fine. The NBA wanted reporters in the locker room no later than ten minutes following the final buzzer. Reporters needed to file their stories, and players apparently needed to vent about the cruelty of the NBA road.

NEW YORK, NOVEMBER 17, 1974. Archie opened his eyes and located the clock mounted on the wall. It was 10 a.m. Archie sprang out of bed and roused his roommate, John Brisker. The two tossed clothes and toothbrushes into their suitcases and hurried downstairs. Too late. The team had departed over an hour ago for La Guardia International and a scheduled mid-morning commercial flight to Atlanta.

Archie stopped at the front desk, where a note from trainer Frank Furtado instructed him to take a cab to La Guardia and catch such-and-such a flight. Furtado didn't have to state the obvious: Archie would be fined for oversleeping and billed for the flight. So would Brisker, who swore that no wake-up call had been placed to their room. Was it an honest mistake? Or had Bill Russell put Furtado up to it for an excuse to fine Brisker? That's what Brisker wanted to know as he and Archie squeezed into the back of a Yellow Cab and disappeared into the glob of late-morning, bumper-to-bumper Manhattan traffic.

When Archie and Brisker arrived fashionably late in Atlanta, Spencer Haywood played it cool, cracking jokes with his trusted fellow

Detroiters and sucking attention in his direction. That was Haywood. He was a boisterous personality. But the boisterous was suddenly punctuated with a sniffle and a cough. Haywood had caught the flu bug in New York and admitted to feeling achy. Haywood vowed to be ready for the Atlanta game in two days.

But it was not to be. After fourteen second-half lead changes the Hawks finally surged ahead for good midway through the fourth quarter to claim the win. Russell, his chin lurching forward, glared his way to the locker room.

"It's got to be the longest speech ever," a ball boy exclaimed while waiting outside for the locker room door to open. Twenty-five minutes and a $1,000 fine later, the door finally popped open. Shortly thereafter players laden with bags rolled out of the locker room. Among the first out was John Brisker, who hadn't gotten off the bench on the road trip. Then out trickled Archie, Haywood, and Brown. They had a midnight flight to New Orleans.

About two hours later their flight descended through the darkness, red lights blinking on the wings, and touched down in New Orleans. The local (Central) time was 12:30 a.m., with the temperature still hovering in the sixties. "Crescent City! I'm home, baby," Slick Watts announced after drawing his first breaths of the sultry swamp air.

When the team arrived at its hotel near Bourbon Street, the desk clerk drew a blank on the reservation and then told everyone to wait while the housekeeping staff prepared the rooms. "The style of this motel is early dump," someone grumped about the décor. While everyone waited, members of the American Power Boat Association, staying at the hotel for their annual convention, passed through the lobby, some having imbibed one Hurricane too many on Bourbon Street and feeling no inhibitions.

"Bill RUSSELL!"

"The Boston Celtics are staying at our hotel."

"That guy over there must be eight feet tall."

At about 2 a.m. the room keys were finally distributed. Time for the Sonics to dream of wrapping up this disappointing road trip with a win in the Crescent City. Game time: less than eighteen hours away.

NEW ORLEANS, NOVEMBER 20, 1974. Hot Rod Hundley was remembered as "the clown prince" of college basketball for his entertaining All-American run at West Virginia University in the 1950s. Now Hundley brought his special brand of showmanship to the microphone as the colorful voice of the first-year New Orleans Jazz. He started each radio broadcast with the signature intro, "They call San Francisco 'the City,' New York 'the Big Apple.' Now swing with me to the Land of Jazz, New Orleans."

Tonight Hundley would swing with his radio audience to creaky Municipal Auditorium, just north of the French Quarter, for the first meeting of the Seattle Supersonics and the New Orleans Jazz, losers of fourteen of their first fifteen games. Though the Sonics struggled early, they came on late to take the lead. "Then Clark took over with four consecutive points—as he has down the stretch on several other occasions—and Seattle had salvaged a [99–95] victory," wrote a reporter at courtside.

Hot Rod Hundley hurried through the postgame stats, noting Seattle remained in second place in the Pacific Division. With that Hundley signed off with his signature line, referring to a popular Vieux Carre watering hole, "Win or lose, I'll see you at Pat O'Brien's." A Hurricane would be waiting, heavy on the rum. Cheers.

# 30

*As we were coming out of the All-Star break, second place in the Pacific Division—and an automatic playoff berth—was up for grabs. We were exactly one percentage point ahead of third-place Portland. But things weren't looking good for us. Our scoring was way down, and we'd dropped from the fourth-best team in the league defensively to the second worst. Remember Bill Russell was supposed to be a defensive genius.*

*What ailed us was that our lineup just kept changing due to injury or illness, and Bill just kept shortening his rotation. I was the one veteran on the roster who could take charge of the offense like KC and Sam Jones used to do in Boston, and Bill had me logging big minutes. I don't want to sound dramatic, but my shoulder remained messed up. If I'd been playing in today's NBA, I'd probably have landed on the injured reserve to get it straight.*

---

Bellevue, Washington, January 31, 1975. Archie opened his eyes and, for a few groggy seconds, racked his brain. Was he in Chicago? Phoenix maybe? Then he heard the soft, rhythmic patter of rain outside his window, and it all came whirling back: last night's redeye flight from Phoenix, the late landing at Sea-Tac Airport, and the early-morning drive north along dark, deserted Interstate 405.

After the All-Star break and fifteen interminable and a few miserable days on the NBA road, Archie was finally in his own bed. Archie had played well on the team's first stops in Houston and New Orleans. Then he had picked up the winter flu bug that was going around and had ho-hum outings in Atlanta and Buffalo. After a long flight to Chicago and a day of hell coughing in a hotel room, Archie had gutted out the next game with the Bulls. Then he had hung in there for the team in Cleveland and Phoenix.

Archie had to play through his hacking coughs. Spencer Haywood and his twenty-one points and nine rebounds per game didn't make the trip. He was hospitalized with viral pneumonia. Fred Brown had a horrible sinus infection, then twisted his right ankle in the Atlanta game. By the Phoenix game bronchitis had leveled Leonard Gray. Bill Russell was also coughing, and Bob Hopkins had an abscess lanced on his foot and hobbled around like a penguin.

With all the bad karma swirling around the team, the Sonics had predictably sputtered on the road, losing four of seven games. That dinged Seattle's season record to 22–26. But the ding was minor enough to keep the Sonics deadlocked with Portland for second place in the Pacific Division.

SEATTLE, FEBRUARY 11, 1975. Happy birthday, Bill Russell. The NBA legend had turned forty-one years young today, and it went without saying that the birthday boy could do with some peace and quiet on his special day. Because Russell still wouldn't elaborate on his surprising refusal to be enshrined in the Hall of Fame, the press had filled in the blanks for him, dragging his mostly spotless national reputation flopping through the mud. Though Russell did his best "I'm rubber, you're glue" in public, it hadn't been fun being treated like an old coot in the press.

To lighten the mood Seattle's marketing guru Bob Walsh had granted all senior citizens free admission to tonight's NBA tussle to mark this old coot's birthday. More important, Russell and the real old coots in the crowd got to watch the Sonics snap their four-game tailspin with a narrow win over the Houston Rockets.

But at the final horn the birthday bash had very nearly descended into an ugly brawl. No, the senior citizens hadn't come to blows again jawing over Babe Ruth and Pie Traynor. It was veteran referee Earl Strom who had "purpled the air with obscenities" and threatened to kick some you-know-what.

The great purpling began after Strom had collected his warm-up jacket from the scorer's table and started his postgame amble toward the tunnel that led to the referees' dressing room, where an ice-cold bottle of Rainier beer and a cigar waited. About thirty steps from the tunnel entrance Strom felt a hand from behind grab his right arm. Strom reflexively turned and saw the hand belonged to a young black woman. Who could forget that face? Oh she of the leather lungs seated directly under the basket. The woman had railed at him all night, and now she and some of her courtside cronies had something more to say about his officiating.

What enraged the woman were Strom's inopportune whistles (delivered with his signature toot, pause, toot-toot-toot). As was whispered around the league, Strom often favored the visiting team, and tonight his inopportune toot-pause-toot toot-toots against the home team fouled out Archie early in the fourth quarter and very nearly cost Seattle the game down the stretch on a questionable charging call on Fred Brown.

Strom glared back, calculating his options. There was one of him and maybe six of them. That's when Strom, known for his cool, assertive demeanor, made a regrettable, split-second error in judgment. He took a step toward the woman and either tried to push or punch her aside.

As the two momentarily tangled, the chivalrous Fred Brown rushed forward to give Strom a swift shove away from the woman, whom he knew well. She was one of Archie's good friends from Detroit. Her name was Sonja.

The shove sent Strom sprawling backward into the lap of more courtside hostility. A man immediately grabbed Strom's arms from behind and trussed him like a Butterball turkey.

"What are you doing hitting a woman?" taunted Brown.

Strom, who'd fought his way up from the streets of working-class Pottstown, Pennsylvania, felt the fan's tight grip and yelled, "If you don't let go, I'll kick you in the balls." The grip tightened, and Strom seethed at Brown, "I'm going to kick your ass."

"Try it," Brown yelled, "I've got ten thousand people on my side."

Before Strom could follow through on the threats, fellow referee Hugh Evans and Bill Russell flew to the rescue. They got the fan to unhand Strom, then pushed and jostled him back onto the court to simmer down.

"Go to your locker room," commanded Russell, now joined by Archie. "It's over."

"I want that son of a bitch," yelled Strom, pointing at Brown while Evans body-hugged his partner for dear life. "I want to kick his ass."

"Go to your locker room. It's over."

Strom finally piped down, and Evans escorted his partner by the arm in the direction of the tunnel. A few feet from the entrance a cup of beer sailed down from the cheap seats like a Molotov cocktail and exploded with a sudsy kapow on Strom's head. Strom shook his fists in righteous indignation and purpled the air with his foulest obscenities yet until two cops finally escorted him into the tunnel and safety. When Strom reached the dressing room, his arms scraped red and beer still dripping down his cheeks and forehead, he paused with a gleam in his eye, looked back at the younger Evans, and burst into a belly laugh. "You think this is bad, you shoulda seen Syracuse back in the old days."

Strom cracked open a brown, twelve-ounce bottle of Rainier Beer and took a long, deep, forgetful gulp. Somewhere in between beers Archie rapped on the metal door of the dressing room. Archie hadn't witnessed the scuffle, but Sonja told him afterward that the whole thing was no big deal. Strom's push was unintentional.

"Sorry, I had no idea that she was your friend," Strom said after Archie explained everything—who Sonja was, why Brown had reacted, the whole nine yards. Strom finally poked his smoldering postgame cigar into his mouth and extended his right hand. As NBA referees loved to repeat: no harm, no foul.

SEATTLE, FEBRUARY 14, 1975. Roses are red / violets are blue / the Supersonics played a basketball game on Valentine's Day / that would soon make Bill Russell stew.

The slumping Portland Trail Blazers rolled into town, having dropped twelve of their last fourteen games, including the last five straight. Bill Walton, milling around before the game in a red lumberjack shirt and a matching red bandana, would be out of action. It was the bone spurs again. And oh yeah, Portland had managed just five road wins all season. In short, this one had all the hallmarks of a Valentine's Day Massacre.

Instead it was the great Valentine's Day Muddle. As advertised, Portland was terrible without Walton. But the Supersonics were equally bad. Up by eight in the fourth quarter, the Supes let Portland rally down the stretch. "Ever watch a couple of drunks fight where nobody lands a punch, but somebody must be declared a winner?" wrote Don Fair of the *Seattle Post-Intelligencer*. That about covered it. Portland threw the final punch to win on points.

Afterward Bill Russell slammed the locker room door for his NBA-allotted ten-minute postgame vent, groping for the proper adjective to place on this low point of the season. He settled on "disgraceful" and added a long spew of four-letter, alpha-male invective to drive home the point that he was at the end of his rope with his humbug gutless wonders. They'd screwed around in practice yesterday, and now this. Russell, still staring darts, finally departed for his mandatory postgame meet-and-greet with the equally humbug members of the media. "Our offense?" quipped Bill Russell. "I think they forgot the plays."

Archie was exempted. He'd gotten the Seattle offense humming early in what amounted to the high point of the evening. Then the ball stopped moving, and the five-man Sonic machine ground to a halt. Doing most of the holding was Spencer Haywood. He jab-stepped his defender, dribbled left, wheeled right, and gobbled up precious time on the shot clock. If red shirts double-teamed him, Haywood more often than not skipped a pass to Fred Brown on the perimeter to salvage the remaining seconds of the possession. "It was one-on-one, schoolyard basketball . . . at its worst," grumped Gil Lyons of the *Seattle Times*.

Two years ago Haywood's schoolyard tactics had been written off as Spencer being Spencer. He'd never met a shot that he didn't think he could make. And yet, having spent many a midnight meal listening to Russell wax poetic about the self-sacrificing Celtics, Haywood clearly knew better. But since his return from pneumonia it was as though Haywood was done being Mr. Nice Guy.

While Russell blew hot, venomous air in the postgame interview, his players slumped around their lockers, sweaty and in various states of undress. Archie, who had taken just seven shots from the field all night for ten points, had already begun his postgame ritual of icing down his bad shoulder. Near him the younger faces looked exhausted. They wore the aches and pains of a long NBA season like unwanted extra gear; each ouch was its own beast of burden to wrap, ice, slather, massage, and hope away.

Most of the players were psychologically spent from six long months of trying to figure out Russell. The Dictator. The Legend. The Enigma. Leonard Gray bristled at the sight of Russell. Freddie Brown often looked straight ahead, refusing to engage Russell's cackling one-liners about his paunch (now gone) and his pack-on-the-pounds body type.

But the fatigue involved more than hurt feelings. It involved dreams. Tom Burleson wanted to show everyone back home around Squirrel Creek, North Carolina, that he was one of the NBA's dominant centers. Though a little thin to bang his way to NBA success, Burleson had several numbers on his side. He stood a legitimate 7 feet 2 inches, possessed a 7-foot-6 wingspan, and had a twenty-nine inch vertical jump. That added up to the Needle rising thirty inches above the goal, when needed, to swat shots or tap them into the hoop. What's more, this proud son of a Green Beret had worked tirelessly in college to master the standard tricks of post play. He had a drop step to wheel around defenders and get to the rim, a soft jump hook taught to him by UCLA's John Wooden himself, and the court vision to whiz passes from the post to teammates flashing to the hoop for lay-ups. Burleson's strong work ethic had paid off in an NCAA championship and the fulfillment of his dream to play pro ball.

Like his collegiate nemesis Bill Walton, Burleson now found that the dream had its own mind-numbing imperfections. Bob Hopkins, the Sonics' practice coach and, by default, head of player development, had never coached a big man of Burleson's caliber at small college Xavier. According to Burleson, it put a big damper on his pro development. Case in point: Hoppy often watched the heavier NBA centers bump Burleson and constantly yelled out to him, "Don't let him push you around! Punch him back. Elbow him. But don't let him do that!"

Burleson quickly discovered that elbowing back against the NBA's 250-pound brick houses was a fool's errand. His sharp elbows only incited them to push back harder and explained why Burleson had been in more brawls this season than any NBA center. He desperately needed Hoppy to teach him how to exploit his height and quickness in the NBA, his main advantages in the post. Hoppy brushed aside the request for tutorials and told Burleson that the cure to all that ailed him was simple: get tougher, dammit!

Russell would impart his wisdom on NBA post play whenever the spirit moved him. But Burleson noticed that Russell didn't have a lot to offer on the offensive end. Scoring wasn't his forte. And yet it was Russell who was now running the offense in Seattle. About a week into the season Russell had scrapped Hoppy's newfangled triangle offense, concluding that his young players weren't up to executing its complicated reads and options. In Russell's dictatorial mind, why run an egalitarian offense? He didn't want Slick Watts or Tal Skinner shooting twenty footers. He had three proven twenty-point-per-game scorers on the roster: Brown, Haywood, and Clark. Get them the basketball.

Russell reintroduced the tried-and-true Celtics offense that he'd rolled out during his first season in Seattle. Though called the Celtics offense, it was hardly a perfect replica. Russell had kept the hard double screens to pick off defenders and squeeze his scorers open. But he'd stripped out most of the ball movement, in and out and from side to side, that had made the Celtics offense hum.

What remained of Boston's offense were isolation plays. When Burleson's number was called, he posted up his defender at the rim, jostled for the advantage, and tried to flip in his jump hook. There was no passing out of the post to set up Haywood or Brown for a better open shot on the perimeter. Barring a double team, tough guys imposed their will on their defenders. Or so Hoppy told Burleson. Burleson found the whole thing utterly predictable, prone to stagnation, and just bad basketball.

The bad basketball had some second-guessing the Legend's coaching credentials. They could snap off his bad in-game decisions like naming songs on the radio. Now joining in the locker-room vent sessions was Haywood. His nearly two-year bromance with Russell was over. Haywood, though still smitten with the idea of Russell's trailblazing image, had tired of kowtowing to it. The Legend was too proud, too prickly, too divisive. John Brisker, whom Haywood trusted like a brother, razzed him continuously for being so chummy with his tormentor. Brisker's barbs had gotten old, and Haywood decided enough was enough. "I was trying hard not to look like [Russell's] bobo," he explained.

Russell seemed to sense the chill in the air with his superstar and turned inward to the Celtic pride that sustained him. Eleven championship rings still trumped Haywood's three All-Pro selections.

Haywood seemed to have reverted to "schoolyard basketball" to reassert himself and his superb athletic ability. As Haywood believed from the tips of his extra-jointed fingers to the soles of his white Adidas sneakers, he was good for thirty points and fifteen rebounds on any NBA night that he chose. What's more, he was good for it whether he committed a defensive boo-boo or refused to be Russell's bobo.

SEATTLE, FEBRUARY 16, 1975. Archie joked that when he had arrived in Seattle last October, it had rained all morning but had given way to clear skies in the afternoon. In November the skies had been clear in the morning but had given way to rain in the afternoon. By December, Archie laughed, it just rained all day, every day.

Despite the heavy umbrella weather, Archie remained happy in Seattle. He'd stayed above the Sonics' fray in his role as the trusted veteran. Bill Russell treated him with respect, and so did the younger players. But he'd never been on a team with such palpable tension between players and coach. There was a story making the rounds about Russell running into the now-retired Jerry West and how the two had spent a few moments rolling their eyes at this new generation. These Baby Boomers didn't play hard enough. They weren't tough enough. They weren't savvy enough. Then there was Russell's pet peeve: they didn't care enough about the game.

Archie could empathize with Russell and West, but he also saw things a little differently. Basketball wasn't meant to lionize the era of Russell and West. Basketball, like Hollywood, continued to evolve into a higher form of entertainment. Twenty years ago a few token black NBA players were encouraged to rebound the misses and pass the ball back to their white teammates for another shot. Today a majority of black players were free to score and thrill America with their jaw-dropping innovations in the air or off the dribble.

The black Boomers inhabited a snappier new dimension that eluded Russell (with his limited offensive skills) and West (with his good but not great athleticism). These black Boomers, joined by Pete Maravich and other uniquely talented white players, constituted the greatest generation of showmen yet to arrive on the pro basketball stage.

Why not open up the game for Haywood, Seattle's doctor of dunk? Or run the offense through Burleson to set up his teammates for alley oops or Fred Brown's high-arching bombs "from downtown"? Why did Burleson, like Jim McDaniels before him, have to play in the spitting defensive image of Russell and his era? That would be akin to expecting John Lennon to croon like Frank Sinatra. The times, like Casey Kasem's Top 40, had moved on to new genres, fresh tastes, and exciting possibilities.

Russell's refusal to dismount his legend and move into the future created not only tension, but also a situation that Archie heard repeated in the locker room: chaos. It was chaotic for the younger players to have seen Russell quoted in the newspaper a week ago as believing their playoff hopes were "in a deep hole, about six feet. I'd say that's the normal depth of a grave." It was chaotic to watch Russell destroy John Brisker's career and engage in mind games with his other whipping boys. It was chaotic for them to second-guess Russell's competence and interest in coaching, and it was chaotic to be blamed for everything that inevitably went wrong.

With just over a month and twenty-five games left in the season Archie was nearing the end of his three-year NBA contract and staring retirement in the face. He didn't want to go out in sheer chaos. He wanted to go out with a triumphant bang, and that meant helping to pull his teammates out of that 6-foot playoff grave. Despite Russell's rhetoric, the Sonics (26–31) remained tied with Phoenix for second place, technically two percentage points ahead of their rivals to the south. The playoffs were there for the taking as a celebrated first for this troubled franchise. Archie would continue pushing, imparting his wisdom, and getting everyone to pull together in the right direction, starting this afternoon against the slumping Los Angeles Lakers.

Like he had done in the Portland game, Archie got the offense rolling in the first quarter. It was the roll in the second quarter that he didn't expect. Archie's left ankle rolled when he landed on some-body's foot. A throbbing pain ran up his leg, and Archie immedi-ately gimped over to the sideline. Experience told him that this was a bad one.

## 31

*I couldn't put any weight on my ankle by morning. It was swollen stiff on both sides, and I faced at least a week on the injured list. One week extended to three, and the team kept losing. By late February I was still on the injured list, and the Sonics flew East for an eight-game, fourteen-day road trip.*

*We beat New York, and Bill was all smiles. It was his first victory in New York as head coach of the Sonics. The next game, we choked big time against Washington. Bill pulled me aside afterward and said he needed me on the court to steady the team. I told him that my ankle still wasn't right, but he wasn't taking no for an answer. Bill was of that generation that if the team needed you, you were expected to play. What could I do as this point in my career? Bill activated me off the injured list.*

---

**H**artford, Connecticut, March 2, 1975. While the CBS Sports crew shuffled around before the game unspooling cords and fastening television lights, Archie and Fred Brown spent some quality time talking basketball with Oscar Robertson. The Big O, now almost a full season into retirement and the color commentator on the NBA *Game of the Week*, remained a total basketball nut. Robertson needled Brown to quit relying on his jump shot at the end of games and drive to the basket instead. Force the referees to make the call. It was pure locker-room analytics a good twenty years before the math whizzes would arrive on the NBA scene with their algorithms. Get a three-point play while the opposition settled for a two-point play.

Archie of course had lived by those three-is-better-than-two words during his career, though one of his problems right now transitioning back into the lineup involved getting to the basket. The bad ankle, though partially healed, deadened whenever he put pressure on it. That became painfully obvious in the second period, when the ball landed in his hands for an easy breakaway lay-up. As Archie glided in for the score, his bad ankle screamed. The lay-up skimmed out, and Bill Russell got the message. Archie wasn't ready to return to action.

Russell didn't need his veteran playmaker this afternoon anyway. Today's go-to lineup—Spencer Haywood, Talvin Skinner, Tom Burleson, Fred Brown, and Slick Watts—dominated the Celtics in the fourth quarter with a mix of hustle and surprising precision. The offense ran through Haywood, positioned just to the right of the free-throw line with the bulky veteran Paul Silas leaning on him. Haywood, looking every bit like an All-Star on national television, leaned back on Silas, faked left, and maneuvered right for either his patented pull-up ten footer or soared straight to the rim, over and over again. With 3:13 to play Haywood converted a three-point play for the lead, and Brown drove to the basket on back-to-back plays, just like the Big O told him to, for two scores (though no three-point plays) that put victory thirty-one in the books for Seattle.

After the usual "grab your bags" late-night rush to the airport, Haywood boarded the team's short flight to Buffalo wearing a funky eye patch. Silas had poked him in the eye twice, badly scratching the cornea and leaving Haywood in wincing postgame agony. Knock on (Hay)wood, scratched corneas usually healed quickly.

BUFFALO, MARCH 4, 1975. The funky eye patch was crinkled up in the garbage can, and Spencer Haywood's cornea had received a clean bill of health. It was Haywood's game that was ailing against Buffalo. Number twenty-four in green fumbled passes, whiffed on wide-open shots, and, worst of all for his all-seeing coach, failed to hustle back on defense. Bill Russell probably would have bitten his tongue earlier in the season. The NBA season is long, and the two could talk it out later at a favorite restaurant, man to man, mentor to student. But with their friendship on the rocks Russell had grown coy toward his former student. With 6:02 left and Seattle trailing but still in the ballgame, Russell benched the guy who had had the monster fourth quarter the other day against Boston.

Buffalo's Bob McAdoo, the NBA's leading scorer, floated like a butterfly along the perimeter and stung like a bee from fifteen feet and under. Bob Hopkins, Russell's court strategist, yelled for the nearest defender to stick like glue to McAdoo on the pick-and-rolls that were leaving him so wide open. About six feet from Hopkins, Haywood sat seething. If looks could kill. "I feel fine," Haywood snapped after the close loss. "I'm just pissed off."

Russell, now using the media to communicate with Haywood, settled on the word "half-assed" to label his team's performance and to dig a little deeper into his star's bruised psyche.

Taking it all in was Archie, a bag of ice balanced on his shoulder and one on his bum ankle. Russell had increased his minutes tonight to nineteen, up from nine against Philadelphia and Boston. Yes, his body hurt all over. But more than ever Archie's veteran leadership was needed on the court to keep this young team focused and Russell's psychological warfare out of their heads.

MILWAUKEE, MARCH 6, 1975. The snow had started falling yesterday evening a few hours after the Sonics had landed in Milwaukee. By midnight five inches had accumulated on the sidewalk outside the hotel. By sunrise it looked like eight inches, with a few stray flakes still swirling down, caught in a stiff, ten-mile-per-hour wind.

By late morning Archie could see through the lobby window that the streets were mostly cleared of snow. But the stiff wind continued, and the temperature remained below freezing. Archie wasn't headed anywhere, though he didn't have to worry about tonight's game. He'd reached an agreement with Bill Russell to sit out the contest and give his ankle a little extra time to heal.

A few players started a card game, while others talked about old times and gossiped about the plight of John Brisker. Last month Brisker had been a no-show for six straight practices, claiming a variety of maladies. Russell put Brisker on the injured list, promising to "give him a call" in five games. Instead Russell prepared to reactivate veteran forward John Hummer, now nearly recovered from foot surgery. Brisker's next stop? Only Russell knew, and he wasn't talking.

The more immediate issue was Spencer Haywood's benching in Buffalo. Everybody had heard the rumor, published a few weeks ago in the *Los Angeles Herald-Examiner*, that Haywood was on the trade block. Was the benching somehow related? Haywood, immensely confident in his talent, scoffed. But he remained "pissed off" about Russell's power play.

Haywood's "Russell fatigue" became obvious against the Bucks. Though his shooting was better tonight, his effort remained "half-assed" and sloppy with the basketball. In the third quarter Russell benched Haywood for a second straight night. While sitting mindlessly on the bench spinning a basketball on the floor, Haywood watched Kareem Abdul-Jabbar terrorize the rookie Tom Burleson.

"Push him back," yelled Bob Hopkins.

Jabbar kept using the lead elbow to drive back Burleson and flick his soft, right-handed sky hook. Finally Russell ordered a double team. Jabbar and his high basketball IQ simply found the open man. More often than not, it was long-range gunner Jon McGlocklin. His six high-arching bombs down the stretch sealed Seattle's fate.

"Why'd you bench Haywood tonight in the second half?" a reporter asked Russell.

"I liked the way the others were playing, and I didn't like the way he was playing."

Haywood made a stop in the Bucks' locker room to check in with some of the Bucks and probably to avoid Russell. "Did I play a bad game?" Haywood asked rhetorically. "Nope, I didn't play, period." When the rhetoric was over, Haywood walked to the door and called out, "See you in Seattle [in a few weeks]. Hope I'll be playing by then."

CHICAGO, MARCH 7, 1975. Frank Furtado, the Sonics' trainer and designated travel agent, glanced up at the flight board in the lobby of O'Hare International Airport. His eyes scrolled down to "K" and Kansas City. The gate for their United flight to Kansas City was that way, Furtado surmised, and everyone proceeded like lemmings "that way." While their fellow travelers gawked at the superhuman height of Tom Burleson ("he must be eight feet tall") or wondered whether that tall black guy was Bill Russell (or Wilt Chamberlain), Archie limped along inconspicuously, shooting the breeze with Fred Brown, also limping from the thigh bruise that he had picked up last night in Milwaukee. One narrow hallway gave way to another, and Archie nudged Brown. Approaching them from the other direction was none other than NBA referee Earl Strom.

The last time Brown had seen Strom, the two had nearly come to blows in Seattle Coliseum. A month later all was forgotten, though the matter remained under review at league headquarters. "Hold me back," Brown yelled to Archie with mock seriousness.

The three bantered like old buddies. Strom finally said he had a flight to catch, and Archie and Brown continued their joint limp to God knows where.

"Our backs are against the wall, I guess," Archie picked up their conversation, referring to the uncertain state of the Sonics.

"When haven't they been against the wall?" answered Brown.

Seattle (31–36) had lost two in a row and dropped three of the five games played so far on the road trip. True, Seattle somehow remained a half game ahead of third-place Phoenix. But for how long? Haywood and Russell were at odds, Archie and Brown were limping, and the Kansas City–Omaha Kings (38–29), their next opponent, were red hot.

KANSAS CITY, MISSOURI, March 8, 1975. Before the Kings game Spencer Haywood sat staring blankly in front of his locker. At 6 feet 9 inches and a rock-solid 225 pounds, Haywood looked bigger than an Oakland Raider and just as menacing.

Haywood, though, had no intention of bashing heads or quarterbacks. As Haywood later explained the blank stare, he was trying to get his head straight. That meant letting go of the anger for Russell that boiled deep within. How had he gone from looking like a million bucks against the Celtics to a spot in Russell's doghouse forty-eight hours later?

Haywood continued staring darkly ahead, and two words—fuck it—popped out of nowhere into his head and poked through the pain. That's right, fuck it. Haywood loved to play basketball. He loved to run, dunk, snatch rebounds, and stand out as the dominant athlete on the floor. He decided to quit obsessing about the stuff that he couldn't control and just play basketball with the passion that was always there.

And Haywood (twenty-two points, seventeen rebounds) did exactly that against the Kings. Making his transition a whole lot easier was the inspired play of Slick Watts. Watts, knowing his team was in trouble, scrapped, clawed, dove after loose balls, and defended like a glove through most of four quarters. Also pitching in big time was Archie. He logged twenty-three solid minutes, providing sixteen points and seven assists. After a month of pampering his bad ankle he could finally put his full weight on it without wincing.

Though the Kings, led by the amazing Tiny Archibald, stayed close through three quarters, the final stanza belonged once again to Haywood. After the win Haywood was back to his old, fun-loving self. So were his teammates. They could do this—not for Russell but for themselves. Up and down the season had gone through sixty-eight games, and the Sonics were suddenly headed back up to better times with fourteen to go.

KANSAS CITY, MISSOURI, March 9, 1975. Archie thought it had been wishful thinking to board the airplane. Snow had been falling for about an hour, guided by stiff gusts of wind. The buzz in coach was that the pilots had better hurry and get into the air while they still could. Then, almost as if on cue, the captain announced over the intercom that they'd been cleared for takeoff.

The stewardesses rushed to their stations, and the large commercial jet rumbled down the runway, the snow now sticking to just about everything, and lifted into the air. For about twenty seconds it was like flying inside a snow globe. But once above the clouds, all that remained was a tranquil blue horizon that, as the passengers would soon discover, had been booby-trapped with frequent pockets of choppy air. The choppiness came from a destabilizing low-pressure system over the Texas panhandle, and the captain warned everyone to buckle in for the next hour or so. Today's flight into Dallas would be a real rodeo ride.

By the third or fourth buck-'em bronco, Archie felt his stomach in his throat, where it stayed for the remainder of the flight. In first class Bill Russell had turned bug eyed. "I'm giving myself fifteen more minutes," he announced to the person sitting next to him. "Then I'm going to barf." A stewardess approached, smiled, and gave him a long, quizzical look. "Are you Wilt Chamberlain?"

Russell snapped his head away from her and immediately let loose into the barf bag. That turned out to be a good move as the rodeo ride culminated with the most terrifying landing of the season. Archie and the rest of the Sonics pushed their way off the plane as soon as the hatch opened. They had just enough time to take a deep breath and consider calling a loved one—or a priest. The team was soon back in the air for what thankfully was a smoother ride to Houston.

The game against the Rockets fit the day's flight pattern. All was a rough ride through most of four quarters. Then Tommy Burleson flew in for a rim-rattling dunk that landed the game in overtime at 110 each. In the extra leg of the journey all was mostly smooth sailing. The Sonics closed out the game and evened out this epic road trip at four and four. "Now if we can just get it together at home," said Russell afterward.

The Sonics would finish the regular season with nine of their final thirteen games in the friendly confines of Seattle Coliseum, where they had inexplicably lost half of their home games this season. That would be the final hurdle in this crazy season: learn how to win before a home crowd that adored them.

BELLEVUE, WASHINGTON, MARCH 14, 1975. The red-eye flight from Houston touched down in Seattle well after midnight, and Archie pulled his Mercedes into the driveway of his home in suburban Bellevue around 3 a.m. Thank goodness the Sonics had the day off tomorrow. Under the dim moonlight Archie scooped his bags from the trunk, stuck the key in the lock, and opened the door to a stack of mail waiting for his return. He fingered through a few of the envelopes, but who was Archie kidding? He needed to get some rest.

When he finally awoke, sunlight poked through the curtains. It had to be around lunchtime. Archie's thoughts drifted through the murk of two weeks on the road. One moment in particular was indelible. Bill Russell had held a practice after the Milwaukee loss. As he was wont to do after a bad loss, Russell ordered his "gutless wonders" to run a lap around the court for each point that Milwaukee had scored. Archie did the math in his head. That came to 110 laps.

"Bill, my ankle. You want me to run all those laps on my bad ankle?"

"Just humor me on this, Archie," Russell answered in a confiding half whisper. "I've got to teach these young guys some discipline."

There was such a strange dynamic on this team. Russell thought he was somehow breaking through and molding character, lap by monotonous lap. But most of these hip youngsters wanted no part of the powerful Russell and his mind games. In some ways the team dynamic was like the old fairy tale of the emperor's new clothes. The players humored Russell's vanity out of fear and worried about his next whim and its crushing influence on their NBA careers.

And now, over the final thirteen games of the regular season, this NBA version of the emperor's new clothes advanced to the final challenge of clinching a playoff berth for the Sonics and the city of Seattle. Would this be Archie's last NBA hurrah? Right now he wasn't sure. If not for the injuries, he remained one of the better playmaking guards in the league. He had showed it the other night against Houston; his ankle was feeling better, and he hit a clutch driving hook in the final minutes of play. In his mind he could definitely play another year. But in his heart Archie wasn't so sure.

SEATTLE, MARCH 14, 1975. In a season filled with strange moments this one was just plain spooky against the Buffalo Braves. With the Sonics ahead early in the third quarter the sellout crowd began the spontaneous chilling chant, "Kill, kill, kill," like a scene from a monster movie or possibly Charles Manson's *Helter Skelter*.

Kill, kill, kill the Sonics surely did, extending their lead to thirty-six points early in the fourth quarter before Bill Russell mercifully gave his starters the rest of the night off. "I don't recall the team hustling more than they did tonight," said a pleased Russell. "That might just be the best game that we've played all year."

Afterward in the Seattle locker room one would have never known that the Sonics were the victors. Archie had bags of ice on his shoulder and ankle. Spencer Haywood had a bad case of bronchitis. Fred Brown tended to a sore hip and a torn rotator cuff in his shoulder. Slick Watts had a bruised tailbone. John Hummer, now activated from the injured list, tended to his surgically repaired foot.

Trainer Frank Furtado cut short the postgame first-aid session.

They had a boarding call to make, followed by a two-hour flight to Oakland. About 2 a.m. the Sonics arrived at their Bay Area lodgings limping, coughing, and just plain feeling blah. That's exactly how the team awoke later that morning, and the sluggishness carried over to the game that evening. The Sonics led 4–0 and 6–5. It was all Golden State the rest of the way. After the thirty-six-point beat down the Sonics caught a late-night flight home, finally landing at Sea-Tac International at 3:35 a.m. They had a game with the New York Knicks in exactly twelve hours and more bad news to come. Haywood, nursing a 101 degree fever in Oakland, was doubtful for the Knicks game.

Fred Brown wasn't in much better shape. Around 5 a.m. he finally drifted off to sleep. But pain shot through his damaged right shoulder whenever he rolled over, which he often did. He couldn't stop thinking about the Golden State disaster. Then his stomach started twisting in four directions at once. By 10 a.m. Brown had turned on a college basketball game on television for background noise to lull him and his stomach back to sleep. An hour later Brown got up and felt his stomach cramp. He had the stomach flu.

Brown forced down a few bites of scrambled eggs and sipped hot tea with honey. The game was at three, and Brown arrived at the Seattle Coliseum looking like something that the cat had dragged in. He consulted with the team physician, who offered a little something to settle his stomach. He gulped it down, but what really bothered Brown was his blurry vision. "I didn't think I'd be able to see the hoop."

The NBA's premier long-range shooter didn't really need to see the hoop against the Knicks. "Downtown Freddie" got hot in the second quarter, and soon nearly every shot that left his hand and damaged shoulder swished, banked, or occasionally rattled through the rim.

It was one of those magical moments that dot an NBA season, and of course his improbable thirty-seven-point performance deserved a fitting fairy tale finish. The Knicks came roaring back in the fourth quarter, and Earl Monroe took matters into his always clutch hands. Every time Monroe wheeled in for the score, Brown found a sliver of daylight on the next possession to sink another of his twenty-foot rainmakers. Then the Pearl stole a pass at midcourt with thirty-six seconds to play and raced in for the score and foul. Monroe added the free throw, pulling New York to within one.

The ballgame now came down to one possession. At eleven on the shot clock Seattle's Jim Fox winged a pass just beyond the outstretched fingers of a Knicks defender and over to Brown. The Pearl waited. The fleeter Brown dribbled Monroe into a screen and then scooted to the baseline, with a help-side defender closing in for the block. Brown, scrunching to make himself smaller and avoid the block, adjusted the release point of his shot to chest level and lofted a soft ten footer straight through the net for the win.

The Sonics had won two in a row at home. Whaddya know?

SEATTLE, MARCH 21, 1975. The Seattle newspapers were running a daily playoff countdown. Right now the Sonics' magic number was calculated at five. That was any combination of Sonics wins and Portland losses that equaled five, and Seattle would be in the NBA playoffs for the first time.

Everywhere Bill Russell went, he fielded some version of the same question: Do you think the Sonics will make the playoffs? There were only so many ways to answer the unknown. Russell, slipping into his more engaged public persona, defaulted to the provocative. "If opportunity knocks, you've got to be there," he said of the playoff run.

But Russell remained convinced that his veterans were too injured to secure a playoff bid, and everyone else was too inexperienced to know how to win. His ego told him that he was the one guy in Seattle who could take responsibility for the team's fate. It was his time to prove to his detractors that the "Seattle Celtics" had arrived.

So Russell brainstormed with his cousin and chief strategist, Bob Hopkins, about pulling off the basketball equivalent of an intervention to get their players the needed strategic help and, though never expressly stated, "idiot-proof" their playoff run. For Hoppy, the basketball-obsessed college coach, the only way forward was to put the focus back on "team." They had to quit this one-on-one monkey business. Hoppy rambled on about back cuts, shuffle cuts, and all the back-to-the-basics stuff that Russell had heard since training camp.

By pure chance the Sonics now had two- and three-day gaps

between games—or long enough to impose some discipline for the stretch run. Hoppy dusted off some of his favorite drills. The gutless wonders would be going back to school, where Hoppy and his famous cousin could feel in complete control of the team's playoff run and a band of players who, to varying degrees, had given up on them.

SEATTLE, MARCH 23, 1975. The Sonics' magic number remained stuck on five. Portland kept winning, and the more team-oriented Sonics had suddenly dropped two straight. More distressing for the Sonics, Fred Brown and his tender right shoulder had endured just two minutes in their last outing, while Spencer Haywood got yanked almost immediately in his return to the lineup. Coach's decision.

Tonight, after two days of rest and rehab, Haywood and Brown had made their emergency return to the starting lineup against the slumping Phoenix Suns. Though both looked okay offensively and logged heavy minutes, the Sonics let this one slip through their fingers.

Afterward Russell kept the locker-room door closed about ten minutes longer than the NBA permitted. A league fine would be forthcoming. But Russell didn't give a damn. He needed to set a few things straight about teamwork, total effort, and pride. It was all the stuff that he and Hoppy had been discussing. As Russell spoke, Haywood tried to subdue his wicked cough. Russell kept going. He wasn't going to let Haywood interrupt him. And yet the cough had already interrupted the train of thought of most in the room. They knew that Haywood's respiratory problem and Brown's numb right arm were the cause of this two-game skid. But all Russell had left to lean on was the hallowed concept of team. If he leaned hard enough on it, his intention seemed to be that maybe Archie, Slick Watts, and some of the rookies would band together to make a dent in that magic number five.

SEATTLE, MARCH 26, 1975. Oh what a difference a few days make. Tonight the Sonics had pulled together at home to thump the Los Angeles Lakers, 110–89. The win, coupled with second-place Portland's loss, dropped the Sonics' magic number to three with six games remaining in the regular season.

As most of tonight's near sellout crowd could attest, the win wasn't a thing of beauty. The Sonics committed twenty-four turnovers and took some terrible shots. But Russell got what he wanted—a team effort—that started before the game with an awkward but overdue chat between Russell and his star, Spencer Haywood.

"For myself, I can say I'm going to do all of those things necessary to win—play tough defense, set picks, move away from the ball, try to set up the other guys—and I'm not going to stand around with the ball," clarified Haywood.

Whether the words were sincere or empty only Haywood could say. But Haywood, still popping pills to tame his cough, finished with twenty-three points and ten rebounds. The star of the game was Archie. With Fred Brown out of action Archie had pulled double duty to knock down a team-high twenty-four points and dish out eight assists to Haywood and crew. It was moments like these that made Archie think he had another NBA season left in the tank.

SEATTLE, MARCH 29, 1975. Archie was on good terms with all his teammates. But he was probably the tightest with Fred Brown. The two always found time to talk basketball, books, politics, business, music, civil rights, Bill Russell, John Brisker, and you name it. So after beating Golden State tonight, it was only natural that the two had sought out each other in the locker room to mark this special moment.

"We need just one more," Brown laughed. "Isn't that something, man?"

Archie concurred and added with a comic lilt in his voice, "The playoffs are where the owners get rich and the players get a little richer." He was referring to the NBA's record playoff pool this season of $950,000, which would be divvied up unequally among the ten entrants.

But this upcoming trip to the playoffs was truly more about pride for Archie than the postseason paycheck. Russell had brought him to Seattle to help lead a young, troubled franchise to the playoffs. Archie had fought through his injuries and all of the dysfunction that had this franchise by the throat. Now he was on the brink of delivering on his end of the bargain in this Sunday afternoon game against the Portland Trail Blazers.

As Archie and his teammates wound their way from the locker room through the cramped hallway with the cheap linoleum floor and yellow glare of the overhead box lights, the energy inside the sold-out arena was incandescent. Seattle had never won a thing in the NBA, and the crowd wanted that monkey off its back. Joining them tonight was owner Sam Schulman. He'd made a rare trip to the Pacific Northwest to be there when his team finally got into the playoffs.

What Schulman and the others got was an extremely heated, low-scoring contest. The Sonics would inch into the lead, and the Trail Blazers would claw right back. In the fourth quarter, with just over eight minutes to go, Portland clawed back once again and finally took the lead. "Fred, let's work together," Russell yelled after Brown, trying to put the team on his aching right shoulder, missed a forced shot.

Portland rebounded Brown's miss, and the crowd went numb for the first time, though thankfully not for long. Portland fumbled away its chance to extend the lead, and the Sonics worked the ball to Spencer Haywood in the corner, the bearded Sidney Wicks shadowing him. Haywood, who'd been locked in and lights out all night, rocked backward as though setting his feet to shoot. Wicks bit on the oldest fake in the book, and, bam, Haywood was gone. As Hayward barreled ahead on the dribble, Portland's 6-foot-11 LaRue Martin slide-stepped over to protect the rim. Haywood rose above Martin's raised hand, cocked his right arm back, and dunked like he was pounding a nail. In the stands, pure, unrehearsed bedlam ensued from Schulman at ground level and cascaded all the way up to the cheap seats.

The Sonics took the lead and every last ounce of momentum in the building. Jim Fox, old Foxy, banked in a ten footer. Brown, working with his teammates, netted two straight jumpers, and Archie added a deuce that pushed Seattle's advantage to eight points with 5:34 seconds to play.

Then Portland clawed right back, somehow, some way. The Sonics countered. Then Portland whittled the lead to four with under a minute to go. The overhead scoreboard flashed, "Let's GO Sonics," and the crowd broke into a spontaneous chorus of the same. Archie tried to find the open man, but nobody in home white was moving.

Finally, with the shot clock down to five, four, three, the ball went to Haywood in the corner. His hurried shot splashed through the rim as the twenty-four-second clock buzzed belatedly. All 6 feet 10 inches of Russell leapt from his seat in a scatter of arms and legs as though he'd been shocked with 120 volts. Flashing "a smile that could be seen all the way to Port Angeles in a fog," the Legend turned and faced his boss, Schulman, in the front row. Schulman, short and balding but looking dapper in his tweed sports jacket and white turtleneck, stood pumping his fists as the scoreboard flashed, "PLAYOFFS."

It was good night, Irene, for the Trail Blazers. Tall Tommy Burleson blocked a pair of shots, and, with two seconds left, Russell removed Haywood (forty points, ten rebounds) from the game and let the crowd roar its utmost approval for number twenty-four's finest game ever in a Sonics uniform. Russell bear-hugged his star, believing that the thrill of victory had just cured all the tension between them.

The final buzzer sounded, and Archie scooped up into his arms a little girl that he knew. "We made it," he said before depositing her back on the floor. "This year, it really was a challenge," he told a reporter a moment later about the playoff quest. "Mainly because this is such a young team. One time during the season, I had my doubts, during that last long road trip. But we kept pulling each other up."

Zollie Volchok, the team's executive vice president and Schulman's trusted right-hand man in Seattle, had asked Russell beforehand whether he wanted boxes of champagne stashed in the locker room for a postgame celebration. Russell had smirked. He told Volchok to break out the bubbly when the Sonics won a playoff series. But the mood in the Sonics' locker room couldn't have been any more effervescent.

"This is what Sam Schulman and I fought for five years ago," said Haywood, referring to his controversial jump to the NBA and, interestingly, making no mention of Russell. "I wanted it. Sam wanted it, the players wanted it, the fans wanted it. We got it." He continued: "I've seen us come from a one-man, a two-man, and a three-man team, and now we're a real team. It couldn't happen to better people, better fans. It's a hell of a feeling."

The Sonics finished with a 43–39 record. Our season-long playoff race had forced us to band together, and the team finally peaked at the end of the season, which is exactly what you want going into the postseason. Everyone now knew their role, and collectively we were confident that the Sonics could make a little noise in the playoffs.

We faced Detroit in the first round in a best-of-five series. It was real hard-nosed playoff basketball that turned intensely physical and often got chippy. But we won the series at home in the final minute of the final game. Our fans went nuts at the city's good fortune, though I can't remember whether Zollie Volchok got to bring in a few cases of champagne in the locker room to celebrate the triumph.

In round two we got the Golden State Warriors and two big problems. One, the Detroit series had done a number on us physically. Fred Brown had broken a finger on his shooting hand, Spencer Haywood had hurt his right foot, and Tom Burleson had bruised ribs. Two, as far as I could tell, Bill didn't believe that we could beat Golden State in a best-of-seven series even if we were healthy. He turned out to be right—we lost to Golden State in six games. But Bill was dead wrong about the heart of this team. We banded together one more time to give Rick Barry and crew, the eventual NBA champions that season, a run for their money. The series ended on a real sour note in Seattle Coliseum when a small mob of fans tried to jump Barry afterward en route to the Golden State locker room. Barry got out of his jam unscathed, but the fans showered him in beer and the worst insults that you can imagine.

This embarrassment to the Sonics and the city had everyone appalled and ready to move on as quickly as possible to baseball season. That included Bill, though for a more personal reason. Despite a magical final month of the season, with its flowering of team and all the higher moral values that sports, at its best, is all about, Bill couldn't claim a second-round playoff defeat as a moral victory or an accomplishment worthy of his NBA resume. His greatness, for better or worse, was denominated in NBA championships, not mere playoff appearances.

So Bill disengaged from the team and its moral victories as soon as the season ended. He was back to muttering about his gutless wonders and telling everyone that this season was just another stepping stone *toward building an eventual* NBA *champion in Seattle. To hasten the rebuild Bill seemed prepared to blow up the entire roster.*

*What about me? Bill said we could talk over the summer, which was perfectly fine with me. I planned to spend the offseason in Ecorse. I'd invested in a Detroit shipping company that had run into a few problems, and that weighed on my mind. I figured that between solving those problems and that never-ending ache in my shoulder, I'd know in my heart whether I had another* NBA *season left in me.*

# 32

*By midsummer I still didn't know whether to play or retire. I really didn't. I stayed in shape, though, playing in a local summer league. Ray Scott, who coached the Pistons, would stop in sometimes, and we would talk basketball. Ray had just traded Dave Bing to Washington for Kevin Porter, and he started telling me that he planned to take advantage of Kevin's ability to run the floor. I told him that he should get a scoring guard to back up Kevin for a change of pace. Ray agreed. What I didn't know was that Ray thought of me as providing that change of pace. So the day before training camp I got a call from Ray saying he'd just swapped a first-round draft choice with Seattle for my rights. Did I want to go another year in the NBA? I told him sure.*

A nn Arbor, Michigan, September 25, 1975. Archie changed into his Pistons practice gear and clicked the metal door out of the locker room. The click rippled through a concrete hallway somewhere in the dim recesses of Crisler Arena, home of the University of Michigan Wolverines. Archie heard the soft thud, thud, thud of bouncing basketballs somewhere in the faraway and followed them down a tunnel to the court. A local television reporter and his camera man, working on a story for the evening news, waited expectantly to greet the new acquisition. Archie slapped hands with the reporter and prepared for the lights, camera, and action.

Archie wrapped up his thirty-second "Hello, Detroit" and proceeded onto the court to greet his new teammates. He knew most of them already. There was Bob Lanier, Curtis Rowe, Willie Norwood, George Trapp, Howard Porter, and Eric Money. Then there was the six feet, 165 pounds of pure piss and vinegar now hoisting jump shots nearby: Kevin Porter. "I wanted a quick-strike team," Scott explained the trade for the quick-strike Porter. "That's the way the NBA was going. Everybody wanted to run like the Celtics."

Scott clapped the practice to order, shadowed by a short white guy with a mop of dark wavy hair. He was Scott's young assistant coach, Herb Brown. Archie had never heard of him, but Brown seemed raring to go. While Brown fidgeted in the background, the 6-foot-9 Scott stood stoically working his way through the usual list of welcomes. Someone pulled aside Archie and told him to hang tight. Yesterday's trade with Seattle, though announced to the media, wasn't official. The trade still had to be approved by the NBA front office, and the Pistons had a call into New York.

Archie had been friendly for years with "Chink," as Scott was known to everybody for his small eyes set into a large head. But lately Chink also answered to "the Cheese," from the "Farmer in the Dell" nursery rhyme that closes with "The cheese stands alone." Scott felt this simple rhyme captured well the lonely plight of an NBA coach. But there was nothing simple or sing-songy about this NBA coach. He was as complex as a Shakespearean figure, self-aware, big thinking, well spoken, and profoundly wise to the ways of the world.

Just then a face that Archie recognized from the front office offered a perfunctory congratulations. New York had given the thumbs up. He was now officially a Detroit Piston. Archie rose from his seat and walked in the direction of his new coach to rotate into the next drill. The clock was now ticking on Archie's final NBA season.

RAY SCOTT WANTED Archie to log maybe twenty minutes per game and, as he had done in Seattle, lend a grounded veteran presence in the locker room. That he could do with his eyes closed and definitely for the money. Archie had inked a one-year, $200,000 contract with the Pistons. Fortunately his agent, Larry Fleisher, had negotiated Archie's big contract three years ago without an option clause, unheard of in the NBA. Had there been an option year keeping his salary well above $200,000, Archie would have never landed with the Pistons, and that would have been too bad. Archie liked the idea of ending his career with his hometown team.

As long as Archie could remember, the Pistons had been owned by industrialist Fred Zollner. He wintered in Miami and called in firings like he was ordering a pizza. He had fired five coaches and four general managers during the team's first eight years in Detroit, all the while the team had wallowed in red ink.

Last year Zollner had sold the Pistons to a group of eleven investors, led by the ultra-wealthy Bill Davidson and his dear friend and lawyer Oscar Feldman. "I said they haven't turned a profit in seventeen years of existence and that I'd be happy to close the deal, but I didn't want any part of it," Feldman recalled telling Davidson. "I want you to take a piece," Davidson replied, "so you'll look after the store for me."

Last June the self-sure Feldman, a former lawyer for the Internal Revenue Service, had officially taken over the store as general manager. He had zero experience in professional sports. Neither did Davidson. But both knew how to pinch pennies and, for now, engage their staff in a tedious corporate group-think.

"We don't have the kind of structure where anybody sits down and says this is the way it's going to be," Scott described Feldman's store. "It's discussed among us from the standpoint: will it be successful or will it be unsuccessful? You sit down and it's discussed among all the departments. That's the way we do it—we brainstorm."

Scott, "the Cheese," had never been more alone. He now had to explain the whys and wherefores of the NBA to a table full of middle-aged businessmen. Though they tried to carry themselves like regular guys, Scott was the only one in the room with any NBA experience. It could be exhausting breaking down the sometimes ineffable five-man dynamics of basketball into easy, measurable concepts and then opening up the floor to a table full of mostly unenlightened critiques. Years ago Scott had listened to Boston's Red Auerbach pontificate on winning basketball, as cocksure and uncompromising as an army general. Auerbach never had to put his strategy up for a vote. Why did Scott, the 1974 NBA Coach of the Year, need to do so?

"It was a mess," Scott said of the new owners. "It's hard for people to invest in something if they don't know how it works. It would be like me, as a basketball player, investing in a high-tech company and saying, 'I'll run it.'"

Adding to Scott's feeling of isolation, the table full of middle-aged men expected Scott to produce measurable progress on their NBA investment. They expected no less than a winning season. Those expectations didn't scare Scott. He liked his team, now built around the quick-strike Kevin Porter and the 6-foot-11, multi-talented Bob Lanier.

But the NBA season is long, and lots of unexpected stuff happens. That's the nature of the NBA's eighty-two-game beast. Scott's real problem was that when the usual stuff happened, these guys in suits would have zero loyalty to him. He wasn't their hand-picked coach, the anointed one who would lead them and the city of Detroit to the Promised Land. Scott was merely the tall guy with the squinty eyes that they'd inherited with their purchase, much like a washing machine in the sale of a house.

Businessmen made their fortunes by identifying problems (real or imagined) and brainstorming solutions around creativity and efficiency. It wouldn't take much of the unexpected to make Scott, a self-described "Zollner guy," the source of their investment problems. That was the ax hanging over the thirty-seven-year-old Scott's head as he began his fourth season in Detroit.

Would the axe fall? Or would Scott keep everyone healthy and winning to keep his place at the table? Those were the two overarching questions as the 1975–76 season got under way in Detroit.

DETROIT, NOVEMBER 28, 1975. All the early-season numbers were adding up for Ray Scott and his Detroit Pistons. Fourteen games into the annual eighty-two-game slog the Pistons sported a 9–5 record, including their current four-game win streak. That put Detroit in first place in the Midwest Division, and tonight the Pistons had taken care of business against the Kansas City Kings, a club that, according to Scott, "beat our pants off" last season.

Another vital number was twelve. All twelve Pistons were contributing to the team's success, and that of course included Archie as the third guard. He averaged nearly nine points and three assists per game. More important, Archie clicked with the other members of the backcourt, and the on-court synergy let Scott rotate guards in and out of the lineup all game to keep everyone fresh and keep his team running at full speed all night.

"I liked this team," said Archie. "Everyone was still getting familiar with each other to start the season and working out a few rough spots. But we played hard, and all the right pieces were there to have a really big season"—assuming the unexpected didn't strike first.

OAKLAND, CALIFORNIA, DECEMBER 9, 1975. Kevin Porter had always played with a chip on his shoulder in Washington. In Detroit he entered his fourth pro season with the level-headedness of a veteran who understood the nuances of the NBA game, and that made it easier for Archie to talk basketball constructively with him.

The two in fact were on great terms in Detroit. For Archie their past disagreements had all come in the heat of competition. They were no longer competing for the same job in Detroit, and that made all the difference in the world. One thing that caught Archie's eye about the new and more mature Porter was that he'd mastered the fine art of playing to the strengths of his teammates. On every trip down the floor he knew which shots Crash Mengelt, Bob Lanier, and his other teammates liked, and he delivered the ball to each on time and in the right place—just like Archie had tried to tell him in Washington.

Tonight against the Golden State Warriors (14–6) Porter had had the ball in the right place the entire second quarter. The Pistons were closing in on a forty-point quarter against the defending NBA champions when somebody in the crowd of 10,087 must have stuck a pin in a voodoo doll. How else to explain what happened next?

With the quarter winding down Porter got the ball to Mengelt in the right place. He dribbled into the lane, absorbed contact, and heard a loud pop as his right knee buckled. "I ran up and down the court two more times," said Mengelt, recalling that he could run straight ahead, no problem. "Then I tried to cut laterally and fell down in a heap."

A doctor manipulated Mengelt's knee and suspected torn cartilage. He advised immediate surgery. Mengelt declined, preferring that the Pistons' team physician in Michigan make the call. Mengelt changed into his street clothes and hobbled to the Pistons' bench midway through the fourth quarter with Detroit now trailing by nine points and just in time to see the next pin stick.

Porter leaked downcourt, and Lanier hit him in stride for one of the safest plays in basketball—the breakaway lay-up. Not this time.

After laying the ball into the hoop, Porter's momentum carried him into the basket support, wrapped in a red pad with a troublesome open seam. Both feet sliced through the seam and a knee smacked hard into the basket support. After impact Porter twisted sideways and "crumpled like a discarded towel" to the floor. He struggled to his feet, attempted a few pained steps, then collapsed. Porter, strapped to a stretcher with a look of disgust etched on his face, rode in an ambulance to the emergency room at nearby Peralta Hospital. The attending physician manipulated Porter's knee. Torn cartilage.

SEATTLE, DECEMBER 12, 1975. The unexpected had struck, and a magical season now seemed cursed. "We'll have to do things a little more intelligently now," said Scott. "We just can't depend on raw talent. We'll just have to be a better basketball team."

A better basketball team often starts with a few lucky bounces, and there were none of them to be had this evening against Seattle (12–13).

With under twenty-five seconds to go in this hard-fought contest Archie swiped the ball from Herm Gilliam—ironically his replacement in Seattle—and had free sailing to knot the score. Watching from the sideline, Coach Bill Russell implored a "miss it" to his preferred higher being and, sure enough, the ball boinked off the rim and back into the hands of Gilliam. He pushed the ball in the other direction, and Fred Brown, who'd been dropping twenty-foot daggers for Seattle the entire fourth quarter, sliced another through the twine to send the Pistons to their third straight loss.

Archie offered no excuses, but the score sheet offered some possible insight into the weird bounce. Archie had logged forty-one minutes, or nearly double his nightly output this season. Though Archie had played well, the physical wear and tear of running sprints with Seattle's Slick Watts and later chasing Brown around screens had taken their toll. "This is the most minutes I've played in two seasons," Archie noted.

Scott, as was his modus operandi, called an all-hands meeting to discuss how to become a better basketball team before moving on to tackle the Portland Trail Blazers, the Pistons' fourth stop on this disastrous five-game western trip. Porter had undergone season-ending surgery in Ann Arbor yesterday to repair his knee. But there was good news on Mengelt. Crash had a strained knee and no apparent structural damage that required surgery. Fingers crossed, Mengelt would be back in three to six weeks.

That left Archie as the heir apparent to Porter's job. His shoulder ached every hour of every day, but he liked this team. Archie had stepped up in Seattle for Russell, and now he'd do the same in Detroit for Scott to help build that "better basketball team."

Or would he? Out of Archie's earshot Herb Brown reportedly lobbied Scott to replace Porter with second-year guard Eric Money. Like Seattle's Watts last season, Money was still growing into his pro career. But Brown contended that Porter's injury might just be a blessing in disguise. In Brown's eyes Money was potentially the better player. The 6-foot speedster just needed a chance to prove himself, and Brown insisted now was the time with the season still young.

The Cheese took a deep breath and decided to give it a shot for a few more games. He was taking a lot of deep breaths lately. Brown could be exhausting.

Brown was also lucky to be in the NBA. The Cheese had handed the job to Brown, a mostly small college coach whom he didn't know, as a favor to Scott's mentor, Haskell Cohen, the league's former publicity director. It was an act of charity that he instantly wished to do over. "I just had that feeling that it wouldn't be a good fit," said Scott. "I didn't know why, much to my regret."

Brown arrived high on basketball strategy, particularly defense, and could wax on about it with a gleam in his eye and song in his heart. While Scott stood stock still during games, intuiting the action, Brown looked like he was being attacked by a colony of Australian fire ants. He jumped, yelled, shrieked, and collapsed to his knees. While Scott could seem impassive, Brown could seem to be giving every inch of his heart to survive the enemy onslaught and send fans home happy until the next time.

Brown also had an uncanny ability to make friends in all the right places. One was Feldman. The two reportedly talked, and that had Scott wondering what they were discussing. Oh yes, "the Cheese" stands alone.

In the final game of Detroit's trip from hell Scott's Pistons, adjusting to more rejiggering of the lineup, stumbled to Portland. More important, Bob Lanier looked woozy and badly winded trying to keep up with the Trail Blazers' Bill Walton. Lanier was as sick as a dog with the winter flu and wincing at the chronic pain in his knee. The chances were good that he'd sit out the final stop on the western road trip against Kareem Abdul-Jabbar and the much-improved Los Angeles Lakers (14–8).

DETROIT, DECEMBER 15, 1975. Five straight losses. Kareem Abdul-Jabbar and the Los Angeles Lakers had squeaked past the visiting Pistons last night, 110–100, to send Detroit's finest home winless on their five-game western swing. The Pistons departed after the game, landing in Detroit during those wee small hours of the morning. All the players snatched their bags from the carousel and departed to catch a few hours of sleep in their own beds.

Ray Scott wished he could be so lucky. His brain was in overdrive. The whirl in his head would probably preclude sleep. Bob Lanier had sat out the Lakers' game as expected, and Jabbar had been like a 7-foot kid in a candy shop. He had feasted for twenty-seven points, eight blocks, six assists, and two steals to go with a career-high thirty-four rebounds. And yet the Pistons had nearly outrebounded the Lakers. In fact the Pistons set not one but two franchise records for offensive rebounding in the game. Those offensive rebounds were there to be snatched by the bundle because the Pistons had shot a pathetic 32 percent from the field. "The Cheese" stood alone, now more than ever.

Scott drove to the office the next day to read his mail and hopefully touch base with general manager Oscar Feldman. The early-season brainstorms with Feldman and crew had trailed off to benign corporate neglect. As best as Scott could tell, Feldman visited the Pistons' offices as little as possible. If Scott needed Feldman's input, he called his absentee general manager at his law firm. They talked on average about twice a week.

Whether he would connect with Feldman today or the "big" owner, Bill Davidson, to whom he also spoke by phone about twice a week,

Scott needed to fill Porter's empty roster spot before their upcoming game against Golden State.

Since joining the starting lineup, Eric Money remained young and sometimes foolish with the basketball. But Herb Brown persisted about keeping him in the starting lineup. Though Archie helped to stabilize the team when on the floor, Brown might have been right. Money and his younger legs provided the best chance to restore Detroit's quick-strike offense and the excitement of the early season. Scott, as he was wont to do, had called a team meeting to lay out the reset in the backcourt for the foreseeable future. Archie wouldn't be happy, but he'd take the reshuffling like a pro. "The Cheese" stands alone.

DETROIT, DECEMBER 17, 1975. The losing streak reached six with another loss to Golden State. "We can win," Ray Scott reassured reporters after a thirty-minute postgame team meeting to communicate "some fundamentals" of team play.

Twenty-three games into the regular season Scott had a brand-new starting point guard in Eric Money and a banged-up center in Bob Lanier. The ornery right knee kept Lanier on the bench for most of the second half. This awkward addition-and-subtraction in personnel had basic defensive rotations arriving late and basic offensive reads missed. The home crowd hooted the miscues. "Put me in, Attles," a local shouted to Golden State coach Al Attles. The Detroit defense was that atrocious.

DETROIT, DECEMBER 23,1975. Nine losses in a row. Tonight the Washington Bullets strafed the Pistons, 120–102, in veteran Dave Bing's triumphant return to his old stomping grounds. "We just can't put a sustained effort together," lamented Scott over the nine-game skid, which tied the franchise record for futility.

DETROIT, DECEMBER 26, 1975. The losing streak was over. Bob Lanier, likely receiving a little something to loosen up his bad knee and ankle, returned to the lineup to pound the Chicago Bulls (7–22) into submission on the inside. Archie and crew took care of the rest from the outside, allowing the Pistons to coast in the fourth quarter to a 102–87 sigh of relief. So weak was the four-team Midwest Division this season that the Pistons (12–15) remained in first place by a half game over Milwaukee.

"The spirit never broke down during the whole losing streak," celebrated Herb Brown. "The players didn't die, not once!"

"The losing streak was a trauma," spoke Scott more sedately. "But I think we're going to be so much better for it in the second half of the season. The players have been striving to make the pieces fit."

Scott smiled and heaved a sigh of relief. He believed January would be a better month. It had to be better than this coldest of Decembers. But it wouldn't. Though Scott couldn't quite perceive it, the clock was now ticking on his career as an NBA head coach. The alarm would strike abruptly, like a heart attack, in just about one month in the middle of a team practice.

SOUTHFIELD, MICHIGAN, JANUARY 26, 1976. There's was always something scheduled at Cobo Arena, and that something always had the Pistons roaming the area in search of an available practice gym. With their own dedicated NBA practice facility still a few years off, the Pistons often gathered at a Jewish community center, a Catholic Church, and, tonight, Southfield High School, a northwest suburb of Detroit.

January had been more of the same for the Pistons. Bob Lanier had fractured his shoulder. John Mengelt, back from his badly sprained knee injury, had sprained his ankle. Howard Porter had just missed a game with back spasms, and Archie, Curtis Rowe, and Mengelt had been out of commission with the flu. All the "unable-to-performs" kept the Pistons as a work in progress, with a 17–26 record and now a half game behind first-place Milwaukee in the Midwest Division.

But with tonight's 8 p.m. practice Ray Scott finally had everyone in uniform for the first time this month. Knock on wood. Herb Brown broke everyone into groups, and immediately balls thudded and sneakers squeaked. About thirty minutes later a metal door squeaked open and in ambled Bill Davidson, Oscar Feldman, and Herb Tyner, the other major Pistons' investor. It was the ultimate grim reaper moment for an NBA coach.

Scott eased on over, and Feldman asked to have a word alone. The four exchanged glances into the foyer and out of earshot of the players. Feldman informed his coach that he was being relieved of his duties due to "a complete breakdown in communications."

"Don't bullshit me," said Scott, not buying the reason. "If there's something there, tell me what it is."

Feldman repeated the explanation as stolidly as a mortician, and the other two nodded in solemn agreement. The 6-foot-9 Scott glared down in disbelief at the three little rich men out of their comfort zones, and the thought crossed his mind that they must have rehearsed the whole charade. A lack of communication? He asked Feldman if he had a replacement in mind.

"Herbie."

Scott walked back into the gym and huddled his players one last time. "There's been a disagreement between me and management," Scott heard himself announce, segueing into a single sentence that he'd just been fired and Brown was their new coach. "I wish you all good luck. Keep playing hard."

With that the Cheese gathered his belongings, snapped open the metal door, and was suddenly alone to parse his absolute shock and anger. Did they have to do this at a team practice in front of all the players? Outside the clear night sky reframed the dreadful moment in a starry chill, and Scott reached for a cigarette. He needed to cut back. But not yet. His mind now ping-ponged between rage and sadness. He'd thrown his blood, sweat, and tears into nursing this badly hobbled team back to health. What would become of it now? Scott had been the only person in the front office with any NBA experience. Now there was nobody.

Scott approached his car, surrounded by all the gleaming, high-end German engineering under the temporary ownership of his now former players. Reserve Howard Porter drove a top-of-the-line Mercedes Benz and bragged to his teammates that he had a PhD in psychology and could read their minds like Dr. Freud. He was lying through his teeth. Porter was the one who'd signed early with the ABA's Pittsburgh Condors a few years ago while leading Villanova University to the NCAA finals. He got caught with his hands in the cookie jar, and the Condors traded Porter's tainted contract to the NBA Chicago Bulls, no questions asked. Porter had bounced around the NBA ever since, a decent pro destined never to be great. And yet the crazy money remained in his pocket to fill up his gas tank and let him live the dream.

The dream was a wicked illusion. Scott knew that now. The NBA wasn't an end; it was a means. It was a sign-here, throw-it-in-the-bank chance one day to earn that doctorate in psychology, invest in a lucrative business, buy stocks, squirrel away bonds, or, as Scott did now, just breathe and stare in everlasting wonder at the stars. Scott reached for the ignition. It was time to depart four topsy-turvy seasons piloting the Detroit Pistons and finally discover what he wanted out of this incredible thing called life.

## 33

*When I was in Seattle, I wore a beard. I kept it trimmed like a lot of other players around the league. But when I started playing for the Pistons, I let the beard grow out. Forty years later in the era of James Harden, a.k.a. "the Beard," people sometimes joke that I was the original NBA "Beard." I don't know about that except to say that my thick beard expressed pretty much where I was in my NBA career. I was the old veteran. And that was cool with me. What I didn't expect is that Ray Scott would be gone by midseason and my role as the bearded veteran would now extend to tutoring his replacement, Herb Brown.*

---

**D**etroit, February 7, 1976. The official explanation was a failure to communicate. But nobody outside the owners' own tight circle knew the real reason for Ray Scott's firing. That included Scott, who would declare forty years later, "I'm still waiting for an explanation."

Scott's best explanation came from Jerry Green, the well-known, ear-to-the-ground local sports pundit, who met privately with him along the Detroit Riverfront shortly before the firing. Green, playing Deep Throat, passed along his strong suspicion that Herbie Brown wanted his job and had general manager Oscar Feldman's ear.

Whether Green was right or wrong, Scott's fate seemed to be sealed by the team's poor attendance. The Pistons, still the least popular pro sports team in Detroit despite a dedicated core group of fans, were fourth worst in the league in attendance at 6,647 per game, down about 850 tickets per night from last season. The new owners equated the slow sales with an outdated product. As prudent businessmen, they had to stir things up. Like slapping fresh packaging on a stale brand of toothpaste, swapping out Scott for his exuberant young assistant would shake things up and bring Cobo Arena back to life. That was mostly Feldman's brilliant idea.

The problem was few Detroiters were interested in purchasing the new toothpaste. "What a joke. What a sham. What a shame," one newspaperman described Scott's firing. Another opted for "viciously unjust," and a third offered this dose of reality: "And now Herb Brown is left with the unenviable task of convincing basketball fans not to meaningfully communicate by staying home."

Brown was off to a predictably rough start. That included tonight's eight-point trimming by the Milwaukee Bucks before a larger crowd of 5,875 not-so-faithful. Most seized any chance to demean Brown and decry Scott's sacking.

To Brown's credit he seemed to block out the boos and the empty seats. His total focus was on transforming the Pistons into *his* winning team. He'd already banished Scott's more traditional NBA playbook with a jazzy, five-man motion offense, a bold attempt to customize strategy to the personnel and "get them to play five-man basketball and to play every game as if it is their last game."

There was absolutely no missing the 5-foot-something man behind all the boldness. Brown had an expansive wardrobe of 1970s super-mod attire, heavy on wide, open collars and loafers with no socks. "Herbie Baby," as the catcallers ruthlessly mocked him, launched into a kneeling, leaping, hand-clapping, occasionally pirouetting dance and rapid-fire, deep-throated chatter that went something like this: "Go hard! . . . Good pass, George! . . . D up, good tough D. . . . See it, George! . . . Way to go, Chris. . . . Go! Go! . . . Get one, get one."

Brown's song and dance fell flat with most of the tall guys on the court. They weren't in the mood or in the moment. They too were trying to process the uncertainty of the past few weeks and come to terms with how they had ended up with this little ball of unbridled energy cheerleading from the sidelines, and it showed tonight. "They didn't play offense, they didn't play defense, they didn't rebound," the *Detroit Free Press* summed up the effort from press row.

Archie was one of the exceptions. He was a pro's pro who played his usual steady floor game, making the smart pass and connecting on five of seven shots from the field to keep the defense honest and stop it from sagging on Bob Lanier. But Lanier was ailing again, though in a new limb. His left elbow was badly inflamed, and it greatly limited his ability to jostle inside and shoot. Compounding the problem, many of the younger Pistons trying to get the ball to Lanier didn't know how to close out games, and that included tonight's fourth-quarter giveaway.

The loss dropped the Pistons (20–29) into second place behind the Bucks in the weak Midwest Division, where all four teams had losing records. Things weren't going to get any easier for the Pistons. The team rushed out of the locker room after the Milwaukee game to reach the airport and another red-eye flight that would start a ten-day, five-game march out west.

LOS ANGELES, FEBRUARY 10, 1976. Archie located his assigned aisle seat and buckled up for the ninety-minute flight to Phoenix. The Pistons had split the first two games of the western road trip, eking out a win against Kansas City and losing by eighteen points a few hours ago to the Los Angeles Lakers. Archie just wanted to put this one behind him. He'd gotten into the game early to guard his former teammate Gail Goodrich, who'd been having his way with the inexperienced Eric Money. Archie quieted Goodrich for a while, then Brown pulled him. Archie plopped down on the bench. What was Herbie doing?

Goodrich got going again, and as he sliced and diced the Pistons defense en route to a thirty-seven-point night, Brown left his defensive stopper seated on the bench. All Archie could do was stare straight ahead while a wee, small voice in his head repeated, "What's Herbie doing?" It was as though he was tone deaf to the rhythms of the NBA game. For "Herbie," as everyone called the young coach, it seemed like every night was a John Phillip Sousa march. Mind over matter. Climb every mountain. Execute, execute, execute. But that's not how the NBA worked. It was pure jazz—Monk, Coltrane, even the block chords of Red Garland—and a continuous improvisation to match up the personnel on the floor. It was played by a bunch of old pros hoping to make as much money as possible while their knees and ankles still could. That meant everybody needed playing time to pump up their numbers and sign that next big contract. Everybody, including Archie in his final season, needed a clearly defined role to shine and feel a part of the team. That's how the pro game worked, and Herbie seemed to struggle either to see or accept it.

"Pass and move," Brown yelled from his knees, where he spent a good part of the game. "Defense, now, defense. Talk, talk. See it."

The Lakers' lead extended to twenty (on a night that Kareem Abdul-Jabbar had scored just eight points!), and Archie sat. Watched. Stewed. The Pistons newfangled offense predictably faltered, and frustration boiled over. Bob Lanier, who had had his bad elbow drained before the game, picked up a technical. So did Money, and Herbie got one for popping off at referee Jim Capers.

And now Archie stared ahead from his aisle seat ready for takeoff. The chances were good that "Herbie Baby" would soon call another of his closed-door "rap sessions" to break down plays, discuss defensive rotations, climb every mountain, and preach his favorite word lately: consistency. Archie told himself to behave. But he'd couldn't. He would have a few things to tell this rookie coach about life in the NBA.

The plane lifted into the air, and with it all the tension of the last few hours momentarily vanished into the clouds, allowing his mind to drift into a pleasant half sleep. Next to him sat teammate George Trapp, fiddling with something or other. While Archie rested, Herbie roamed. The coach soon worked his way over to Trapp to make a point. Herbie was always teaching, always pitching some impenetrable point. Half asleep, Archie heard Herbie call out, "Isn't that right, Shake?" followed by a whack to his shoulder.

Archie startled and opened his eyes to Herbie's wide, toothy, expectant grin. Archie shut his eyes again without uttering a word. That throb of tension in his head returned. NBA coaches didn't roam the plane whacking their ten-year veterans while they slept. And what was he doing calling him "Shake?" Respect was earned in the NBA; it wasn't given.

The next night in Phoenix against the sinking Suns (21–27, last in the Pacific Division), the Pistons starters fell behind early and, with the ailing Lanier sitting this one out, struggled to score and defend. To start the second quarter Herbie waved in Archie and veteran forward Howard Porter. Less than four minutes later the two were back on the bench. Archie stared straight ahead. So did Porter. What was Herbie trying to prove?

At halftime the Pistons were in a seventeen-point hole, and Herbie started in about team effort. His eyes darted to Archie and Porter. Neither, he snapped, seemed interested in competing tonight. Speaking directly to Archie, he said, "I could tell from last night that you wouldn't be ready to play," referring to the airplane incident.

Archie doesn't remember exactly what he shouted back. But anger overcame him. Archie reminded his accuser that he had played hard every night over the last ten years, and now he played hurt every night. If Brown had a problem with him, they could talk about it behind closed doors. But no college coach had the right to question his professionalism.

Herbie, pretty scrappy himself, yelled something back. This only enraged the 6-foot-8 Porter, who leapt to his feet ready to take out the college coach from CW Post. A few players grabbed a hold of the flailing Porter, and moments later the team staggered back out to the court, still unsure of exactly what had just transpired in the locker room.

With Archie and Porter still angry at the end of the bench, Brown got back to coaching. He had a game to win. "Nice play, Chris," he yelled. "Pass and move. Way to go!"

The chatter, punctuated with yells, once again fell on mostly deaf ears, and Archie sat wondering why a rookie coach would pick a fight with his veterans. It made no sense. By the fourth quarter the Suns' lead had risen to twenty-one points, and Brown cleared the bench, except for Archie and Porter. The two veterans—"the Beard" and "the Geezer," as Porter was known—were in the rookie coach's doghouse.

ECORSE, MICHIGAN, FEBRUARY 17, 1976. The clock was tick-tick-ticking on Archie's NBA career. By the end of the Western trip Archie and Herbie Brown had patched things up—or made them as good as things would ever be between them. Archie was back in the nine-man rotation, playing maybe twenty minutes per night, and Brown was back in his ear with unsolicited advice. ("Right, Shake?") But the Pistons (20–33) had dropped four straight, seven of their last ten games, and owned the third-worst record in the NBA.

As bad as it sounded, the Pistons somehow remained plopped in second place of the Midwest Division, just two games behind front-running Milwaukee. If the NBA postseason were starting today, the Pistons, woeful record and all, would make the Western Conference playoffs for holding down second place. For now this made the injury-plagued Pistons hands down the luckiest unlucky team in pro sports.

Archie resented having to break in a rookie coach so late in his career. That's not what he'd signed up for. As Archie sat in his home in Ecorse, he thought about his brash rookie signal caller. Herbie wasn't a bad person. He was just the polar opposite of the calm, cool, and communicative Ray Scott. Scott was a players' coach; Brown was perceived in the locker room as an owner's coach. He was Feldman's guy. While Scott had a gift for building team unity, Brown preached strategy. Like Jack Ramsay back in Philadelphia, Brown was a college coach trying to prove his chops to a pro basketball audience. Dr. Jack had struggled to make it work but was starting to figure out the NBA in Buffalo. Maybe one day Brown would do the same. It just wouldn't be this season. The Pistons, after all, had nobody in the front office with NBA experience. It had walked out the door with Scott.

DETROIT, FEBRUARY 20, 1976. Dave Bing and the Washington Bullets were back in town on this cold Friday night, and 5,309 Pistons fans had hazarded the extreme February chill for another two-hour group grumble about the state of their team. In the parking lot a gaggle of the disgruntled passed out fliers urging a boycott of the next home game against Cleveland. The fliers asked Pistons fans, like autoworkers, to go on strike until that blankety-blank Oscar Feldman found some real basketball people to run the operation.

The mood only worsened inside the arena. During warm-ups Crash Mengelt, in and out of the Pistons lineup all season with injuries, sprained his left ankle. When Mengelt finally hobbled to the bench in street clothes midway through the first quarter, the Pistons already "looked like a team that would have preferred to be somewhere else." The boos, vented with open hostility, were at times so vicious that it made Feldman seem like a heroic figure for even showing his face in Cobo Arena.

At halftime, with the Pistons down by seventeen and showing no signs of snapping out of it, many were thinking of driving to Greektown for a nightcap at Hellas or maybe Nikis. Those who exited early for moussaka and the first round of drinks missed the Pistons' best half of basketball all season. The transformation started when Archie and Howard Porter rotated onto the court with about nine minutes left in the third quarter. The change in personnel brought instant defense, and this tougher mindset led to long defensive rebounds and some quick scores that, two minutes later, had the offense back in gear, playing inside-out through Lanier. The boos turned to cheers, and suddenly the Pistons weren't so terrible after all.

Porter slammed home an offensive rebound. Al Eberhard stood his ground to take an offensive charge from the runaway freight train called Wes Unseld. The crowd roared, and the Bullets' once comfortable lead had devolved into a double-digit deficit by early in the fourth quarter. "Everybody was doing it!" shouted Herbie after the final buzzer and his first career win over an NBA team of note.

The next night the Pistons were in Buffalo, where they extended their win streak to three with a two-point, come-from-behind win over a pretty good Braves team. What's more, for a second-straight game Detroit inexplicably dominated the fourth quarter. The Pistons now returned home for a Wednesday tussle against Cleveland and just in time for Fan Boycott Night.

DETROIT, FEBRUARY 25, 1976. There's no telling how successful Fan Boycott Night really was. Attendance had remained atrocious after Ray Scott's firing, and just over 4,800 scabs crossed the imaginary picket line, though mostly to raise more Cain at Oscar Feldman's Pistons. The fans booed, occasionally hooted, and frequently hollered as the Pistons battled the Cleveland Cavaliers nearly evenly through three quarters. But the Pistons faded early in the second half, falling at the final horn by seven points.

The Pistons closed out February at home with a 97–93 win over the New York Knicks, pulling them to within a half game of the first-place Milwaukee Bucks in the Midwest Division. Brown's team (24–34) finally seemed to be headed in the right direction, and with twenty-four games left in the regular season, they still had plenty of time to make the playoffs.

But there was a shadow hanging over February. Many players, though not all, were both tired of Herbie's nonstop yelling and befuddled by his substitutions, which cut into their playing time and led to all variety of second-guessing. Off the court they accused their coach of playing favorites.

For Archie, the bearded veteran, the season couldn't end fast enough. His body ached, as was always the case in February, but this time around, at age thirty-five, playing injured and at maybe at 60 percent of his former All-Star ability had taken a toll on him. Archie could feel the churn now in the pit of his stomach: it was time to retire.

LOS ANGELES, MARCH 19, 1976. Chick Hearn, the long-time radio voice of the Los Angeles Lakers, had his own homespun line of telling his listeners across Southern California that the guys in yellow and blue were about to win another one. "The game's in the refrigerator," he would start. "The door's closed, the light's out, the eggs are cooling, the butter's getting hard and the Jell-O's jiggling."

Tonight Hearn could have declared the Jell-O jiggling at halftime. Though the Lakers led by just twelve points, the Pistons forgot to bring their defense to the Forum. Hearn's team scored in big bunches during the third quarter to boost the lead to twenty, and the only entertaining moment came later in the half, when Laker guard Gail Goodrich got hacked on a lay-up and lost his cool when the man in the striped shirt, Bill Jones, swallowed his whistle. "You son of a bitch," he yelled and took two steps in the direction of Jones, drawing a whistle, though not the one that he'd wanted. Goodrich had been tossed from the game for, yes, swearing.

After the game it was the Piston players doing all the swearing. The fifteen-point beatdown marked Detroit's eighth loss in its last ten games. More telling, the Pistons had sunk to the second-worst record in the NBA, marooned seventeen games below .500. While those numbers might have caused some players in the other NBA divisions to jump out of windows or call their shrinks, the Pistons remained remarkably just a half game out of second place in the woeful Midwest Division and a fateful trip to the playoffs.

Most of all, today's game wasn't supposed to have blown up in their faces. Quite the opposite. Bob Lanier, the team captain, had called a special players-only meeting to grab this season by the scruff of its neck once and for all. To a man the Pistons were frustrated—tired of all the injuries, tired of Herb Brown, tired of all the fourth-quarter meltdowns, tired of all the losing. "The spiritual vibes just came," said Lanier. "We decided that, hey, we're going to be here together. We're going to play together, and the coach is going to be here whether everybody likes him or not."

And then all those spiritual vibes blew up in their faces, and before they knew it, the Jell-O was jiggling. With thirteen games left in the regular season the losing had to stop now. Tonight. The team had to get back to the basics. One by one they threw in their hands. Archie, Curtis Rowe, Eric Money, Al Eberhard, Howard Porter, Crash Mengelt, Lanier. They would end the season strong and make the playoffs, not for Herbie, not for Oscar Feldman, not for Bill Davidson. They'd do it for each other.

Three nights later the Pistons were back in Cobo Arena against the slumping Buffalo Braves, and, as they say in church, the spirit was with them. The Pistons shouted out a sixty-point Hallelujah in the first half, dominating the backboards and running at will on the Braves. The third quarter brought a predictable trial of faith as Buffalo's high-scoring Bob McAdoo got going and so did the hometown hecklers. They chanted "Sweet George" for crowd favorite George Trapp to get into the game. When "Herbie Baby" ignored them, unflattering signs were unfurled over the balcony. But the fourth quarter brought redemption. The Pistons, who never trailed in the game, closed out this six-point win the old-fashioned way, by pounding the ball inside to Lanier (thirty-four points, eighteen rebounds).

NEW YORK, MARCH 23, 1976. This was Archie's last trip as a professional basketball player to Madison Square Garden. Ah, the Gah-den: all the women in pant suits and furs, the street hustlers in cheap polyester and platform shoes, and the balding, middle-aged white men with bad complexions and cigars extending from their mouths like extra appendages. Archie wasn't feeling too nostalgic about his final lap around the NBA. Not in the Garden. Not in Chicago Stadium. Not really even a few nights ago in the Fabulous Forum, where Archie had played in the very first basketball game. For Archie there was no region reserved deep in his cerebral cortex for the pomp and nostalgia of it all. The NBA was a business. Nothing more, nothing less.

Tonight business was good. The Pistons closed the deal on the Knicks for a second-straight win. The game ball went to Eric Money, who, in his own words, had played "close to my best game ever," connecting on eleven of fourteen shots from the field and pitching in six assists.

Sonny Hill, the Philadelphia broadcaster who was now working for CBS Sports, stopped by the Pistons' locker room to say hello to Archie, whom he'd famously nicknamed "Shake and Bake" about seven years ago. All eyes were on Mr. CBS. His network had just killed its scheduled broadcast of an upcoming game between the Pistons and the Philadelphia 76ers. Why? ABA refugee George McGinnis, in the midst of a breakout first season with Philadelphia, had just blown out his knee. "Why take us off the screen just because George McGinnis got hurt?" bantered Lanier while icing down nearly everything from shoulder to toe. "We need exposure! When you're losing, people just step in your face."

Hill chuckled, explaining it wasn't his call. But the Pistons, just four days removed from their fateful players-only meeting, were suddenly back playing winning basketball, CBS Sports be damned. The Pistons (28–43) were now a half game behind the Midwest Division's second-place Kansas City Kings, led by the amazing Nate Archibald.

In the remedial math of this historically bad division, if the Pistons could defeat the Kings tomorrow night and leapfrog into second place, it might just be enough to get into the playoffs. The Kings played seven of their remaining nine games on the road, while the Pistons closed out the regular season with six of their last ten games at Cobo Arena.

DETROIT, MARCH 24, 1976. Kansas City's Nate Archibald played like poetry in motion. There was absolutely no wasted movement as the 6-foot southpaw navigated the open court on the dribble. Play up on him, and he faked, spun, or crossed over his dribble, creating a fresh angle to outfox the pressure, all the while churning his body forward, like a downhill runner in football, and working his way to the rim to find space to flick a pass or, more often, to shoot. "Basket Archibald," the Cobo public address announcer punctuated the early action.

Herb Brown tried mixing up Detroit's defense to confuse Archibald, but the Kings had settled into a comfortable rhythm, connecting on more than 60 percent of their shots midway through the second quarter. That's when the Cobo faithful began the chant for "Sweet George" Trapp, also known around the arena and on WJR-AM radio as "Instant Heat." When his soft jump shot was on target, to quote Bob Lanier, "There is no one better at this game."

Tonight Sweet George got into the game with five minutes left in the first half and the Pistons down by two. Trapp's first shot whooshed through the wickets, and the temperature and decibel level rose instantly inside Cobo Arena. Trapp made a steal, then another, and then another for an easy score. The Kings turned tentative, and Sweet George and the Pistons closed out the half on a 13–4 run to take a nine-point lead to the locker room.

While Herbie talked second-half strategy, Archie couldn't help but get caught up in the excitement of the moment. Sure, he was ready to retire. But what a beautiful way to end his career. As Archie liked to say, "All I ever wanted in the NBA was to win." So it was only fitting that he go out with a bang, surrounded by a bunch of winners who refused to quit on each other or let themselves be defined by their losing season record.

In the second half the Pistons pounded the ball inside on the Kings. Lanier didn't disappoint. Neither did Trapp, Curtis Rowe, Al Eberhard, Eric Money, Chris Ford, Howard Porter, Crash Mengelt, or, of course, Archie Clark. For once this season everything went right for the Pistons in the second half, and Gus, the dancing, beer-bellied vendor in Section 3C, saluted what would be the biggest win of the season with an awesome two minutes of twisting, heartfelt joy. At the final buzzer the scoreboard flashed 130–117, and the Pistons were back in second place in the Midwest Division and sitting on a three-game win streak.

DETROIT, APRIL 2, 1976. Make it a seven-game win streak. After racking up wins over Chicago (twice) and Portland, the Pistons tonight topped Pete Maravich and the New Orleans Jazz, 116–102, and they did it without the services of Bob Lanier in the second half. "Bob-a-Dob," as he was called, took an inadvertent elbow to the back of the neck late in the first half that sent him thudding to the floor with no sensation on the left side of his body. Though the feeling quickly returned, the doctors called it a cervical spine injury. Prognosis: he'd be fine in a few days.

Some in the past had questioned Lanier's dedication to the game, often off the record. Not this season. Lanier had struggled through tendonitis in both knees, a broken bone in his shoulder, a badly inflamed elbow, and now a spine injury. There was no quit in him. In fact, if not for the team doctor, Lanier would have likely returned to the game in the second half, stiff as a board but as always effective.

No Lanier meant a heavy dose of Roger Brown, the backup center that the Cobo unfaithful loved to hate. Big Roger had been booed mercilessly in Detroit since his arrival two months ago, not for his deficiencies but for his perceived link to the unpopular Herb Brown. Yesterday Lanier had "begged and pleaded" in the newspaper "for fan support" to help power the playoff run. As a sign of progress, tonight the fans barely mustered a boo for Big Roger.

The Pistons (33–44) now needed either one more win or a Kansas City loss to clinch a playoff spot. "There was more doubt about this one than there had been in other years," Archie admitted, referring to his career-long string of making the NBA playoffs. "I even doubted it myself just a little at one time, and that's not my way."

DETROIT, APRIL 4, 1976. CBS Sports should have been there. The Persistent Pistons, their seven-game win streak snapped the night before in Chicago, were hell-bent to clinch a playoff spot tonight against the Philadelphia 76ers. George McGinnis, though ailing, was back in uniform for the 76ers, and so was Bob Lanier for the Pistons after having sat out the Chicago loss as a precaution to give the spinal injury one more day to heal.

It was by any measure a heck of a game, with the lead flip-flopping throughout the second half. Then with six seconds left and the Pistons ahead by two, Lanier was fouled. Who better than the team captain to seal the victory and put the Pistons into the playoffs. He was the one who had called the players-only meeting in Los Angeles about two weeks ago to rescue the season. He was the one who had almost single-handedly kept Detroit in the game in the final minutes, scoring six of its final ten points.

Lanier, a 77 percent free throw shooter, stepped to the free-throw line and calmly sank both attempts. Archie pumped his fist. He was going to the playoffs one last time.

Seated at his locker afterward, covered in ice bags and tape, was Bob Lanier, his laughter "bouncing off the walls like a loose basketball." The man long known around newsrooms as a bad interview was now almost giddy with perspective on this luckiest of unlucky seasons. "I'm amazed at how in the hell we stuck together," he would repeat over the next few days almost like a mantra.

Archie thought about his first playoff series in 1967 against the then San Francisco Warriors with a young Rick Barry. Now if the Pistons could get past Milwaukee in a best-of-three miniseries, an older Barry and the defending NBA champion Warriors would be waiting. Funny how history repeats itself.

---

*I really wanted to win the Milwaukee series, and, as my last NBA hurrah, I had a big game to help close out the series. Golden State waited in the wings, and they eked past us en route to the NBA title.*

*And just like that my NBA career was over. I cleaned out my locker with career numbers of more than eleven thousand points and three-thousand-plus assists. Not bad for a pro career that was nearly derailed because of a stupid racial quota system. During my ten seasons I had joined others to reform an oppressive labor system and build a better game for the generations to come. In fact, while I wrapped things up in Detroit, the final signatures were being signed to settle the Oscar Robertson case. The settlement brought free agency and laid the foundation for today's multi-billion-dollar business.*

*But my real passion has been looking out for the well-being of retired NBA players. I was a founding member of the NBA Retired Players Association to help my NBA brothers tackle the many challenges of life after basketball. It's to those brothers that I dedicate my story!*